TRIBES OF UTTARANCHAL

TRIBES OF UTTARANCHAL

A Study of Education, Health, Hygiene and Nutrition

B.S. BISHT

Publications

KALPAZ PUBLICATION

DELHI - 110052

Tribes of Uttaranchal
A Study of Education, Health, Hygine and Nutrition

Rs. 750

ISBN : 81-7835-320-2

Published in 2006 in India by
Kalpaz Publications,
C-30, Satyawati Nagar,
Delhi-110 052
E-mail : kalpaz@hotmail.com

Lasertype Setting by: Tact Computer Graphics, Delhi
Printed at: Salasar Imaging System, Delhi

Contents

Preface

Education, health, hygiene and nutrition are the prerequisites of human resource development. The world community, therefore, unanimously insists on works for the education and health of mankind so that a common man can achieve the best of his life. Today, in one way or the other, education and health have become the prime concerns of governments of all countries of the world. The governments are working through their own agencies for imparting education and health services to their citizens. The role of WHO in this field, has been crucial and of immense importance particularly the assurance of good health reiterated through WHO declaration "Health for All By 2000 A.D.", so is the case of literacy.

India, one of the biggest democratic countries of the world, has its commitment to the creation of a society free from poverty, ignorance and diseases so that equality, freedom and justice can be made accessible to all the citizens of the country in general and the rural poor and tribals in particular. In this context there has been efforts made by the central and state governments for expanding educational, medical and health services through their various agencies since long. A number of voluntary organizations also have come forward for implementing various schemes related to education, health, hygiene and nutrition. There are assertion of having achieved the targets of literacy as well as of health. In this backdrop, the main thrust of this ambitious 'Research Project' is to investigate scientifically the actual situation of education, health, hygiene and nutrition among the tribals of Uttaranchal.

In fact this 'work' is a product of prolonged mental exercise, conversations, discussions, experiences, meetings, exchange of ideas and investigations. Various agencies, academicians and hard-working curious associates have imparted their contribution to accomplish this 'Venture'. This would not have been accomplished, if the University Grants Commission, New Delhi had not approved it through its impartial and transparent screening pattern for financial assistance. I am really thankful to the Commission for financial assistance it granted and also to the concerning office-bearers for their cooperation they rendered whenever needed.

There are still many kinds of helping hands to whom I owe my sense of gratitude. Without their benign help this work would not have been completed. Dr. (Smt.) Sarojani Devi Bisht, remained very sincere, serious and hard-working to her duties throughout the work. She also deserve my thanks. Actually I have no words of appreciation for the part she played for the accomplishment of this work. She is in real sense a co-sharer of this venture.

The last but not the least, I am truly indebted to the tribal people who inspired me from the very beginning for undertaking 'Researches' on the unique and peculiar aspects of tribal societies. I shall feel myself oblized and academically successful if my research findings can help a little in the betterment and wellbeing of the tribals.

B.S. Bisht

1
Introduction

Education, health, hygiene and nutrition are the prerequisites of human resource development. The development of a given community depends to a large extent on the educational standard, health, hygiene and nutritional conditions of its population. Viewing to this reality, the education, health, hygiene and nutrition have been included even in the list of human rights on priority basis. In fact these are the basic amenities of human resource development without which no man can achieve excellence in life. These amenities are linked directly or indirectly to the 'Right of Life'. The International Bill of Human Rights of United Nations states that, "Every human being has the inherent right to life. This right should be protected by law. No one shall be arbitrarily deprived of his life." According to the Supreme Court, 'Right to Life' includes right to live with human dignity and all that goes along with it viz. the basic necessities of life such as nutrition, clothing and shelter and facilities for reading, writing and expressing oneself in diverse forms freely moving about and mixing with fellow human beings. In this way the right to education, health, hygiene, nutrition, clothing and shelter are held to be implicit in the right to life because of their inherent fundamental importance (Mathew: 1988:19-22). In regard to 'Right to education' the judgement of the 'Supreme Court' in *Unnikrishnan, J.P.* Vs *State of Andhra Pradesh* (1993:1 Sec. 645) is considered a land mark judgement which declares that every child up to fourteen years of age has fundamental right to primary education. This judgement has far reaching consequences for children in general and for weaker sections in particular. Free and compulsory education for children envisaged by Article 45 of the Constitution, if implemented, can be an effective measure to eradicate child labour which prevents them from developing themselves as dynamic citizens.

Even in Bandua Mukti Morcha Case [(1984) 3 Sec. 161] the Supreme Court held that 'Right to education implicates in and flow from the right to life guaranteed by Article 21 of the Constitution of India. The court held that the right to education has been treated as one of the transcendental importance in the life of an individual and has been recognized not only in this country but also in the world. In another case of *Mohini Jain* Vs. *State of Karnataka*; (1992) 3 Sec. 668)], the importance of education has been duly and rightly stressed. Without education the objectives set forth in the 'Preamble of the Constitution' can not be achieved.

In fact the 'Right to education' consists in Part IV Article 41, 45 and 46 of the Constitution, proves its importance to the citizens of India. Even some of the Articles in Part III of the Constitution, viz. Article 29 and 30 also speak of education. The Supreme Court held that the right to education is implicit in the right to education except in accordance with the procedure prescribed by law. Thus, the judgement in Mohini Jain case affirmed that "right to education flows directly from right to life." The Supreme Court has also stated that the question pertaining to the level and choice of education can be answered only in the light of the provisions contained in the Directive Principles of State Policy.

Article 41 of the Constitution says that the state shall, within the limits of its economic capacity and development, make effective provision for securing the right to work, to education and to public assistance in case of unemployment, old age, sickness and disablement and in other cases of undeserved wants. Article 45 says that the state shall endeavour to provide, within a period of ten years from the commencement of this Constitution, for free and compulsory education for all children until they complete the age of fourteen years. Thus, only the Article 45 speaks of a time limit, no other article does. It was a time bound plan imposing an obligation on the state to implement it before 1960. But even after 50 years the state has not been able to provide free education to the children below 14 years of age in India even after the stipulation of the period more than four times in Article 45. The same is the case of the Scheduled Castes, Scheduled Tribes and of the women's education. In this regard the Supreme Court observed that the allocation of available funds to different sectors of education in India was not on the basis of priorities determined by the Constitution of India. The Constitution contemplated a crash programme being undertaken by the state to achieve the goal set-out in Article 45. But actually what happened is more money is spent and more attention is directed to higher education than to primary education. In this matter rural sector and the weaker sections of the society referred to in Article 46 were neglected more. This policy of the Government was against the constitutional policy as is described in Article 41, 45 and 46. This inversion of priorities has been commented upon adversely by educationists and economists.

The Supreme Court observed that the education is the second highest sector of budgeted expenditure after defence. A little more than three per cent of the Gross National Product is spent on education. In comparison to many countries, India spends much less on education in terms of the proportion of Gross National Product. In spite of the fact that educational expenditure continues to be the highest item of expenditure next only to defence. The resource gap for educational needs is one of the major problems. Most of the current expenditure is only in the form of salary payment. Thus ultimately, it is a question of resources and resourcewise expenditure. This country is not in a happy position. While allocating the available resources, due regard should be paid to the wise words of the founding fathers in Article 45 and 46. Though higher education is important there should be proper balancing of various sectors of education.

Article 46 commands that the state shall promote with special care the educational and economic interests of the weaker sections of the people and in particular of the Scheduled Castes and Scheduled Tribes. The underlying concern in Article 46 is that, "Since education gives knowledge and knowledge gives power, the preservation of means of knowledge among the lowest rank is more important to the public than all the property of all the rich men in the country. It is the tyrants and bad rulers who are afraid of spreading education and knowledge among the deprived classes".

In fact the significance of education can not be neglected. Spread of education among all sections of the societies has been the foremost priority for a progressive nation. It is rightly stated that, if the nation is to be freed from slavery and bondage, the general mass has to be enlightened through education. Of course, education is the only means to salvage the human society from superstition, ignorance and subjugation to evil forces.

It is widely accepted by social thinkers, social reformers and social scientists that education as an agency, institution and media has a significant role to play in bringing about social transformation, progress and development in society. It makes all the persons fit to realize the world around them and tackle the problems whatsoever it may be with rational and scientific approach. Singh (1995:140) has aptly stated, "Education helps in shaping the personality by creating conditions which sharpen the menial abilities and intelligence of an individual. It helps in creation of an insight through rational understanding into the social phenomenon. At the pragmatic level education equips and trains a person to perform one's role adequately. At the societal abstract level, education helps in creating general ethos of enlightenment. At the societal pragmatic level, education is an important factor in status determination in contemporary society. Education provides one of the status indices to objectively assess the status mobility of an individual in social system."

The importance of education to people's life has been accepted for a long time in every society and in all stages of human development. The standard of education is viewed as an indicator of the progress and development of any society. The welfare Government of India has therefore adopted a number of education policies for its citizens in general and for the weaker sections of society viz. Scheduled Castes and Scheduled Tribes, in particular. Educational concessions, stipends at various levels of education, free welfare hostels, boarding schools exclusively meant for the tribes are some of the steps taken for popularising the education among the tribals. Besides these facilities reservation of seats and relaxation in criteria for admission to the technical and other educational institutions under the control of governments, the central and state have also been provided to the Scheduled Castes and Scheduled Tribes students. These educational schemes have, no doubt, a positive impact on the educational standard of the tribals as is obvious from the decadal literacy related data which show that literacy rate of Scheduled Tribes was 11.30 per cent in 1971, 16.35 in 1981, which has gone up to 29.60 per cent in 1991.

During last three decades, the average annual growth-rate of the ST literacy has been 0.70 per cent only. The slow rather very poor progress of education among Scheduled Tribes is the manifestation of the failure of the educational strategies adopted by the governments at state and central level. Today there is a wide gap between literacy rate of the general population which is 52.2 per cent in comparison to the Scheduled Tribe literacy percentage, i.e., 29.60 only. The gap of the S.T. literacy rate vary from state to state and tribe to tribe. As the educational statistics of scheduled castes and scheduled tribes, Ministry of the Human Resource Development, show that the variation among states is from 17.16 per cent in Andhra Pradesh to 82.73 per cent in Mizoram. Seven states and union territories have less than 29.60 per cent, which is the all India S.T. literacy figure. In other words, we can say that two-thirds of the total S.T. population has been at a literacy level less than the all-India S.T. average and less than half of the literacy level of the total population. The Scheduled Tribe female literacy rate vary from 4.42 per cent in Rajasthan to 78.70 per cent in Mizoram. The five states namely Rajasthan, Andhra Pradesh, Orissa, Madhya Pradesh and Bihar constitute altogether 51.69 per cent of the female S.T. population in the country but continue to remain below the national average of S.T. female literacy during 1981-1991 decade. Thus, it is evident that S.T. female population has a literacy level below 20 per cent. On the contrary, five states and Union Territories, i.e., Lakhshadweep, Mizoram, Kerala, Nagaland and Sikkim have been able to make more than 50 per cent of their S.T. female literate. This variation of literacy is also viewed from one tribe to another. For example, in Kerala the Kochu Velan and Kattunayakam have literacy rates of 75 per cent and 1.96 per cent respectively (Singh: 1995 : 21).

The scheduled tribe communities of Uttarakhand also exhibit the variations and divergencies from one tribe to another in all sectors of their life in general and in the educational sector in particular. The literacy percentage among the Bhotiyas of Uttarakhand is very high, i.e., approximately 73 per cent while the Rajis have only 5 per cent literacy. This variation is the result of the variation of economic statuses of both the tribes. The tribal community like that of Bhotiya who is economically well off is comparatively more prone to education while the poor and deprived tribes like that of the Rajis and the Buxas of Uttarakhand are still backward and illiterate. Thus, in view of the general literacy pervaded among the general masses in general and among the Scheduled Tribes in particular the Govt. of India has followed a policy, i.e., education for all by 2000 A.D., and has made every possible effort to achieve it.

In this context the problem of education and tribal education in particular, has assumed an urgent importance. Education has a key role in providing a status and position in society but it is still neglected in rural areas particularly in tribal areas. The disparity of percentage of literacy of tribal and non-tribal population is an outcome of indifference to tribal areas particularly with reference to educational facilities. It seems the dimensions and problems of tribal education could not be properly understood. Even the special provisions made for the tribal education could not produce fruitful results. Today the different issues often raised in the context of tribal education as stated by Chaudhuri (1992" XXXIV) are:

(i) Disparity of literacy between tribal and non-tribal on the one hand and within the tribal communities on the other, including sex-wise variation,

(ii) Suitability of educational system including curriculum, course, medium of instruction and the utilization of traditional institution in this context,

(iii) The problem of dropout, stagnation and wastage particularly the problem of retention of education,

(iv) Tribal education to be examined in isolation or as a part of general education,

(v) Inequality in enjoyment of educational facilities and its consequences. These issues deserve to be chewed for bringing out a better line of action particularly in the field of tribal education.

Other important aspects of human life are "Health, Hygiene and Nutrition" which altogether ascertain psycho-physical, social, economic and cultural status of an individual. Basically all the three elements, i.e., health, hygiene and nutrition are interrelated and positively correlated with each other. Health status of an individual depends, to a large extent, on the hygienic conditions and nutritional pattern. Health is essentially a basic requirement to lead a normal socio-economic life. And it is essential to have an appropriate feeling for a healthy life. Besides this, the hygiene and hygienic conditions are fundamental to health. In fact there are ample evidences that the higher level of nutrition, improvement in environmental sanitation and adoption of better health care and hygienic practices have made possible improvement in the health status of the population. Thus health care is intrinsic to the well being of the people. Health status of the people determines the average expectation of life, number of persons in the productive age bracket, production, productivity, earning capacity, employment and finally welfare (Gopal: 1986 : 1-2). Thus we may term 'health' as one of the important indicators of human resource development. To a large extent, development of a given society depends on the health status of its populace. It is therefore the Health Assembly of World Health Organization in an international conference on primary health care at 'Alma Ata USSR' unanimously decided with 134 governments majority including India and 67 other UN representatives that primary health care for all is essential and that it has to be an integral part of social development in the spirit of social equity and justice. India is a signatory to the resolution and is committed to the attainment of the 'Goal of health for all by 2000 AD' through universal provision of comprehensive primary health care service. Thus, the statement of the National Health Policy, 1982, signifies a formal commitment of the government of India to the attainment of this objective. In this context targets were set for lower mortality rates and a higher life expectancy. Besides this the aim was to reduce the infant mortality rate from 120 to 60 per thousand, the crude death rate from 15 to 09 per thousand and to raise the life expectancy from 52 to 64 years by the turn of this century (ICSSR and ICMR 1981). In its report ICMR and ICSSR acknowledged this fact that, "Health is a function, not only of medical care, but of the overall integrated development of society, cultural, economic, social and political (ICSSR and ICMR 1981 : vii). K.V. Narayan (1977 :10) has aptly stated that "Nutrition, environmental sanitation, literacy and other socio-economic factors play a greater role than the narrowly defined health care services in determining the physical, mental and social well-being of people, especially in the early stages of development." If we look at the health care system prevalent among the people we find a certain difference in between the health care system observed in urban or civilized modern societies and that of the traditional indigenous or the tribal communities. In traditional tribal health care system there is an important role of medicinal herbs, roots, tubers and healing practices based on Ayurvedic, Unani, Sidh as well as nature cure and yoga system. Besides this the magico-religious aspects have equally an important place in the healing practices observed by the tribal people. It is so because the tribals relate sickness, death and good health to the curse or goodwill of the deities worshipped by the respective tribal community. Mahanti (1995 : 34) has aptly remarked that, "Tribal health-care-systems are based on herbal medicine, Ayurvedic medicine and other related systems like sidh and yoga victuals alongwith a strong leaning towards magico-religious spirits at bay."After declaration of the 'National Health Policy' by the Ministry of Health and Family Welfare, Government of India in 1982, stress is being given on the provision of preventive, promotive and rehabilitating health services to the people, representing a shift from medical care to health care and from urban to rural population. The emphasis is on achieving 'Health for all by 2000 A.D.' through primary health care approach and attaining the long-term demographic goal of a net reproduction rate of 1 per thousand by the year 2000 at the lowest feasible levels of mortality. In particular it has been emphasized that the infant mortality rate should be below 60 per 1000 live births and the expectation of life at birth should increase to 64 years and the birth rate should be reduced to 21 per 1000 population by the turn of the century. Through the framework of the seventh and eighth Five Year Plans and the 20-Point Programme steps are already underway to implement the policy (VHA of India, 1983).

Thus, in view of the literacy programme and National Health Policy which have specific goals and targets to be achieved through primary health care approach, which mainly consists of various health- related programmes like maternal and child health care, control of water-borne and sanitation-related diseases, nutrition programmes, control of mortality due to respiratory diseases, control of malaria, control of STD, prevention of AIDS control of scabies, control of leprosy, control of TB, prevention of Pulse and Polio etc. In this context, the main objective is to assess the existing state of education, health, hygiene and nutrition among the Scheduled Tribe communities, namely the Rajis, the Tharus, the Buksas and the Jaunsarese of Uttarakhand. Besides thus an effort has also been made:

1. To study the existing education, health and nutritional conditions in tribal areas with a view to finding out any impediments amenable for the problems related to education, health, hygiene and nutrition.
2. To study the role and perception of the tribals themselves towards the health and nutrition pattern.
3. To study the role of the state government and the non-voluntary organization in the field of health and nutrition of the tribals

particularly in normal and crisis situation.

4. To study the newly emerged class (tribal elite class) from among the tribals particularly in the context of its role and perception towards the health and nutrition and also to study the patterns of social mobility.
5. To provide viable policy oriented solution to eradicate the causes responsible for the problems related to health and nutrition and also for their betterment.

References

Singh, B.S., 1995 ; *Tribal Education in India*, Inter India Publications, New Delhi-15.

Gopal, K. Rani, 1996: *Health Status of Tribals*, A.P.H. Publishing Corporation, New Delhi-2.

Indian Council of Social Science Research and Indian Council of Medical Research, 1981, Health for All: An Alternative Strategy, Indian Institute of Education, Pune.

Voluntary Health Association of India, 1983, Seminar on the National Health Policy- A Report, New Delhi-110016.

2
Conceptual Analysis

Education, Health, Hygiene and Nutrition are some of the terms frequently used by people and interpreted according to their necessities and vested interests. As, for instance, these terms are generally coined by politicians for their vested interests, chewed, digested and discussed by policy-makers as to show their keenness on the basic issues of human life and considered as the prerequisites of human resource development by academicians. Today these terms have become more common and of prime concern for NGO's as to extract funds from different agencies to carryout their projects in regard to education, health, hygiene and nutrition among the marginalized and vulnerable groups. Nevertheless the unending discussion on education, health, hygiene and nutrition have remained almost the same without any solution.

Even WHO has realised education, health, hygiene and nutrition as the prime concerns of human development and declared its commitment for making available education as well as health for all by 2000 A.D.

In this very context, an objective effort has been made particularly for two prime purposes: (i) to evaluate the existing educational, health, hygiene and nutritional status of the tribes under study, and, (ii) to assess the viability, relevance and achievement of the declaration of WHO. In this way the endeavour, in brief, tends to present a lucid analysis of education, health, hygiene and nutrition among the tribes in retrospect and prospect.

But before we present the findings and analysis as desired the conceptional analyses of the terms, viz. education, health, hygiene and nutrition is necessary.

In fact the terms education, health, hygiene and nutrition have been conceptually analysed in different ways by different philosophers, thinkers, scholars and scientists. The need of the hour which is realised most today is to consider unanimously and of giving them a unified meaning. Keeping this in mind a brief account of the conceptual analysis is being presented here:

Education

It is an ever known fact that education is an important and powerful means of social change, which ultimately paves way for modernization process in a given society. Education has ever been a source of enlightenment, knowledge, cognizance, dominance and power. It has functional importance to the well being of mankind in the universe. Though there are controversies about the role of education. Nevertheless the expansion of education even in the most backward communities has not been deterred. Sharma (2001:205) has aptly stated that, "Controversies regarding the role of education have not deterred massive expansion of education all over the world. Education has been perceived largely as a source, both material and cognitive. As resource education becomes power, a means of control and domination in the hands of those who are highly educated over those who are less educated and illiterate. Besides this education is a means of socialization. It generates and creates a scientific approach, a sense of rationality, work culture and paves the way of development. It poses a structure against conservatism, traditionally and opens up the door of modernity and transformation. The processes like social mobility as well as occupational mobility, in real sense, are intrinsic to education. The caste, class, linguistic and communal barriers can be loosened only through the expansion of modern education. It can be helpful in creating a social atmosphere free from all those biases which are birth based or man-made. On the contrary, education has some paradoxical implications too. It divides human society into educated and uneducated groups. The modern and backward classes by and large are the outcome of education. The social, occupational and spatial mobility which ultimately set free mankind from its traditional moorings is possible only through education. There are the attributes of education which are considered widely throughout the world and every welfare government of any country is therefore committed to impart education to its citizens."

In India, under Articles 29 and 30 of the Constitution, certain cultural and educational rights are guaranteed. For instance, Section (1) of Article 29 guarantees the right of any section of the citizen residing in any part of the country having a distinct language, script or culture of its own. Section (2) prohibits any discrimination based on religion, race, caste, language or any of them in the matter of admission to state or state aided educational institutions. Section (1) of Article 30 provides that 'all minorities, whether based on religion or language, shall have the right to establish and administer educational institutions, discriminate against any educational institution on the ground that it is under the management of a minority, whether based on religion or language. Besides this, some special provisions have also been made for the dissemination and promotion of education in tribal and backward areas. The states and union territories of India have some constitutional liabilities for providing education to all sections of society in general and to weaker sections including Scheduled Tribes, Scheduled Castes and Other Backward Classes in particular. For this very purpose there is a certain provision of budget in every state and union territory in every financial year. Even in advanced countries of Western Europe, education is mainly supported and funded by the state. In this context the Marxist Educational Praxis (MEP) advocated by Lenin and others is essentially a theory of practice to bring about change and modernization (Bottomore Tom, et. al. (eds); 1985:144-145 quoted by Sharma, K.L. (2001 : 206-207). The main components of the MEP are; (i) There should be free public education, compulsory and uniform for all children, assuring the abolition of cultural or knowledge monopolies and of privileged forms of schooling. The purpose of this theory was to weaken the role of the family in social reproduction, to bring up children under less unequal conditions, to utilise the socialising force of the community. As such hierarchy of schools would vanish, and the role of family and parentage remain checked. Such a theory can ensure coexistence of education and equality. Mahatma Gandhi campaigned for compulsory education for all which incorporated elements of basic education which would facilitate employment to the educated, (ii) The MEP emphasises on the contribution of education with material production. The aim is to bridge the gap between physical and mental work, between conception and education by assuring to all full understanding of the producing process, (iii) Education has to assure an all-round development of the personality. The aim is to activate the individual in all spheres of social life including consumption, leisure, creation and enjoyment of culture, participation in social life, interaction with others and self-fulfilment (auto-creation). The realisation of this objective requires the transformation of the social division of labour. Various tribal and feminist movements in India have focused on this particular aspect in relation to education. Tribals in particular need education which can touch upon the totality of their social life. Formal education alone would not do justice to them, (iv) The community is assigned a new and vast role in the process of education. This changes the in-group relations in the school which implies more open relations between school and society, and a dialogical relation between teacher and taught. This can be possible only if school is treated as a community rather than a formal bureaucratic organization.

French sociologist Emile Durkheim considers education as an eminently social thing in its origins and in its functions. He conceives education as intimately related to a society's structure. For Durkheim 'education reflects and maintains the society and it can only partially change it.' (Sharma: 2001:208).

Viewing the powerful and an immensely important agent of personality development as well as a basic constituent part of social transformation, the 'education' has been considered as a variable element in the present study. An attempt has been made to understand the educational status of the study units, their perception towards education, their educational behaviour, their responses of the respondents towards educational infrastructure exists in their area and finally their aspirations towards the education of their coming generation. This information will incontestably reflect the overall educational scenario of the tribals.

Health

As an important issue the theme of health has gained enormous popularity and universally in all cultures, societies and at all times. But in spite of being a universal phenomena we see a cultural variation in regard of the concept of health and its implications. It is therefore the notion related to health varied with the variation of cultural system, space, time and situation. The meaning and definition propounded in different times by different scholars and thinkers prove not only the difference of opinion about the concept of health but also its importance and indifference to the mind of the people. The oldest definitions of health used to be "Health is the absence of disease." Even today 'health' is termed in the same frame of reference by the people in general. In some cultures, health and harmony are considered equivalent, harmony being defined as "being at peace with the self, the community, god and cosmos." The ancient Indians and Greeks shared this concept and attributed disease to disturbances in bodily equilibrium of what they called 'humorous' (Park: 1997 : 11).

In fact 'health' is not perceived the same way even by the professional groups, e.g., biomedical scientists, social scientists, health administrators, ecologists, etc. This resulted in different concepts of health, viz : the biomedical concept, the ecological concept, the psychological concept and the holistic concept. Biomedical concept views 'health' as an 'absence of disease'. It is perceived that if one was free from disease then the person was considered healthy. This concept is based on the given theory of disease which dominated medical thought at the turn of 20th century. Ahmed (1979) has stated that, "The medical profession viewed the human body as a machine, disease as a consequence of the breakdown of the machine and one of the doctor's tasks is repair of machine." The biomedical concept of health is a narrow view and unable to answer some of the major health problems caused by malnutrition, chronic diseases, accidents, dry abuse, mental illness, environmental pollution and population explosion. In the present day context the biomedical concept of health is not adequate as to perceive the 'health' in its broad perspective. This lacking gave birth to the ecological concept of health which viewed health as a dynamic equilibrium between man and his environment and disease maladjustment of the human organism to environment. Dubos (1965) stated that, "Health implies the relative absence of pain and discomfort and a continuous adaptation and adjustment to the environment to ensure optimal function." Thus the ecological concept raises two issues, viz. imperfect man and imperfect environment. History argues strongly that improvement in human adaptation to natural environments can lead to longer life expectancies and a better quality of life even in the absence of modern health delivery system (WHO; 1986).

Apart from biomedical and ecological concepts of health the psychological concept perceive 'health' as a socio-psychological phenomena because it is influenced even by the social, psychological, cultural, economic and political factors of the person concerned. Hence these factors should be taken into consideration in defining and measuring health. Thus the health must be viewed as a biological and social phenomena.

The holistic concept of health synthesizes all the concepts viz. the biomedical, the ecological and the psychological and implies that all sections of society have an effect on health in particular agriculture, animal husbandry, food, industry, education, housing, public works, communication and other sectors. The holistic model corresponds to the view held by the ancients that, "health implies a sound mind in a sound body, in sound family, in a sound environment'. Thus, the main emphasis of the holistic model is on the promotion and protection of health.

Health is defined by different people in a different manner. In other words it can be stated that there is no consensus about the meaning and definition of health. In *Webster Dictionary,* health is defined as 'the condition of being sound in body, mind or spirit especially freedom from physical disease or pain'. According to *Oxford English Dictionary,* Health means a state of being well in body or mind, that condition in which its functions are duly and efficiently discharged" (Thomson : 1995 : 626). World Health Organization (WHO) has defined the term 'health' in the preamble of its constitution as, "Health is a state of complete physical, mental and social wellbeing and not merely an absence of disease or infirmity." In 1978 this statement has been amplified to include the ability to lead a "socially and economically productive life" (WHO : 1978 : Health for all, Sr. No.I). But the WHO definition has been criticised widely as being too broad. It is argued that the health must be seen as process of continuous adjustment to the changing demands of living and of the changing meaning we give to life. Hence 'health' can not be termed as static because it is a dynamic concept. It helps people live well, work well and enjoy themselves. Many people consider WHO definition of health as an idealistic goal than a realistic proposition. Some people consider WHO definition irrelevant to everyday demands as no body qualifies as healthy, i.e., perfect biological, psychological and social functioning. However, the WHO definition of health is broad and positive in its implications because it sets out the standard of positive health. It symbolizes the aspiration of people and represents an over all objective or goal towards which nations should strive. People do not consider WHO definition of health as an 'operational' definition. WHO study group (1957 : Techs. Rep. Ser. No. 667) has therefore suggested an operational definitions which viewed health in two senses, i.e., a broad sense and a narrow sense. In a broad sense health can be seen as a condition or quality of the human organism expressing the adequate functioning of the organism in given conditions, genetic or environmental. In a narrow sense, health means (a) there is no obvious evidence of disease and that a person is functioning normally and (b) the several organs of the body are functioning adequately in themselves and in relation to one another, which emphasizes a kind of equilibrium or homeostasis.

In recent years a new philosophy of health has come into being which may be stated as—health is a fundamental human right, health is the essence of productive life and not the result of ever increasing expenditure on medical care, health is inter-sectoral, health is an integral part of development, health is central to the concept of quality of life, health involves individuals, state and international responsibility, health and its maintenance is a major social investment, and health is world-wide social goal.

In this way health is a multidimensional concept. The WHO definition envisages three dimensions viz. the physical, the mental and the social, while some other people talk about many other dimensions like, spiritual, emotional, vocational, philosophical/cultural, economic, environmental, educational, nutritional, curative and preventive.

Physical dimension of health denotes the perfect functioning of body. It defines health biologically in which every cell or organ of body is functioning at optimum capacity and in perfect harmony with the rest of the body. A good complexion, a clean skin, bright eyes, lustrous hair, firm flesh, not too fat, a sweet breath, a good appetite, sound sleep, regular activity of bowels and bladder and smooth, easy, coordinated body movements are some of the signs of physical health. The physical health can be measured by self assessment of over all health, inquiry into symptoms of ill health and risk factors, inquiry into medications, inquiry into levels of activity, inquiry into use of medical service, standardized questionnaires for cardiovascular diseases, standardized questionnaires for respiratory diseases, clinical examination, nutrition and dietary assessment and biochemical and laboratory investigations. At the community level the state of health may be assessed by such indicators as death rate, infant mortality rate and expectation of life.

Mental dimension of health deals with an important component of health, i.e., mental health. Sartorius (1983) defines mental health as, "a state of balance between the individual and the surrounding world, a state of harmony between oneself and others, a coexistence between the realities of the self and that of other people and that of the environment." Though mental health is an essential component of health yet there is no precise tool to assess the state of mental health. However, assessment of mental health can be made by administering a well structured questionnaire by an experienced interviewer. There is nothing like established indicators of mental health, yet psychologists have mentioned some attributes of a mentally healthy person. For instance; a mentally healthy person is free from internal conflicts; he/she is not at war with himself, he/she is well adjusted and accepts criticism and is not easily upset, he/she searches for identity, he/she has a strong sense of self-esteem, he/ she knows him/her self, his/her needs, problems and goals, he/she has good self-control-balances rationality and emotionality, he/she faces problems and tries to solve them intelligently, i.e., coping with stress and anxiety.

Social dimension of health, as Fillenbaum (1984) has stated, "includes the levels of social skills one possesses, social functioning and the ability to see oneself as a member of a larger society." Social health takes into account that every individual is part of a family and of wider community and focusses on social and economic conditions and well-being of the whole person in the context of his social network. Social health is rooted in "Positive material environment" (focussing on financial and residential matters), and "Positive human environment" which is concerned with the social network of the individual."

Spiritual dimension of health refers to that part of the individual which reaches out and strives for meaning and purpose in life. It is the intangible "some thing" that transcends physiology and psychology. It includes integrity, principles and ethics, the purpose in life, commitment to some higher being and belief in concept that are not subject to "state of the art" explanation (Eberst: 1984:99-104).

Emotional dimension of health deals with 'feeling' of an individual. The feelings of an individual have psychological impacts and thus influence the physical health of the person concerned. The experts in psychology have been successful in isolating the mental and emotional dimension but could not establish the standardized indicators as to assess the emotional health so far.

Another dimension of health is a vocational dimension, which is related with the work of an individual adapt for one's existence. Work has both physical and mental impacts. Physical work is usually associated with an improvement in physical capacity while goal achievement and self-realization in work are a source of satisfaction and enhanced self-esteem.

Besides this, there are numerous other dimensions which have direct or indirect impacts on human health. Thus it may be concluded that health is multidimensional concept which should be viewed in the context of various aspects which altogether determine the health status of an individual and a community at large. Since every community has its own racial origin, physiology, biology, sociology, ecology, environment, culture and economy which varies from other communities, hence the health standards vary from community to community and also among cultures, socioeconomic groups, social classes, age-groups etc. etc. This concludes that health may not have universal standards of measurements because health is a relative concept. However there are some common determinants of health which are as follows :

Determinants of Health

There are numbers of factors which influence health. These factors categorised broadly into two categories, i.e., the internal factors and external factors. Internal factors can be understood more precisely in terms of genetic factors which lie with in the individual and the external factors can be termed as the environmental factors which lie outside of the individual and influence him/her as an external force. These factors interact constantly and that interaction may be health-promoting or deleterious. Thus, conceptually the health of an individual and a community as a whole may be considered to be the result of interactions of these factors. The factors can be generalized and outlined as; heredity, environment, lifestyle, socio-economic conditions, health and family welfare, services and other factors like food intake pattern, education, occupational status, developmental standard etc.

Indicators of Health

The aforesaid conceptual delineation presents the nature of 'health' its various concepts, dimensions and determinants. But there are questions that always come to mind how 'health' can be measured? who is healthy? how a health status can be assessed? which are the criteria of health assessment? It is evident that health is multidimensional concept and each dimension is influenced by various known and unknown factors.

Therefore health must be measured multidimensionally. No doubt health measurement is a complicated one because health can not be defined in exact measurable terms. However, there are some indicators which may be classified as: mortality indicators, morbidity indicators, disability rates, nutritional status indicators, health care delivery indicators, utilization rates, indicators of social and mental health, environmental indicators, socio-economic indicators, health policy indicators, indicators of quality of life, etc. Besides this there are some other indicators viz. (i) social indicators-which are divided into twelve categories; population, family formation, families and households, learning and educational services, earning activities, distribution of income, consumption and accumulation, social security and welfare services, health services and nutrition, housing and its environment, public order and safety, time use, leisure and culture, social stratification and mobility (U.N. Dept. of Economic and Social Affairs (1978). Social indicators, statistical paper Series M. No. 63). (ii) Basic needs indicators, which includes calorie consumption, access to water, life expectancy, deaths due to disease, illiteracy, doctors and nurse as per population, rooms per person, GNP per capita (Sheehan and Hopkin: 1979). (iii) Health for all indicators: For monitoring progress towards the goal of health for all by 2000 AD, the WHO (1981) has listed the following four categories of indicators; (a) Health policy indicators—political commitment to health for all, resource allocation, the degree of equity of distribution of health services, community involvement, organizational frame-work and managerial process, (b) Social and economic indicators related to health; rate of population increase, GNP and GDP, income distribution, work conditions, adult literacy rate, housing, food availability, (c) Indicators for the provision of health care; availability, accessibility, utilization, quality of care, (4) Health status indicators; low birth weight (percentage), nutritional status and psychological development of children, infant mortality rate, child mortality rate (1-4 yrs.), life expectancy at birth, maternal mortality rate, disease specific mortality, morbidity-incidence and prevalence, disability prevalence.

The mortality indicators may be considered in terms of (i) crude death rate, (ii) expectancy of life, (iii) infant mortality rate, (iv) child mortality rate, (v) under 5 proportionate mortality rate, (vi) maternal mortality rate (vii) disease-specific mortality rate, and (viii) proportional mortality rate. The crude death rate may be defined as the number of deaths per 1000 population per year in a given community. Life expectancy is another important mortality indicator which is considered as a good indicator of socio-economic development in general. As an indicator of long-term survival, it can be considered as a positive health indicator. It has been adopted as a global health indicator. A minimum life expectancy at birth of 60 years is the goal of Health for all by 2000 AD. Child mortality rate is another indicator related to the overall health status in early childhood (1-4 years). It can be defined as the number of deaths at the age of 1-4 years in a given year, per 1000 children in that age-group at the midpoint of the year concerned. Under 5 proportionate mortality rate reflect both infant and child mortality rates. In communities with poor hygiene, the proportion may exceed 60 per cent. High rate reflects high birth rates, high child mortality rates and shorter life expectancy. Maternal mortality rate denotes the greater proportion of deaths among women of reproductive age in most of the developing world. Besides this the mortality rates can be computed for specific disease. The simplest measures of estimating the burden of a disease in the community is proportional mortality rate, i.e., the proportion of all deaths currently attributed to it. The proportional mortality rate from communicable disease has been suggested as a useful health status indicator, it indicates the magnitude of preventable mortality.

Mortality indicators have been the most popular indicators of health status in a given community which are probably the most often used even today. Besides this morbidity indicators of health status are equally important because morbidity indicators are used to supplement mortality data to describe the health status of a population. Generally for assessing ill health in the community the following morbidity rates are used - (i) incidence and prevalence (ii) notification rates (iii) attendance rates at outpatient departments, health centres etc. (iv) admission, readmission and discharge rates (v) duration of stay in hospital and (vi) spells of sickness or absence from work or school (WHO, 1987; Techn. Rep. Ser., No. 587).

There are disability rates too to assess health status in a given community. The disability rates related to illness and injury have come into use to supplement mortality and morbidity indicators. The disability rates are of two types; (i) Event-type indicators and (ii) Person-type indicates. Fillenbaum : 1984 and Wilson and Drury : 1984: 5:83-106. Event- type indicators include (a) number of days of restricted activity (b) bed disability days (c) work-loss days or school loss days within a specified period. On the contrary the person-type indicators include (a) limitation of morbidity, viz. confined to bed, confined to house, special aid in getting mound either inside or outside the house, (b) limitation of activity, viz., limitation to perform the basic activities of daily living (ADL), e.g., eating, washing, dressing, going to toilet, moving about etc., limitation in major activity, e.g., ability to work at a job, ability to house work etc. WHO (1981) in Health for all series No. 04 has mentioned about three important nutritional states indicators as to assess the health status of the people. They are (i) Anthropometric measurements of preschool children, e.g., (a) weight and height, mid-arm circumference (b) heights and weights of children at school entry and (c) prevalence of low birth weight (less them 2-5 kg.).

There are some health-care delivery indicators which are frequently used for assessing the health resources and facilities distributed in a given society. These indicators also include the provision of health care which ultimately determine the health status of the people. Health care delivery indicators include—(a) doctor-population ratio (b) doctor-nurse ratio (c) population-bed ratio (c) population per-health sub-centre (e) population per traditional birth attendant.

Utilization rates of the health services also give some indication about the care needed by a population and also their health status. Health care utilization and health needs of the population indicate the attitude of the population towards health services and the health care system. For example—(i) Proportion of infants who are fully immunized against the 6 EPI diseases (ii) proportion of pregnant women who receive antenatal care or have their deliveries supervised by a trained birth attendant (iii) percentage of the population using various methods of family planning (iv) bed occupancy rate (i.e., average daily inpatient census/average number of beds) (v) average length of stay (i.e., days of care rendered/ discharges) (vi) bed turnover ratio (i.e., discharges/average beds).

There are some indirect measures pertaining to social and mental health of the people. These measures can be termed as the indicators of social and mental pathology which includes suicide, homicide, other acts of violence, battered-baby and battered wife syndromes and neglected and abandoned youth in the neighbourhood. These indicators provide a guide to social action for improving the health of the people.

The environmental indicators relating to the pollution of air and water, radiation, solid wastes, noise, exposure to toxic substance in food or drink also have deciding impacts on health status. Besides this the safe drinking water and sanitation facilities available to the people also determine their health status hence may be considered as the environmental indicator of health.

There are socio-economic indicators too to measure the health status. These indicators include- (a) rate of population increase (b) per capita GNP (c) level of unemployment (d) dependency ratio (e) literacy rates especially female literacy rates (f) family size (g) housing the number of persons per room, and (h) per capita calorie availability.

The 'health policy indicator' is also an important indicator of health care system and therefore the health status of the population. Health policy indicators as such are related with the political commitment which includes (i) proportion of GNP spent on health services (ii) proportion of GNP spent on health-related activities (including water supply and sanitation, housing and nutrition, community development) and (iii) proportion of total health resource devoted to primary health care. These indicators, by and large, determine or reflect the health status of the population.

Indicators of quality of life which can be considered in terms of mortality rate, infant mortality in particular, morbidity data available, life expectancy and literacy are some of the indicators for assessing health status of the people.

Thus, it may be concluded that there are a number of indicators for assessing the health statue of the population residing in a given community. Each indicator has its own importance in assessing, rather reflecting the health status, health care system, health resources and also attitude of the people towards health and health related aspects, i.e., the health system. All the indicators have almost equal importance in the measurement pattern of the health status. It is so because any indicator is not adequate as to measure sufficiently and completely the health status of a given population. It is so because the term 'health' is itself a multidimensional and multifactoral. A number of factors determine the health status of an individual which can broadly be categorised as biological and non-biological factors. Both the factors have a number of implications and health related impacts. Besides this 'health' has different dimensions too. In real sense, health can adequately and absolutely be viewed in terms of its various dimensions. Thus keeping in view of the multifactoral and multidimensional nature of health, the researcher has taken into practice all the indicators as cited in the aforesaid analysis for studying the health status of the tribes under study.

Hygiene

The word 'hygiene' is derived from 'Hygeia', the goddess of health in Greek mythology. She is represented as a beautiful woman holding in her hand a bowl from which a serpent is drinking. In 'Greek mythology' the serpent testifies the art of healing which symbol is retained even today. Hygiene is defined as "the science of health and embraces all factors which contribute to healthy living" (Park : 1997 : 39). Hygiene is basically a major part of health education which consists of two aspects, i.e., (i) personal hygiene, and (ii) environmental hygiene. The personal hygiene aims at promoting the standards of personal cleanliness within the setting of conditions where people live. Personal hygiene includes bathing, clothing, washing hands and toilet, care of feet, nails and teeth, spitting, coughing, personal appearance and inculcation of clean habits in the youngsters. Environmental hygiene has two aspects (i) domestic and (ii) community hygiene. Domestic hygiene consists of home related aspects, such as use of soap, need for fresh air, light and ventilation, hygienic storage of foods, hygienic disposal of wastes, need to avoid pests, rats, mice and insects. While the community hygiene is concerned with basic sanitary services consisting of water supply, disposal of human excreta and other solid and liquid wastes, vector control, food sanitation and housing which are fundamental to health.

Nutrition

Another important aspect is 'nutrition pattern', nutritional status, nutrition related awareness and behaviour of the tribes. But before going to the factual analysis of the tribal communities it is pertinent to understand the 'nutrition' as a concept so that the nutrition related observations can go in a proper and meaningful direction. Broadly speaking, nutrition may be defined as the science of food and its relationship to health. Primarily it is related to the part played by nutrients in body growth, development and maintenance. The term 'Nutrient' or food factor is used for specific dietary constituents such as proteins, vitamins and minerals. Nutrition as such is a broad concept. Since the study deals primarily with nutritional aspects of the tribal communities, hence the concept 'Nutrition' will be viewed in terms of dietary pattern, assessment of nutritional status, nutritional problems and nutritional programmes. Besides this, the attitude, behaviour and awareness of the tribals under reference will also be helpful in understanding the nutritional aspects of the tribals.

'Nutrition', in general, is the science of food. But the food concept has been changing through the ages. The use and importance of food for human beings has been recognized at all ages. But in general good food means "maintaining a nutritional status that enables us to grow well and enjoy good health". In early 19th century, protein, carbohydrate and fat were recognized as energy yielding foods therefore, much attention was paid to their metabolism and contribution to energy requirements (Aykroyd : 1970 : Sl. No. 24). The discovery of vitamins at the turn of the twentieth century has added a new chapter in the history of the nutrition science. By 1950 all the presently known vitamins and essential amino acids were discovered and thus nutrition gained recognition as a scientific discipline with roots in physiology and biochemistry (Park: 1997 : 392).

In due course of time, particularly during the first decade of the country some diseases caused by nutritional deficiency came into existence and this incident has extended the influence and scope of the nutrition science in other fields too - in agriculture, animal husbandry, economics and sociology. The Green Revolution and the White Revolution by and large have been the result of the new knowledge gained in the field of nutritional science. More so the problem of nutrition also attracted the international attention for the first time as a cause of social problem.

At international level the League of Nations initiated its activities in the field of nutrition and later continued by FAO, WHO and UNICEF.

During eighties and nineties the significance of nutrition science tremendously increased due to its association with some diseases like infection, immunity, fertility, maternal and child health etc. In recent years, the nutrition science has come out of laboratories and association with epidemiology. This association of nutrition science and epidemiology has given birth to a new concept which we call nutritional epidemiology. The epidemiological methods are now used even in the planning and evaluation of nutritional programmes. In the present-day context 'nutrition science' is considered as the cornerstone of socio-economic development and thus the nutritional problems are not medical problems but are multifactoral with roots in many other sectors of development, such as, education, demography, agriculture and rural development. With the campaign of 'Health for all by 2000 A.D.' promotion of proper nutrition has been considered one of the eight elements of primary health care (WHO/ UNICEF-1978). Even the nutritional indicators have been developed to monitor health for all and nutrition is now being integrated into primary health care systems to promote health and nutritional status of the people.

Assessment of Nutritional Status

"The nutritional status of an individual is often the result of many interrelated factors. It is influenced by the adequacy of food intake both in terms of quantity and quality and also by the physical health of the individual" (WHO; 1978 : 514). In general nutrition is commonly related to food pattern. It is a known fact that food is a bio-chemical process and product which sustains life. But it is not merely the source of bio-chemical needs, it also has a cultural dimension which helps a person to determine his food and nutrition habits and choices (Doshi : 1995 :11). Each society has its own culture which determines its food related tastes, norms, behaviours, values and even the acceptance and rejection of a particular item of food. Besides this, there are great geographical variations which determine the crop pattern and also the quality and quantity of food stuffs. This geographical variation also ascertain the dietary pattern which is directly related to nutritional quality. In fact, food is of different types. It varies from one region to another, from one ethnic group to another, from one culture to another. Even in the same region, culture and ethnic group there are varieties of foods. Aykroyd (1966 :1) says there are 'proximate principle' which explain the main bulk of foods. For him proteins, fats and carbohydrates are termed as 'proximate principles' "they are burnt or oxidized in the body to provide the energy for various activities of life." The proximate principles also have the components of vitamins, minerals and water. Thus the dietary principles include proteins, fats and carbohydrates and also vitamins, mineral salts and water. The foods contain all these principles in varying proportions. On the basis of these dietary principles, Aykroyd classified the food as : cereals, pulses, nuts, oilseeds, vegetables, fruits, milk, milk products and fast foods. Harper and Spencer (1987 : 1) have classified the food commodity into ten groups as; (a) cereals and grain products (b) starchy roots, tubers and fruits (c) pulses, nuts and oilseeds (d) vegetables (e) fruits (f) foods of animal origin (g) fats and oils (h) sugars and syrups (i) spices and other condiments, and (j) other foods not classified above including yeast, algae and fermented products. The classification of food commodities made by the scholars can be used for food analysis as well as for intra and cross-cultural comparison of any community. Simoons (1991: vii-xiii) has scientifically classified the food habits of Chinese into eleven categories as; (1) cereals and pulses (2) roots and tubers (3) cultivated vegetables (4) seaweeds and other algae (5) fruits (6) edible nuts, like fruits and seeds (7) flesh and fowl (8) fish, turtles and tortoises (9) eggs (10) spices and flavourings, and (11) beverages including dairy products. Thus, it may be concluded that there is no unanimity about food in different societies. In advanced and modern societies the food imply different meaning in comparisons to the backward or traditional societies. In other words we can say that every ethnic group has its own tradition of food classification. Despite this cultural variation about food classification, there is one traditional way of classification of foods into hot and cold in one form or the other is found in all the societies (Doshi: 1995 : 38). The hot-cold dichotomy is also known in the folk medicine of China, Burma, India an Sri Lanka. Luzzi (1987 :97) observed that, in Tamil Nadu hot food is avoided at puberty for girls. Non-vegetarian food too, for this purpose, is an avoidance. Out of a total of 1067 non-vegetarians, egg-consumers and qualified non-vegetarians, 837 (78.4 per cent) avoided all or some non-vegetarian item of diet at menarche, Jelliffe (1966) has carried out extensive nutrition work in villages of third world countries. On the basis of the empirical study he has outlined five major food classification viz. (1) Cultural super-food—It includes staple food, and regarded as the main source of calories. This category of food has emotional attachment to the people who preferentially consume it without any comprehension of its nutritional value. For example, rice is considered to be a staple food in south India. (2) Prestige Food— this category of food is specific to certain ceremonies and festivals and sometimes meant for prestigious people also. This is comparatively an expensive category of food. For instance, there is a tradition of prepaiing non-vegetarian food particularly meat while a maternal uncle visits to his nephews (sisters' sons) house in Kumauni community in Uttarakhand.

(3) Body-image food—with reference to hot and cold concept of disease, body-image-food is based on the ancient Hindu classification of body physiology into 'dosa' (humours). The importance of this classification is that, in addition to illness, food, herbs and medications are usually classified into these categorise. (4) Sympathetic Magic Food—this food is taken on the assumption that it affects its consumer. "This basic premise incorporated in sympathetic magic is that natural phenomena, such as the phases of the moon, position of the planets or season of the year directly affect the human body, or man as part of nature." (5) Physiological Groups of Food—some foods have physiological specifications for example, there are particular foods for pregnant women and old people.

Jelliffee's classification of foods appears to be culture-oriented and therefore seems to be more relevant to the traditional sections of the society particularly of Indian society. Even in the study of good culture of the tribals we have sufficient instances corresponding to Jelliffee's classification of food.

Thus, we may conclude that food is an important segment or component of nutrition and a determinant factor of health composition. Food may be used as an indicator to assess the nutritional status of an individual. Besides this, there are various techniques of assessments of nutritional status which are as follows: (i) Clinical examination (ii) Anthropometric (iii) Bio-chemical evaluation (iv) Functional assessment (v) Assessment of dietary intake (vi) Vital and health statistics, and (vii) ecological studies. All the techniques.used for evaluations of nutritional status are not exclusive but complementary. However, these 'Anthropometric' measurements are the most commonly used methods of assessing the nutritional status of a community. Since the procedures are complicated and standardisation has been difficult, WHO offers the following guidelines : (i) Overall assessment of a population requires a wide sample studies may concentrate on children below the age of 5 years who could serve as indicators (2) For areas of priority action height/weight and height/age could be considered to assess the nature of the problem. (3) In evaluating the impact of a programme, Anthropometric measurement have a dual function : they provide information on the nutritional status of children and are indicators of the programme's impact on the population as a whole. (4) In emergency situations where a cutoff point is necessary, height/weight can be used for screening to select those who need priority attention (5) sequential measurement is useful in studying the effect of seasonal changes in food supply or disease prevalence and for identifying alterations in growth at an early age. (6) Anthropometric assessment of individuals is undertaken to find out if growth is proceeding satisfactorily and naturally a single measurement is not useful.

Thus the Anthropometric measurements are useful not only for the assessment of the nutritional status of a given community but also for planning the programmes for health care. In the present study food pattern, dietary intake and ecological factors are scientifically discussed for the nutritional assessment of the tribals under study. Because the clinical examinations and anthropometric measurements in sociological studies have no relevance, nevertheless it was practically impossible to implement these techniques in the field study.

An Overview of the Literature

For a long time the tribals have been the focus of study for philosophers, physiologists, anthropologists, sociologists and historians. A bulk of descriptions is available about the different aspects of tribals viz. physiological, social, cultural, economic and socio-psychological, etc. Scientists, applying various approaches, tools and techniques, have been engaged in the study of the various aspects of tribal life. Indian tribes, which constitute about 9 per cent of the total population of the country have also been studied by the scholars of different disciplines from different points of view. While presenting an overview of the literature pertaining to the tribal studies, the demographic, linguistic, racial, cultural, economic, educational, health, hygiene and nutritional considerations have been taken into account for discussion here. So that a precise and explicit scenario of the tribals till the date in India and the studies carried out so far about them can be presented.

D.N. Majumdar (1965:253) has demarcated tribal population of India on the basis of geographical propinquity into three geographical zones viz. the north, north-eastern zone; the central or the middle zone; and the southern zone. The tribal areas of eastern Kashmir, east Punjab, Himachal Pradesh, Northern U.P. (Uttaranchal), Assam and Sikkim fall in the first zone. The central or the middle zone includes Bengal, Bihar, Southern U.P., Southern Rajasthan, Madhya Pradesh, Northern-Bombay and Orissa. Northern Rajasthan, southern Bombay and Bastar form the peripheral areas of this zones. In area and population of the tribals this zone comes first among the three zones. The southern zone comprises east Hyderabad, Mysore, Coorg, Travancore, Cochin, Andhra Pradesh and Chennai.

Taking into account the historical, ethnic and socio-cultural relations, B.K. Roy Burman (1972:5) has divided the tribal communities into five territorial groupings (1) North-East India comprising Assam, NEFA, Nagaland, Manipur and Tripura, (2) The Sub-Himalayan region of North- and North West India, comprising the Northern sub-mountain districts of

U.P. and Himachal Pradesh as a whole including the areas transferred from Punjab, (3) Central and East India comprising West Bengal, Bihar, Orissa, Madhya Pradesh and Andhra Pradesh, (4) South India comprising Chennai, Kerala and Mysore, (5) Western India comprising Rajasthan, Gujarat and Maharashtra.

B.S. Guha (1944) has made three broad geographical divisions of the Indian tribes. These are: (1) North and North-Eastern zone which includes Leh, Simla, Lusai hills, eastern Kashmir, eastern Punjab, Himachal Pradesh, Uttaranchal, and the hills of Assam. The major tribal communities living in this zone are, the Gaddi, Gujjar, Lamba, Khampa, Kanota, Lahaula, Jaunsari, Bhotiya, Tharu, Naga, Kuki, Khasi, Kachari, and Rabha tribes. (2) Central zone consists of Bengals, Bihar, southern U.P., south-Rajasthan, Madhya Pradesh, northern Mumbai and Orissa. The tribal communities living in this area are the Santhal, Oraon, Ho, Khariya, Birhor, Bhuyan, Gond, Baiga, Kond, Kota, Chenchu, Vehara, Korawa, Munda, Kol and Bhil and (3) The southern zone which includes Hyderabad, Mysore, Coorg, Travancore, Cochin, Andhra Pradesh and Chennai. The main tribal communities of this region are Chenchu, Kota, Kuramba, Baraga, Toda, Kadar, Malayan, Warli, Irula and Palayan.

Based on the Anthropometric and other related data Herbert Risley has made first ever scientific effort of making racial classification of the people of India including the tribes. He classified the people of India into seven racial types. These are (1) Turk-Iranian, (2) Indo-Aryan, (3) Seytho-Dravidian, (4) Aryo-Dravidian, (5) Mongolo-Dravidian, (6) Mongoloid and (7) Dravidians. These seven types can be reduced into three basic types viz. the Dravidian, the Mongolian and the Indo-Aryan. According to Risley the first two types would account for the racial composition of tribal India.

On the basis of the physical characters, artifacts, customs, folk tales, languages and the evidence of migration of people, A.C. Haddon has stated that the oldest habitants of India must have been the pre-Dravidian jungle tribes who he defines merely as an existing stratum. He regards the central Indian tribes as the autochthons of India and the Brachyephalic element as post-Mongolian and Alpine in origin.

Guha (1944) has classified the Indian tribes into six racial types. These are (1) The Negrito, (2) The Proto-Australoid (3) The Mongoloid, (4) The Mediterranean, (5) The Western Brachycephals and the Nordic. Guha states that the ancestry of the present tribal population is traced chiefly to the first three types. The Negrito is regarded as the earliest racial element as found among the Kadar. The central Indian tribes are assigned to the Proto-Australoid race and the North-North Eastern to the Mongoloid race. The Palaco-Mediterranean stock is also held responsible for the ancestry of some tribal communities. Regarding the racial composition of tribal India Guha has stated that - (i) the Kadar, the Irula and the Paniyan of south India with frizzly hair have an undoubted Negrito strain, (ii) the tribes of middle India belong to the proto-Australoid stock (iii) the Brachycephalic Mongoloids of north-eastern India with typical features of face and eyes, (iv) a slightly different Mongoloid type with medium stature, high head and medium nose living in the Brahmaputra valley.

Indian tribes belong to different language families. Prominent anthropologist D.N. Majumdar (1963:255-256) has divided the Indian tribes into three broad geographical regions. In the North and North-Eastern region most of the tribal people speak some form or the other of Sino-Tibetan and Tibeto-Burman language. While in some North-Eastern tribal areas there is an admixture of the Mon-Khmer (Austrid) speech, as is observed among the Khasis. It has been estimated that in the Naga hills, apart from numerous dialects sixteen languages are spoken. In the central zone, the Austric family of language is dominated, although important tribes like the Oraon, the Kolam, the Khond and the Gond speak languages having a Dravidian affinity. The Austric speech family includes the Kol and Munda languages and dialects of the central and the eastern India. Such languages and dialects deal with the Santhal, Mundari, Ho, Kharia, Bhoomij, Garo and Khasi languages and dialects which are mainly spoken in Bihar, Orissa, Bengal, and Assam. In the south the tribal people speak some form or the other of some Dravidian language like Tamil, Telgu, Malayalam and Coorgi. The Kadar of Travancore and Cochin speak a Malayalam dialect. Thus it is observed that the geographical regions denoted by Majumdar correspond roughly to three linguistic zones.

Alike the geographical, racial and linguistic variations we also observe cultural variations among the tribal communities of India. Bisht (1994:9) states "Some tribal communities have got the cultural position in the composite cultural system of Indian society, some are passing through the transitional period while some are still cling to the pivot of their traditional moorings. Some tribal communities have constantly been moving towards the urban and the industrial centres and following the respective cultural traits, some intend to move towards the glorified and glamourous world of urbans while some have still maintained their isolation in their age old habitations". Varrier Elwin (1963:263) categorised Indian tribes into four cultural categories (i) Those who are most primitive, live a joint community life and cultivate with axe, (ii) Those who are more individualistic, less occupied with axe cultivation, more used to outside life and generally less simple and honest than the first category (iii) Those who, under external influence, are already on way to the loss of their tribal culture, religion and social organization, and (iv) Those who are said to be the representatives of the old aristocracy of the country who retain much of their original tribal life who have won the battle of culture contact. Majumdar (1963 : 265-266) has classified Indian tribes on the basic idea of distance from rural-urban groups, i.e., : (1) those who are culturally most distanced from rural-urban groups (ii) those who are under the influence of rural-urban groups and have developed discomforts and problems and, (iii) those who are in contact with rural-urban groups and have acculturated into rural or urban cultures. A tribal welfare committee appointed by the Indian Conference of Social Work (1952) suggested four cultural categories of the Indian tribes, viz. (i) tribal communities (ii) semi-tribal communities (iii) acculturated tribal communities, and (iv) totally assimilated tribes.

In view of the planned social change and the process of cultural transformation that took place particularly in post-independence era, the cultural scenario of the tribals reflects some other types of images. It is observed that tribal communities which have completely assimilated themselves with non-tribal cultures are now in the process of re-tribalization as to maintain their status-quo. In fact, the tribals having achieved maximum benefits of the constitutional provisions, government welfare and development policies and programmes as well as of the reservations appear to be perturbed by doubts of losing the benefits meant for the STs, due to their high socio-economic status. They are forming different tribal organizations and motivating their people in the name of the protection of tribal interests, tribal status-quo and tribal culture. In real sense they are making a pressure group as to maintain their status-quo so that their coming generations can avail the benefits of the welfare policies and programmes meant for the STs. While there are tribal communities which are socio-economically and educationally backward and able to assimilate themselves neither with the non-tribal culture nor with their in-group tribal elites. There are still some tribal communities which are not at all in the position of tribalism nor are they in the process of culture transformation. A deformed type of cultural position in which neither any basic tribal character exists nor the people are able to assimilate with out-cultures. This cultural position is some sort of identity loss and can be termed as 'Ritualism'. Without knowing the implication of any institutional norms as well as of the planned process of development people follow the things only by nodding acquaintance. In brief, it can be concluded that culturally Indian tribes can be categorised into three major categories: (1) the tribal communities which are in the process of re-tribalization, (2) those tribal communities which are in the process of sanskritizatlion and, finally (3) those tribal communities which are in the state of ritualism.

Besides this there is also an economic gradation of the Indian tribes. Economically the tribal communities vaıy from one another. Even the impact of various planned processes of development has been proved to be uneven throughout the tribal population. Majumdar (1963 : 267-268) has categorised the Indian tribes into four groupings. These are : (i) the tribes dependent on forests and dwell in forested regions with food gathering type of economy, (ii) those tribal communities which have an economy midway between food gathering and primitive agricultural types, (iii) those tribal communities depending upon some form of agriculture with forest produce as a secondary support, and (iv) a new category of tribesmen engaged in industries with the effect of 'push' and 'pull' factors.

Nicboer has classified the Indian tribes into seven economic types, these are (i) gleaners (ii) hunters (iii) fishers (iv) settled agriculturists of lower grade who also hunt wild animals (v) agricultural nomads or hunter-agriculturists (vi) superior farmers who have complex implements, and (vii) nomad-shepherds. Ernest Gross describes five forms of tribal economy - (i) collectional economy (ii) cultural nomadic economy (iii) settled village economy (iv) town economy and (v) metropolitan economy. Jacob and Stern have divided the primitive economy into two major parts (i) Hunting, fishing and food gathering economy, the type includes (a) simple food gathering economy (b) advanced food gathering economy (ii) Agricultural and pastoral economy which includes (a) simple agriculture and pastoral economy (b) advanced agricultural and pastoral economy. Thurnwald (1933) has classified the primitive economy into seven types: (i) homogeneous communities of hunters, trappers and food collectors (ii) homogeneous communities of hunters, trappers and agriculturists (iii) graded society of hunters, trappers, agriculturists and artisans (iv) herdsmen (v) homogeneous hunters and herdsmen (vi) ethnically stratified cattle breeders and traders, and (vii) socially graded herdsmen with hunting, agricultural and artisan population.

It is observed that different thinkers have their own viewpoints and experience about the economic life of the tribals. These classical classifications of the economic gradation of the tribal economy have lost their relevance in the present-day context. Today any tribal community cannot be identified with any particular occupation because each and every tribal community is engaged in more than one occupation. It is so because single source of subsistence is not sufficient for the fulfilment of various needs even of the tribals today. The tribals therefore follow more than one occupation for their subsistence. Majumdar (1955 : 138) has aptly stated that, "The grading of the tribes on the basis of their economic life and occupation and in accordance with any approved scheme of classification is indeed difficult as most of the tribes possess either 'marginal' cultures or follow more than one occupation. The tribal stage does not provide for any specialization of function and as such a variety of occupations are followed by a tribe".

Today Indian tribes can also be classified on the bases of their religious beliefs. According to census reports of 1961 and 1991 Indian Tribes can be classified into six religious groups. These are (i) Hindu (ii) Christian (iv) Buddha (iv) Islam (v) Jain and (vi) others. Approximately 90 per cent of the tribal population in India follow Hindu religion while the rest 10 per cent belong to Christianity, Buddhism, Islam, Jainism and other faiths.

Thus it is obvious that Indian tribes belong to a variety of racial stocks, linguistic families and also differ from each other on the bases of cultural system, economic gradation and religious faiths.

At the global plane as well as in India, social scientists have been interested in the study of the tribals and their different aspects of life. If we prepare an account of the literature of the tribal studies, we have bulks of material about them. Since the main object of the present study is to bring forth the scientific reality of educational, health, hygiene and nutritional status of the tribals of Uttaranchal, it will be relevant to present an overview of the related studies only. In this context there are references of various studies which are as follows:

Studies on Tribal Education

It is believed that the education is the only means by which all sorts of developmental processes can be planned, implemented and have fruitful results. As the people will be in a position to overcome the problems through awakening and creating their awareness which is possible only through education. It is only education that makes the people aware of their rights, liberties, interests, duties and dealings. If we turn over the pages of history we envisage a variety of thoughts, ideas and principles underlying education in the policies and thoughts of different organizations and thinkers. As, for instance, in the pre-independence India, the British Education Policy was typical, limited and extended to a certain group of people. In India the only aim of British Education Policy was preparing a breeding ground for clerks. Gandhi's basic education policy was to make an individual a self-reliant, self-sufficient and patriot. Tagore's educational thought of new realization was an exception. Loknaik Jaiprakash Narayan was against the traditional system of British education policy. In the context of educational policies and thoughts of great personalities, the government of free India made various educational policies and incorporated new ideas when and where it was felt so. With this view in mind the educational facilities were extended even to the backward tribal areas and the tribal people along with the whole of the Indian society was motivated. No doubt there is tremendous progress in literacy percentage among the people of India in general and of the tribal people in particular. The available data given in the following Table 2.1, exhibits the real picture of literacy percentage of general masses and of the Scheduled Tribes in India.

Table 2.1. Literacy in India

Year	*General Literacy Percentage*	*ST Literacy Percentage*
1901	5.35	NA
1911	5.92	NA
1921	7.16	NA
1931	9.50	0.75
1941	16.10	NA
1951	16.67	NA
1961	24.02	8.54
1971	29.45	11.29
1981	36.23	16.35
1991	52.21	29.60

Source : 1991 Census report.

The 1991 census data imply that out of 100 ST persons approximately 70.40 per cent are illiterate. The census report 1991 also exhibits that there is great variation between the literacy level of the Scheduled Tribes, Scheduled Castes and Non-SC, Non-ST population. Some available census data showing the level of literacy among the SCs, STs and Non-SCs,Non-STs can be presented as follows :

Table 2.2. Level of Literacy among Different Sections of Indian Society Literacy Percentage of Scheduled Castes, Scheduled Tribes and General Population

Census Year	*Scheduled Castes*	*Scheduled Tribes*	*Non-SC Non-ST Population*	*Literacy gap between Non-SC-Non-ST and*	
				SCs	*STs*
1961	10.27	8.53	27.86	17.59	19.33
1971	14.67	11.30	33.80	19.13	22.50
1981	21.38	16.35	41.30	19.84	24.87
1991	37.41	29.60	62.25	25.24	33.05

Source : Educational Statistics of Scheduled Castes and Scheduled Tribes, Ministry of Human Resource Development 1993.

Reviewing the educational status of the tribes in India, Singh (1995:31) concludes that "The literacy percentage is still at a low level and has been moving up slowly. Further, tribal education has been marked by certain disparities. Some of them are in common with education among other sections of the population: inter-state, inter-region, urban-rural, male-female. It is also characterised by ethnic, i.e., inter-tribe and inter-district disparities which are peculiar to the tribal milieu."

Sachchidanand (1995 : 38-49) has elucidated the role and need of non-formal education in tribal areas. Non-formal education is meant to cater to the needs of school dropouts in the 9 to 14 year age bracket. The curriculum includes literacy, numeracy, environmental studies, social awareness, general science, health and hygiene and socially productive activities. A large number of non-formal centres have been started in various tribal areas in the country. This is in addition to the national adult education programme which caters to the needs of adults in the age group 15 to 35 years. In this programme besides literacy and numeracy, stress is laid on creating awareness of the surroundings and upgrading traditional skills with a view to augmenting the income of the adults. An empirical evaluation of the academic aspects of non-formal education programme in Bihar, made by NCERT, New Delhi (1986), reveals that most of the centres were running in unsatisfactory locations. In some centres learners have to brave the sun and the shower alike; there is hardly any provision for drinking water. Many centres were located so close to the cows and buffaloes that the whole place stinks with dung and filth. It is futile to expect that the learners can get an idea of clean habits, good health and meaningful education if the centres are run under such conditions. Out of sample of 20 centres in Kanke (Ranchi) and Chainpur (Gumla), 11 were poor in academic achievement, 7 were average and only two were good.

Most of the tribes in India have their own traditional institutions for educational purpose which cater the need of their social, cultural and economic education. There are informal institutions which impart education in the realm of social norms, customs, traditions, culture, behaviour patterns, economic system and religion to the people particularly the adolescence and the youths of the community. These informal institutions are known by different names in different tribal communities. Such as, Naga-Morung, Munda-Gitiora, Abors-Mosup, Oraon-Dhumkuria, Gond-Ghotul, Mikir-Terang, Kuki-Z Walbuk, Bhotiya-Ran-ban-chim and Garo-Nokpanti. In this context Ambasht (1995 : 50-59) has made an illustration about the role of Dhumkuria and Gitiora in learning process. Steward (1954 : 142) has stated that institution (i.e., Dhumkuria or Gitiora) serves as psychological agency for proper personality formation, parental overprotection leading to prolonged-dependence spells disaster for later life. Sachchidanand (1994) states, "In social affairs Dhumkuria acts for the entire village and knits together the local population". These institutions are the best effective source of imparting sex-education to the growing youths which is earnestly needed in the present day context when the dangers of AIDS are hovering all around. But the decaying of such institutions has created a gap which needs to be revamped.

Kohli (1995 : 66-67) has made an attempt of studying the moral values through informal education among Adi, Apatani and Nishing tribes of Arunanchal Pradesh. He concludes that the strategy for the value oriented education policy, besides having common norm for the whole nation, may include moral lessons imparting folklores/folk songs from one's own society.

Lakshmaiah (1995 : 117 -133) has conducted a comparative study of two blocks in Ranchi district in former Bihar state. This study aims at (i) assessing the existing pattern of education and educational facilities available to the tribes, (ii) identifying the constraints which impede the process of education, (iii) identifying the reasons of differential success of the government and non-governmental organizations in delivering educational inputs and (iv) studying the impact of education on the life styles of tribal students. This study concludes that education in isolation cannot bring about social change. Similar changes ought to take place in other spheres also. It tends to support that simultaneous efforts in socio-economic and educational spheres are bound to be necessary to realise desirable development and social change.

Joseph Bara (1996 : 32-55) has conducted a study on 'Western education and rise of new identity among the Mundas and the Oraons of Chotanagpur 1839-1939. Bara observes that while western education was a factor behind the rise of an articulate tribal leadership, its uneven diffusion combined with growing agrarian crisis, social development among Christian converts and urbanization to produce certain side effects.

S.N. Ratha (1992 : 3-4) has made an evaluation of literacy in tribal India. He concludes that only 16.35 per cent (1981 census) tribals in the country are reported to be literate. The difference between the literacy level of the general population and the tribal population is 19.88 per cent. Wide differences are observed in the literacy level from tribe to tribe. There are tribes who have achieved a very high level of literacy to the extent of 100 per cent, whereas some are still at less than one per cent level. The gulf between the literacy levels of the tribal population and the general population is also considerably high.

Barman (1992:15-21) has conducted a sociological study of education among the Lepchas of Darjeeling. The inferences of this study are based on the fieldwork done by the author himself in the village

Ngasey under Kalimpong-1 Gram Panchayat of Darjeeling district. The author observed that in the Ngasey village the enrolment rate for the school-age population is cent-per cent. Stagnation and dropout rate is also not very high, i.e., 17 per cent only which is shared by male and female, which means a steady development in education among them. In the village the Lepcha literacy rate was 88 per cent in comparison to 25.50 per cent of the total Lepcha literacy in the district. More than 50 per cent literate adults had secondary standard education while 64 per cent of total literate crossed primary stage of education. This reflects a bright sign of overall development of the tribal people.

R. Chandra (1992:22-34) has presented an appraisal of the situation of education in Nilgiri tribes of Tamil Nadu. The conclusions are drawn on the basis of a fieldwork conducted among the tribes of Nilgiris during the year 1978-1983. The author observed that six tribal groups of Nilgiris, viz. the Toda, Kota, Irula, Kurumba, Kattu Naicken and the Paniya, dwell at different heights and areas. The author finds that the Toda have the maximum literacy rate yet it is the Irula and some group of the Kurumba who are maximum in number in Government Tribal Residential School Centres. The author has takes into account the 'Modernity' measurement scale for assessing the education and its implication on tribals. For him modernity is a strong indicator of transformation of any society if it is to be assessed from development or progress point of view. Lastly, the author concludes that the efforts of state level planning and execution of education programme among the tribals has been rewarding. Education, irrespective of its status and priority given to it and infrastructure provided for this cause, seems to have made positive impacts and produced results.

In an analysis of educational and economic achievements and trend thereof among the Scheduled Tribes of West Bengal, A.K. Das (1992:35-45) illustrated that the communities found to be educationally advanced are also economically better-off. But they cover an insignificant fraction of the total scheduled tribe population. Thus, it indicates a positive relation between economic status and educational achievement. Das also stressed that the comparatively more affluent section of the community is utilising and sucking up more and more of the benefits of welfare programmes and the poorer section is left behind. If this is allowed to continue the gulf between the two sections will widen and ultimately lead to disintegration at the community level.

M. Kundu (1992:46-53) is of the opinion that the tribal education in India is beset with a multiplicity of problems some of which are really very complex and need a deliberate, concerted systematic approach for the solution. He advocates for designing an effective pedagogy for tribal education in India. For this purpose a great deal of anthropological and sociological study of tribals is necessary because the study of their culture, folklore, traditions, customs, superstitions and attitudes will help in planning courses, educational programmes, writing textbooks and diagnosing cultural conflicts. Das also advocates for 'compensatory education programme' for the tribal learners as to check the 'cumulative deficit'. Thus pre-schools with child-care and health components should be established to remedy the tribal learner's deficiency and to prepare him for school. Pre-schools should cater to the improvement of child's physical and mental health, emotional and social development, conceptual and verbal skills and motivation to learn. Besides this, ethnic studies should be incorporated in the school curriculam for both tribal and non-tribal students. The ethnic studies will broaden the ethnic perspective, develop in both the groups mutual understanding and enable them to understand their own culture and be proud of it. It will discourage ethnocentrism and help them to learn to function within and across cultures. Das also states that there is an urgent need of changes in the existing system of education by (i) adapting schools and the system of educating tribal cultures, (ii) imparting education in tribal mother tongues, stressing development of reading skills, preparation of textbooks, methods of teaching and community involvement. Mathur (1992 : 54-98) has conducted a study on tribal education in Kerala with special reference to G.R.B.T. Schools located in the Wyned Valley, the most important tribal pocket of the state. The inferences of the study are based on the data gathered with the help of 'schedules' prepared for this purpose. Besides this, personal interviews were made with the teachers and other members of staff. Some local people, parents of the students were also interviewed for the collection of information. Actual conduct of classes by teachers, hygiene habits of children, their class room behaviour and leisure time behaviour were also observed. The study concludes that the functioning of the GRBT Schools cannot be considered a grand success or as an utter failure at present. In the GRBT Schools the students are provided with freeships, free boarding and lodging besides an incentive of Rs. 10/- to the parents per child. However, despite some progress, the desired benefit has not reached the tribal children so far.

B.K. Roy Burman (1992 : 161-169), has made a suggestive comment on the prevailing pattern of tribal education, status of research and sociological dimensions for projecting the future. He states that, "As part of the overall strategy of nation building and in pursuance of the Directive Principles of State Policy, the Government has provided a number of incentives and facilities for children belonging to STs and SCs. These include stipends and scholarships, free books and uniforms, hostels and boarding grants. A number of states have initiated steps to increase enrolments and retain children in schools. Special coaching programmes have also been arranged to enable the Scheduled Tribes children to overcome their environmental handicaps and educational backwardness. Notwithstanding the promotional activities, the levels of literacy of the Scheduled Tribes remained low as is obvious from the data pertaining to the literacy level of the scheduled tribes in preceding decade census reports. Further, presenting an over-view of the pattern of spread of tribal education and of the status of empirical research, he (Burman) states that "for projecting the future of tribal education the requisite research based data are not available. In the absence of the same, some of the theoretical formulations of various scholars and some hypotheses are presented. These would indicate the massive work that must be done for systematic educational planning among the tribals." In the interest of systematic educational planning of the tribals, Burman has presented a number of hypotheses which will require careful verification. Thus Burman has suggested some essential sociological dimensions for projecting the future planning of tribal education.

Sinha (1992:173-183) has conducted a case study on 'University Education among the Tribals of Chotanagpur : Sinha stated that the tribal people in Chotanagpur region are educationally backward. During British time, the university education was available only to the elite and the tribal people could not think of this education. After independence this outlook changed and government became more interested in the education of weaker sections of the people including tribals. The data based on a sample study of 200 tribal students of different facilities of Post-Graduate Departments in Ranchi University show that most of the tribal students (63.5 per cent) are interested in Arts including Commerce subjects, while 10.5 per cent, 1.00 per cent, 13.00 per cent and 11.00 per cent students belong respectively to Science, Agriculture, Law, Technical and Educational (B.Ed. and M.Ed.) subjects. Describing the aims of university education among tribals, their fulfilment, conspicuous tribal problems, Sinha has suggested some points for university education of the tribals.

S. Narayan (1992 : 184-194) had made a study on, "Education : Then and now among Oraon children of Barambe village of the Mandar Block of Ranchi District in Bihar State". This study aims to highlight the educational scene of the Oraon children in its traditional past context. The author states that the Oraons of Chotanagpur had their traditional institutions for imparting education to its young ones. Dhumkuriya known as Jonkherpa in their language, is the youth dormitory for boys and a youth dormitory locally known as Palerpa is for the girls. In traditional system of education was imparted by the youth dormitories at period of transition from childhood to adult life. The indigenous system was designed to train a child for group life and consequently attention was focussed on the group rather than the individual. But the Dhumkuriya has largely disappeared in many Oraon villages due to the propaganda carried on by the Church and Social Welfare workers. The establishment of schools in villages also seems to have adversely affected the institution. Apart from informal education the Oraons of Barambe have the facilities of formal education. Such facilities are extended to them through the institutions run by the Government or by the missionaries. But the response to such facilities is very poor. It is so because the children are considered economic asset of the family therefore the Oraon parents were of the opinion that except the months of October, November, December and January they are not in a position to send their children to school as they help the family economy.

Maulik (1992 :195-202) has presented a study report on "Mode of subsistence and response to elementary education in some tribes of Orissa". The report was based on the data gathered from eight tribal communities; the Kharia, Santhal, Bhumij, Bado Gadaba, Bhattada, Koya, Bhuiyan and Kissan. The report concludes that forest-based economy of the tribals is rapidly changing without any sustainable alternative. Children are often inducted in the family economic activities. The areas, where these tribal folks share the ecozone with other non-tribal communities, attraction or response to education is better. At the same time the present form of primary education does not offer any solution to produce an efficient tribal person fit to draw as much benefits from the field or forest.

Besides this there are several studies pertaining to the problems of tribal education in India. In this context, Kurup (1992 : 205-212) has presented an overview of the tribal literacy in India and also pointed out some problems of tribal education. For Kurup the major problems pertaining to the tribal education are related to language, teachers, attendance, topography and climate, school timings, school going children, purpose of education, syllabus, poverty, adjustment, agencies of education, leadership and administration.

In order to understand the problem of tribal education Nagla (1992: 213-214) has made an effort for examining the tribal education policy and the sub-plan for tribal development in southern Rajasthan. For assessing the spread of education amongst STs Nagla has taken into consideration the factors like; level of literacy, enrolment of tribal boys and girls, educational institution, residential facilities for tribal students, other assistance programmes, etc. The analysis is based on secondary information gathered from census Deptt., Social Welfare Deptt., Department of Planning, Department of Education, etc. Nagla comes to the conclusion that "despite the considerable investment in the field of education, and the progress made, we have yet to achieve the goal of universalization of elementary education and the complete eradication of illiteracy. The poor economic condition of the tribals combined with age-old traditions are largely responsible for their indifference as well as apathy towards education. Apathy is more pronounced in the case of girls' education."

An evaluation of the problems of education in tribal areas has been presented by Lakshmaiah (1992: 225-239) in an article entitled; "Problems of Education in Tribal Areas on the Basis of the Facts and Figures Available from Different Sources". He concludes that the overall existing position of education in tribal area is far from satisfactory in spite of various incentive schemes and other development measures initiated. As a whole the system of education is beset with various problems which hinder educational development for tribals.

Moreso, the empirical studies undertaken by the social scientists, the committee reports also exhibit a number of problems of tribal education. Elvin (1960) suggested that the tribal education should be linked with their traditional crafts, arts, inherent talents and skills. The report of the Scheduled Area and Scheduled Tribe Commission headed by U.N. Dhebar (1981) concludes that the poor economic condition, lack of proper equipment in schools and communication facilities, unsuitable medium of instruction, inappropriate content and coverage of syllabus were major hurdles in tribal education. Joshi (1982) stated that prevailing ignorance among tribals, reluctance of parents towards education, unhappy school atmosphere and medium of instruction and the family environment of the tribals are responsible factors for the incidence of high dropout among the tribal students.

Lakshmaiah and Yadappanaver (1986) undertook a study on educational facilities for tribal students in Paderu Samithi, Visakhapatnam. They observed that the schools, hostels and Ashram schools were not properly equipped and maintained, thus, inadequate to meet the educational requirements. For them the single teacher schools, differential attitude of parents towards girls' education and policy of admission into Ashram schools and hostels were found as bottlenecks.

In another study conducted in Ranchi district by Lakshmaiah (1987) it was observed that the Christian missionary schools were faring well in comparison to the schools under government management. This study reveals that the medium of instruction, lack of sufficient finances, mis-utilization of stipend and scholarship, improper implementation of incentive schemes and conflicting relations of government and Christian management were the main constraints of tribal education.

Sachchidanand (1992) talked about the structural constraints in the education of Scheduled Tribes and Scheduled Castes. For him these are ecological, socio-economic, and psychological constraints and the constraints of the educational system in the education of the Scheduled Tribes and Scheduled Castes due to which the spread as well as progress of education among the tribals has remained poor.

Behura (1992 : 255-265) has pointed out some constraints in tribal culture that are repugnant to formal education in tribal areas. For him the home atmosphere, the school atmosphere, language, tribal economy and the economic role of tribal children, their sex life (i.e., laxity of sex and the exposure to sex-life relatively in early age) are some of the factors that hinder the growth of formal education among the tribes. He asserted that the tribal culture embodies not only growth-negative values. But there are indeed growth positive or at least growth-neutral values also. No culture is negatively oriented towards development or modernization. What is necessary for the development planners and executives is the appropriate orientation to grasp and comprehend objectively the ethos or genius of the target culture to which development plans must be attained.

A.K. Danda (1992 : 266-293) has made an exercise which deals 'how scheduled tribe students tend to evaluate the programmes specifically drawn and implemented by the government for their benefit. For this purpose Danda interviewed 225 high school students and 1783 college students all belonging to Scheduled Tribes. The respondents were classified on the basis of states, sex, and hostellers, and non-hostelries for analysis. It was observed that mostly the students irrespective of their status (they live in), sex, hostellers or non-hostelries and even education standard do not agree with the preposition that the special provisions for Scheduled Tribes destroy their interest today. Though there is little percentage of the students in all categories who support this preposition, however the bulk of students in all categories fell that the matter is not applicable to their cases.

Studies on Tribal Health, Hygiene and Nutrition

Health, hygiene and nutrition are inter-related aspects which jointly ascertain the health status of an individual. Health, as such, depends to some extent on the food-ideology of a given community. It is aptly stated that, "Food ideology refers to the practices associated with consumption of food, i.e., the usual or customary items preferred and selected, the rituals of eating under variable circumstances, eating territory, eating times and frequency and meal climate. It has been defined as attitudes, beliefs, customs and taboos affecting diet and nutrition. The concept of food ideology is comprehensive and includes what people think about each of the different items that might be considered as food. It also includes people's concern about the effects of eating various foods in their health and well being. It is within the concepts to find out what kinds of foods people think are suitable for individuals and categories of people, i.e., the old, infant, sick, pregnant and lactating mothers. It also takes within its scope as to what kinds of foods are suitable in certain conditions, for instance, menstruation period or pregnancy (Eckstein, Eleanor F. 1980 : 222).

The food ways of a community are determined by the food ideology of the people. The food ways include customary patterns of activities associated with acquisition, preparation, serving, consumption and storing of food. The food habits on the other hand, refer to the practices related to consumption of food, i.e., the customary items preferred and selected and eaten under different circumstances.

Doshi (1995) has conducted a case study of the tribals of Rajasthan within the framework of food in culture. This leads him to discuss various aspect of tribal food habits, food preparation, food preference, hot and cold food and ceremonial food. Doshi attempted to develop a theory of tribal stratification on the basis of food habits as indicators. The class view of diet, disease and health is also illustrated by him. He also brings within his focus the need for an adequate national food policy.

Narayan (1997) has made a study on health and development in India. The basic objective of the study was to identify inter-sectoral linkages in the development and, in the process, to explain the interstate variations in the health status in India. In studying the inter-sectoral linkages, the primary emphasis was on the relationship between health status, health care services and other components of socio-economic development such as education, status of women, infrastructure, agriculture and industry. The inferences of the study were based on secondary data gathered from fifteen major Indian states accounting for ninety-six per cent of the country's population. The study argues that the improvement in health status is an outcome of development measured not in terms of per capita income but in terms of overall socio-economic conditions. The decrease in mortality rates and increase in life expectancy imply wider percolation of benefits from the development process. The composite index of development was also closely associated with the literacy rate among the Scheduled Castes. The Scheduled Castes being the most deprived social group in India, the correlation of composite index with their literacy provides ample evidence for its sensitivity to the distributional aspects of the development process.

Akhtar and Verhasselt (1990) have presented a rich literature on disease ecology and health. Through case studies from Latin America, African and Asian countries 'Disease Ecology and Health' investigates environmental framework of health and disease and encompasses aspects, such as, the geochemistry of health and disease in Sri Lanka, framework of research and teaching in medical geography in Maxico, Dracunculiasis in Togo, alcohol consumption and health problems in Southern Africa, malnutrition in rural Haryana, food distribution system in India and health care in Hong Kong. The information presented in the book identifies imbalances in health care provision and outlines ways to minimise these through health care planning.

Dissanayake (1990:75-92) has conducted a study on 'Human Health Problems in Sri Lanka'. The study subsumes that the bulk of Sri Lanka's health problems are deeply rooted in the environment. Deaths caused by water-related diseases have increased rapidly in the past few years.

Matzke (1990:121-128) has made a study on 'Health Consequences of Tsetse Zone Expansion in Zambia'. Matzke is of the opinion that the Tsetse flies are links in a series of interrelated health problems unique to Africa. This study illustrates some possible health consequences of these Tsetse range shifts with special reference to the case of Zambia. It also suggests a research agenda which flows from these consequences.

Freund (1990 : 145-153), has completed a research work on 'Child health and Nutrition in Zambia'. The main focus of the study was to investigate the problems of delivering health services to remote rural population and to evaluate and monitor the impact of primary health care. The major emphasis of the study is on women and children and involves an assessment of child health, status, nutrition, maternal/ reproductive data and the utilization pattern of health services. The study concludes that the national-level health statistics and health centre records show an increase in malnutrition admission and mortality. The study has also shown that the most severely malnourished are either not brought to the health centres even when they are accessible or are treated with traditional medicines when health facilities are inaccessible. Moreover there is a whole complex of socio-cultural factors (e.g., food distribution patterns, attitudes regarding the cause of disease etc.) that make the situation worse. Finally the study emphasizes the importance of health education and community outrich efforts by health workers to help overcome these obstacles.

Aggarwal (1990:155-164) with a view to estimate the determinants of malnutrition with a comparative analysis for different geographic areas, has conducted a study on 'Malnutrition in Rural Haryana'. The study was carried out in ten purposefully selected villages from three derived ecological zones so as to reflect the varied physical, socio-economic and cultural conditions of the Haryana state. The study concludes that malnutrition in children in Haryana was related to several inter-related factors, i.e., environment, sanitation, income, demography, dietary pattern, sociocultural aspects prevailing in the study area.

In another study Freund (1990 : 235-243) has described the research findings on 'Household Health Surveys and Health Indicators'. The fieldwork was focussed on two rural areas. The site-selection was based on three criteria: (1) that primary health-care be in its initial stages of implementation (i.e., training of community health workers); (2) that they should be sufficiently remote from large urban centres; and (3) that the two areas chosen should be different in term of environment so that comparisons and contrasts could be made. It was the long-term community-based study being conducted in Zambia. The study comes to the conclusion that there are indicators/factors viz: (i) Socio-demographic-community dependency ratio (number of children and adults over age 60 as compared to 14-59 years), sex-ratio, education of household head, average house-hold-size, (ii) Sanitation/environment, house type, pit latrines by total households, environmental risk conditions, (i.e., swampy, cold), (iii) nutrition-annual average-income, soil fertility, periods of drought, percentage of children, under-weight (health records and measurements), land cultivated/household, existence of marketing infrastructure, number of female-headed households, (iv) maternal/ reproductive-age at first pregnancy, survival ratio by gravid category, infant mortality rate, under five mortality, pregnancy wastage (still births and miscarriages), reported difficulties in child-birth, anti-natal attendance, (v) health service utilization-geographical distance of health facilities, accessibility of health facilities (roads, transport), adequacy of health facilities (drugs, staff, equipment). Finally the study concludes that all the indicators are interrelated and no single indicator or category can provide an accurate picture of a community's health status.

There are ample case studies on 'Health care Planning' out of which the case studies conducted by Phillips (1990), Iyun (1990) and Henkel (1990) are of great importance. Phillips conducted a case study on 'Health care Planning in Hong Kong'. The study provides information on the ways in which one rapidly modernizing and quite wealthy country within the tropics has developed its health system in recent years. Western medicine, centralised planning (with regional execution) and strict adherence to get guidelines given personnel limitations—have all influenced Hong Kong's medical advances.

Iyun (1990) in a case study on, 'Health Care Planning and Distribution of Health Services in Oy State, Nigeria', has tried to analyse the spatial pattern of health facilities and the major factors that have influenced the location of hospital services in Ibadan city which is the largest indigenous urban centre in Africa. The study describes that the inhabitants of the city suffer mainly from diseases, such as, diarrhoea and gastroenteritis, malaria, pneumonia, tuberculosis, eye diseases, measles, malnutrition, hypertension and chicken pox. Ibadan city offers a variety of health services, provided by state government, federal government, local government, church missions and private proprietors. The study also provides information about the spatial patterns of the hospitals in Ibadan, historical development of hospital services in Ibadan, and finally the planning implications of the spatial pattern of health facilities. The study concludes that the Ibadan city needs more health units in order to provide an efficient health care delivery system to the population and also suggests that it should be made mandatory nationally for new urban layouts to set aside spaces for the provision of social services.

Maro (1990:293-301) has completed a study on 'population distribution and health facilities in Tanzania. In the study the researcher has presented a brief discussion of the pattern of population distribution which is followed by an outline of government policy and targets of health care. The study investigates that the population is unevenly distributed in Tanzania but the government commitment to socialist transformation based on the rural areas led to the villagisation programme that saw the entire rural population collectivised into more accessible, nucleated settlements. Health facilities and services have been provided keeping in view the patterns of population distribution to ensure that such services have maximum accessibility. However, the quality of health services in rural Tanzania is generally inadequate.

Henkel (1990 :303-313) has also made a study of 'Health care services in Zambia'. This study was undertaken in order to understand and analyse the spatial structure of presently existing health-care systems and also in order to make meaningful proposal for planning. The study comes to the conclusion that the urban areas were much better of in terms of medical supply at independence than the rural areas. But this situation has been reversed to a great extent at least if the population/bed ratio is applied as a measure.

Swain (1998) presented an overview of the studies and the articles on 'health and nutrition in Tribal areas'. The review of literature confirm that not only is there a lack of information but also that there is some misinformation, such as the view that tribals are ill-fed but well-nourished. In general the studies available are inadequate in numbers and quality and are lopsided in approach.

Singh (1995 : 17-32) presents very lucidly an overview of tribal health in Indian context. Extracting some relevant points for the draft prepared by UN working group on indigenous people. Singh states that (i) Article 23 narrates that indigenous people have the right to determine and develop priorities and strategies for exercising their right to development. Indigenous people have a right to determine and develop all health, housing, and other economic and social programmes affecting them and as far as possible, to administer such programmes through their own institutions.

Article 24 describes that indigenous people have the right to their traditional medicines and health practices including the right to protection of vital medicinal plants, animals and minerals. They have also the right to access without any discrimination to stall medical institution, health services and medical care.

Article 28 states that States shall also take effective measures to ensure, as needed, that programmes for monitoring, maintaining and restoring the health of indigenous peoples, as developed and implemented by the people affected by such materials, are duly implemented. While Article 29 has provision that they (indigenous people) have the right to special measures to control, develop and protect their science, technologies and cultural manifestations, including human and other genetic resources, seeds, medicines, knowledge of the properties of fauna and flora, oral traditions, literatures, designs and visual and performing arts.

Singh also refers the recommendation contained in the report of the committee of MPs and Experts (January 1995) that health and education should be the first charge on the finances of Panchayat in Scheduled Areas and Tribal areas on coming into being in pursuance of the Constitution (Seventy-third Amendment) Act 1992. More so, Singh has also presented a lucid account of information pertaining to specific diseases affecting tribals, state of tribal mental health, genetic environment, tribal medicine, family planning and welfare and health delivery system in tribal areas. Singh concludes, in the perspective of health of members of the tribal communities, in interacting factors, i.e., (a) effect of environment inhabited by a tribal community (b) behavioural pattern, cultural pattern and life-style of a community (c) hereditary and genetic determinants, and (d) health care delivery services particularly with reference to cultural constraints need to be analysed and appreciated clearly. Singh observed that issues concerning tribal health, nutrition and genetic-environmental aspects are obscure, having been under-researched. He suggests that the tribal health problems should not be viewed in a purely technological frame, but should have a human perspective. For Singh, the tribal communities in general and primitive tribal groups in particular, who are particularly exposed and disease-prone, do not have the basic health facilities. Being the next exploited, most neglected and most disease-vulnerable with a high degree of malnutrition, morbidity and mortality They are the people who need health care the most. Their misery is compounded by their poverty, ignorance of causes of diseases and a hostile environment. For raising the level of tribal health, a multi-sectorial holistic effort is a sine qua non. Preventive and immunisational measures are necessary. Hygiene and sanitation have to be introduced de rigeur. Health education is essentially simultaneous. The socio-economic condition of the tribals needs to be raised to an appropriately high level so that he can afford for himself and his family, in fact the entire community, a sufficiently nutritious diet, hygienic surroundings and disease-free living.

Mahanti (1995:33-38) concludes in an article on 'Tribal Health in India: Retrospect and Prospect' that the important issues regarding 'tribal health in India needs to be discussed, debated on and looked into from different angles as well as feasibility and practicability in the remote areas. Mahanti suggests, this need be given proper importance by medical institution, medical research units, major hospitals, proponents of different systems of medicine, tribal research institutions, anthropologists, sociologists, ethno-botanists as well as NGOs associated with traditional medicines, alternative systems of health care as well as integrated health care system in our country.

B. K. Roy Burman, an eminent social scientist, in his key-note-address, in a seminar on 'Tribal Health' has stated that the tribal health should be viewed holistically and in the overall perspective. Burman is of the opinion that disorders in tribal physical systems are not merely medical manifestations but connected environmentally also. More so, cultural practices determine incidence of diseases to a considerable extent. He states that an assessment indicates that 80 per cent of the tribal population is afflicted with water-borne diseases.

The recommendations of the Seminar on "Tribal Health" held on 26-27 Oct. 1994 indicated that the question of tribal health should be considered comprehensively and in this context the physical, psychological, socio-cultural, economic, environmental and other concerned aspects would have to be taken into accounts. While dealing with tribal problems the dynamics of tribal societies must be kept abreast and there has to be sensitivity to the ideals, ideas and beliefs of the tribal societies.

Social scientists are of the opinion that the tribal health system is based on two-fold plank of psycho-somatism and herbal knowledge. While dealing with tribal health system, the approach should be understood properly. They suggest for documentation of herbs, flowers, roots, seeds, plants and other sources of traditional medicine. Tribal medicine-men should be trained in some of the elementary allopathic practices to enable them to become instrumental for quick relief among tribals in simple disorders. An intensive health education programme relating to all aspects like preventive, curative, environmental, nutritional and sanitational should be launched. The on-going health related programmes like, maternal and child health, control of water-borne and sanitation-related diseases, nutrition programmes, control of mortality due to respiratory diseases, control of malaria, prevention after epidemics like meningitis, control of STD, prevention of AIDS, control of scabies, control of leprosy, control of TB, detection of genetic diseases, e.g., sickle-cell, G-6-PD deficiency and genetic counselling (Singh: 39-46).

Basu (1995 : 57-92) has presented a review of the available literature on health and its correlates of tribal women to indicate the existing status, to identify the gaps of knowledge and to suggest a possible plan of action. Basu observed that health status of tribal women has been examined in the light of several parameters like; sex - ratio, female literacy, marriage practices, age, nutritional status and mother's health, forest ecology and women's health, child bearing and maternal mortality, maternal and child health care practices, family welfare programmes, sexually transmitted diseases and genetic disorders. In the review account Basu discussed the findings of the available studies in the context of the parameters; sex-ratio, female literacy, marriage practices, age at marriage, fertility and mortality, life expectancy, nutritional status and mother's health, maternal and child health care practices and family welfare programme.

Patel (1995:137-147) describes about awareness of tribal health and medical care in Madhya Pradesh. Patel concludes that due to low literacy level the general awareness of the tribals was low about modern health care. On the contrary the tribals in general had strong faith in supernatural power which largely had been attributed to create health hazards. The tribals have belief on supernatural forces, tribal medicines, herbal medicines, but today by and large, transmission of knowledge about tribal medicines to the successor is being more and more feeble as the transfusion of the same has not been regular and unimpeded from both sides, i.e., from the remitting end and from the receiving end. Lastly, Patel suggests for some preventive and constructive measures for better health status of the tribals.

Verma and other (1995 : 163-170) are of the opinion that the tribal communities can be arbitrarily divided into three groups depending upon their size : (i) diminutive (less than 1000 in population) (ii) Moderate sized (1000-10,000) in population (iii) large-sized (more than 10,000 in population). The health problems of these three groups of tribal communities are also different. Verma and others have studied the diminutive tribal groups in Andaman and Nicobar islands especially the Andamanese, the Onges, and the Shompens and observed that the diminutive tribal communities are undergoing a demographic decline and facing extinction unless intervention is done to redress the multifactorial causes for their reduced growth.

K. Rani Gopal (1996) has made a full length study on the tribals and their health status with special reference to the tribals of

Visakhapatnam district of Andhra Pradesh. This is a study in retrospect and prospect regarding the health status of the tribals. The study deals with the analysis of medical and health facilities in the tribal areas of Visakhapatnam and their nutritional status. The indicators of health status, awareness and utilization of health services have also been examined. The study concludes that backward sections of the society are deprived of the benefits of development due to their economic and social backwardness. Scheduled Tribes lag much behind compared to other fellow beings. The basic problem of the tribals in general is that of poverty which leads to low health status. Hence the health facilities must be expanded and should be within the reach of the tribals. Sufficient incentives must be provided to medical personnel so as to encourage them to work in those parts. The indicators of awareness and utilization of health services, viz. school health service, MCH activities and immunization programme, indicate that utilization of health services is increasing but not upto the mark due to illiteracy. In this context, the study stresses on spread of literacy among tribals.

Bairathi (1991) has made an attempt to study the tribal problems in the present context as a whole with special emphasis on the interplay of culture, economy and health care practices of the Saharias—a tribal community of Rajasthan in given eco system. It is assumed that poor health is an indicator of social and economic backwardness of any society. Hence, efforts are being made by the government to improve the health of Saharias by making modern health facilities accessible to them. But the health status of Saharias is still very poor. Tuberculosis, pneumonia, titanus, anaemia, etc. are the most common diseases found among the Saharias which take a high toll of life every year. Unhealthy climate, malnutrition, traditional health care practices, and non-accessibility to modern amenities in public health are the common causes of high morbidity and mortality among the Saharias. The study suggests that the government should provide health education to the Saharias, they should be acquainted with the benefits of proper dieting and living cleanly and inhygienic conditions. The governments emphasis should be more on preventive medicines than on curative which is very expensive for the poor tribals.

Srivastava and North (1995 : 17-30) have comprehended various perspectives of health pinpointing health hazards in different socio-cultural scenario, especially focussing on developing countries. They have tried to relate development, industrialization, food, technology and trends in food habits, alcoholism and drug addiction with the growing health problem, Srivastava states that, 'hazards related to health are essentially a biological and physiological phenomena but these have a very close affinity with culture'. The attitude of people towards health and its related hazards is governed by customs, traditions, values and pattern of interaction directly or indirectly. In Indian context the problem of health hazards is guided by religious beliefs, dogmas and practices. Srivastava has comprehended health hazards in different spheres of society viz. nutrition and diet, food adulteration, food additives, alcoholism and drug addiction. To eradicate health hazards dedication process must be conducted under strict medical supervision, strict enforcement of law against the drug pedlars.

Karkal (1995 :31-50) presents a detailed analysis on 'Women and Health in India.' Karkal states that poor health conditions in India affect women far more than men. The patriarchal attitude of the society neglects women and their nutritional and medical needs. The female specific health problems, higher incidence of anaemia among women due to nutritional discrimination against women and inadequate reimbursement of the monthly blood loss, malnourishment, discrimination by gender, a variety of occupational diseases, early marriage, etc., are some of the reasons for poor health status of women.

Chaudhuri (1994:124-136) states that every culture has its own beliefs and practices concerning diseases and evolves its own system of medicine in order to treat diseases in its own way. If the health policy meant for the tribals is to be formulated, it is important to study these traditional practices and their implications for modern medicine. In this context there are some issues, viz. supernatural beliefs related to disease and treatment, role and position of traditional medicine-men in the society, reasons for illness and treatment, disease, treatment and community, interaction of traditional and modern systems of medicine need to be considered critically.

Basu et al. (1989) has carried out detailed and in-depth study among the various tribal groups of Bastar district, Madhya Pradesh, and also among the primitive Kutia Khond tribal groups of Phulbani district, Orissa. The major objectives of the Bastar study were: (i) to ascertain socio-economic and socio-cultural characteristics, mating-pattern, preferential marriage alliance, nutritional status, physical growth and health seeking behaviour (ii) to determine fertility, mortality, morbidity trends, sanitation, hygiene, parasitic load and genetic environmental disorders (iii) to determine the high risk tribal families and to formulate effective future health care strategies. The study concludes that the tribal groups have specific problems, some of those are built in problems of these communities and some are imposed upon them which jeopardize their overall development and progress inclusive of their health. Therefore the health care delivery system should be designed for specific needs and problems by their personal involvement.

There are studies on health and nutrition problem of the tribals but comparatively meagre than that of the general population. Patankar (1994 : 152-157) aptly stated that studies pertaining to health and nutritional status among different tribal groups are few. The overall nutritional status of the tribal community is the outcome of several interacting factors : effects of environment in which the tribals live, behaviour pattern and life styles of the tribals, health care delivery, service in tribal areas, constraints in accepting modern health status of the tribals. Patankar has made an attempt to review the studies pertaining to health and nutritional status of the tribals.

Luwang and Singh (1981) have conducted a study on 'Protein Energy Malnutrition (PEM) among the Under-Fives of a Hill tribe Population of Manipur' and found that 53.3 per cent have normal weight and 42.6 per cent varying degrees of malnutrition. They observed that PEM had significant association with age, being highest in the second year and lowest under six months. Worm infestation, diarrhoea and dysentery, chronic respiratory infections were predisposing factors to malnutrition. Age and dietary intake were found to be significantly associated with it. Calorie deficit was the major constraint.

Mishar, Raddy and Tewari have conducted a study on 270 tribal pre-school children from Banda district in U.P. and found that prevalence of mild, moderate and severe degrees of malnutrition to 54.5 per cent among children between 13-36 months of age, and 62.7 per cent among the children over 36 months of age. Nutritional deficiency manifestation like Bitot spots, xerosis, angular stomatitis, glossitis were more prevalent in severe and mild malnutrition, i.e., 19.5, 11.7 and 33.8 per cent in grade III and 5.1, 3.8 and 24.4 per cent in grade II respectively. Besides this the studies conducted by Dava (1983), Devadas (1984 ; 21; 315-322) Hanumantha Rao (1989) and Sarupriya (1988; 25:281-286) on the nutritional status of the tribals are of great importance.

Yadava (1944) has carried out an empirical study on some aspects of tribal communities of Dudhi Block in Mirzapur district, U.P.: Habitations and personal hygiene, diet and alcoholism, disease and treatment, pregnant mothers and infants, traditional medicinemen and medical practices were some of the aspects of this study. Finally the study comes to the conclusion that different aspects of tribal life jointly affect their health status. However, the role of the traditional medicine-men seems to be important and effective in tribal areas under study.

Bhowmick (1994) has conducted a fieldwork based study in different parts of eastern India especially the main locale of the four tribes : the Toto, Lodha, Kheria and Birhor (those tribes pursue pre-agricultural economy for their existence). Bhowmick, through this empirical study, comes to the conclusion that in spite of various welfare measures there are constraints, non-responsiveness on the part of the groups and unplanned thinking by the planners, that have obstructed the development of the tribals. Bhowmick observed that the tribals (under study) even today live in a very precarious condition. Health, hygiene and sanitation have no meaning for them, he states, that the basic difficulties in respect of health and hygiene are to—(i) provide good drinking water, (ii) acquaint them with the primary health centres and acquaint them with the health guides, who will lake initiative, regular survey and report to the nearby health centres. Bhowmick (1994: 133-314) cited an example, 'Even most of these tribal groups have only one piece cloth to cover their body. More precarious is the condition of their womenfolk who are found sometimes to wear half of a cloth piece and dry up the remaining portion either in the sun or in the wind. Under such circumstances of chill penury, it is futile to consider about their health and hygiene. Therefore (he suggests) to improve their health and hygiene it is the prior condition to bring about a condition of stability in their income and impart thereafter education on the basis of which they can afford to have the facilities of modern medicines.

Das and Shah (1991 :177 :190) have made an attempt to understand the pattern of contraceptive use and extent of utilization of maternal and child health (MCH) services among certain tribal groups of Dang district of Gujarat state. This survey-based study concludes that the Dangis are still traditional in their outlook as far as the health care of their women and children is concerned. They rely more on traditional practitioners like the 'dai' who conducts the delivery and various 'bhagats' who prescribe medicines. Such a situation calls for immediate redressal by programme implementation in order to improve their reach to two important components of MCH services among women and children.

Naidu and Gurumurthy (1994: 204-222) carried out a study in two mandals, viz. Kalyanadurgam and Beluguppa of Anantpur district in Andhara Pradesh on infant mortality in relation to health practices among Sugali Tribals. The study comes to the conclusion that infant mortality is higher among the women whose deliveries took place at home, conducted by indigenous/traditional 'dai' or relatives/neighbours and used an unhygienic or unscientific instrument for cutting the umbilical cord and also dressed it with indigenous medicines. Poor pre-natal care and post-natal care received from indigenous medical practitioners, magic of the witches/sorcerers, offerings to God, self-medications (herbal medicine) are also responsible for higher mortality among infants. Maternal risks factors and tetanus are the main causes of death during neo-natal period while dysentery, diarrhoea and meningitis are responsible for deaths during post-neonatal period. The researchers suggest for providing health education to women and also about the scientific method of conducting delivery, immunization for children, and, health care for both mothers and children.

Mishra, Pandey and Sinha (1991 : 243-255) have carried out an in-depth study on some aspects of curative health care among the aged a study in a tribal block of Madhya Pradesh. The study comes to the conclusion that the situation of the aged in the tribal population is not better than the other communities. They are comparatively prone to sickness but given least priority in treatment. Even the aged persons themselves do not take care regarding their health. The behaviour of other family members in general is also of negligence. To improve the situation, regarding the health care of the aged, the government should take initiative to plan health services for them at the village or panchayat level.

Palta et al (1998:25-28) conducted a study on the 'Kamar' tribals of Madhy Pradesh and made an attempt to see the impact of nutrition and health education on the Kamar families. The study summarizes that there is favourable and encouraging response of the tribals towards nutrition and health education. The tribals seem to be receptive to the information about balanced diet, mixed diet, importance of fruits and vegetables, right cooking practices, nutritional care of vulnerable sections and the use of diet during illness. Palta et al suggest for more intensified and enlarging efforts, nutrition education to the Kamars as to check the declining trend of the Kamars in particular and for the wellbeing of the tribals in general.

Goyal et al (1998 : 29-39) conducted a study on the 'health and social aspects of tribal adolescent girls in tribal development blocks of Betul district in Mdhya Pradesh. The analysis of first-hand information reveals that there is poor trend in the health and nutrition status of the tribal adolescent girls. The higher age of menarche of the tribal adolescent girls is a possible indicator of their lower health and nutrition status. As the national average age of menarche is 13.5 years while the average age of the study group was 15 years. It is also obvious from the discussion that the girls are aware of their social discrimination, importance of education, need for sex education. They also know well that they are deprived of all this only because of obsolete, inhibiting social system which kill the exuberance and natural growth of their lives.

The treatment pattern is an important part of health status. To a large extent it determines the health, longevity of life and even psycho-physical state of an individual. In tribal areas, we observe a number of treatment patterns used by the traditional medicine-men for the treatment of the ill people. In this context we have some studies conducted by the learned scholars on the treatment patterns prevalent in tribal areas. Patel (1991 : 10-19) carried out a study on the traditional treatment method of the Baiga tribe in Madhya Pradesh. Patel observed that the Baigas are known for their socio-cultural uniqueness. They observed a number of religions, dietetics, evil spirits and sinful and sacred act related notions about diseases and also corresponding remedial solutions. They have the notions about taboos and also about the results of the violation of taboos. By and large these traditional postulation have effective impact on the health status of the tribals.

Chakravarti (1998 : 249-268) carried out a study on health management and care for the elderly of rural West Bengal. This exploratory research has threefold objectives: (i) it seeks to explore the health condition of the elderly in a multi-ethnic rural setting of West Bengal, (ii) it examines the day-to-day experience of the rural families with respect to care-receiving rights and care-giving responsibilities for the seniormost members, and (iii) it analyses the role of family, kin, neighbours and other members/institutions/associations which are involved in elderly care. This small scale empirical study of the health management and caring system of the elderly outside the urban area points to the severe health problems faced by the old people. Despite poor economic conditions, the family still plays a major role in elderly care. The complexities of the progeny and daughter-in-law in care giving affairs suggest its potential for a social change. The care-receivers could hardly attune themselves to the pace of change. The feeling that the old members are burdens on the family could be understood from the experiences of the elderly. The voice of change, especially those of the daughters-in-law are now being heard more and more loudly. The sons on the other hand are becoming passive day-by-day. A sort of 'matrilocal' tendency seems to be apparent among them with the alternation of women's status in the family.

Barua and Phukan (1998 : 351-362) have made an attempt to discuss the socio-religious aspects in relation to health and well-being of the Sonowal Kachari of Assam. The study comes to the conclusion that the Sonowal Kachari reflect their beliefs and dependency on traditional rites and rituals whenever someone suffers from illness. There are many beliefs and restrictions associated with health and welfare of the people which are strictly followed by them. As people are emotionally attached to them, there develops a fear psychosis that eliminates violation of the traditional beliefs and practices. They still have a firm belief that deities and spirits are responsible for particular diseases. If properly worshipped, they may get the desired result. So they continue to perform the traditional rites and rituals to overcome the effect of such deities.

Palta (1988:29-35) presents the findings of an exploratory survey conducted among the 'Bhumia Baigas' of Baiga Chak in Mandal district of Madhya Pradesh. The objective of the study was to investigate existing pattern of food consumption, nutrient intake and to suggest possible approach to improve nutrition and health improvement in the area. Besides this hygiene and health conditions have also been studied. The study concludes that the diet of the Baigas is quite monotonous specially that of the poor class. Variety of food items is greater in the average and rich class.

However the diet of 85 per cent of the Baiga population (poor and average class) is deficient in calories. Though the protein intake from the food consumption was found to be normal in the poor class and even above the normal requirement for the average and rich class, yet the protein quality can definitely said to be low as it is mainly derived from maize, rice and other millets. The Baigas by habit are not clean. Their clothing is scanty, the skin is more exposed to infection. The surroundings of their dwellings due to rearing of cattle, pigs, and fowls is unclean which leads to malaria and other fevers. Finally the report suggests nutrition and health improvement through extending health and hygiene education and also by providing safe drinking water near their dwellings.

Palta (1993 : 1-9) has also made an attempt to present an overall picture about the food consumption pattern and nutrient intake of one of the important tribes of Madhya Pradesh. Type and pattern of food consumption, food habits, cooking practices of various foodstuffs, socio-economic aspect of health and nutrition have been the main areas of study, besides this some action programmes have also been suggested for better health and nutritional status.

Patel (1993 :13-15) has conducted a detailed study on the Koraku tribe of Chhotanagpur, Madhya Pradesh, and presented briefly the food habits, food pattern and nutritional status of the Koraku tribe. Patel states that Korakus are both vegetarian and non-vegetarian and used to alcoholic drinks. Liquor prepared by Mahuwa is used by men, women and children of the Koraku tribe. Due to this drinking habit the health status of an average Koraku person is very weak.

Sharma (1997 : 45-46) has carried out a study on 'Prevalence of Protein calorie malnutrition among the tribal school children of Shankerpur and Chureha village of Baikunthpur Tehsil of Surguja District, M.P. and found that 91.30 per cent children are having malnutrition, and only 8.70 per cent belonged to normal range. Sharma observed that lack of health awareness, health education, ignorance of proper health checkup of the children are responsible for such crisis of malnutrition.

Goyal and Goyal (1997 : 48-52) have made a study on health and diseases of the tribal elderly of Betul district, M.P. and found that there is prevalence of bronchitis (16 per cent), cataract (26 per cent), arthritis

(20 per cent) and other diseases like anaemia (16 per cent) and dental caries (16 per cent) which are above the national average. Besides this, hypertension, corneal opacity, genetics urinary, skin disease, piles, arthritis and hernia are very common among the tribal elderly. Besides this the elderly tribals are also suffering from psychological problems. .

Sunawal and Singh (1997 : 53-64) carried out study on the nutritional status of Rag Pickers and Agarbatti makers in Indore city and observed that nutritional intake is very low in both the groups. There is deficiency of calcium, fat and protein in their food due to which they are underweight and prone to malnutrition.

Lakra (1997 :43-47) has carried out a research study on the health and nutritional status of women of Khairwar tribes of Surguja district in Madhya Pradesh. The study comes to the conclusion that the excessive workload, scarcity of food, fertility in monotonous succession land them with anaemia and malnutrition. Lack of insight into the problems of women, like repeated pregnancies, abortions, prolonged lactating, parasitic infections etc. increases ill-effects on their health. It is suggested that urgent remedial measures must be taken to promote child survival and safe motherhood and to checkup the declination in the population of this tribe a policy should be formulated at state level.

Palta and Aghaniwanshi (1999 : 91-96) prepared an anthropometric profile of the Hill Korwas of Sarguja district, M.P. and concluded that nutritional status of 'Hill Korwas' cannot be termed as adequate. Their height, weight, mid-arm circumference, BMI and relative body weight percentage are much lower than their urban and rural counterparts.

Vaishnav (1995 : 52-56) has conducted a study on 'bio-cultural study of diet and nutrition on Gamit tribe of Gujarat. Socio-cultural factors affecting diet and nutrition, socio-cultural and religious beliefs regarding food, food recommended by society for infant, child, old-age, during pregnancy and nursing period, drinking habit and smoking, average daily intake of various food groups are studied thoroughly. He concludes that the consumption of calories, protein, niacin, thiamine, phosphorus and iron are satisfactory, while consumption of fat, riboflavine are low, vitamin A, C and calcium are very low compared to recommended allowance.

Besides the review of the literature as cited above there are still a number of tribal studies conducted by social scientists, anthropologists, psycho-analysists and medical scientists of India and abroad particularly in reference to the health, hygiene and nutritional status of the tribals. In this context the scholarly work of some western thinkers, viz. Clements (1932), Sigerist (1951), Ackrknecht (1955), Evance Pritchard (1937),

Rivers (1924), Frake (1961), Franklin (1963), Turner (1963), Grounds (1964), Langness (1965), Rubel (1964), Rodrique (1963), Romand (1965), Maclean (1965), Lieban (1966), Schwartz (1969), Fabrega et al (1978), Riessman (1974), Milsum (1974), Netting (1973), Robinson (1977), Makeowa (1977), Ford Ann and Food (1980), Kroeger (1980), Berg and Adlex Nissen (1974), Britten Brown and Altman (1940), Mackintosh (1934), is of great importance.

Ishwaran (1968) has conducted a study in Sheopur : A South Indian village and observed that the diseases are divided into four types according to the rural postulations. These are: (i) God gifted general illness (ii) God gifted serious disease (iii) diseases as a result of physical factor and (iv) epidemics or illness due to witchcraft or sorcery. He concluded that the medicine-men, patient, treatment pattern and the whole medical system is determined by the well-established social norms.

Bodding (1925 :1-127) has carried out a study on 'The Santhals and Disease' and explored the causes of different diseases prevalent among the Santhals and also analyse the diseases in the frame reference of superstitions and also interpreted the role of traditional medicine-men and Ojhas and also of the patient behaviour.

Elvin (1942,1942a, 1947a, 1947b, 1950) has a deep understanding on the tribals and their various aspects of life—health, hygiene and nutritional status. He concluded that among the tribals of Mandala, health and medicine related beliefs and practices are closely related with culture.

Besides this Marriott (1985), Carstairs (1955), Gould (1965), Fuchs (1964), Harper (1966), Naik (1964), Shukla (1973), Bhatia (1975), Opler (1963), Khare (1963), Valunjkar (1967), Hasan (1967), Mann (1967), Vyass (1970), Chowdhari (1971), Vidhyarthi (1974), Kumar and Maitra (1975), Karana (1976), Banerji (1982), Kakar (1977), Mital (1977), Naidu (1959), Kuriyan (1982, 1985), Panikar (1984), Naik and Sharma (1985), Trakaroo (1985), Banerjee (1986), Raju (1986), Ramalingaswami (1987), Dais (1989) and Banerjee (1989) have carried out detailed and scientific studies on the different aspects of tribal health, hygiene and nutrition in the frame reference of their socio-cultural systems and also made significant comments on the modern medical system and the primary health care services meant particularly for the tribals of India.

Review of the Studies on the Tribals of Uttarakhand

If we turn over the pages of history and make an objective review of the literature available in the writings of our predecessors, we come to the conclusion that the ethnic groups of Uttarakhand have attracted the attention of the pilgrims, travellers, administrators, traders, ethnographers, anthropologists and sociologists. We have no doubt, detailed informations about the people of Uttarakhand and also about their socio-cultural and economic life. Since long Uttarakhand has been the abode of various ethnic groups who are known for their racial socio-cultural and economic distinctiveness. This can be proved by the information we observe in the writings of Atkinson (1882), William Crooke (1896), Latham (1896), etc. Out of the various ethnic groups of Uttarakhand, our main concern is with the study of four tribal groups, namely, the Rajis, Tharus, Buxas and Jaunsaris.

Since long all the tribal groups under study have been the focal point of research studies for the scholars of different disciplines. In this context the information we found in the writings of Atkinson, and Crooke can be considered as the base line data about the people of Uttarakhand Himalaya in general and the tribal groups under study in particular. Apart from this information, there are some worth quoting scholarly works about the tribal groups of Uttarakhand which are as follows :

Bisht's (1982) work on the Rajis of Uttarakhand considered to be a pioneer study on the Rajis. There had been scanty information about the socio-economic life of the Rajis. But it was Bisht who conducted an empirical research work for the first time on the Raji tribe. The study of social structure and organization of the Raji tribe has been the main objective of his study. Using the structural-functional approach, he studied various aspects of the Raji social system and presented a holistic picture of the Raji community. Bisht observed that the Raji community is in diminution process. Even today they are leading a sort of primitive life and are in a state of semi-nomadism. Some of the Raji families still dwell in caves and depend on crude type of 'Ijarani Kheti' and labour. Even today they collect the jungle products for their sustenance. Socially the Raji tribe is divided into five 'Dharas'. Bisht has also presented some references on their poor health, nutrition and hygienic conditions. Bisht (1990) has made a further study on the problems of socio-economic development of the Raji tribe and found that inaccessible habitations, unfavourable agro-climatic conditions, scattered settlement pattern, transportation and communication gap, illiteracy, invalid human capital, indebtedness and land alienation, superstitious nature of the people and constraints related to Govt. policies and their implementation pattern have been the main hindrances on the way of their development.

Bisht (1994) has made a detailed empirical study on the process of cultural transformation among the Scheduled Tribe Communities of Uttarakhand. In fact through this study Bisht made an attempt to evaluate the process of cultural transformation on the Bhotiyas, Rajis, Tharus, Buxas and Jaunsaris of Uttarakhand Himalaya in the frame reference of the various processes of planned changes, Govt. policies, welfare measures and tribal and non-tribal interrelation system. The study concludes that the process of culture transformation of the tribals and the planned processes of change be positively correlated at first sight say overtly but covertly these planned processes, i.e., the welfare measures, statutory provisions, reservation policy, etc., have turned the tribals of Uttarakhand towards tribalism with the result they are inclined to maintain their tribal identity as to receive constantly the benefits meant for the tribals in every walk of life even in infinite future.

Besides this, Sherring (1907), Chattopadhyay (1934), Pannalal (1942) have also presented some scanty references on the different aspects of the Bhotiya community. Chatterjee (1975) carried out a study on the Bhotiyas of Indo-Tibetan border of Uttarakhand. This research work consists of a sociological survey of ideological convictions, customs, mode of social behaviours and attitudes of the tribal people. Rahul (1970) concentrated his study on the religious patterns among the Bhotiyas. Dabral (1965) also studied the religious beliefs and practices of the Bhotiya community of Uttarakhand. Pant (1935) studied the social economy and the Bhotiyas and described their trade pattern with Tibet-China and also with Uttarakhand.

Srivastava (1958) carried out a study on the cultural dynamics among the Tharus. Amir Hasan (1979) conducted a study on the process of change occurring on the Buxa community of Nainital Tarai. Sharma (1976) has made a study on micro-level planning and analysed the process of development of tribal region of the hill districts of Uttar Pradesh. Mukherjee (1963) made a comparative study and the kinship system of two polyandrous communities, i.e., the Jaunsaris of Jaunsar Bawar and the Todas of Nilgiri. During the last two decades some research students have also presented their research dissertations on the different aspects of the tribals of Uttarakhand. But the overall evaluation of the research findings of the studies on the tribals of Uttarakhand depicts that none of the scholars has tried to touch the vital issues like education, health, hygiene and nutrition pattern of the tribals. With a view to bridging this gap of knowledge, this work, with the objectives as cited in Chapter No. 1, is being carried out by the author.

Incontestably this piece of work will be able to present scientifically the picture of education, health, hygiene and nutritional status of the tribals of Uttarakhand. It will also present the relevance and viability of various government sponsored schemes and also the efforts of the NGOs in the field of education, health, hygiene and nutrition of the tribals of Uttarakhand. Thus the present research work has both academic as well as practical importance for the academicians of different disciplines and for the policy-makers.

References

Ahmed., P.I. and Coelho, G.V., 1979 : *Towards a New Definition of 'Health'*, Pleum, New York.

Aykroyd, W.R., 1970: *Conquest of Deficiency Diseases*, FFHC Basic Study, No. 24, Geneva, WHO.

Aykroyd, W.R., 1966 : *The Nutritive value of Indian Foods and the Planning of Satisfactory Diet, Sixth revised edition by C. Gopalan and S. C. Balasubramaniam*, ICMR, New Delhi.

Akhtar, Rais and Yola Verhasselt, 1990 : *Disease Ecology and Health*, Rawat Publications, Jaipur (Rajasthan).

Ackrknecht, E.H., 1995. *A Short History of Medicine*, Ronald Press, New York.

Behura, N.K. 1992 : "Constraints in Tribal Culture for Formal Education", *in Tribal Transformation in India* ed. by B.D. Chaudhuri, Inter-India Publications, Delhi-15.

Burman, B.K. Roy, 1972: "Tribal Demography", in, *Tribal Situation in India* (ed.) by K. S. Singh, Indian Institute of Advanced Study, Simla.

Basu, Salil, 1995 : "Health Status of Tribal Women in India" in, *Tribal Women in India*, (ed.) by Bhupender Singh and N. Mahanli, Inter-India Publications, New Delhi-15.

Bairathi, S., 1991 : *Tribal Culture, Economy andHealth*, Rawat Publications, Jaipur.

Basu, S.K., 1989 : "Factors Affecting Fertility and Mortality Behaviour Among Tribal Population Groups of Bastar District (M.P.)", in, *Health and Family Welfare Services in India* (ed.) by B. Jena and R.W.Pati, Ashish Publishing House, New Delhi.

Basu, S. K., Jindal, A., Kshatriya, G., Chetlapalli, S.K., and Khan, A.S. 1990: *Genetic and Socio-Cultural Determinants of Tribal Health : Kutia Konds of Phulbani District, Orissa*, Annual Report, NIHFW, New Delhi.

Bhowmick, P.K. 1994 : *Primitive Tribal Groups in Eastern India*, Gyan Publishing House, New Delhi-2.

Barua, I., Phukan, R., 1998 : Socio-Religious Aspects of Health Among Sonowal Kachari, in, *The Eastern Anthropologists*, ed. by J.S. Bhandari et al, Ethnographic and Folk Culture Society, Lucknow- 24.

Barman, P.B. 1992 : Education Among the Lepchas of Darjeeling : A Sociological Study, in, *Tribal Transformation in India*, Vol. IV, ed. by B.D. Chaudhuri, Inter-India Publications, Delhi-15.

Burman, B.K. Roy, 1992 : Pattern of Tribal Education, Status of Research and Sociological Dimensions for Projecting the Future, in, *Tribal Transformation in India,* Vol. IV, ed., by B.D. Chaudhuri, Inter-India Publications, Delhi-15.

Chandra, R., 1992 : Education in Nilgiris Tribes - An Appraisal, in, *Tribal Transformation in India*, Vol. IV. ed. by B.D. Chaudhuri, Inter-India Publications, Delhi-15.

Chakrabarti, P., 1998 : Health Management and Care for the Elderly, in, *The Eastern Anthropologists*, Vol. 51, No. 3, ed by J.S. Bhandari et. al., Ethnographic and Folk Culture Society, Lucknow.

Clements, F.E., 1932. *Primitive Concept of Disease*, University of California Publications in American Archaeology and Ethnology, pp. 185-252.

Chaudhuri, B.D., 1994 : Tribal Health and Medicine : Socio-Cultural and Environmental Dimensions, in, *Tribal Economy, Health and Waste Land Development*, ed. by Neeti Mahanti, Inter-India Publications, New Delhi-15.

Dhebar, U.N., 1961 : *Report of the Scheduled Areas and Scheduled Tribe Commission.*

Danda, A.K., 1992: Response of Scheduled Tribes Students to Special Provisions; in, *Tribal Transformation in India*, ed. by B.D. Chaudhari, Inter-India Publications, Delhi-15.

Dave, P., Divakaran, M., and Majhithir, V., 1983 : *Nutritional Status of Under Fives in Limkhada, Panchmahals, Gujarat.* Report from the Department of Child Development, M.S. University, Baroda.

Das, A.K., 1992 : Education and Economic Achievements and Trend thereof among the Scheduled Tribes of West Bengal, in, *Tribal Transformation in India*,Vol. IV, ed. by B.D. Chaudhuri, Inter-India Publications, Delhi-15.

Devadas, R.P., Chandrasekhar, V. and Bhooma, N., 1984: Nutritional Outcomes of a Rural Diet Supplemented with Low Cost Locally Available Foods. Impact on Preschool Children from a Tribal Community, *Indian Journal of Nutrition Dietetics.*

Das, N.P. and Shel, U., 1991: Contraceptive Prevalence and Maternal and Child Health Care Status among Tribals, in, *Tribal Demography in India*, ed. by R.N. Pati and Lalitendu Jagatdeb, Ashish Publishing House, New Delhi.

Dubos, R.C., 1965 : *Man Adapting*, New Haven, Yale University Press.

Dissanayake, C. B., 1990 : Human Health Problems in Sri Lanka, in, *Disease, Ecology and Health* (ed.) by Akhtar and Verhasselt, Rawat Publications-Jaipur.

Doshi, S.L., 1995 : *Anthropology of Food and Nutrition*, Rawat Publications, Jaipur.

Eckstein, Eleanor E., 1980 : *Food, People and Nutrition*, AV Publishing Company, Inc. West Port, Connecticut.

Eberst, R.M. 1984 : Jr. *School Health*, 54 (3).

Elvin, Varrier, 1960 : *Report of the Committee on the Special Multipurpose Tribal Blocks*, Calcutta.

Fillenbaum, G.G., 1984 : *The Well-being of the Elderly*, WHO Offset Publ. No. 84.

Freund, Paul J., 1990 : Child Health and Nutrition in Zambia in, *Disease Ecology and Health* (ed.) by Akhtar and Verhasselt, Rawat Publications, Jaipur.

Gopal, K. Rani, 1996 : Tribals and Their Health Status; A.P.H. Publishing Corporation, New Delhi - 2.

Goyal, S. and Goyal, R., 1997 : Health and Disease of the Tribal Elderly, in *Bulletin, Tribal Research Institute*, Bhopal, ed. K.V. Singh, Director Tribal Research Institute, Bhopal, M.P.

Guha, B.S., 1944: *Racial Elements in Indian Population*, Oxford Pamphlet on Indian Affairs, Oxford University Press, Bombay.

Goyal, S., Goyal, S. and Goyal, N., 1998 : "Health and Social Aspects of Tribal Adolescent Girls in Betul District of Madhya Pradesh", in *Bulletin of the Tribal Research Institute*, Bhopal, ed. by T.R. Sahani, Vol. XXVI, No. 1.

Hanumantha Rao, D., Brahman, G.N.V., and Prahlad Rao, N., 1989 : Diet and Nutrition Survey Among the Onges. *Nutrition News* 1988.

Harper, Laura Jane and Maryellen Spencer; 1987 : "Food for Thought: An Approach to the Study of Food in Culture", in, *Food and Nutrition*, Vol. 13, No 1, FAO, UN.

Hankel, Reinhard; 1990: Health Care Services in Zambia, in *Disease Ecology and Health*, ed. by Akhtar and Verhasselt, Rawat Publications, Jaipur, Rajasthan.

Iyun. F, 1990 : Health Care Planning and Distribution of Health Services in Oyo State, Nigeria, in, *Disease Ecology and Health* ed., by Akhtar and Verhasselt, Rawat Publications, Jaipur, Rajasthan.

Joshi, N.D., 1982: *Tribal Education in Kerala* - Adult Education and Development, Kerala.

Jelliffe, D.B., 1966 : The Assesssment of the Nutritional Status of the Community, *World Health Organization, Monograph Series*, 53, Geneva; WHO.

Karkal, Malini, 1995 : "Women and Health in India", in, *Health Hazards, Gender and Society* (ed.) by Indu Mather and Sanjay Sharma, Rawat Publications, Jaipur.

Kohli, Y. P., 1995 : Moral Values through Informal Education, in, *Tribal Education in India*, (ed.) by, Bhupendra Singh and N. Mohanti, Inter-India Publications, Delhi-15.

Kurup, A. M. 1992: Extent and Problems of Tribal Education, in, *Tribal Transformation in India*, ed. by B.D. Chaudhuri, Inter-India Publications, Delhi-15.

Lakshmaiah, T., 1995 : "Educational Facilities, Problems and Impact- A Comparative Study of Two Blocks in Ranchi District in Bihar State", in, *Tribal Education in India* (ed) by B. Singh and N. Mohanti, Inter-India Publications, Delhi-15.

Lakshmaiah, T., 1992: "Problems of Education in Tribal Areas," in, *Tribal Transformation in India.*, ed. by B.D. Chaudhuri, Inter-India Publications, Delhi-15.

Lakshmaiah, T., 1987 : *Educational Facilities, Problems and Impacts; A Comparative Study of Two Blocks in Ranchi District of Bihar state*, NIRD, Hyderabad.

Lakshmaiah, T., and Aravind Yadappanavar, 1986 : *A Study of Educational Facilities for Tribal Students—Problems and Impact in Paderu Samithi, Visakha Patanam Distt. A.P.* , NIRD, Hyderabad.

Lakara, I., 1997 : "Health Status of Women of Khairwar Tribes of Surguja District", in-*Bulletin of the Tribal Research Institute*, Bhopal, M.P., ed. by S.K. Sood, Director Tribal Research Institute, Bhopal, M.P.

Luzzi, G. Eichinger Ferro, 1980 : "Food avoidances at Puberty and Menstruation in Tamilnadu", in, *Food Ecology and Culture* (ed.) by, J.R.K. Robson, Gordon and Breach Science Publishers, New York.

Maio, P.S., 1990: "Population Distribution and Health Facilities", in, *Disease Ecology and Health* ed. by Akhtar and Verhasselt, Rawat Publications, Jaipur, Rajasthan.

Mathur, P.R.G., 1992 : "Tribal Education in Kerala", in, *Tribal Transformation in India*, Vol. IV., ed. By B.D. Chaudhuri, Inter-India Publications, Delhi-15.

Mishra, D.K., Pandey, G.D., and Sinha, P.K., 1991 : "Some Aspects of Curative Health Care Among the Aged; A Study in a Tribal Block of Madhya Pradesh," in, *Tribal Demography in India*, ed. by R.N. Pati and Lalitendu Jagatdeb, Ashish Publishing House, New Delhi-26.

Mahanti, N., 1995 : "Tribal Health in India: Retrospect and Prospect", in, *Tribal Health in India* (ed.) by, Bhupender Singh and Neeti Mahanti, Inter-India Publications, New Delhi-15.

Mishra, C.P., Reddy, D.C.S, andTiwari, I.C., 1986 : "Some Epidemiological Determinants of Anthropometrically Determined Grades of Malnutrition Among Harijan and Tribal Pre-school Children", in, *Indian Journal of Nutrition and Dietetics*.

Majumdar, D.N., 1963 : *An Introduction to Social Anthropology*, Asia Publishing House, Bombay.

______1955: *Races and Cultures of India*, Asia Publishing House, Bombay.

Malzke, Gordon, 1990 : "Health Consequences of Tsetse Zone Expansion in Zambia", in, *Disease Ecology and Health* (ed) by, Akhtar and Verhasselt, Rawat Publications, Jaipur, Rajasthan.

Maulik, S. K., Ghosh and Anita Ghosh Maulik, 1992 : "Mode of Subsistence and Response to Elementary Education in Some Tribes of Orissa", in, *Tribal Transformation in India.*, ed. by B.D. Chaudhuri, Inter-India Publications, New Delhi-15.

Narayan, S., 1992 : "Education; Then and Now Among Oraon Children", in, *Tribal Transformation in India*, ed. by B.D. Chaudhuri, Inter-India Publications, New Delhi-15.

Nagla, B.K., 1992 : "The Problem of Tribal Education in Southern Rajasthan", in, *Tribal Transformation in India*, ed. by B.D. Chaudhuri, Inter-India Publications, New Delhi-15.

Naidu, V.N. and Gurumurthy, G., 1991 : "Determinants of Infant Mortality in Relation to Health Practices Among Sugali Tribals in Andhra Pradesh", in, *Tribal Demography in India*, ed. by R.N. Pati and L. Jagatdeb, Ashish Publishing House, New Delhi-26.

Naryana, K.V., 1997 : *Health and Development*, Rawat Publications, Jaipur, Rajasthan.

NCERT, Delhi 1986: *Report of the Empirical Evaluation of Academic Aspects of Non-Formal Education Programme in Bihar*, Delhi.

Patel, M.L., 1995 : "Awareness of Tribal Health and Medical Care in Madhya Pradesh", in, *Tribal Health in India* ed. by Bhupender Singh and N. Mahanti; Inter-India Publications, New Delhi-15.

Patnakar, M., 1994: "Diet and Nutritional Status of Tribals in India with Special Reference to Children", in, *Tribal Economy, Health and Wasteland Development*, ed. by Neeti Mahanti, Inter-India Publications, New Delhi-15.

Palta, Arun, Vishwakarma, M., Sharma, R, 1998: "Impact of Nutrition and Health Education on the Kamars", in, *Bulletin of the Tribal Research Institute, Bhopal*. ed. by T.R. Sahni (IAS), Vol. XXVI, No. 1.

Palta, A., 1988 : "A Study of the Food Consumption Pattern of the Baigas in Baigachak Region of M.P.", in, *Bulletin of the Tribal Research and Development Institute, Bhopal*, ed. by V.K. Jajoria, Govt. of M.P., Bhopal.

_____1993 : "A Study on the Food Consumption Pattern and Nutrient Intake of the Oraons of Jaspur Nagar State,in, *Bulletin of the Tribal Research and Development Institute Bhopal*, Vanya Prakashan Bhopal, M.P., ed. by K. Devgan, Director, Tribal Research Institute, Bhopal.

Patil, A.D., 1993 : *Koraku Janjati*, Vishwabharati Prakashan, Nagpur.

Palta, A. and Aghaniwansi, M., 1999: "Anthropometric Profile of the Hill-Korwas of Surguja District", in, *Bulletin of the Tribal Research Institute, Bhopal*, M.P., ed. by T.R. Sahani, Director, Tribal Research institute, Bhopal.

Park, K., 1997 : *Preventive and Social Medicine*, Banarasidas Bhanot, Jabalpur, 001.

Phillips, David R., 1990 : "Health Care Planning in Hong Kong", in, *Disease Ecology and Health* ed. by Akhtar and Verhasselt, Rawat Publications, Jaipur, Rajasthan.

Ratha, S.N., 1992: "Literacy in Tribal India: An Evaluation", in, *Tribal Transformation in India*, Vol. IV, (ed) by Buddhadeb Chaudhuri, Inter-India Publications, Delhi-15.

Risley, H.H.; 1969 : *The People of India*, Delhi.

Singh, Bhupender, 1995 : "An Overview of Tribal Health", in, *Tribal Health in India*, Ed. by. Bhupender Singh and N. Mahanti, Inter-India Publications, New Delhi-15.

Srivastava, A.L. and A. North, 1995 : "Galaxy of health Hazards in Various Socio-cultural Scenario", in, *Health Hazards, Gender and society*, ed. by Indu Mathur and Sanjay Sharma, Rawat Publications, Jaipur.

Sarvpriya, S., and Mathew, S., 1988 : Nutritional Status of Tribal Adolescents of Village Gogunda, Rajasthan, *Indian Journal of Nutrition and Dietetics*.

Sharma, K.K.N., 1997 : "Prevalence of Protein Calorie Malnutrition Among the Tribal School Children of Shankerpur and Churcha Villages of

Baikunthpur Tehsil of Surguja District, Madhy Pradesh", in, *Bulletin of the Tribal Research Institute, Bhopal*, Vanya Prakashan, Bhopal, M.P., ed. by, K.V Singh, Director, Tribal Research, Institute, Bhopal.

Sharma, K.L., 2001 : *Reconceptualizing Caste, Class and Tribe*; Rawat Publications, Jaipur.

Sonwat, R., and Singh, V., 1997 : "Nutritional Status of Rag Pickers and Agarbatti Makers in Indore City", in, *Bulletin of the Tribal Research Institute*, Bhopal, ed. by. K. V. Singh, Director, Tribal Research Institute, Bhopal.

Sartorius, N., 1983 : *Bulletin.* WHO, 61(1)5.

Sheehan, G. and Hopkins, M., 1979 : *Basic Needs Performance*, ILO, Geneva.

Simoons, Frederick J., 1991; *Food in China :A Cultural and Historical Inquiry*, CRC Press, Boston.

Swain, S., 1998 : "Health and Nutrition in Tribal Areas", in, *Antiquity to Modernity in Tribal India*; by S.C. Dube, Inter-India Publications, New Delhi.

Singh, B., 1995 : *Tribal Education in India*; Inter-India Publications, New Delhi-15.

Sachchidanand, 1995 : "Non-Formal Education in Tribal Areas", in, *Tribal Education in India* (ed) B. Singh and N. Mohanti, Inter India Publications, New Delhi-15.

Steward, George, H.; 1954 : *Sex and Social Order*, Penguin Books.

Sachchidanand; 1954: "The Morung and Dhumkuria : A Study in Contrast", *Journal of Bihar Research Society*, Vol XL, Part-4.

Sinha, A.K., 1992 : "University-Education Among the Tribals of Chotanagpur-A Case Study", in, *Tribal Transformation in India*, Vol. IV, ed by B.D. Chaudhari, Inter-India Publications, Delhi-15.

Sachhidanand, 1992 : "Structural Constraints in the Education of Scheduled Tribes and Scheduled Castes", in *Tribal Transformation in India*, ed. by B.D. Chaudhuri, Inter-India Publications, Delhi-15.

Signerist, H.E., 1951: *A History of Medicine*, Vol. 1, Oxford University Press, Fair Lawn. N.J.

Thompson, Della, 1995 : *The Concise Oxford Dictionary*, Oxford University Press, Delhi.

Thurnwald. R., 1933 : *Nomads Encyclopaedia of Social Sciences.*

Verma, R. C., R.C, Das, G.P. and Kaur, M., 1995 : "Genetic and other Health Problems of Tribal Communities", in, *Tribal Health in India*, ed. by B. Singh and N. Mahati, Inter India Publications, New Delhi-15.

Vaishnav, T.K., 1995 : "Bio-cultural Study of Diet and Nutrition on Gamit Tribe of Gujrat", in, *Bulletin of the Tribal Research Institute, Bhopal*, M.P., ed. by K. Devagan, Director Tribal Research Institute, Bhopal, M.P.

WHO, 1986 : Concepts of health behaviour research, Reg. Health paper No. 13, SEARO, New Delhi.

WHO; 1978 : *Bulletin.* WHO 56(4)519.

WHO, 1981 : *Health for all*, Sr. No. 6.

Wilson, R.W. &T.F. Dairy, 1984: Ann Rev. Pub. Health. Quoted from K. Park, *Preventive and Social Medicine*, Banarasidas Bhanot, Jabalpur, 01.

WHO, 1989, *Global Nutritional Status: Anthropometric Duplicators Update.*

3
Methodological Perspective

'The Education, Health, Hygiene and Nutrition of the Tribals of Uttarakhand' has received quite a little attention in sociological studies. No doubt, there are studies about the educational status of the tribals but the problem of health, hygiene and nutrition has been taken up in a very superficial manner. In fact, there is urgent need for more specific problem oriented approach on education, health, hygiene and nutrition of all the societies in general and the tribal communities in particular. The data thus achieved on this problem can help in policy making on education, health, hygiene and nutrition. The need of the hour is to carry out the study in depth with scientific manner about the problem in hand. It is therefore planned to study the problem in tribal settings with a view to understand the educational, health, hygiene and nutritional status of the tribals of Uttarakhand.

Uttarakhand is basically a hilly area with a narrow strip of Tarai Bhabar plain belt in its foothills. A variety of ethnic groups have been living here for a long time. The five tribal communities, which constitute about 3.54 per cent of the total population, also reside in this region. Incontestably the tribal communities and their demographic aspects of community life like socio-cultural, economic and racial etc. have been studied by the social scientists, administrators and anthropologists. But the education, health, hygiene and nutrition related aspects are almost neglected in their writings. This is an endeavour to bridge up this gap of knowledge. In real sense the present study is an attempt to have familiarity with the problem and to achieve new insights into it. So that its findings can be helpful in formulating a more precise research problem and also to develop hypotheses for further studies and researches. As there is not much research material in socio-anthropological discipiine about health, hygiene and nutrition. It was really difficult to make a meaningful explanation of the problem on the basis of the existing available data in terms of framing some research hypotheses particularly about the situation of education, health, hygiene and nutrition of the tribals of Uttarakhand. Hence to bridge up the gap of knowledge this study aims at studying accurately the characteristics and situation of education, health, hygiene and nutrition of the tribals under study. The factors which affect the education and its prevalence, health, hygiene and nutrition of the people will also be discussed systematically and objectively as to achieve the scientific conclusions of the study under investigation. In this context the exploratory-cum-descriptive research designs have been used for more precise scientific investigation of the problem.

In fact, in sociological discipline there has been a little scope and area of research of social variables affecting education, health, hygiene and nutrition and of the settings in which these variables occur. In such cases the formulation of hypothesis is likely to be trivial. However a little experience about the study problem, study units and the study area can pave the way for a scientific research. In such cases when there is a little understanding about the study problem and thc area where it lies the use of exploratory research design is appropriate, Jahoda and Cook (1969 : 52) have aptly remarked," In the case of problems about which little knowledge is available, an exploratory study is usually most appropriate. "Keeping in view the nature, attributes as well as the postulations of exploratory research design the survey of literature and a review of related studies conducted so far has been made for gaining deeper insight into the problem. Chapter No. 2 of the report, which deals with the conceptual analysis and review of literature, is an attempt made in accordance with the postulations of the exploratory research design. At this step the researcher has presented extensively an analysis of the concepts used in the study. The concepts, first of all, have been narrated according to the thoughts presented by earlier authors, scholars, philosophers and scientists. After that the researcher has conceptualized the concepts in view of the nature and objectives of the study under investigation. So that the concepts can be viewed in a particular frame of reference. In this context some indicators and parameters have been structured and included in the questionnaire. More so a review of literature pertaining to tribal education, health, hygiene and nutrition has been presented in the report with a view to understanding the methods, approaches and tools applied in different studies by different scholars, and also to understand the findings of studies conducted by scholars. Thus the survey of the existing literature has helped in developing insight into the problem in hand and also pinpointed towards the gaps of knowledge which ultimately paved the way for the formulation of research questions of the present study. The survey of literature also helped in the selection of tools, techniques, methods and approaches of the study. The forthcoming delineation deals about it.

In exploratory researches the use of experience survey is of great importance for gaining insight into the problem called upon to study. In view of the relevant formulation and application of the tools, techniques and approaches for collecting first-hand field information the use of 'experience survey' is essentially important. In this context, before the commencement of the research work a pilot survey of the 'tribal area' was conducted by the principal investigator. Even the universe of the study was selected only after the completion of the pilot survey of the whole tribal areas of Uttarakhand. It was found that the tribal villages have different locations, different geography and demography. Even the socio-economic conditions and infrastructural facilities, were quite different from one tribal village to another. There were tribal villages located nearby market centres and road communications with comparatively better infrastructural facilities, on the contrary, there were villages having inaccessible location with no infrastructural facilities. There were villages with large population while some have very scanty and small population. It was of course the 'experience survey' that has paved the way for an appropriate selection of the field of the study as well as of the study units out of the diversified tribal areas.

Developing of tools and techniques of a research and the collection of relevant first-hand information are the important steps in a research work. The experience survey, which aims at developing insight into relationships between variables paves the way for tools construction and their application in data collection. In the present study three interview-schedules; the village schedule, nutrition assessment schedule and household schedule have been structured as the study tools. Besides this, other study equipments were also used for the collection of relevant first-hand information. The case studies which are proved to be 'insight-stimulating' approach have also been prepared in the study. Thus, the present research work has been designed according to the postulations of exploratory research design.

In the study we were concerned with various aspects of the study group. In this very context the demographic structure of the study group, their ecological settings, profile of their habitat, society and economy, sample profile, infrastructural facilities and their use in the study area by the target groups, and the role of government agencies particularly in regard to education, health, hygiene and nutrition of the study group, etc. have been taken into consideration for study. In this way the present study is concerned not only with the exploration or formulation of the research problem or working hypotheses and the tools, techniques or methods of data collection but also with the objective description of the existing position of the different variables and also about their correlation with one another.

Thus, the present study is based on exploratory-cum-descriptive research designs which can be proved by the procedure applied in the research work and can also be understood by the following analysis:

The Study Problem

If we look into the existing literature available on the tribals and their different aspects we come to know that there are controversies in thoughts and findings of scholars and researches conducted so far even by the social-scientists of high academic repute. In spite of the spate of researches on tribals and their different spheres every new scholar/ researcher underestimates the earlier studies and their findings and asserts the need of some more studies or researches and thus prove relevance of one's study even if it is nothing more than the repetition of the previous studies or sometimes the manipulation of studies done by earlier scholars. No doubt the subsequent researches pave the way for more scientific/ objective conclusions provided that such studies are based on scientific undertakings, not on speculations or mere nodding acquaintance. If we go through the studies related to the education, health, hygiene and nutrition among the tribal communities in India, we see that there is still a lot to work empirically. Swain (1998 :184) has aptly stated that 'there are few studies on health and nutritional states of India's tribal communities'. Dube (1988 :333), on the basis of research findings and the data presented by different scholars about tribal education, has stated that tribal education in India presents a dismal scene. It is characterized by low enrolment, especially of girls, high drop out, drift and wastage, limited numbers of high achievers and little credibility. It is so far a variety of reasons; ambiguities and contradictions in plannings; an undifferentiated approach towards the entire lot of tribes; amorphous definition of aims, without focus on the needs of particular tribes or their regional clusters; lack of cultural sensitivity and no visible gain within a closed structure of economic opportunities. Massive inputs in the educational endeavour, therefore, do not show proportionate benefits. However there are census reports which depict comparatively a tremendous decadal progress in literacy percentage and in educational status of Indian tribes. At the same time there are tribes who are still far away from educational facilities and health services. Viewing these dissimilarities, gap of education and literacy percentage as well as of health, hygiene and nutrition related problems the government of India has launched its campaign, i.e., 'Education and Health for all by 2000 A.D.' In this very context the study problem of the present research work has been formulated so that the education, health, hygiene and nutritional condition of the tribals, namely, the Tharus, the Buxas, the Raji and the Khasas of Uttarakhand (now Uttaranchal) can be understood and the relevance of the various concerning policies and programmes can be enumerated.

Universe of the Study

The universe of the present study consists of the tribal area of Uttarakhand inhabited particularly by the tribals namely the Tharus, the

Buxas, The Rajis and the Khasas. Though there are mainly five Scheduled Tribe communities in Uttarakhand namely the Bhotiyas, the Tharus, the Rajis and the Khasas. But the present study has been confined only up to the empirical study of the four tribal groups except the former one, i.e., the Bhotiyas. At present the Tharus with 53406 population are living in 141 villages of Sitarganj and Khatima Blocks in Udham Singh Nagar district of Uttaranchal. The main concentration of their population is in Khatima Block. Ratanpur a Tharu village of this Block has been purposefully selected for study. The Buxa tribe with 31037 population is spread over in 173 villages of three districts of Uttaranchal, namely, Udham Singh Nagar District, Nainital District and Dehradun District. In Udham Singh Nagar District Bajpur has been comparatively a Buxa predominant block in Uttaranchal. 'Bannakhera' a Buxa village of Bajpur block, has been purposefully selected for study. The Rajis, the aboriginal tribe of Kumaun Himalaya, has been confined to eight villages of three blocks of Pithoragarh district. Dharchula Block has maximum Raji population. Kimkhola a Raji village of Dharchula block has been selected purposefully for study. 'Basaya', a Khasa village in Kalsi Block of Dehradun district, is also selected for study. In this way out of the vast and scattered tribal area, i.e., the universe of the present research work, only four tribal villages, one from each tribal community has been selected purposefully for study.

In fact all the four tribal communities under reference of Uttaranchal were categorised as Scheduled Tribes in Jun 1967. Since then all possible efforts have been made under constitutional provisions for overall development of the tribals. For instance, rehabilitation scheme, agricultural development schemes, housing schemes, employment generation schemes, medical and health care services, literacy programmes, child and women welfare schemes, scheme for drinking water, electricity and road communication, integrated tribal development programmes etc. are some of the schemes which have been launched in tribal areas for their alround development. Besides this, they have been provided the facility of reservation in different spheres of life.

It is presumed that Scheduled Tribe communities alongwith SCs and OBCs, have suffered through the ages due to inequalities in social, economic and educational fields in comparison to certain forward castes. To minimize these social and economic dissimilarities and to safeguard their interests many social provisions were made in the Constitution of India. The reservation policy of government is an effort which tends to eradicate the present social, educational and economic disparities caused by social discrimination in the past. In this backdrop, the tribal villages, having approximately larger population, located comparatively in an accessible locations and have opportunity of availing the developmental and welfare facilities under various government provisions, have been purposefully selected for study. It is presumed hypothetically that, "the various development programmes meant particularly for the promotion of education, health, hygiene and nutritional status of the tribals, have successfully carried out throughout the tribal area and the tribes under reference have successfully availed these facilities". How far this hypothetical presumption is correct and to what extent the national goal of 'Health for all and Education for all by 2000 A.D.' can be achieved by the government, are some of the research questions which are to be answered through the empirical study of the four tribal villages, i.e., Ratanpur the Tharu village; Bannakhera - the Buxa village; Kimkhola—the Raji village and Basaya, the Khasa village of Uttaranchal.

Units of the Study; Sampling Procedure and the Samples of the Study

All the four purposefully sampled tribal villages are the study units of the present project work. It is expected that the selected villages have substantial development work done and the tribal people under study area have an experience of the impacts of the process of developmental schemes. But for an in-depth study of the problem and for collecting firsthand objective information about education, health, hygiene and nutrition the tribal families of the selected tribal villages are the focal points of observation. The family-wise information can produce an objective picture of the whole of the villages and its development. With this view in mind each family of every selected tribal village has purposefully been selected as a focal-unit of the study. Besides this, we also concern with the collection of the relevant, reliable, intensive and factual information as to answer the research questions outlined for the study. For this purpose one member from each family, mainly the head of the family, has been sampled purposefully as the informant of the study. In this way out of the total four tribal villages 347 families constitute altogether the observed group of the present project work. Out of the observed group one member (head of the family) from each family is selected as the respondent of the study. Thus the total number of the respondents is 347.

Tools and Techniques of Data Collection

In the present research work we need a variety of information as to reach the scientific conclusions. Hence viewing the nature and objectives of the present research work firsthand information have been collected through interview-schedule, observation and case study method. In order to maintain the objectivity all the relevant tools and equipments have also been used as and where it is felt necessary.

In this context three 'Schedules' viz. the Village-schedule, the Nutrition-assessment schedule and the Interview-schedule were constructed for obtaining first-hand information about the study problem. (Sec Annexure No. ii, iii and iv). In fact, first of all we need a base line data pertaining to the observed group, so that the information related to ecological settings of the village, infrastructural facilities available in the village, health and medicare pattern, sources of drinking water, state of employment generation schemes etc. can be obtained. The Village-schedule thus structured consists of the questions related to different aspects of the village. For instance, the introductory question deals with village profile, its geographical location, habitation pattern, economic structure in general, resources available in the village. The questions related to infrastructural facilities available in the village subsume these questions which can give information about educational facilities, medical and health care services, supply of drinking and irrigation water, transport and communication pattern, employment pattern, public distribution system and the food and drinking habits in general. Thus, it is tried that the information collected through village-schedule can give complete information about the study area. The village-schedule as a primary source of primary information has been administered on the village head, i.e., Sabhapati and simultaneously the village records, which is retained generally by the village-secretary, have also been used as the source of information. Mostly the questions are closed in nature.

The nutrition-assessment-schedule also includes the questions related to different aspects of the study unit. The introductory questions give basic information about the respondent units, on the basis of which we have prepared case studies about some of the cases related to the study problem. The questions pertaining to the nutrition assessment consist of the clinical and anthropometric measurements, food habits, drinks, food consumption, dietary pattern of different age-groups in the family. The nutrition-assessment schedule has been applied on some particular cases about which a case study has been prepared.

Lastly, 'Interview-schedule' with closed and open-end questions was constructed. This schedule was administered mainly on the head of the family. It gives the information about the household head, his family, his/her perception about education, health, hygiene and nutrition etc. Even the health status of the family members, life-expectancy in the family, cases of sickness in the family, socio-religious and environmental aspects of health, level of fertility and mortality, hygienic conditions—personal hygiene, environmental and domestic hygiene, community hygiene, sanitary services etc. have been studied through interview-schedule method.

Besides this the use of weighing machine for the measurement of weight of the pre-school children, school-going children, teenagers, adults and aged persons, flexible steel tape for the measurement of chest-circumference, upper arm circumference, etc., anthropometer rod and a vertical measuring rod for the measurement of stature/height and holtain skin fold caliper for the measurement of skin fold thickness have been used in the study. More so, in order to substantiate the conclusions scientifically the camera has also been used during the field work.

The observation is another relevant method used for the collection of primary information in the present research work. In fact, observation is a primary tool of scientific inquiry. It becomes a scientific technique to the extent that it (1) serves a formulated research purpose, (2) is planned systematically, (3) is recorded systematically and related to more general propositions rather than being presented as a set of interesting curiosa, and (4) is subjected to checks and controls on validity and reliability (1969: 2000). Even in scientific researches the use of observation method is considered reliable and of great importance. Goode and Hatt (1952 : 119) have aptly remarked, 'science begins with observation and returns to observation for its final validation'. In the present study we went up to the sampled villages in a very planned way, contacted each and every household head and the family members, established rapport by telling them what our objectives were, we convinced them honestly, made them aware about the benefits of the study and its findings for both the investigators as well as of the study groups. In this process the assistance of the educated tribal youths was sought. When the tribal people of the study area were convinced and considered our friendly presence and community participation with heart, only then the commencement of the present empirical research work could be possible. This state of full participation could follow the filling of the 'schedules' and taking the measurements of the study units successfully. It was really a hard job which required a lot of patience, perseverance, persistence, painstaking ability, prudence and overall the friendly and brotherly treatment plus scientific insight respectively with the study group and the research work. During this tedious, tough, tiresome, time-taking, prosaic but an adventurous and philanthropic scientific undertaking the longing to show something by deeds predominantly motivated us. Throughout this endeavour we used an observation guide scientifically constructed before the commencement of the real research work as to escape from oblivion. Thus the primary information was collected through accurate, suitable and well-tested techniques and equipments.

Secondary information, in the form of published public records, research papers, reference books, research studies done by earlier scholars were also used where-ever needed.

Analysis and Interpretation of Data

"After the data have been collected, the social scientist turns his full attention to their analysis and interpretation, a process consisting of a number of closely related operations. It is the purpose of analysis to summarize the complete observations in such a manner that they yield answers to the research questions. It is the purpose of interpretation to search for the broader meaning of these answers by linking them to other available knowledge. Both these purposes, of course, govern the entire research process; all preceding steps have been undertaken in order to make their fulfilment possible" (1959 : 386). Scientific analysis and interpretation of the compiled data is the creative aspect of research which makes possible the attainment of the scientific inferences and yields the answers of the research questions and also verifies the validity of the working hypothesis. The bewildering heap of collected data do not lead to any scientific conclusions unless they are not generalized in a systematic manner. In fact, science is built with facts as a house is built with stones but collection of facts is no more a science as a heap of stones is no more a house (Morris: 1960 : 509).

The data collected through primary and secondary sources are so unsystematic, scattered and meaningless that no scientific conclusion can be drawn out of them unless they are not processed and analysed in a planned and meaningful way. Galtung (1967:108) states, "Analysis of data refers to seeing the data in the light of hypotheses or research questions and the prevailing theories and drawing conclusions that are as amenable to theory formation as possible." Only after the systematic processing, the analysis and interpretation of data can produce scientific conclusions. The process of data analysis passes through different measurable steps to obtain the generalized findings of any research work. Those steps can be elaborated as follows : (i) classification or categorization of data - in fact the data we collect through different sources and different tools and techniques remain in a very unarranged and scattered form. To make them meaningful and sensible it is necessary to group or categorise them on the basis of resemblances or likeness in nature into different groups or categories. This process of arranging the data in groups or classes according to resemblances and similarities is technically called classification, (ii) Coding : Coding is a important step in scientific analysis. It is basically a technical procedure by which data are categorised. "Through coding, the raw data are transformed into symbols—usually numerals—that may be tabulated and counted. The transformation is not, however, automatic, it involves judgement on the part of a coder (Jahoda and Cook, 1959 : 410). Young (1968 : 211) stated, "Coding consists of setting up classes or categories to be used in presenting the data and then assigning a symbol, usually numerical to each answer which falls into a predetermined class."

Tabulation

Tabulation is a part of the technical process in the statistical analysis of data. The essential operation in tabulation is counting to determine the number of cases that fall into various categories (1969 : 406-407). In other words, we can say that the process of arranging the data in an orderly manner into rows and columns capable of being read into two directions is called tabulation.

In the present study the data collected through different sources have been classified on the basis of likeness or similarities. Particularly the information obtained through various types of questions viz. open-end questions, closed questions, structured questions, multiple choice questions etc. included in the interview-schedule, has been classified and then arranged in columns in an orderly manner so that the elucidation of the data can be possible. The classification and tabulation of the data was made entirely by manual method.

Statistical Analysis of Data

In the technical process of analysis and interpretation of data, the statistical analysis of tabulated data is an important stage on which scientific findings of any study are based. On the basis of the tabulated data, we have calculated statistically the responses obtained in regard to different variables. And, the correlation between education and health, hygiene and nutrition has been enumerated. By statistical analysis it has also been tried to present the qualitative data into quantitative form which is regarded comparatively more authentic and reliable even in sociological researches.

Inferences about Causal Relations Among Variables

The statistical analysis of data follows the interpretation to achieve scientific inferences about the causal relations among the variables. The facts statistically drawn have thoroughly been interpreted and the inferences of the study have been drawn. It is assumed that the findings will pave the way for further researches in sociological discipline and new dimensions in health and nutrition-related studies in general and in tribal and marginalized groups in particular will also be evolved.

References

Jahoda, M., and Cook, S.W., 1969 : *Research Methods in Social Relations*, Mathew and Co. Ltd. 11 New Fitter Lane, E.C.4., U.S.A.

Goode, W.J. and Hatt, P.K., 1952 : *Methods in Social Research*, Mc-Graw Hill Book Co., New York.

Morris, R.T., 1960 : *The Tow-Way Mirror, Cultural Status in Foreign Student Adjustment*, University of Minnesota Press.

Galtung, J., 1967: *Theory and Methods of Social Research*, London.

4

Demography, Habitat and Ethnography of the Tribes of Uttarakhand

The main objective of this chapter is to provide a lucid account of the profile of the demography, habitat and ethnography of the tribals of Uttarakhand. This effort will help us in understanding the existing status of the tribals of Uttarakhand as a whole. In fact the nature of the population, ecological background, habitations and the ethnographic traits of a given community altogether ascertain its present state of being, i.e., the nature of the society, culture and economy. By and large it is the socio-cultural and economic system which determines the human life in general and the status of education, health, hygiene and nutrition of its population in particular. With this view in mind the profile of the demography, habitat and ethnography of the tribals of Uttarakhand is being presented here in its historical background.

It is well understood that under Article 342 of the Constitution of India certain tribes have been specified as Scheduled Tribes in the country. Almost all the states and union territories, except the state of Punjab and Haryana and Union Territories of Chandigarh, Delhi and Pondicherry, have Scheduled Tribe population. Uttarakhand (now Uttaranchal state), a hilly region of Indian sub-continent has also five tribal communities which have been specified as Scheduled Tribes by constitutional order 1967. Before we talk about the socio-economic profile of the tribals of Uttarakhand and their habitations, it will be more pertinent to give a general look on the scenario of the tribals of Indian subcontinent. In this context it may be noted that India has the second largest concentration of tribal population after that of African continent. As per 2001 census, tribal population of India is about 8.08 per cent of the total population of the country excluding the population of Jammu and Kashmir where census could not be conducted due to disturbed situation. If we look into the population distribution of the tribals we find that about 87 per cent Scheduled Tribe population is concentrated in the central belt covering 8 states of Madhya Pradesh, Orissa, Bihar, Maharashtra, Gujarat, Rajasthan, Andhra Pradesh and West Bengal. About 10 per cent in the Norlh-Eastern region and about 3 per cent are in other states. Madhya Pradesh has the highest concentration of Scheduled Tribe population, i.e., 1.54 crore which is about 23 per cent of the total Scheduled Tribe population in the country. There are 360 Scheduled Tribes (sub-tribes being many more) speaking more than 100 dialects in this zone. There are five major tribes, namely the Gonds, the Bhils, the Santhals, the Oraons and the Minas, each having a population more than 74 lakhs, 55 lakhs, 42 lakhs, 20 lakhs and 18 lakhs respectively. There are five small tribes found in Andaman and Nicobar Islands, namely, the Great-Andamanese, the Sentenelese, the Onges, the Jarwas and the Shompens, each having a population of 28, 80, 98, 200 and 214 respectively. Thus the Gond is the single largest tribe and the Great Andamanese is the smallest tribe in the country (Verma: 1995).

Under the Constitution of India a comprehensive special provisions have been made for protection and development of Scheduled Tribes. The special provisions relating to the interests of the Scheduled Tribes are contained in the Articles -15(4), 16(4), 19(4), 19(5), 23, 29, 46, 164, 275(1), 330, 332, 334, 335, 338, 342 and fifth and sixth schedules of the Constitution. These articles have provisions for all round development of the Scheduled Tribes in the country.

The Scheduled Tribe communities of India present a complex and composite socio-economic and cultural scenario. The Scheduled Tribes in the country belong to a variety of linguistic families, racial stocks and also differ from one another in regard to their economic standard, religious faiths, cultural system and social status (Bisht: 1994: 14). It is also substantiated from the writings of Majumdar (1963 : 253), Burman (1972), Guha (1944), Dube (1965), Risely (1915), Haddon (1963:257-258), Elwin (1963:23), Thurnwald (1933), Dubey (1998), Singh (198), Mishra (1998), Singh (1997-98), Chaudhuri (1990-92) and Raha (1989) etc. etc.

Like other states and union territories in the country, Uttaranchal, a newly formed state also have Scheduled Tribe population but in a very scanty and scattered form. Out of total 5926147 population of Uttarakhand the Scheduled Tribes constitute only 3.54 per cent with 209838 population (Bisht: 1996: 161-170) of the state. The Bhotiyas, the Buxas, the Tharus, the Rajis and the Khasas (Jaunsaris) are the Scheduled Tribe communities dwelling in Uttarakhand since the time immemorial. The population of the former four tribal communities is predominantly concentrated in Kumaun region while the last tribal community is exclusively found in Jaunsar-Bavar area of Garhwal region. A brief demographic sketch of the Scheduled Tribes of Uttarakhand can be given as follows.

Demography of the Tribals of Uttarakhand

It is a known fact that systematic caste-wise enumeration of population was introduced by the Registrar General of India in 1881 and discontinued in 1931. In this context, figures of caste-wise population beyond 1931 are not available. But assuming the inter se rate of population growth of various castes, communities and religious groups over the last half a century has remained more or less the same, it is possible to work out the percentage that all these groups constitute of the total population of the country (Singh 1996 ; 18). Working on the aforesaid assumption the Scheduled Tribe population in Uttarakhand may be presented in the following Table 4.1.

It is obvious that every district of Uttaranchal has more or less tribal population. But the concentration of the major part of the ST population reside in rural areas. As 94.50 per cent of the total tribal population belongs to rural areas while the rest 5.50 per cent to urban centres. The population distribution of STs also show that maximum 90,020 tribal population dwell in Nainital (including U.S. Nagar district) district which is preceded respectively by Dehradun, Pithoragarh, Chamoli, Almora, Uttarakashi, Pauri and Tehri with 84,046, 15,140,10,073, 2739, 2300,1502 and 615 population.

The average sex-ratio is 930 females per thousand males and the literacy is 23.56 per cent. The highest 1056 females per thousand males are in Pithoragarh urban area while the lowest 440 females per thousand males are in Pauri urban area. It is noteworthy that the Dehradun district with maximum ST population has 889 females per thousand males only. So far as the average literacy per cent is concerned, Dehradun with maximum tribal population, has the lowest per cent of tribal literacy. i.e., only 29.36 per cent while Tehri with minimum tribal population has maximum tribal literacy, i.e., 63.27 per cent. The per cent figure related to literacy also exhibits that in urban areas tribal literacy is comparatively more than in rural areas. It is so because of two main reasons, that is, (i) the urban impact motivates even the tribal people towards education and also make them realize the importance as well as the need of education in the present-day context. It is one of the reasons that tribal literacy in urban areas is much greater than in the rural areas. The urban-rural variation in tribal literacy particularly in Almora, Pithoragarh, Chamoli, Dehradun, Nainital and Uttarakashi is the result of urban-rural impact, (ii) There are urban centres where the tribals are engaged either in some vocational profession or in service pursuits after getting education, whatsoever their place of birth and domicile. But this pattern show the spatial literacy per cent, and enumerate comparatively more tribal literacy per cent or sometimes 100 per cent tribal literacy in urban areas. As we observe in the case of Tehri urban area where tribal literacy is seen 100

Table 4.1. Districtwise Scheduled—Tribe Population in Uttarakhand

District	Total- (T) Rural- (R) Urban- (U)	Population	% of Scheduled-Tribe Population to total population	Sex ratio (Females Per 1000 Males)	Literacy Percentage		
					Persons	Male	Female
Almora	T	2739	0.33	949	46.57	61.39	31.55
(including	R	2044	0.26	1018	44.55	60.76	27.87
Bageshwar)	U	695	1.30	773	60.36	65.91	55.24
Nainital	T	90020	5.84	9.44	19.04	31.59	6.12
(including	R	88061	8.49	947	18.71	31.15	5.95
U.S. Nagar)	U	1959	0.39	814	48.61	64.96	25.07
Pithoragarh	T	18313	3.23	995	47.62	62.41	32.51
(including	R	15140	2.89	982	44.66	59.96	29.07
Champawat)	U	3173	7.53	1056	68.94	79.87	57.57
Chamoli	T	10073	2.26	1062	45.88	63.11	29.43
(including	R	7939	1.92	1113	40.03	58.11	23.56
Karn Prayag)	U	2334	5.76	907	60.79	74.81	45.70
Dehradun	T	84046	8.20	889	18.64	29.36	6.08
	R	81005	15.88	898	18.13	28.78	5.72
	U	3071	0.60	684	61.31	67.43	48.45

(Contd. Table 4.1)

District	Total- (T) Rural- (R) Urban- (U)	Population	% of Scheduled-Tribe Population to total population	Sex ratio (Females Per 1000 Males)	Literacy Percentage		
					Persons	Male	Female
Pauri	T	1502	0.22	744	26.16	40.22	6.55
	R	1358	0.28	784	19.35	32.55	2.35
	U	144	0.18	440	80.99	87.64	62.50
Tehri	T	615	0.11	1312	51.35	63.27	42.11
	R	548	0.10	1491	52.46	59.09	35.29
	U	67	0.20	456	100.00	100.00	100.00
Uttarkashi	T	2300	0.96	909	40.84	57.53	20.01
	R	2240	1.01	908	40.28	57.04	21.58
	U	60	0.35	935	59.61	71.88	40.00
Uttarakhand	T	209838	3.54	930	23.56	35.64	10.43
	R	198335	4.27	935	22.03	34.06	9.03
	U	11503	0.89	843	62.27	73.79	48.28

per cent. Besides this, tribal literacy also depicts a considerable variation in regard to male-female literacy ratio. There is 35.64 per cent male literacy against 10.43 per cent female literacy. This broader gap in respect of male-female literacy depicts the lesser interest and awareness of tribal women towards education. The population related data also depicts that the Scheduled Tribe population in Uttaranchal is comparatively very low in comparison to other Himalayan states in the country.

If we take into account the tribe-wise population and the status of the tribals in Uttaranchal we come to the conclusion that there is great variation in regard to population size as well as of the socio-economic and cultural status of the tribals. It is already mentioned that the tribe-wise census has not been conducted in the country after 1931. However if we take into consideration the available tribe-wise population as the base line data and calculate the population growth as per-rate we observe in general census, we find the following tribe-wise population figures in Uttaranchal (Bisht: 1996:163).

Table 4.2. Tribe-wise Population in Uttaranchal (%)

Tribes	*Bhotiya*	*Buxa*	*Tharus*	*Rajis*	*Jaunsaris*	*Total*
Population	31014	28685	68197	567	81375	209838
Per cent	14.78	13.67	37.5	0.27	38.78	100.00

It is obvious that Jaunsari with 38.78 per cent of the total tribal population in Uttaranchal is the largest tribal group. At present total population of Jaunsaris (81375) is scattered over 356 villages of Chakrata and Kalsi Development blocks of Dehradun district.

The Tharu is the second largest tribal group of Uttarakhand. It constitutes 32.50 per cent of the total tribal population of Uttaranchal. The total population of the Tharus, i.e., 68197 is spread over 141 villages of Sitarganj and Khatima-Development blocks of newly formed Udham Singh Nagar district (previously this area was the part of Nainital district) of Uttaranchal. The Tharus are also found in Lakhimpur-Khiri, Gonda, Behraich and Gorakhpur districts of U.P. But 60 per cent of the total Tharu population is concentrated only in Sitarganj and Khatima blocks.

14.78 per cent of the total tribal population of Uttaranchal is formed by the Bhotiyas. According to available information total population of the Bhotiyas stands 31014 which is spread over 291 villages of Pithoragarh, Uttarkashi, Chamoli and Almora Districts of Uttaranchal.

The Buxas have 13.67 per cent population of the total Scheduled Tribe population of Uttaranchal. Its total population, i.e., 28685 is spread over in approximately 173 villages of Dehradun, U.S. Nagar and Nainital districts of Uttaranchal. But the main concentration of the Buxa population is in Bajpur, Gadarpur, Kashipur and Ramnagar of Kumaun region. Besides this, the Buxas are also found in Kotwali and Afajalgarh Blocks of Bijnor district of U.P. But the major part of the Buxa population is confined in Uttaranchal.

Raji, the smallest tribal group of Uttaranchal has only 565 population which is 0.27 per cent of the total tribal population of Uttaranchal. The Raji population is confined only in eight villages of Didihat, Dharchula, Kanalichhina and Champawat (now a separate district) Block of Pithoragarh district in a very scanty manner.

Thus as far as the numerical strength is concerned the Jaunsaris can be termed as the largest tribal group in Uttaranchal which is preceded (in terms of population size) respectively by the Tharus, the Bhotiyas, the Buxas and the Rajis. But as far as literacy is concerned, the Bhotiyas stand first which is preceded respectively by the Jaunsaris, Tharus, Buxas and the Rajis. Numerically Uttaranchal has only 0.16 per cent tribal population of India which is less than the tribal population of any state and union territory in the country.

Physical Features of Tribal Habitat in Uttaranchal

The tribal population is found in almost all parts of Uttaranchal. As per historical records the tribals are the autochthonous people of the land and are believed to be the earliest settlers in Uttaranchal region. At present the district-wise distribution of tribal population in Uttaranchal (as shown in Table 4.1) shows their present existing settlement status. But if we go back to history we find that their original habitations in Uttaranchal were confined in remote hilly, forested and foot-hill areas and they used to lead their life with their age-old traditional ways of living which can more precisely be termed as the primitive way of living. With the course of time the transformation process took place and the status-quo of the then tribals changed and the present tribal-scenario came into existence which we will delineate in forthcoming discussion. One can deny the impact of history in the determination of present and future. So is true in regard to the ecology which includes the habitations and its impact in the determination of socio-cultural system of a given community. It is a must to understand the present tribal scenario in Uttaranchal in its historical background. With this view in mind a brief account of the historical background of Uttaranchal and its people-particularly of the tribal people is indispensable in the analysis of the existing profile of tribal habitations in Uttaranchal.

Physical Features of Uttaranchal and of the Tribal Habitations

The area of Uttaranchal extends between latitudes 28°44' and 31°25' N and longitudes 77°45' and 81°1' E. It spans over 51,225 km^2 area and supports a population of 59,26,146 persons out of which the Scheduled Tribe population is 209838. At present there are about 15117 rural and

64 urban settlements in Uttaranchal. The Scheduled-Tribe population live in about 970 rural and approximately 45 urban areas spread over 27 blocks of thirteen districts of Uttaranchal. Approximately 94.50 per cent tribal population lives in rural areas while the remaining part, i.e., approximately 5.50 per cent live in urban areas.

Physiographically, Uttaranchal comprises all the five latitudinal physiographic-geological zones, i.e., the Tarai Bhabar, the Siwalik with Dun, the Lesser Himalaya, the Great Himalaya and the Trans-Himalaya. (Pant: 1996:45).

The northern fringe of the Indo-Gangetic Plains with 10-25 km. wide and stretching from Tanakpur in east to Dehradun in west is known as Tarai zone. It is originally the homeland of the Tharus and the Buksas of Uttaranchal. But in due course of time the refugees from Pakistan and Bangladesh and some other ethnic groups settled down in this region. Today it is one of the most developed area of newly formed Uttaranchal state. The adjoining 10-20 km. northern wide belt of Tarai is known as Bhabar. This zone is formed by coarse gravels in which all streams disappear and causing water scarcity. We can also find some migrated tribal population of Bhotiyas, Buxas and Khasas who have settled-down here in some rural and urban settlements. The northern area of Bhabar zone ranging from 700 to 1200 mtr. is known as Siwalik zone. We find very thin tribal population in this zone. The 70 km. wide zone in the north of the Siwalika range is called the Lesser Himalayas. This is densely populated area of Uttaranchal. In this region we can observe the settlement of the Bhotiya, Raji and Jaunsari tribes of Uttaranchal. The winter houses of Bhotiya tribe lie in this area. With the end of the Lesser Himalayan ranges the Great Himalayan region starts. The northern belt of Uttaranchal, ranging 30 to 50 km. in width and 3000 mtr to 7000 mtr. in altitude is known as the Great Himalaya. This belt comprises of high peaks and glaciers. Generally the summer homes of the Bhotiya tribe lie in this region. The unfavourable, harsh and rigorous climatic conditions and the tumulous, rugged and fragile land structures have been responsible for scanty habitation in this region. The famous peaks of religious importance like Nandadevi, Panchachuli, Badrinath, Kedarnath, Trishul, Chaukhamba, Bandarpunch, and Kamet are also located in the Great Himalayan region. Besides this, the famous glaciers like Milam, Pindari, Khatling and Gangotri are also situated in this region. The northern most belt with 49 km width of Uttaranchal is known as Trans-Himalayan belt. This is one of the most thinly populated area with approximately 20 to 30 temporary summers settlement of the Bhotiya tribe.

Atkinson (1996 : 270) has also stated 'To the north in the inter-alpine valleys of Bhot, we have a tribe of Tibetan origin and whose affinities are found in the trans-Himalayan tribes of Hundes. They are known as Bhotiyas by the people of the lower hills, who in turn are designated Khasiyas by the Bhotiyas, whilst the people of the adjoining portion of Tibet are known as Hunas or Huniyas. In addition to the tribes already enumerated there are the Rajis or Rajyas, the modern representatives of the Rajya-Kiratas and the Tharus and Bhuksas of the Tarai lowlands and traces of the Nagas and Sakas, whilst other contend that we have here also old Baktrian (yavana)". Jaunsar-Bawar, a homeland of the Khasa Tribe or the Jaunsaris is situated in the CIS-Himalayan region. It forms approximately half of the Dehradun district and located at the north-western corner of the Uttaranchal state. It lies between the longitude 77°42' to 78°5' east and latitude 30°31' to 31°2' north. The area is roughly oval in shape with its major axis laying north and south. Jaunsar-Bawar is surrounded by the boundaries of Tehri-Garhwal in east, north-east and south-east, by Himachal Pradesh in west and north-west and its sourthern part is adjacent to Dehradun itself. Jaunsar-Bawar is constituted by its two constituent parts, i.e., the Jaunsar which forms the lower part of this region and the Bawar which includes the northern parts of this region. Topographically, Jaunsar-Bawar is a hill appanage of the Dun, to which it has no physical resemblance. It is constituted entirely of rugged mountains and gorges.

The most striking features of Jaunsar-Bawar topography have been summarized in the District Gazetteer of Dehradun (1911:6) as follows; 'Even in the hills, Jaunsar-Bawar has the character of being one of the wildest and most rugged tracts, affording naturally very little level ground, and that only in small patches. The mountains are peculiarly rough and precipitous, there is much cliff and rock and few villages so that the cultivation is necessarily small and very laborious (Majumdar, 1963:19). The mountains of Jaunsar-Bawar belong to the cis-Himalayan system. The Kharamba is the highest peak 10075 high, Deoban near Chakrata is 9331 feet while Chakrata itself is 7076 feet above the sea level. The water system of the region consists of two lines, that of the Tons and the Jamuna respectively. The Tons in its upper course carries a larger volume of water than the Jamuna and runs down to the north-east and encircles the northern and eastern sides of Jaunsar-Bawar. Jamuna has its origin from the Jamnotri glacier in Tehri-Garhwal and runs southward and encircles the eastern and southern borders of Jaunsar-Bawar. It is finally joined by the Tons at the south-western corner of this pargana and runs south-west in the name of Jamuna. Thus the whole of the Jaunsar-Bawar is practically encircled by these two rivers.

The climate of Jaunsar-Bawar varies greatly from place to place according to elevation which ranges from 3000 feet to 10,075 feet high from the sea level. It has three seasons in the year: the cold, the hot, and, the rainy. The cold season starts in November and remains up to March, the hot season starts from April and continues to June while the rainy season begins partially by the end of June and remains till September. In October there is pleasant weather with occasional scanty rainfall. The rainfall in this region is moderate which is recorded average 70" annually. The heaviest rainfall is recorded in the month of July and August while May and June are the months when mercury rises to the highest in a year. The winter is severe and snowfall is heavy in the villages located in Bawar area at the elevation of five to seven thousand feet above the sea level.

The Jaunsar-Bawar area has an inferior quality of land with rugged and rocky hills. The soil is often porous and water drains away. But besides the water source there are some fields of good loam and good clay. Jaunsar-Bawar is rich in minerals and forest wealth. Among the fruit trees walnut, peach, apple, pear, apricot are very common. The Kharif and Rabi are the two main crop reasons. The former starts in June and ends by October while the later begins in October-November and ends by April and May. The rice (Paddy), kodu (Manduwa), maize, potato, ginger, tobacco, chaulai are the major Kharif crops which have comparatively better yield, while wheat, barley, mustard and some pulses are the major Rabi crops. Besides this, turmeric, chillies, onions and tomato are also produced in this region. Potato, ginger, turmeric, chillies and tomato are the cash crops. Agricultural yield in Jaunsar-Bawar area is very poor which hardly meets even the local needs.

In agricultural economy, the animal husbandry is of great importance. The Jaunsaris lead an agricultural-cum-pastoral life. Hence cattle are reared for twin purposes—ploughing fields and for milk products. Cows, ox, buffalos, goats, sheep are reared commonly by the people. They get meat and wool from sheep and goats. Woollen clothes and blankets are made of wool for their own use. Besides this, pigs and fowls are also reared by lower castes only.

The Himalayan borderland laying with the southern part of Tibet and stretching from Vyans valley in east to Niti and Mana in west has been the homeland of the Bhotiyas since the time immemorial. We have some references in *Himalayan Gazetteer* Vol. II, part I, which states that, "when we pass to the north of the great snowy peaks, we get among different people, the Bhotiyas. Bod, the native name for Tibet, corrupted by the people of India into Bhot, has given rise to the name Bhotiya for the border tribes between the two countries (Atkinson : 1996: 388). It is evident that the appellation 'Bhotiya' is derived from Bod the native name for Tibet and thus the Bhotiya is basically a territorial group. Besides this the term 'Bhotiyas' is used commonly for the border tribes living in between both the countries. Sherring (1906), Smith (1930), Pant (1935) etc. are also of the opinion, "If a straight line is drawn between Askot and Kapkot, the area to the north of this line will constitute the region locally known as the 'Bhot' or the Bhotiya tract which is entirely different from the remaining south-eastern portion of the rest. But this delineation excludes the Mana and Niti groups."

Apart from the pages of history if we turn our attention to the hearsays, folk tales and folk songs prevalent for long throughout Uttaranchal and its populace we come to know that the Bhotiyas are the aboriginal tribes of the Indo-Tibetan borderland. Their existence has been noted along the snowy ranges of the Indo-Tibetan border by scholars, pilgrims and travellers. Even today it is believed that different Bhotiya groups have been living in seven different river valleys of Uttaranchal after which they have derived their name. For example, the Bhotiyas living in Vyans and Chaudans-a Kali-river valley of eastern border of Uttaranchal are respectively known as Vyansis and Chaudansis, the Bhotiyas of Darma - a Dholi-river valley, are Darmias, the Bhotiyas of Johar a Gori-river valley, are Jauharis. These four Bhotiya-groups belong to Kumaun region of Uttaranchal. The rest three Bhotiya-Groups namely, the Marchas the habitant of Bishnu-Ganga-river valley in Chamoli, the Tolchha resident of Dhauli-Ganga-river valley in Uttarakashi district and the Jads - aboriginals of Jad-Ganga-river valley in Chamoli. Niti and Mana are the two main Bhotiya villages along the river Dhauliganga (west), in Garhwal region of Uttaranchal. The Bhotiyas living in different valleys have generally, two settlements. First the winter settlements located in lower Himalayan valleys and the second summer settlements situated on the high altitude of the Himalayan ranges. If we take into account these two settlements we find that these settlements are located at the elevation of 3000' to 12330' from the sea level. The Bhotiyas practise seasonal movements with their livestock. They come down in low lying valleys with their live-stock in winter and turn back to high hills in summer. The process of seasonal movement has been termed as 'transhumance' by the geographers and the anthropologists. The Bhotiyas have been traditionally a trader-cum-pastoral community with partial agricultural economy, hence they have been termed by different names by different scholars. Such as Sashi (1979) has termed them as 'Trader nomads', Pant (1935) named them as semi-nomads and nomads, and Kharakwal (1971) 'transhumant' community. In Nepal the migration process followed by the Bhotiyas has been described as 'transhumance' by Furer-Haimendorf (1975-1981). Thus the Bhotiyas have double settlement pattern between which their cyclical movements go on throughout the year.

The Raji, a little known tribe of Kumaun Himalaya in Uttaranchal is an aboriginal tribe who is said to be the habitants of Askot and its adjacent forest area on the Kali river. At present the Raji clusters which are eight in numbers have settled down in the hilly and forest area of Dharchula, Didihat and Champawat Tehsils of Pithoragarh district. The locality, where the Raji clusters are settled, can be termed as Raji-village or the Rauturha, as denominated by the neighbouring people. The Raji-habitations are located at the elevation of 2000' to 6000' from the sea level. The steep hilly slopes, amidst dense forests with small huts, surrounded by small terraces give impression of existence of human life. When we proceed nearer and nearer we meet the Raji people in a very isolated state there. In fact the Raji habitations are situated in a very lonely, aloof, inaccessible and distant forest and hilly regions. Their places of dwellings are still far from the means of direct transportation. Exceptionally there is only a Raji village-Kimkhola which is, located by the road side. Besides this, there are some small Raji clusters who are still living in caves. The 'Phanpu-Odhiyar' on Jaulajibee-Dharchula motor road is one of the caves where a Raji family lives for a long time.

It is observed that the climatic conditions of the Raji settlements vary as according to the variation of the altitude of the habitations. In general almost all the settlements have no suitable life and agro-climatic conditions. The Raji people are leading their life in a very miserable and adverse life conditions (See Bisht's writings 1993, for more detail) because the places of their habitations are not suitable for healthy life conditions.

We have two more tribal communities—the Tharus and the Buksas in Uttaranchal. The foot-hill Tarai and Bhabar areas of Kumaun in east and Garhwal in west has been the home-land of Tharus and Buksas since the time immemorial. We have some written references about their habitations. Atkinson (1996 :371) states "In the country lying along the foot of the Kumaun hills from the Kosi eastwards we have a tribe known as 'Tharus' which may be traced further east to the Bagmati river. They are the dwellers in swamps and are great rice cultivators and are proof against malaria. They even dread visiting the plains, where they say they suffer severely from fever. To the east they are neighbours of the 'Mechis', a tribe of similar character living in the thickest part of the Tarai forest lying below eastern Nepal, Sikkim and Bhutan". Even today the Tharu population is scattered over Nainital Tarai (now U.S. Nagar district) to Gorakhpur in east. But the major part of their population is concentrated in Khatima and Sitarganj tehsils of Uttaranchal. The places of their habitations have been known as 'Tharuwat' means the region where 'Tharus' live since long. In this way it is said that the 'Tarai land' of the then Nainital district, particularly Khatima and Sitarganj used to be owned by the Tharus. They had the real ownership of the Tarai.

On the other hand, "The Buksas or the Bhoksas, a tribe somewhat similar to the Tharus are found in the Tarai and Bhabar from the Pilibhit district in the east and Chandpur on the Ganges in the west and a few scattered colonies also occur in Dehradun" (1996 : 371). In fact the Buxas are known as the original habitants of the Tarai and Bhabar plains of Uttarakhand including Pilibhit and Bijnor districts of Uttar Pradesh. At present the population of Buxa tribe is spread over in the Tarai plains of Dehradun, Pauri, U.S. Nagar, and Nainital districts of Uttaranchal and also in Bijnor district of U.P. (Bisht: 1999:212). Besides this, the Buxa population is spread over 17 villages of Sirmaur district in Himachal Pradesh (Singh and Shukla: 1990:83). In U.S. Nagar district, the Bajpur, Kashipur, Gadarpur, Rudrapur Blocks, in Nainital district Ramnagar Block, in Dehradun district, the Doiwala and Sahaspur blocks and in Pauri district the Dogadda block have been the homeland of Buxa tribe. In U.S. Nagar district, the region where the Buxa tribe has been dwelling for a long time is known as 'Buxar', i.e., the homeland of the Buxas. It is believed that before partition 'Buxar' area was owned by the Buxas only and the then Nainital Tarai (now U.S. Nagar district) was the main residing place of the Buxas where about 60 per cent of the total Buxa population was concentrated. No doubt their settlement in Tarai is of ancient date. In the Ain-i-Akbari the name 'Bhuksar' was given to the tract occupied by them up to recent date (Atkinson 1996:372). The Tarai area of U. S. Nagar district where the major Buxa population live, lies immediately south of the Bhabar region. This Tarai region is situated between 28°43' and 29°26' north latitudes and between 78°53' and 80° east longitudes with an average breadth of 18 kms and stretches from the Sarada in the east to pargana Kashipur in west (Hasan : 1979: 8). Basically this area was full of forests and swamps. There was endless farming mainly of paddy and sugarcane. With due course of time this green belt has been transformed into an industrial area and big market centres. The climate of the Tarai, all the year round, is trying. Owing to proximity of hills, the circulation of air being very much retarded, the direct and refracted heat makes it hot and sultry. In the month of August and October when the forest undergrowth, grows up, the climate is extremely malarial. But today with the introduction of health and medicare programmes malaria has almost been eradicated, however, the rainy and winter seasons have unhealthy impacts on the people. We can observe overtly the impact of the topography of the Tarai region on its populace and also on their socio-economic life. Even the health, hygiene and nutrition is highly affected by the topographical aspects of the region.

Ethnography of the Tribals of Uttaranchal

When we talk about the ethnography of a given community there we mean an objective study of the ethnic traits and the activity of members of that particular social group and also the description and evaluation of such trails and activities which altogether present the ethnic and socio-cultural identity of that particular social group or the community. Ethnography is basically an approach used generally in anthropological and sociological studies which aims at the holistic scientific study of a given community. Since we have also an objective of studying the tribals of Uttarakhand in its holistic perspective in general and their educational, health, hygiene and nutritional status in particular which is possible only through a scientific approach. The ethnographic approach along with other relevant methods has been helpful in achieving the objective of the study.

In this context if we take into account the geographical classification of Indian Tribes made by Prof. B.K. Roy Berman, an eminent anthropologist, we can categorise the Scheduled Tribe Communities of Uttaranchal as the 'tribes of sub-Himalayan region of the north and north-west India'. We have also references of earlier eminent scholars who denote the origin, racial affinity and also socio-cultural history of the tribals of Uttaranchal in a very scanty form. In general, the scholars are of the opinion that the Bhotiyas, the Rajis, the Tharus and the Buxas have the Mongoloid racial traits while the Jaunsaris or the Khasas have Mediterranean racial traits. Moreover we have a number of legends and speculations made by earlier scholars about the appellation and etymology of the tribes under study. We think that the tribe-wise description will be relevant enough in reviewing their status in the present day context. With this in mind the tribe-wise ethnographic interpretation of the tribes of Uttaranchal is as follows :

The Bhotiyas

Etymologically the term 'Bhotiya' refers to the habitants of 'Bhot' the region of Indo-Tibetan border of Uttaranchal Himalaya. In fact, the term 'Bhot' is a corrupted form of 'Bod' the native name for Tibet which was corrupted by the people of India into 'Bhot'. Even today 'Bhot' has not altogether lost its proper meaning, it is still applied generally to the tract north of the great peaks without reference to physical or political boundaries, though in Kumaun it is now more commonly used to signify the country within the snowy range south of the Tibetan frontier. It is rather an ethnographical than a geographical expression intending the country inhabited by Bhotiyas....... It will be convenient here to use the word 'Bhot' and 'Bhotiya' in this restricted sense: (Atkinson: 1996:368-369). Thus etymologically the term 'Bhotiya' in corrupted form is derived from 'Bod', i.e., Tibet and also connects its roots in a proved way, with ancient Tibetan community. Atkinson aptly states that 'the Bhotiyas themselves are of Tibetan origin is sufficiently shown by the language that they speak, by their mongolian caste of countenance, and those unmistakeable peculiarities that belong to the Tibetan race, and which are as well marked in them as in the Huniyas themselves (1996:369). But the Bhotiyas do not admit this generic term 'Bhotiya'and their assignment with the Huniyas of Hundes. Chatterjee (1975:138) is of the opinion that the term 'Bhotiya' stands for a generic term of several distinct-ethnic groups which share many features in common. At the same time each group also exhibits certain sets of distinctive features which may be unique for one or more groups but not shared by the rest.' In fact the different ethnic groups named after different river valleys but known as Bhotiyas in general are of different origin. Chatterjee states that 'the Bhotiyas of all the seven river valleys have no common origin. There has been a lot of admixture of different ethnic strains in the past. It has also been recognized by many authors that there are Aryans, Scythians or Shakas, Tibeto mongols, Nepalis and Gorkhalis. Rahul (1970:140-151) says that 'the Jad (the Bhotiyas of Uttarkashi) claim to have come from Kinnaur in Himachal Pradesh. The eastern Bhotiyas used the term 'Shakas' to indicate their origin—its phonetic similarity with Shakas (the Scythians, a branch of Nordic Aryans) is generally underlined.' Even the Bhotiyas do not agree with the generic term 'Bhotiya' as is used to denote them. As stated by Atkinson (1996:368) 'In the traditional account of the colonization of the Bhotiya valley in which Milam is situated and which is given hereafter, they declare themselves the offsprings of a Rajput immigration from beyond the snows that succeed a Sokpa colony, but they are usually called Sokpas themselves.' Crooke (1896) is also of the opinion that, 'They (the Bhotiyas) call themselves Raghubansi Rajputs and trace their origin to Bhutwal in Nepal. They fix their immigration into Northern Oudh in the region of Nawab Asafuddaula (1775-1797). They now present a curious instance of Non-Aryan origin who are now in a short time completely Brahmins.' Whatever been the origin of the Bhotiyas, their physical features speak the story of their Mongoloid racial affinity.

The Bhotiya is basically a patriarchal, patrilocal and patrilineal community but the aged woman in the family also wield the status of female head and termed as 'Mulin-Rani', i.e., the queen of the hearth. The women in general have honourable position in the community. Both the male and female jointly perform their liabilities without any complication of formal pattern of division of labour. Joint families are predominantly found in rural areas while there are mostly nuclear families in urbans where only service class or business class Bhotiyas live. The Bhotiyas is an endogamous community who follow monogamy in general. But the widow/widower and divorced remarriages do take place. Besides this sororate and levirate marriages are also observed among them. Some preferential marriages like cross-cousin marriages are also practised among the Bhotiyas. They observe different ways of getting life mates.

Marriage by capture, marriage by elopement, marriage by mutual consent and the formal marriages are some of the prevalent ways of getting mates. The impact of education, modernization and urbanization in every walk of their socio-economic and cultural life cannot be ignored. The status of Bhotiya woman is respectful and venerable.' In every respect her life is not gloomy. She does not have to face any sort of discrimination due to being female. Moreover she enjoys some privileges in family as well as in community life. She is the best host to attend the guest. She offers open heartedly the cup of wine with her pretty hands and unblemished feelings to the newcomers. She sings and dances even before her family members without any hesitation and social taboos. She does not observe any 'Parda' with her in-law as is observed in many non-tribal 'Savarn-Hindus.' No incest taboos are laid down on the Bhotiya woman. Thus the nature, activities and the social norms related with the womenfolk, show that the status of women in Bhotiya community is prestigious, venerable and equal to that of man (Bisht: 1994:180-181). The role of Bhotiya women in every walk of community's life is of great importance. Somewhere she is 'Mulin Rani' the queen of the hearth, somewhere Sya-sya, somewhere 'Tisya', somewhere 'Ran-bang-khenti'..... But every where she plays a decisive role in community's life.

The Bhotiyas are basically a trader community. This community is known as the international-traders' community who used to perform their trades in between China (Tibet) and India. But today a considerable number of the Bhotiya population is engaged in government services and also in settled business pursuits. We can observe an effect of various government policies and development programmes on their economic life too. Besides this, the Bhotiya is an agricultural-cum-pastoral community. Weaving of woollen yarn and making woollen stuffs like Dan (Carpet), Chutka, Thulma (a type of blanket), sweater and also their traditional costumes have been the speciality of the Bhotiyas. They rear goats and sheep which have multipurpose uses in Bhotiya community. They can get raw wool and meat from the goat and sheep and also use them as transport animals. They also rear Jhibus (Yaks). Mostly the Bhotiyas subsist on wheat, maize, rice, kodo, Bhat or Soyabean and some locally produced vegetables, fruits and roots. They have alcoholic beverages and also smoke beedis, tobacco and cigarettes. But the percentage of alcoholic drinks and of smoking is gradually declining in younger generations.

Mostly the Bhotiyas are Hindus by religion. They worship 'Shiv-Parvati' and other local Hindu Gods and Goddesses as the neighbouring non-tribal Hindus do. They also observe birth and death related rituals like Hindus. Birth and death pollution is observed by them which ends after a certain period and with some ceremonial performances. But in spite of being Hindus the eastern Bhotiyas, i.e., the Darmis, Vyansis and Chaudansis do not take the services of Brahmin priest for any ritual performances. On the contrary the Jad Bhotiyas of Jad-gang valley are Buddhists. But none of the Bhotiyas profess Islam,Christianity, Jainism and Sikhism till the date.

Jaunsaris or the Khasas

Generally the territorial group of people living in Jaunsar-Bawar area in Uttaranchal is known as 'Jaunsaris'. The 'Jaunsari' is thus a composite term which consists of the people of different sub-groups. Some of them enjoy high social status while some other have comparatively a lower position among the Jaunsaris. Majumdar (1962:64-69) talks about three-tier structure of caste hierarchy in Jaunsar-Bawar and arranges them hierarchically as follows: (i) on the top, there is a dominating group of 'high castes' including Brahmins and Khasas (Rajputs), (ii) In the middle, there is a number of castes which form an intermediate group including Badi, Sunar, Jagdi, Nath, Lohar, Bajgi etc., and (iii) At the bottom, there is a low caste, which includes Koltas in general and at some places also Dom, Mochi etc. Thus the sub-groups viz. Brahmin and Khasa (Rajput) constitute that part of the Jaunsaris which we call Khasas and the rest sub-groups share the appellation 'Kolta'. Majumdar (1940) further says, 'despite some intermixture with Mongoloids of the Upper-Himalayas or with the Doms of the lower regions the Khasas are clearly distinguishable from the Proto-Australoid or Mongoloids, who form the bulk of the tribal people. He talks about their (Khasas) true mediterranean features.' Atkinson (1982: 353) states that, 'Jaunsar-Bawar' a representative Khasiya tract forms a very important link between the almost Hinduised Khasiyas of Kumaun and their brethren converts to Islam on the ethnic frontier in the mountains of the Hindukush, and apparently gives customs and practices of the Khasiya race in full force at the present day which distinguished them a thousand years ago. Bisht (1994:22) states that the Khasas which include Brahmans and Rajputs are basically of the Aryan origin which later on converted into 'Malechchhas' due to the non-observance of the Aryan cultural traits (Bisht: 1994:22).

The anthropometric measurements show that the Khasas are below medium in height with a long head shape. They have long and narrow (thin) nasal structure with a convex upper bone. They have fair complexion with light brownish colour. But the Koltas are of dark complexion and look like the Doms. In fact today the whole of the Khasa community as such does not present any clear-cut physical features which embodies any particular racial origin. It is of course the outcome of the medley of different racial waves in the past.

At present the Khasa community is stratified into different caste-groups. The Brahmins, the Rajputs and the Koltas are the three hierarchical stratas in the community. The upper caste Jaunsaris have socially sanctioned affinal relations with one another. Intermarriages between the Brahmin and the Rajputs do take place. Mostly, we observe evidences of hypergamy than the hypogamy. Lineage has important role in regulating the marriages among the sub-caste groups.

The Khasa is basically a polyandrous community. For this social feature the Khasas claim their origin from the Pandavas of Mahabharata. Majumdar states, 'In the Mahabharata the Khasas are expressly mentioned amongst the northern tribes who brought presents for Yudhisthira'. Briffault (1927:671) has also stated that, 'the Khasas hold festivals in honour of the Pandavas' who are their favourite deities. Many important spots in Jaunsar Bawar are supposed to have associations with the Pandavas. They have temples dedicated to the 'Pandavas' called 'Pandavon-ki-chauri'. The courtyard of the temple is called 'Pandavon-ka-agana'. The central feature of their festivals is the 'Pandav-dance." At present the fraternal-polyandry has been transformed into bi-polyandry, polygyny and monogamy. However we can observe ample evidences of fraternal polyandry in the remote rural areas of Jaunsar Bawar. In fact the economic factor and education have simultaneously played an important role in determining the type of the marriage and the pattern of its observance.

The Jaunsaris are basically an agricultural-cum-pastoral community. Its economy has been based on a crude type of cultivation and animal husbandry. With the introduction of education and other welfare measures by the Government, the traditional economic system is transforming gradually and their dependence on agriculture and animal husbandry is decreasing day by day. Yet the remote rural areas of Jaunsar-Bawar still follow their traditional pattern of subsistence. They extract wool from the sheep and manufacture woollen stuffs for their own use. 'Pankhi', Thumba', 'Khurshay' are some of the woollen items made by them for their own use. A cooperative system is followed in agricultural and other social activities and religious functions. About 5 per cent Khasas are engaged in other subsidiary jobs which consists of service, labour, business and handicraft.

In general the status of woman in polyandrous Khasa community is prestigious. She is respected by all in the community. But for the objective assessment of her status and role in society the measurements, standards and the value system of the community which altogether define her position, need re-evaluation. In this context we observed that in the Khasa community there are 'double standards' of measurement for women. The married women have to follow certain taboos, restrictions and norms at her in-laws place and she is termed as 'Rain'. But when the same woman comes back to her natal place she becomes free from all sorts of taboos and restrictions and is supposed to avail all sorts of freedom. At her father's place she is known as 'Dhyan'. In both the cases the attitude and treatment of the community members towards 'Rain' and 'Dhyan' varies. As a 'Rain' she enjoys all sorts of privileges, respect, affection and love of family members as well as of the community as a whole. At the same time at her natal place as 'Dhyan' (married and unmarried both) no doubt she has freedom and no restrictions but she loses all the privileges and respects of the community members as she enjoys as a 'Rain' at her in-laws's place. There is clear-cut division of labour among the women. A Khasa woman, other than the female head rotates throughout the day like a wheel in a cart in daily routine of agriculture and animal husbandry. Today some educated Khasa women have government jobs. Education and economic dependence of women have changed their attitude towards fraternal polyandrous system. Such group of women prefer monogamy while the illiterate women still cling with their traditions of polyandrous society. Bisht (1994:190) has aptly remarked, 'the position of Khasa woman' who is still persists in remote villages, particularly in polyandrous type of families, is very pitiable while in monogamous type of families, her position is comparatively better.

The literacy percentage among the Khasas is 19.07 per cent which is comparatively lower than that of the national ST literacy percentage. The male literacy is 29.79 per cent in comparison to female literacy that is only 6.43 per cent. The infrastructural facilities are not upto the mark. There are understaffed primary schools. The same is the case of primary health centres. But where ever such facilities of education and medical care are available the Khasa people seems inclined to avail them. They have positive attitude towards development policies.

The inter and intra-tribal relations are viewed only in certain walk of life. The economic and political spheres are only the centres where the Khasa-people interact with out groups, may be non-tribal and/or tribal. Besides this, within community itself there is restricted inter-caste relations. The commensal and connubial relations of the Khasa Brahmins and Rajputs with low-caste Jaunsaris like Kolta, Bajgi, Dom etc. do not take place. However in economic sector cooperation between the landlords, artisans and in agricultural serfs exists in terms of employer and employee which is transformed of Jajmani system.

The Rajis

Generally a generic term 'Ban Raut' is used by the local people to denote the 'Rajis' of Kumaun-Himalaya. 'Ban-Raut' means the forest dwellers who subsist on forest and forest-produces. The Rajis have been a community of food gatherers, small game-trappers and the 'Ijarani-Kheti' cultivators (a sort of agricultural pattern as is followed by the tribals of Northeast India-called Zooming cultivation) until recently. The Rajis were the nomadic people of Kumaun Himalaya who have been rehabilitated by the Govt. efforts, on slopes of the steep hills of Kumaun mainly in Didihat and Dharchula Tehsils. By the end of the nineteenth century their forefathers were traced around the forest region of Askot on the Kali river. Crooke (1896) states that, 'Rajis were found in Askot and in small numbers along the lower Himalayan ranges of Kumaun and were dependent on primitive type of cultivation and the making of vessels out of wood for their livelihood.'

The Rajis are said to be the descendants of Kiratas who once lived to the west and east of the present settlement of the Rajis at Askot on the Kali. In a report of Mr. Traill, the first Commissioner of British Kumaun, it was said that the 'Rajis represent themselves as descendants of one of the aboriginal prince of Kumaun who with his family fled to the jungles to escape the destruction threatened by a usurper. Under the pretension of royal origin, the Rawats or Rajis abstain from offering to any individual whatever his rank, the usual eastern salutation (Atkinson : 1996:335-366). With the course of time the Rajis of today have changed their traditional attitude of social intercourse and they equally reciprocate the salutation to the outsiders, all the visiting outsiders and also to the neighbouring twice born Hindus. However, a general trend exists there that the non-tribal neighbouring people, treating them of the royal descent, make their salutation to the Rajis first who then reciprocate them in a respectable manner.

William Crooke has affined Rajis with the non-Aryan affinities while Atkinson talks about the racial mixture of Tibetans and Khasas in their physical features. Majumdar (1944 : 148) relates them to Mongolian race, Pritchard, in his writing *Ethnology of the British Colonies* (p. 132), conjectured that 'the Rajis would be found to resemble the other numerous aboriginal tribes found along the Himalayan Border, all possessing 'the physical character of the Bhotiyas in general and very unlike the Doms, (1966:366)'. Latham too expresses his conviction that the Rajis are similar to the Chepang of Nepal. But today (1993:17) 'the countenance and the physical traits of the Rajis in common do not present any clue to look into their racial affinity. Today no Mangolian traits can be observed in the physical appearance of the Rajis. Today by physical appearance and caste countenance the Rajis have whitish complexion, average height, straight and scanty hair with slight brownish in colour, intermediate headed type with medium nose, round to long face with half or there about ears and small eyes with grey pigment. Thus the Rajis are very much alike the low caste Hindus and unlike that of the Bhotiyas. It appears that the medley of different ethnic elements for ages has caused the disappearance of the original racial elements among the Rajis. They (the Rajis) at present exhibit a mixed racial traits of Aryo-Dravidian and Mongoloid in common (1993 :170).

The Rajis have their own dialect which is quite different from that of neighbouring tribal and non-tribal communities. However, they can speak and interact in Kumauni-Pahari-dialect as well as in broken Hindi language. 'The scanty vocabulary of the Raji language supports the connection of the Rajis with the tribes of Nepal From their language it would appear that they are of ordinary aboriginal stock like the Kirantis, a still further reason for identifying them with the Rajya-Kiratas of the Purans (1996:367). Some scholars are of the opinion that the Rajis belong to the Himalayan group of the Tibeto-Burman family of languages.

Socially the Raji community has been divided into five major 'Dharas' namely the Askoti-Pal, the Dinshi Pal, the Baitara, the Baluwakoti Aeri and the Kwaintola. 'Dhara' is a clan group, the membership of which is achieved by birth. The people follow the rule of Dhara exogamy. It (Dhara system) is a vertical division of the community (Bisht: 1993:60). The Raji is a patrilineal, patrilocal and patriarchal community. However, there are evidences of Gharjawain system (in which the groom lives in his wife's father's residence after marriage), as well as the dominance of women in family matters. Bride-price has crucial role in mating alliances. Child marriages do take place. The marriage of a girl before puberty is regarded essential. Hence the girl is married before fourteen years of age while the boys are married in between 15 to 20 years of age. The Raji is a monogamous community, yet polygyny, in some exceptional cases, is also socially sanctioned. The formal negotiation, mutual consent and elopement are some of the socially sanctioned ways of acquiring mates. Widow remarriages, sororate and levirate marriages are also practised. Divorce (ladau) and divorced remarriages are permitted. A mark of vermillion and nose-ring are the symbol of a married woman. The family for the Rajis is an association of a husband, wife and their unmarried children. It can be termed as a nuclear family. The nuclear families are predominant among the Rajis. The eldest male in the family has the headship yet the eldest woman equally shares the privileges in practice. Male equigeniture is a general rule of inheritance.

The Rajis are Hindu by religion. Naming, marriage and death are the main rituals observed by them. They worship various gods and goddesses as are worshipped by their neighbouring Hindus. They also believe on spirits, goblins, ghosts and demons. Their religious beliefs and practices are transforming in the direction of Hindu culture. Today they observe the rite of cremation of their deads rather than to bury them. They celebrate Deepawali and Holi. Some local festivals like

'Bishpati', 'Pusurhi' and 'Gamara' etc. (predominantly celebrated by Kumaunies) are also observed by them.

The Rajis, the food gatherers, invisible traders, and hunters of one time, are now settled agriculturists. But the crude type of hilly terrace farming has pushed them back to profess some subsidiary economic pursuits like wage-earning through physical labour and collection of seasonal food from the jungle and other natural resources for their subsistence. In true sense the economy of the Rajis stands in between food gleaning and settled agriculture. In spite of being assisted by various Government agencies the Rajis could not get proper benefits. They are deprived of basic amenities like education, health, hygiene and nutrition.

The infrastructural facilities are almost absent from their habitations. No doubt, various schemes related to agricultural development, animal husbandry, education, health services, nutrition, drinking water, women and child welfare, employment generation etc. have been launched in the Raji areas but these schemes could not receive their desired target of development. Research findings speak of a number of inhibitions amenable for the socio-economic deprivation of the Rajis. However, the ecological factors, socio-cultural factors, government schemes and their implementation pattern are some of the major factors which have obstructed the way of development of the Rajis and perpetuated their unending pauperism.

The Buksas or the Buxas or the Bhuksas

The Buksa is a primitive tribal group of Uttaranchal Tarai. They claim, according to Elliot, 'to be Panwar Rajputs and assert that their chief Udayjit, was driven from house in a quarrel that he had with his brother Jagat Deo, the Raja of Dharanagar and come to dwell with a few dependants at Banbasa on the Sarda. Udayjit had not been there long before his aid was solicited by the Raja of Kumaun whose territories required defence against some of the neighbouring powers. Success attended the efforts of the Panwar and the gratitude of the Raja induced him to offer his defenders an asylum in his territories. Upon this they are represented to have left Banbasa and to have taken up their residence in their present abode (Atkinson 1996: 372). Crooke (1896) has stated a legend according to which the Buksas came from Dakhin while others have specifically stated that they migrated from Delhi. Crooke stated that, 'Jagat Deo was a worshipper of Goddess Durga and offered his head to her. The Buxas claim to have brought the deity Durga, now known as Kashipur Devi, to Tarai and even today offer Nariyal (Palmnut) in worship to the deity as a symbol of his head. Some Buksas are of the opinion that Raja Jagat Deo had two sons, Chittaur and Nandhaur. The Tharus are the descendants of the former while the Buksas are stated to have descended from the *latter*. The etymology of the term 'Buksas' leads to a number of legends. It is observed that 'the Bhuksas are not of the Rajput origin but the absence of any historical clue has resulted in a number of legends to prove their Rajput ancestry. Even today the aged Buksas admit that at the time of their migration to Tarai and Bhabar area, everyone was not the descendant of the Rajput for there were the people belonging to different castes who merged into one community due to some adverse geo-social circumstances and dispensed all the previous caste and class barriers which later on emerged as the Buksa community (1994:33). So far as the physical traits are concerned it is further stated that, 'an average Buksa possesses an average height with stout built. Both the male and female are of whitish or dark complexion with broad face, oblique eyes, flat nose, thick lips and black hair. The beard and moustaches of a Buksa is very scanty. Such a countenance and physique eventually give no clue of any particular racial origin of the Buksas. It is rather a convas of a mixed racial traits which came into existence as an outcome of the mixture of different racial elements occurring due to the entrance of different ethnic groups in Uttaranchal (1994 : 33-34). However, there are scholars who affined them with Mongolian racial slock. Sero-generic studies suggest a higher incidence of gene B (23-29 per cent) than A (18-24 per cent) and a low value of A_2 (07 per cent), in the ABO blood group system. The Rh blood group distribution shows the principal chromosome to be R_1 (44 per cent) a higher occurrence of R_0 (15 per cent) and a moderate value of R (6 per cent); gene N scores a high value (45 per cent) in the MN system only a few of them are non-tasters (9 per cent) for PTC taste (Garg, et. al., 1981 :157-168)."

The etymology of the term 'Buksa' leads to a number of stories as to prove the exactness of the appellation used for this tribal community. As for example "some Buxas of Bijnor area are of the opinion that their ancestors had the long beard quite resembling the 'Bok', (a he-goat) found in the adjoining hill provinces of their settlements and thus called Boksas or Boxas or Bhuksas. Some Buxas relate the etymology of their name with the English word 'bogus' which later on changed into 'Buksa. Some aged Buxas of Nainital Tarai (now U.S. Nagar District) are of the opinion that 'Bhuksa' is a corrupted form of 'Sarva-Bhaksi' mean, 'Bhakosane wala' means omnivorous. It is said that at the earlier stage of their settlement in Tarai they used to devour everything as to keep their body and soul together and thus called 'Bhaksi' which gradually converted into 'Bhoksa'. With the passage of time this nomadic community adhered to this appellation 'Bhuksa' under the pretension of their 'Rajput Origin' (Bisht: 1994:31-32). Today this community is pronounced as 'Buxa', 'Bhuksa', 'Boksa' by different people. But in this inscription it is being presented as the 'Buksas and Buxas'.

Apart from the racial and serological analysis the Buksas of today have more resemblances to the low-caste Hindus particularly in their habits and customs. They claim to be Hindu by religion. Atkinson (1882:372) has also stated that 'They are now in every respect in their habits and customs Hindus of the ordinary low caste type and employ Gaur Brahman Purohits in their marriage and funeral ceremonies'. Hasan (1970:25) says that, 'The Buksas are one of the most Hinduised tribes of India. They themselves claim to be Hindus and to prove that they are authentic Hindus, they point out that they originally belong to various Hindu castes and sub-castes for Kshyatriyas to Sudras, who decided to merge into one class under special circumstances in the hoary past.' Even today they worship various gods and goddesses of the Hindu pantheon, like, Shiv-Parvati, Krishna, Lord Rama etc. They have a number of local deities too, the Kashipur Devi, the Atariya Devi, the Ilavas Devi, the Basundari Devi, the Sundari Devi, the Gamkheri Devi are some of the Goddesses they worship. Besides this, the Bhumsen (Bhuyian), the Sankariya and some Buxa Gods they worship on different occasions. The Buksas also believe in spirits and goblins. The Mani Ram Thekedar, the Kothan Padhan, the Dalpuriya, the Buxaro Padhan etc. are some of the spirits they worship.

Previously, the whole of the Buxa community was divided into two major sects i.e. the 'Guruware' and the 'Deviware.' The Buxa who used to worship 'Gurunanak Dev' were known as 'Guruware' and the Buxa worshipping Devi were of 'Deviware' sect. Besides this, there were Buxas who had a faith on Islam. It is said the Buxas have been in contact with Muslims for more than four hundred years. The existence of 'Muswani' gotra among the Buxas of Dehradun proves this fact. Crooke (1896 : Vol. 11) states, Two Muslim saints, 'Sarwar-Lakhi' and 'Kalu Sayyed' are worshipped by the Buksas. 'Zahir Aulya Pir' is quite popular among the Buxas of Bajpur who mention that the 'Pir' was originally a 'Kshatriya' who later embraced Islam. He is also offered flowers and 'Matka' (earthern pot in worship). There are scholars who talk about the impact of Christianity on the Buxas of Bajpur and Dhamola area. But today we hardly trace the impact of Christianity on the behaviour pattern of the Buksas. Even the impact of 'Sikhism' mainly the faith and trust on Guru Nanak's tenets is decreasing day by day on the Buxas. It is so because the 'Sikh community has emerged in the Tarai as landgrabbers and exploiters. The popularity of Guru Nanak is therefore decreasing day by day among the Buxas because they associate the popularity of Guru Nanak with their exploiters and prefer to be known as 'Deviware' rather than Guruware. But the existence of 'Guruware' sect proves the impact of 'Sikhism' on the Buxas of Tarai.

The Buksas are endogamous and divided into various clans (gotras) named after their sub-caste groups and the place of dwellings called

'Khera'. Elliot has mentioned 15 Gotras of the Buksas while Shukla (1974) has stated 56 'Gotras' named after their 'Kheras' or the places of habitations. Every 'Gotra' is exogamous in nature. The 'Gotra' is a basis of vertical division of the Buksa community hence inter-gotra marriages do take place without a feeling of social-hierarchy of any kind.

The Buksa is a patriarchal, patrilocal and patrilineal community. Both the nuclear and extended type of families exist among the Buksas. It is a male dominated community but the female equally wield equal position in different walks of life. They do not observe any particular pattern of life-cycle rituals. But the impact of neighbouring Hindus has resulted in some ceremonial observances of the rituals like 'Chhati-Karm', 'Namkaran', marriage, death and cremation. The marriage by negotiation is a formal way of acquiring mate among the Buksas. This sort of marriage is followed by some ceremonies like Mangani, Ganana, Ratjaga, Haldi, Chhaie Katana, Worship of Gamkheri Devi, Nauta, Bhatlagana, Fere, Pachaherhi, Vidai and Gauna (1997 :189-191).

Besides the formal way some other ways like, marriage by mutual consent and elopement, widow remarriage, divorced marriage, levirate, levirate-senior marriage, sororate, marriage by exchange, Gharjawain marriage are also observed by the Buksas. They also observe some prohibitions like incest taboo, gotra and Khera exogamy and community endogamy. Cross cousin marriages are prohibited.

The Buksa is an agriculturist community. Almost all the Buksa population is engaged in agriculture and agricultural associated jobs. Pressure of increasing tribal population, their pressing needs and fragmentation of land due to growing generations have caused the problem of land alienation among some Buksa families. The primitive way of living, illiteracy, introverted nature of the Buksas in general, unawareness and the lack of employment opportunities have perpetuated their ages old pauperism. However, some self-employment generation schemes have provided some of the Buksa youths an opportunity of employment other than agriculture. The Buksas also rear tamed animals like buffalo, cows, ox, goat, horse etc. The economy of the Buksas is thus based on agriculture and animal husbandry. Besides this they also earn their living as a daily labourer and by service in private and government sectors. According to an estimate out of the total Buksa population the workers constitute 31.90 per cent (56.83 per cent male and 43.17 per cent female). Out of them 93.35 per cent are engaged in primary sector- (67.21 per cent as cultivator, 26.14 per cent as agricultural labourers, 1.65 per cent are engaged in household industry, i.e., basketry while the remaining 5 per cent are engaged in various occupations) (Singh : 1994:148).

No doubt, the government sponsored schemes and programmes have positive impacts in the development of infrastructural facilities in

Buxa areas and process of socio-economic transformation is on the way to progress but the target of overall development of the Buksa community as a whole is beyond reach till the date.

The Tharus

The scholars have no consensus about the racial origin of the Tharus. Risely (1915:313) has stated that the Tharus represent mixed racial features which are mostly nearer to the Mongolian race. Majumdar (1944:70) is of the opinion that, "the Tharus claim Rajput origin on the mother's side and Bhil on the father's but the Mongolian features are dominant among them and even the skin colour is yellow brown and oblique eyes are numerous." A legend prevalent in general, states that, "Tharus are of the Rajput origin and they relate themselves to the Sisodiya dynasty of Rana Pratap of Chittaurh". But, Majumdar (1942:33) an eminent anthropologist, has proved through the racial and serological survey that there are no traces as to affine the Tharus with Sisodiya Rajputs of Chittaurh. Nesfield (1885:37) relates them to Dravidian race on the basis of their physical features. While Crooke (1973:118) is of the opinion that the Tharu is a mixed tribe with some Mongolian and some Dravidian blood who occupy the Malarious Tarai at the foot of the lower Himalayas. Mahalanobis, et. al (1949:89-324), stating the physique of an average Tharu, say that the Tharus are on an average of below medium height with a round head tending towards a broader shape. They have a short nose and a round or oval face. We have references about their blood groups too. Singh (1994:1138) referred that, "In the ABO blood group they show a higher incidence of gene B (29-37 per cent) than gene of with 40 to 50 per cent of gene O. A relatively higher gene, M (70.75 per cent) in the MN system has been observed among them. They show a very low frequency of non-sectors (42 per cent) for ABH secretion in saliva, and non-taster individuals (18 per cent) for PTC taste ability. In the Rh distribution they show a high incidence of R_1 (70 per cent) R_0 (8 per cent), and low frequency of R_2 (11 per cent) with the presence of R_2. In finger dermatoglyphic features, they exhibit a higher incidence of whorls and low percentage of arches and a high value of pattern intensity index. Bisht (1994:30) has stated that,.....the physical appearance of the Tharus even today express itself their Mongolian strains. They have got the medium height, round face with yellow brown complexion, medium to short nose, oblique or slant eyes and straight hair.

There are different opinions about the 'Etymology' of the term 'Tharu'. In the census report 1887 the term 'Taruwa' has been used to denote the Tharu tribe. It is said that the term Tharu' has been derived from the term 'Taruwa' which means to get a wetting due to constant heavy rainfall occurring in the Tarai area and the people living in that area were called

'Taruwa' which later on converted into 'Tharuwa' and then Tharu. According to Nesfield (1885:115) the term 'Tharu' has been derived from 'Thar' which was locally used for the 'forest dwellers' (Jangal Niwasi) these days. Since, those people have been living in forest area for a long time hence called 'Thar' which gradually transformed into 'Tharu'. In Oudh Gazetteer (1887:126) the etymology of the term 'Tharu' is from 'Tahare' which means to make a halt or camp. Since, those people migrating from other areas made their camp in Tarai area hence called 'Tahare' which later on began to be known as 'Tharu'. In the *Journal of Asiatic Society of Bengal* (1887:450) the term 'Athawaru' has been used to name this tribe. In those days the term 'Athawaru' was used for the eighth day of ones', means the person who was compelled for the forced labourer to one's master's place once in a week was 'Athawaru' which later on converted into the term 'Tharu'. Crooke (1896:381) admits that the term 'Tharu' has been derived from the term 'Daru' (wine). Since the people of this community were very much foppish of 'Daru' (wine) or alcohol hence called in a due course of time as 'Tharu'. Nowells (1904:120) has indicated this tribe with the appellation 'Tharuwa' which means a 'Wayfarer' or traveller. Since persons of this tribe have a capacity of walking on foot very speedily hence they were called 'Tharuwa' the corrupted form of which was 'Tharu'. Apart from these connotations we have a reference in the North-Western Provinces Gazetteer (1881:354) that the term 'Thatharan' or 'Thithurana' was used for the Tharus which means to quake or to runaway. Since the Rajput queens were frightened due to the killings of Rajputs in the battle fought between the Mughals and the Rajputs and ranaway with their servants and settled down in the Tarai of Uttar Pradesh. Later on the queens had offsprings from their servants who were known as 'Tharu-Rana'. Navil (1904:107) has stated differently that the kings of the Tarai were once defeated by the userpers or the invaders coming from outside and their queens absconded with their servants and grooms towards the jungles of Tarai. In due course of time they had marital relations with their servants (i.e., the grooms and the Chamars) and the offsprings of whom were called respectively the Tharus and the Buxas of Tarai. The Tharus belong to the central group of the Indo-Aryan family of language. They use Hindi languages for inter-community communication and use Devanagari script for writing.

Socially the Tharus of Uttarakhand Tarai are divided into seven endogamous groups viz. Ranas, Bukhasas, Garhaurha, Dhanara, Khunka, Jugiya and Saunra. Hierarchically the Ranas hold a superior social status and are in majority of population, while the Bukhasas, Garhaurha, Dhanara, Khunka, Jugiya and Saunra hold respectively lower position. The Tharu is a monogamous community, the lineage of whom runs in father's line. It is a patriarchal and patrilocal community. However the women wield higher, dominant and venerable position in the society. In 'Gharjawain marriage system' the groom live in bride's place after marriage. The Tharus are Hindus by religion. However, there are Tharu families who follow Radha-Swami pantheon in their religious life. The impact of Christianity is also observed on some Tharu families. Some Tharus have been converted into Christianity by Christian missionaries recently. But the number of Christian Tharus is very nominal. Holi, Diwali, Teej and Charai are the main festivals observed by the Tharus. They have their own gods and goddesses. The worship of 'Bhumisen' is of great importance in the Tharu community. Besides this, they also worship ghost, goblins and spirits. In spite of being Hindus they observe, only three life cycle rituals, namely, the naming ceremony, marriage and death or cremation. In the performance of the rituals they do not call Brahmin priest rather they take the services of their traditional priest called 'Bharare.'

Among the Tharus the child marriage is common and socially sanctioned practice. Generally the girls are married before 11 years of age, that is to say, before puberty and the boys are married before 13 to 14 years of age. The marriage by negotiation, in which the role of a mediator called 'Maspatiya', is a simplest and formal way of acquiring mates. The formal marriage is performed with some rites namely- Dikhanauri (Tika) which takes place in an early age of the girl and boy, 'Puchhahu', Chula Baithan, Bhumia-Poojan, Sar-Dena, Tel-Chadawa, Pahrawa, Bhaudi, Kanyadan, Bhanwar and finally the Gauna only then the bride is supposed to live with her in-laws house. Apart from the formal way, the court marriage-which occurs due to premarital love affair and discontent of parents of this affair. The widow remarriage-which consists of Chutkata and Uthan marriage, sororate, levirate, levirate-senior, divorced-marriage are some other ways of acquiring mates. (See Bisht, 1997: 147-173 for detail).

Economically the Tharus are self-sufficient. They fulfil their limited needs of food, shelter and clothes with their own efforts. Agriculture is their age old occupation. They have been termed as rice-cultivators of swamp area of Tarai. Besides this animal husbandry, fishing, food collection from the nearby jungles etc. are some other sources of their subsistence. The Tharus are skilled craftsmen. Their women are skilled in making basketry of different type. Rope making, mat-weaving, cot making and manufacturing of agricultural equipments are their specialities. Besides this the Tharus are also employed in different government and private jobs. Thus the service both, Government and private, wage-earning through physical labour and business of small scale are some subsidiary sources of their income. According to an estimate 35.85 per cent of their population constitutes a workers group. The percentage of women among the workers is only 41.68 per cent whereas among males it is 58.32 per cent. Of these workers the majority is of the cultivators which constitute about 82.43 per cent of the total workers, agricultural labourers constitute 1.24 per cent, and the rest 7.33 per cent are engaged in other occupations.

The infrastructural facilities in 'Tharuwat' area is in developing stage. The school facilities with certain incentives have been made available to the Tharus. An Ashram Type school is being run by the Government in Khatima Block, Primary Health Centre has been established within the reach of the tribal area. Irrigation and drinking water is supplied through tubewells, handpumps and pipelines. Every Tharu village has been linked with one-way motorable roads. The tribal areas have been electrified. But the maintenance of all these infrastructural units is not upto the mark. Hence these facilities are unable to produce the desired fruits. For instance, the literacy percentage among Tharus is only 19.46 per cent; for the males it is 26.23 per cent and 5.84 per cent for the females.

It is thus obvious that the tribal scenario in Uttarakhand presents a composite picture in which every tribal group has its own identity, peculiarity and life-style. They have almost different surroundings and ecological settings. Virtually the status of education, health, hygiene and nutrition is different. Exactly how these factors affect their basic amenities of vital importance will be discussed in the forthcoming chapters.

References

Atkinson, E.T., 1996 : *The Himalayan Gazetteer* Vol. II-I (Reprint), Natraj Publishers, Dehradun.

Burman, B.K. Roy, 1972 : "Tribal Demography" in *Tribal Situation in India*, ed. by K.S. Singh, Indian Institute of Advanced Study, Simla.

Bisht, B.S., 1993 : *Raji: A Tribe of Indo-Nepal Border of Uttarakhand*, Vivek Prakashan, Delhi-7.

Bisht, B.S., 1997 : *Uttaranchal - Gramin Samuday, Pichhadi Jati Avam Janjatiya Paridrasya*. Almora Book Depot. Mal Road, Almora.

Bisht, Sarojani, 1999 : "The Buxas of Uttarakhand"- Habitat, Society, Economy and Transformation, in- *Backward Communities in India*, ed. by. B.S. Bisht, Gyan Publishing House, New Delhi.

Bisht, B.S., 1994 : *Tribes of India, Nepal, Tibet Border Land*, Gyan Publishing House, New Delhi.

——— 1996 : "Uttarakhand Ki Janjatiyan Avam Janjatiya Samikaran", in, *Uttarakhand Today* (ed.) by K.S. Valdiya, Shree Almora Book Depot, Almora.

Burman, B.K. Roy, 1972: "Tribal Demography," in, *Tribal Situation in India*, ed. by. K.S. Singh, Indian Institute of Advanced Study, Simla-5.

Chaudhuri, Buddhadev, 1992 : *Tribal Transformation in India*, (ed), Inter-India Publications, New Delhi.

Crooke, W, 1973 : *Races of Northern India*, Cosmo Publications, New Delhi.

Chatterjee, B.B., 1975 : *Bhotiyas of Indo-Tibetan Border of Uttarakhand*, RP, ICSSR, Documentation Centre, New Delhi.

Crooke, W., 1846 : *Tribes and Castes of North-West Provinces and Oudh Region* Vol. II, Calcutta.

Chaudhuri, Buddhadeb, 1990 : *Tribal Development in India-Problems and Prospects* (ed.) Inter-India Publications, New Delhi-15.

Dube, S.C., 1965 : *Manav or Sanskriti*, Raj Kamal Prakashan, Delhi.

Dube, S.C., 1998 : *Antiquity to Modernity in Tribal India-Continuity and Change Among Indian Tribes*, Vol. I, Inter-India Publications (ed.) New Delhi-15.

Garg, S.K., R.S. Negi and A.R. Sankhyan, 1981: *A Serological Analysis of the Bhoksa : A Scheduled Tribe of Uttar Pradesh*, Acta Anthropo Genetica, 5 (3).

Guha, B.S., 1944: *Racial Elements in Indian Population, Oxford Pamphlet on Indian Affairs*, Oxford University Press, Bombay.

Furer-Haimendorf, Vonf. 1975 : *Himalayan Traders*, Murray : London.

——— 1981:.*Asian Highland Societies*, Sterling Publishers, New Delhi.

Hasan, Amir, 1979 : *The Buxas of the Tarai*; B.R. Publishing Corporation, Delhi.

Haddon,A.C, 1919: "The Wondering People, in, *Social Anthropology* ed.by D.N. Majumdar and T.N. Madan, Asia Publishing House, Bombay.

Kharkwal, S.C., 1971: "The Uttar Pradesh Himalaya", in, R.L. Singh ed. *India: A Regional Geography*, National Geographical Society of India, Varanasi.

Majumdar, D.N., 1963 : *An Introduction to Social Anthropology*, Asia Publishing House, Bombay.

Mahalanobis, P.C., et. al., 1949: *Anthropometric Survey of the United Provinces-A Statistical Study*, Sankhya IX.

Mishra, S.N., 1998 : *Antiquity to Modernity in Tribal India- Ownership and Control of Resources Among Indian Tribes*, Inter-India Publications, New Delhi-15.

Majumdar, D.N., 1963 : *Himalayan Polyandry*, Asia Publishing House, Bombay.

Majumdar, D.N., 1994 : *Races and Cultures of India*, Asia Publishing House, Bombay.

Majumdar, D.N., 1942: "TheTharus and Their Blood Group", in, *Journal of Royal Asiatic Society of Bengal*, Vol. III, part I.

Majumdar, D.N., 1955 : *Races and Cultures of India*, Asia Publishing House, Bombay.

Nesfield, J.C., 1885 : *Description of Manners, Industries and Religion of the Tharu and Buxa Tribes of Upper India*, Calcutta.

Pant, B.R., 1996: "Physical Geography and Demographic Characteristics of Uttarakhand", in, *Uttarakhand Today*, by. K.S. Valdiya, Shree Almora Book Depot Almora.

Pant. S.D., 1935 : *The Social Economy of the Himalayas*, London, George Allen and Unwin.

Rahul, R., 1970 : *The Himalayan Border Land*, Vikas Publications, New Delhi.

Risely, H.H., 1915 : *People of India*, Delhi.

——— 1997 : *The Scheduled Tribes*, Oxford University Press, Delhi.

Rahà, M.K., 1989 : *Tribal India-Problem, Development, Prospect*, in two vols. (ed.), Gian Publishing House, New Delhi.

Singh, S.N., 1996 : *Reservation Policy for Backward Classes*, Rawat Publications, Jaipur.

Singh, K.S., 1994 : *The Scheduled Tribes*, Oxford University Press, Walton Street Oxford New York.

Singh, V.P. and Shukla, B.K., 1990 : "Buxa Janjati Me Jeevan Sathi Ka Chayan", in, *Manav*; Year -18, Vol. 3,1990, Ethnographic and Folk-culture Society, Lucknow.

Smith, W. Robertson, 1903 : *Kinship and Marriage in Early Arabia*, London.

Sherring, C. A., 1906: *Notes on the Bhotiyas, Almora and British Garwal*, Calcutta, Asiatic Society, Bengal.

Sashi, S.S., 1979 : *The Nomads of the Himalayas*, Sundeep Prakashan, New Delhi.

Singh, Bhupender, 1998: "Antiquity to Modernity" in *Tribal India—Tribal Self-Management in North-East India* (ed.), Inter-India Publications, New Delhi-15.

Singh, K.S., 1998 : "Antiquity to Modernity" in *Tribal India—Tribal Movements in India* (ed), Inter-India Publications, New Delhi.

Thurnwald R., 1933 : "Nomads", *Encyclopedia of Social Sciences*, Delhi.

Verma, R.C., 1995 : *Indian Tribes through the Ages*, Publication Division Ministry of Information and Broadcasting, Govt. of India, New Delhi.

Vaishnava,Y.D., 1983: *Land and People; Himalayan Districts of Uttar Pradesh*, Sri Almora Book Depot, Almora.

5
Area and Sample Profile

Purposefully selected four tribal villages namely; Kimkhola—the Raji village, Ratanpur - the Tharu village; Bannakhera, the Buxa village; and Basaya - the Khasa village constitute jointly the study area of the present project work. Overtly all the four tribal villages are located in Uttarakhand region but the ecology and the geographical situation of all the villages is different from each other. The following village-wise profile gives an understanding of the study area which is based on personal experiences of the author gained through observation method.

Kimkhola—the Raji Village

Out of the total eight Raji villages, Kimkhola is the sampled Raji village of the present project work. This village is situated in Dharchula Block of Pithoragarh district. Dharchula is the interior-most block not only of the Pithoragarh district but of the Northern India which is located on the fringe of Tibet and Nepal and thus constitute international boundary of India with Tibet in north and Nepal in east. Geographically the regions falling within 'Dharchula block' are located at the height of 3000' to 12000' from the sea level. There are regions which experience the impacts of different sharp climatic variations the limits of which go beyond the imagination of the common masses. There are snow covered high Himalayan peaks on the one hand, and the deep river valleys on the other. The network of Kali, Dhauli and Gori rivers and their tributaries has an important role in shaping the geography and ultimately the life-style of the populace of this region. There is diversified flora and fauna system throughout the region caused by geographic variations. The deep river valleys where climatic conditions are comparatively better, we observe a thick population which becomes more and more thicker during winter because the people living in high altitude comes down to their winter-homes situated in those valleys. The Bhotiyas, the Anwals, the hill non-tribal Kumaunis and the Rajis are the major ethnic groups living predominantly in this area.

Besides the Pithoragarh-Dharchula motor road, Kimkhola, the Raji tribal village is located at 70 km far from the district headquarter and above 3700' from the sea level. The distance of Kimkhola village is 360 km from Haldwani the headquarter of the project work. From Haldwani the Kimkhola village can be approached by two different routes. First the Haldwani-Dharchula motor road via Dhaulichhina, Berinag, Sheraghat, Thal, Didihat, Jaulajibee and Kimkhola. The second routes is Haldwani-Dharchula motor road via Almora, Pithoragarh, Jaulajibee and Kimkhola. Both the routes can be travelled either by bus or by car/taxi from Haldwani.

Kimkhola, the residing place of the Rajis is basically a 'Tok' (sub-village) of Kimkhola village panchayat. Different non-tribal sub-caste groups like Brahman, Rajput and Scheduled Castes live in this village panchayat area. The peculiarity of the village is that each sub-caste group has its own separate residential area, however they are functionally interrelated with each other.

The total geographical area of the village is 60 sq. Nali, i.e., approximately 3.5 acres of land out of which 57.14 per cent acre of land is cultivable 14.28 per cent acre is a waste land and 28.28 per cent acre of land is residential. In fact the Rajis of Kimkhola village are rehabilitate in forest land. Geographically this is a rugged and sloped hilly terrain which is non-irrigated and quite unsuitable for agriculture. The residential area of the Raji' tribe is locally known as 'Rautuda'. It is basically a lease land allotted to the Rajis by the government under the rehabilitation scheme. 'Rautuda' the residential area of the Rajis in Kimkhola is virtually surrounded by dense forest in north, west and south and in east by the river Kali. The small Toks, situated respectively in the north, south and west are the Panchakana village, the Bhoktirwa—a Raji village which is now desolated, and Ganagaun—a Raji village. In the east the Kali river makes the boundary with Nepal-kingdom.

The Kimkhola is situated besides the Pithoragarh-Dharchula motor road and can be approached from Kimkhola sub-bus-stop. A steep hilly bridlepath links the village. The village is located at a distance of 70 kms from district headquarters, 24 kms from Tehsil and Block headquarters, 04 kms from the bus station, police station, post office and market centre at Jaulajibee. There is no facility even of primary education for the tribal children in the village. The only 'Agan-Badi' primary school run by Harijan and Social Welfare Department of Uttar Pradesh is presently not in working order. The remaining ashes make a clue of the existence of the school in the village in part 2. The same is the case of primary health centre and hospital. The tribal children can avail the facility of primary as well as the school level education only by traversing the distance of eight km. The High School, Intermediate and Govt. Degree

College are situated in Baluwakot which is about eight km. far from Kimkhola. There is an 'Ashram Type School' for the tribal children. But the enrolment of the Raji children is very nominal. The economic condition of poor Rajis does not allow them to avail the facilities even of the primary education with incentives. However some parents enrol their children in Ashram Type School with the intention to avail the incentives in the form of school dress only. As soon as the children get the dress, their motto ends and when they visit their parents during vacations, they do not come back to school again. This is only the reason of absenteeism and dropouts of the Raji children in schools. At present, the total population of the Rajis is 107 out of which 65 (60.74 per cent) are male and 42 (39.26 per cent) are female. If we deduct the pre-school population out of the total population we find that the literacy percentage among the Rajis is approximately 51.51 out of which the male literacy is 86.28 per cent and the female literacy is only 13.72 per cent. This is lower than State as well as National tribal and non-tribal female literacy. The age and sex-wise education standard of the Rajis may be presented in the Table 5.1.

Since, Kimkhola, the Raji village is situated near the river valley with the elevation of 3700' from sea level and surrounded by high sub-Himalayan ranges the climate of this village is somewhat uneven, rather, contrast. During winter the rising fog from the river and the snowfall on the mountain peaks of the surrounding areas cause severing cold vis-a-vis the summer and the rainy seasons are respectively very hot and full of humidity. There is heavy rainfall during rainy season and medium to heavy snowfall during winter. In summer, particularly in May and June of every year, there are hail stones followed by heavy rains. Such type of climatic condition is quite unfavourable for agriculture related jobs. It is the reason that the economy of the Rajis is of primitive type which is based on jungle products, food gathering, crude type of cultivation, fishing and physical labour. The people hardly manage their livelihood. In a slopy mountainous region small terraces have been made by the Rajis. Some coarse type of crops like, Maduwa (Kodo), Bhat (Soyabean), maze, paddy etc. are sown in 'Kharif', while wheat, barley and 'Masoor' etc. are sown during 'Rabi'. But the meagre agricultural yield push the tribals towards their age old traditional pattern of subsistence. Even today their livelihood is based on jungle products, wage-earning and crude type of agriculture. The Rajis also rear tamed animals like cows, bullocks, buffaloes and goats but in a very rare quantity. Bullocks and goats have multipurpose uses for the Rajis. But the milching cattle and the concept of milk in their nutritional index have no place. They are used to live with nature and natural laws. The Raji women collect fodder and fuel wood from the jungle and sell it in the nearby Jaulajibee market; thus the petty

Table 5.1. Age and Sex-wise Educational Standard of the Rajis of the Kimkhola Village

Age Group	*Sex*	*Illiterate/ Pre-School*	*Primary & Preprimary*	*Junior High School*	*High School*	*Inter-mediate*	*Under-Graduate*	*Post-Graduate*	*Total %*
0-5	M	06	-	-	-	-	-	-	66
	F	02	-	-	-	-	-	-	02
5-10	M	-	14	-	-	-	-	-	14
	F	03	05	-	-	-	-	-	08
10-15	M	-	12	-	-	-	-	-	12
	F	05	02	-	-	-	-	-	07
15-20	M	01	06	01	-	-	-	-	08
	F	01	-	-	-	-	-	-	01
20-25	M	01	01	01	-	-	01	-	04
	F	03	-	-	-	-	-	-	03
25-30	M	-	2	02	-	-	-	-	04
	F	02	-	-	-	-	-	-	02
30-35	M	-	-	-	-	-	-	-	-
	F	02	-	-	-	-	-	-	02
35-40	M	01	2	01	-	-	-	-	04
	F	04	-	-	-	-	-	-	04
40-45	M	01	-	-	-	-	-	-	01
	F	04	-	-	-	-	-	-	04

(Contd.)

(Contd. Table 5.1)

Age Group	Sex .	Illiterate/ Pre-School	Primary & Preprimary	Junior High School	High School	Inter-mediate	Under-Graduate	Post-Graduate	Total %
45-50	M	04	01	-	-	-	-	-	05
	F	03	-	-	-	-	-	-	03
50-55	M	-	-	-	-	-	-	-	-
	F	01	-	-	-	-	-	-	01
55-60	M	05	-	-	-	-	-	-	05
	F	02	-	-	-	-	-	-	02
60-65	M	02	-	-	-	-	-	-	-
	F	02	-	-	-	-	-	-	02
65-70	M	-	-	-	-	-	-	-	-
	F	-	-	-	-	-	-	-	-
70 & Above	M	-	-	-	-	-	-	-	-
	F	03	-	-	-	-	-	-	03
Total	M	21	38	05	-	-	01	-	65(60.74)
	F	35	07	-	-	-	-	-	42(39.26)
Grand Total		56	45	05	-	-	01	-	107 (100.00)

Table 5.1 (b) Demographic Profile of Raji Respondents

Age Group	Sex	Marital Status			Educational Status							Occupational Status			
		Widow	Widower	Married	Illiterate	Primary	J.High School	High School	Inter-Mediate	Under-Graduate	Post-Graduate	Agriculture	Service Govt.	Service Private	Labour
< 25	M	-	-	01	-	-	01	-	-	-	-	-	-	-	01
	F	-	-		-	-	.	-		-	-	-	-	-	-
25-30	M	-	01	02	-	01	02	-	-	-	-	-	-	-	03
	F	01	-	-	01	-	-	-	-	-	-	-	-	-	01
30-35	M	-	-	01	-	01	-	-	-	-	-	-	-	-	01
	F	-	-	-	-	-		-		-	-	-	-	-	-
35-40	M	-	01	02	01	02	-	-	-	-	-	-	01	-	02
	F	02	-	-	02	-	-	-	-	-	-	-	01	-	01
40-45	M	-	-	-	-	-	-	-	-	-	-	-	-	-	-
	F	-	-	-	-	-	-	-	-	-	-	-	-	-	-
45-50	M	-	-	05	04	01	-	-	-	-	-	-	-	-	05
	F	-	-	-	-	-	-	-	-	-	-	-	-	-	-

(Contd. Table 5.1 (b))

Age Group	Sex	Marital Status				Educational Status						Occupational Status			
		Widow	Widower	Married	Illiterate	Primary	J.High School	High School	Inter-Mediate	Under-Graduate	Post-Graduate	Agriculture	Service Govt.	Service Private	Labour
50-55	M	-	-	01	01	-	-	-	-	-	-	-	-	-	01
	F	-	-		-		-		-	-	-	-	-	-	-
55-60	M	-	-	04	04	-	-	-	-	-	-	-	-	-	04
	F	01	-	-	01	-	-	-	-	-	-	01	-	-	-
60-65	M	-	-	02	02	-	-	-	-	-	-	-	-	-	02
	F	-	-	-	-	-	-	-	-	-	-	-	-	-	-
65-70	M	-	-	-	-	-	-	-	-	-	-	-	-	-	-
	F	-	-		-	-		-	-	-	-	-	-	-	-
70 & Above	M	-	-	-	-	-	-	-	-	-	-	-	-	-	-
	F	01	-	-	01	-	-	-	-	-	-	01	-	-	-
Total	M	-	02	18	12	05	03	-	-	-	-	-	01	-	19
	F	05	-	-	05	-	-	-	-	-		02	01	-	02

amount earned is spent to meet out the dire need of daily fooding. While men either take the job of sawing timber wood on contract basis or make the stone-wall fencing on daily-wage basis. In leisure time the menfolk can be seen in market place or playing cards in their own place. By and large the womenfolk is the axis of the Rajis economy. The Rajis are not farsighted people. They do not have the tendency of saving things may be that foodgrains or money or any food item. They desire to earn as much as is necessary for the present day. So far as they have the things or food items they do not make any further effort for more items until the things do not come to end. Their indolent habits have pushed them to pauperism and perpetuated the unending poverty and backwardness.

Even today the Rajis depend virtually on natural resources even for drinking water, fuel wood, fodder, building material and food items- like rhizome, edible roots, fruits and vegetables. But the prolonged pressure on nature, especially on forests, has reduced the natural sources to its end and the paucity of all these things has made the life of the Rajis very troublesome. Even the day long tour to the core zone of the farthest dense forests and the hard toil do not pay the desired results. Generally they collect the jungle products, may be that fodder or fuel wood at the first day and sell it next day. Thus, the tasks they used to perform in a day now take two days due to the scarcity of the natural resources in the vicinity of village surroundings.

In general, the housing-condition in the village of Kimkhola is harsh and troublesome. We observe three types of housing pattern in the village. There are some 'Pucca' houses made up of stone-bricks plastered over by mud and with black-stone slates roofing. The second category of the houses is of mixed type, which are built-up with stone plus mud walls and thatched over by grass roofing. A special type of oily grass called 'Babyau' is used for roofing. And the third category is of huts constructed by straight wooden logs and roofed by the grass. The 'pucca' houses are double storied. In ground floor the tamed animals are kept while the first floor is used by family members for familial activities. The rest two type of houses have single storey which is used for dwelling purposes of the tamed animals as well as of the family members. As a whole the housing condition and the living pattern is not suitable from hygienic point of view. The filthy surrounding, the combined system of living of human beings and the cattle, absence of hygiene-related sense have caused the health problem for the Rajis. There is no provision of separate kitchen, bed-room, drawing room, toilets and even of ventilation in the house or hut. All the familial tasks are performed in a single-room, single storied huts or houses. The backside of the house or hut is the permanent receptacle for urination and the nearby terraces or the water course is used for latrine. The people just sit besides the path for evacuation which is generally run over the children who enter into their abodes without washing feet. This process causes various diseases. To escape from cold the people either pass their nights in the ground floor of the house where the cattle are also kept or fomet the fire. Thus the constant vicinity of animals and of smoke rising from fire cause many kind of disorders in human body.

The Kimkhola village is still deprived of any kind of infrastructural facilities. So far as educational facility is concerned, even the primary or under primary level school is not available in the village. Even the basic amenities like drinking water, electricity, medical facility etc. are not available in the village. No doubt, the pipeline of drinking water is present in the village but the supply of water is very casual there. The same is the case of electricity, the electric-line has been installed in the village but without current. The decaying erected wooden logs with hanging electric wires having no current can be seen there. There was time during eighties to mid-nineties when an 'Agan Badi' type of primary school was run by the 'Harijan and Samaj Kalyan Vibhag' of U.P. but today we can observe only its remains in the form of broken single room school-building, some broken chairs, one table, one blackboard, one 'Hindi Alphabet-Chart' etc. In an 'Ashram Type School' situated in Baluwakot about 8 km from Kimkhola village, every facility of boarding and lodging is available for the tribal children. Even school dress once in a year and stationery with textbooks are provided to the tribal children there. Some needy and self-motivated guardian do enrol their children in 'Ashram School' but the school records show a very poor results in regard to the Raji children. As the Table 5.2 shows year-wise (session-wise) enrolment of the Raji children in different classes.

The figure shown in the Table 5.2 prove the poor response of the Rajis towards education. The number of the Raji children enrolled in different years in different classes in 'Ashram Type School, Baluwakot' belong to the whole of the Raji community not only of the Kimkhola village. No doubt the percentage of the Raji children from Kimkhola village is higher than other Raji villages. It is so because the Kimkhola village is situated comparatively at a short distance than of the others. The enrolment pattern also exhibits that in lower classes the number of the Raji children is more as the class or standard goes up the enrolment decreases. It shows the tendency of dropouts among the Raji children. In fact, the information gathered from the study-group show, that the Rajis are not aware of education and its importance in personality development. How the illiterate parents can motivate their children towards education? Besides this the poor economy always discourages the people and poses obstacles on the way to schooling children. It is true that the

Table 5.2. Academic Session-wise Enrolment of Raji Children in Different Classes.

Academic Session	Class/Standard												BA/BSc			MA/MSc		Total
	I	II	III	IV	V	VI	VII	VIII	IX	X	XI	XII	I	II	III	I	II	
1993-94	2	1	–	2	1	–	–	–	–	–	–	–	–	–	–	–	–	6
1994-95	1	2	–	–	–	1	–	–	–	–	–	–	–	–	–	–	–	4
1995-96	1	1	2	–	–	–	1	–	–	–	–	–	–	–	–	–	–	5
1996-97	–	1	–	2	–	–	–	1	–	–	–	–	–	–	–	–	–	4
1997-98	6	1	–	–	2	–	–	–	–	–	–	–	–	–	–	–	–	9
1998-99	4	7	1	–	–	2	–	–	–	–	–	–	–	–	–	–	–	14
1999-00	1	1	3	1	–	2	–	–	–	–	–	–	–	–	–	–	–	08
Total	15	14	6	5	3	5	1	1	–	–	–	–	–	–	–	–	–	50

Raji children having six years of age and above lend their hands in economic activities of the family or help the family in other ways. As they look after the cattle or the infants while the parents or elders of the family are out for earning. Some time they collect fodder or fuel wood from the nearby jungles and fetch drinking water. In such a situation, how can the parents persuade their children for any unproductive undertakings like education having no instant economic output?

There are a number of health and medicare related programmes launched in rural areas. These programmes aim at improving the health conditions of the people and also to save them from different life-killing diseases. Besides this there is a provision of hygiene and nutrition related programmes for the betterment of the health of the people in general and the tribal people in particular. In the present study an attempt has also been made to assess the impact of various programmes and also the responses of the study units. In Kimkhola Raji tribal village, the tribal people are not aware of any health and medicare related programmes, like national family welfare programmes, universal immunization programme, maternity and child health programme, national malaria eradication programme, national tuberculosis eradication programme, school health programme and control of communicable diseases programme. However, the tribal people have expressed their cognizance about national leprosy control programme. A Raji tribal man suffering from leprosy is admitted in leprosy-hospital at Baluwakot for a long time. This incident has made the Raji people familiar with leprosy programme. Other programmes like installation of sanitary latrines, improvement of dietary patterns and infant-rearing practices have no meaning for the Raji people. No efforts have been made in this direction so far. The Raji people accepted that some personnels of health department visit periodically in the village as asked about the health problems of the people in general and of children, infants and mothers in particular. The vaccination programme periodically or as per health-departmental schedule is earned out in the village. But the tribal people have no knowledge of any vaccine and the reason of the vaccination. Almost all the Raji people under study area express their ignorance about any health and medicare programmes, hence they are not satisfied with the programmes and their results. However, they are partially satisfied with the vaccination programme and also with the maternity and child-health programme. As they experience the visits of ANM or mid-wife or medical-personnel at their places who just enquire about their well-being and inoculate the vaccine and provide them medicines in need and also persuade them for family planning. But the conservative, introvert and illiterate jungle people have no meaning for such advocacy or suggestions made by the personnel.

The Kimkhola Raji village is deprived of any kind of planned and institutionalize health care system. There is no Government Hospital. Even the sub-public health centre could not be established within the easy reach of the tribal people. There is no private hospital or any indigenous system of medicare like Aurveda, Siddha, Unani, Tibbi and Homoeopathy. But sometime the members of the Red Cross Society visit the Kimkhola village to provide them medical aid at their door steps. Thus the absence of any kind of medical facilities has compelled the Raji people to cling to their age-old pattern of indigenous treatment-like exorcism, magico-religious practices and crude-herbal treatment.

The primary health care services which include primarily the health education, the promotion of proper nutrition, adequate and safe drinking water, proper sanitation, maternity and child health care, family planning, prevention and control of endemic diseases the school health services like health appraisal of school children and school teachers with monthly check-up, remedial measures and follow up referral services and first-aid treatment of minor ailments by teachers etc., do not exist in the village. The Raji people are not aware of any kind of primary health care services hence they have no opinion about it.

Drinking water is positively correlated with the health condition of a person. Clean water bears good and positive effects on human body while polluted water has ill effects. With this assumption in mind it was tried to understand the source of drinking water of the Rajis and also the quality and up-keeping pattern of the drinking water system. We observed that there exists tape water supply in the village as well as there is spring at a distance of 100 metres. But the up-keeping system at the drinking water place is almost unhygienic. People use the same place for all purposes may be that of cleaning used kitchen-utensils, dirty clothes, bathing, even washing hands after evacuation. The surrounding remains full of dirt rather polluted which has always ill effects on their body.

The Raji people use fire-wood for cooking and fomentation purposes. In a small sized huts there is dense smoke which has always ill effects on human lungs. The respiratory problems, like Asthama even in early age are caused by long sitting near the smoky fire in the hut or room of the house having no ventilation. In fact the burning fire is only the natural way out to get rid of cold in hilly Raji areas. But the ignorant of the ill-effects of smoke the Raji people constantly sit beside the fire since birth to the end of their life as to save themselves from cold so catch respiratory problems that ends their life. They use kerosene oil to lit the lamps for lighting purposes during night. In the absence of kerosene, they use thin sticks of pine wood called for 'Jharo' for lighting purposes. Due to availability of the fire woods in jungles they do not use any other material like cow-dung-cakes etc. for fuel. LPG has no meaning for them, they are still unaware of LPG and solar power system.

The village economy of the Rajis is based on under developed agriculture. The tribal people perform crude type of terrace farming which is insufficient to meet out their needs, hence they earn wages as daily wage earners. They also collect forest products like edible roots and fruits. They collect fuelwood and fodder for selling in the nearby Jaulajibee market and for their non-tribal neighbourers. At present there are only two persons employed in Government Service and the rest of the Raji population has no permanent source of income.

They have small terrace farming in the slopy hill region of Kimkhola village. They cultivate the terraces twice in a year and sow Rabi and Kharif crops in rotation. But the yield of terrace farming always remains very inadequate so does meet their food requirements only for few months in a year. In fact the traditional way of agriculture is the reason of poor yield. They do not use advanced seeds, chemical fertilizers and insecticides for better agriculture yield. Only organic manure, provided that it is available, is used in terrace farming. The utilization pattern even of the organic manure, i.e., the 'Gobar Ki Khad' is very unscientific. In the cultivated terraces they just disperse the organic manure which gradually dries-up and does not produce the desired results. Thus, the crude type of agricultural farming has pushed them back to profess other subsidiary sources of subsistence.

Though the government agencies have planned and executed various development schemes like IRDP, JRY, REGS, REP, NREP, SFJA and MFALDA in general even for the Raji tribals. A special self-employment generation programme was also launched for the Raji youths in Jaulajibee, a nearby market centre of the Kimkhola village. Under this programme, training camps were held and a certain amount of stipend of Rs. 150/- per month was paid to the learners and a tool-kit was provided to each trainee. But this effort could not produce the desired results. The tools provided to the trainees were either rusted or sold by the trainees for petty amounts. Thus the poor, illiterate and ignorant Rajis have no meaning of development and employment generation schemes. Only the thing they need is cash or kind which can instantly satisfy their burning need of food, clothing and shelter. Today they have no patience, no endurance, no perseverance, no skill, no aspiration, no ambition but only hunger that keeps them busy in collecting food through available and known resources on the one hand, and also make them look intently towards the percolation of subsidised Government Schemes. In fact the development, self-employment and subsidized loan schemes have transformed simple primitive jungle people, i.e., the Raji's into indolent and lazy people. By and large the Raji people of the Kimkhola village have not benefitted up to the target mark.

So far as the public distribution system is concern, a fair price ration shop is available at about one km. far from the Raji village. The people can have the ration, such as, wheat, rice and other items of daily use as kerosene, sugar etc. at concessional rates. The quantity of all the items is decided as per-unit of the family. In an interview the Raji people said that they need every item available on concessional rates from the ration shop but it is the poverty and lack of money that deprived them of availing this facility. Hence they do not ask the shopkeeper even the per-unit quantity of the goods sanctioned for the tribals. In their words "*Paise ho to puchhai, aur janane ki koshish karain, Jitana dam utna mal milhi jata hai.*" i.e. 'if there is money, there is meaning of asking about the quantity allotted per-unit per-family. If we have money we can get easily the items we desire'. In fact the Raji people have no purchasing power, hence the public distribution system through fair price shop has no meaning for the poor Rajis. However, the people having purchasing power virtually take the benefit of it in the name of the poor Rajis. There are Raji people who even do not know about the schemes meant for their welfare. There is no source of information even of the basic amenities like education, health, hygiene and nutrition. Sometimes some government departmental officials on duty visit the villages at day time, means on their working hours but they do not meet the tribal people because the tribals gone for their jobs. In such cases whoever the people, may be that aged or children, they meet, they ask about the schemes and other related information. In this way the officials, no doubt, perform their duty but the receptivity of the Raji people in general remains nil.

Kimkhola village is linked by foot-path from the motor road. The people can visit the nearest market place, i.e., Jaulijabee on foot or after traversing some distance on foot they can also travel by bus. But the block, tehsil and district headquarters can be reached only by bus. The village has no facility of post and telegraph. In fact the post and telegraphic facilities have no use in Raji tribal area because they have very limited network of relations and they believe in personal visits to their relations or sending messengers on some particular occasions.

The food habits of the Raji people are somewhat different from the rest of the neighbouring non-tribals. In general they take 'Kalewa' called 'Kalau' in the morning which consists of 'Roti of a coarse grain', i.e., the Kodo or maize or the Roti of Kodo and wheat flour mixed with fine salty mixture made up of salt grinded with red or green chilly, coriander leaf and garlic. But the use of these items is based on the availability of the items. Sometimes, due to non-availability of the necessary items, the people drop the idea of *kalau* and manage for the mid-day meal called the 'Chhakala Ko Khano', i.e., the lunch. Cooked rice, (if rice is available), Fanau-made up of Kodo-flour with some rice or sometime without rice, Bhatya made of Bhat (a type of soyabean), Jaulo prepared with rice, butter milk and flour are the main items prepared at midday. In case of cooked-rice, i.e., Bhat, 'Chudakani' an adhesive preparation made up of fried Bhat (soyabean) with kodo or wheat flour is used in place of 'Dal'. Sometimes they make the preparation of some edible roots like 'Gethi', 'Tarud', 'Bhekuna', etc. collected from jungle. Tender shoots of Sinna (nettle) is their favourite vegetable. In the evening they prepare Roti of Kodo, maize, wheat, barley whatever is available and take it with the preparation made up of either some edible roots or vegetable of 'Bhichhu ghas'. An adhesive made up of Bichhu ghas and Tarud is their traditional preparation. The Rajis grow Bhat and masoor in their small terraces in Kharif and Ravi seasons respectively. But no oil seeds are grown. In the name of beverages, the Raji families having milching cattle drink 'Mattha or milk, otherwise there is no concept of milk, mattha or other healthy drinks. However, the people are fond of alcoholic drinks they buy from local people. 'Kachchi sarab', or the alcoholic drink of any kind, Bidi, Tambaco, Bhang, Charas are used generally by male members. While some Raji women also smoke. It is notable here that the use of food items other than alcoholic drinks or smoking, is subject to their availability. There is no regularity of food and food items. The availability of food items decide whether the oven will be lit up or not. The people manage alcoholic drinks and the smoking items by hook or by crook. The local market and local brewers are the sources from where they can have the smoking items and alcoholic drinks. Moreover, the supply of wine-pouch even in the remotest area has made easier the supply of alcoholic drinks even in the tribal areas.

Bannakhera—The Buxa Village

Bannakhera, a Buxa village is one of the 173 Buxa villages in Uttaranchal. As already mentioned the Buxas have been the original owners of the Tarai and Bhabar plains of Uttaranchal inducting Pilibhit and Bijnor districts of Uttar Pradesh. At present the population of the Buxa tribe, i.e., approximately 13.62 per cent of the total Scheduled Tribe population of Uttaranchal, is spread over in Tarai plains in Dehradun, Paurhi and Udham Singh Nagar district of Uttaranchal. In Udham Singh Nagar district the Buxa population is spread over mainly in Bajpur, Kashipur, Gadarpur and Ramnagar Blocks. Bannakhera, the sampled village is situated in Bajpur Block. From Haldwani, the Bannakhera village can be approached by bus or taxi. It is about 60 km. far from Haldwani and located beside the Haldwani-Bajpur motor road. When we travel through Haldwani-Bajpur motor route (westward from Haldwani) there comes a bus-stop namely 'Bannakhera market'. From here the Bannakhera (Majara-Bhudi) the study area is situated at about 6 km far from the bus stop which can be approached either by one's own vehicle or by asking for lift in frequently moving tractors or motorcycles or by hiring a tonga. The last alternative is 'on foot' march to reach the village. In fact the village Bannakhera Majara-Bhudi is linked by a metalled road constructed by the Cane Society Bajpur.

Bannakhera is one of the large Buxa villages of Bajpur Block. It falls within Bannakhera village panchayat. In this village panchayat 'Majara-Bhudi' is inhabited predominantly by the Buxas while the Bannakhera village panchayat as a whole is inhabited by different caste-groups including Buxas, Sikhs, Ray-Sikhs, Jat-Sikhs, Majavi-Sikhs. Among the Hindus Brahmin, Kshatriya, Sudra are the main caste-groups living here. Bannakhera has an area of 526.732 Hectare or 1316.822 Acre land. Out of which 1144.522 acre is cultivable, 1135.252 acres is irrigated land while the rest 9.312 acres is non-irrigated. 28.602 acres is waste land, 45.502 acres is residential and 98.202 acres of land is forested.

The village is surrounded by Bhikampuri Gram Sabha in east, Kela Banwari Gram Sabha in west, Belparao in north and Reta Gram Sabha in south. The village is located at a distance of 50 km. from district headquarters Rudrapur, 40 km. from Tehsil headquarters, 12 km. from Block headquarters and 12 km. from the police station. While the rest of the facilities like bus station, local market centre, post office, primary sub-health centre, Govt. A.P.H.C., Pvt. dispensary, Primary school and Junior High School are located within the periphery of Bannakhera village panchayat. So far as medical aid is concerned the additional sub-public health centre and a private dispensary have very limited facilities. The needy people can have only first-aid facilities there. So far as educational facilities up to Junior High School standard are concerned the shortage of teaching staff, lack of teaching material, library, school building, furniture and other sanitary related infrastructure is very common in all types of schools, may be that a government or private. The High School and Intermediate College are located at a distance of 4 km. in Gajraula from the village, while the Govt. Degree College and Post-Graduate College are located respectively at a distance of 12 km (at Bajpur) and 40 km (at Kashipur) from the village. There is a People's Training School at Haldwani which is located about 56 km from the village.

The total population of the village is 1856 out of which 485 are of the Buxas. Among the Buxas 53.60 per cent are male and 46.40 per cent are female. So far as literacy is concerned 68.04 per cent Buxa population is illiterate out of which 41.51 per cent is of male population and 58.49 per cent is of female. The Table 5.3 shows the age and sex-wise educational standard of the Buxas of the study area.

The climate of the village is very hot during summer. There is heavy fog during winter, the sun shines hardly from 12.00 Noon to 4.00

p.m. The rest of the time the area remains covered by fog. There is casual heavy rain fall during rainy season and the climate is humid.

The economy of the village is based on agriculture. Some Buxas are also daily wage labourers in private, government and semi-govt. industrial undertakings. Some are agricultural labourers and there are only a few persons who are employed in government services. The Table 5.4 shows the education-wise occupational status of the Buxa male and female of the village.

The people live in Kachcha houses made up of wooden logs, grass and viscous soil collected from ponds. They use hand-pump installed by the villagers themselves as well as by the government for drinking water. There are tube-wells for irrigation purposes. Generally the well off Buxas have their own tube-wells while some tubewells are installed by the government under irrigation scheme. The Buxa people have no other natural resource available in village surrounding. They collect fuel wood and timber from forests. They also collect some seasonal jungle products such as vegetables, herbs and tubers but they are not dependent on jungle products for their sustenance.

The infrastructural facilities likes education, road, communication, electricity, drinking water, medicare system, telecommunication, post-office etc. are not upto the mark. No doubt, there is a primary and junior high school located in the village but the shortage of teaching and non-teaching staff has defeated the aims of the schools. For example there are clear vacancies of six teachers in a primary school out of which only two teachers have been posted in the school. It is questionable, how two teachers can manage five classes at a time. Besides this the teachers working at the school are not paid even monthly salary in time. During field work, the teachers made us known that they were not paid salary for the last four months. The same is the case of junior high school. Besides this, the school setups in the village have no sufficient school buildings, there is no proper and permanent drinking water, no toilets, no sweepers, no fourth-class employees, no library, no reading room, no proper arrangement of seating of the students and no furniture. Such a condition of the schools can never meet its aims. It is the reason that the enrolment of the students in different classes is very thin and their performance is not satisfactory. The teachers generally upgrade the children up to junior high school level in home examinations whatso ever their performance is, but they cannot pass any board examination. Hence the number of the board examination pass students is very few in the village. The following table gives an impression about the position of the students in different classes during the last five years.

It is observed that in the last five years, i.e., from 1996-2000, the total enrolment of the Buxa children in different classes, i.e., from first

Table 5.3. Age and Sex-wise Educational Standard of the Buxas

Age Group	Sex	Illiterate	Primary	Junior H. S.	High School	Inter-mediate	Gra-duate	Post-Graduate	Other	Total	%	G. Total	Per-centage
0-5	M	28-1 =27	-	-	-	-	-	-	-	27	50.00	54	11.33
	F	31-1 =27	-	-	-	-	-	-	-	27	50.00		
5-10	M	22	15	-	-	-	-	-	-	37	56.06	66	13.60
	F	24	05	-	-	-	-	-	-	29	43.94		
10-15	M	07	18	05	-	-	-	-	-	30	54.55	55	11 .34
	F	12	11	02	-	-	-	-		25	45.45		
15-20	M	05	06	11	05	-	-	-	-	32	58.80	55	11 .33
	F	15	06	02	-		-	-	-	23	41.82		
20-25	M	08	04	07	04	-	-	-	-	23	60.52	38	7.83
	F	13	01	01	-	-	-	-	-	15	39.48		
25-30	M	08	08	05	02		-	01	-	24	52.18	46	9.49
	F	21	-	01	-	-	-	-	-	22	47.82		
30-35	M	10	07	03	02	-	-	-	-	22	55.00	40	8.25
	F	16	01	01	-	-	-	-	-	18	45.00		
35-40	M	06	07	02	-	-	-	-	-	15	42.86	35	7.22
	F	19	01	-	-	-	-	-	-	20	57.14		
40-45	M	07	03	01	-	-	-	-	-	11	47.82	23	4.75
	F	12	-	-	-	-	-	-	-	12	52.18		
45-50	M	10	05	-	-	-	-	-	-	15	83.33	18	3.71
	F	03	-	-	-	-	-	-	-	03	16.67		
50-55	M	05	-	-	-	-	-	-	-	05	45.45	11	2.27
	F	06	-	-	-	-	-	-	-	06	54.35		

(Contd.)

(Contd. Table 5.3)

Age Group	Sex	Illiterate	Primary	Junior H. S.	High School	Inter-mediate	Gra-duate	Post-Graduate	Other	Total	%	G. Total	Per-centage
55-60	M	03	01	-	-	-	-	-	-	04	40.00	10	2.07
	F	6	-	-	-	-	-	-	-	06	60.00		
60-65	M	03	01	-	-	-	-	-	—	04	57.14	07	1.44
	F	03								03	42.86		
65-70	M	05 03	-	-	-	-	-	-	-	05	62.50	08	1.65
	F									03	37.50		
70 & above	M	10 09	-	-	-	-	-	-	-	10	52.63	19	3.92
	F									09	47.37		
Total	M	136 (41.84%)	75 (75%)	34 (82.92%)	18 (100%)	-	-	01 (100%)	-	264	54.43	485	100.00
	F	189 (58.16%)	25 (25%)	07 (17.08%)	-	-	-	-	-	221	45.57		
G. Total		325 (100%)	100 (100%)	41 (100%)	13 (100%)	-	-	01 (100%)	-	485	100.00		
%		68.04	20.62	8.45	2.69	-	-	0.20	-	App. 100			

Table 5.4. Education and Occupation Status of the Buxas of 'Majara Bhudi, Bannakhera'

Education	Sex	*Occupational Status*								*Dependant Population*								
		Agri	*Service (Govt.)*	*Service (Pvt.)*	*Wage earning*	*Agri. & Labour*	*Agri. & Service*	*Business*	*Agri. & Busi.*	*Agri.*	*Govt. Service*	*Pvt. Service*	*Labour*	*Agri. & Labour*	*Agri. &*	*Businness*	*Agri. & Busi.*	*Total*
Illiterate	Male	45	-	-	27	-	-	-	-	31	-	-	33	-	-	-	-	136
	Female	66	-	-	40	-	-	-	-	32	-	01	40	-	-	-	-	189
Primary	Male	24	-	-	27	-	-	02	-	15	-	-	07	-	-	-	-	75
	Famale	04	-	-	02	-	-	-	-	14	-	02	03	-	-	-	-	25
Junior H.S.	Male	19	-	02	10	-	-	-	-	02	-	01	-	-	-	-	-	34
	Female	03	-	-	02	-	-	-	-	02	-	-	-	-	-	-	-	07
High School	Male	08	01	02	01	-	-	01	-	-	-	-		-	-	05	-	18
	Female	-	-	-	-	-	-	-	-	-	-	-	-	-	-	-	-	-
Inter-mediate	Male	-	-	-	-	-	-	-	-	-	-	-	-	-	-	-	-	-
	Female	-	-	-		-	-	-	-	-	-	-	-	-	-	-	-	-
Graduate	Male	-	-	-	-	-	-	-	-	-	-	-	-	-	-	-	-	-
	Female	-	-	-	-	-	-	-	-	-	-	-	-	-	-	-	-	-
Post-Graduate	Male	-	-	-	01	-	-	-	-	-	-	-	-	-	-	-	-	01
	Female	-	-	-	-	-	-	-	-	-	-	-	-	-	-	-	-	-
Others	Male	-	-	-	-	-	-	-	-	-	-	-.	-	-	-	-	-	-
	Female	-	-	-	-	-	-	-	-	-	-	-	-	-	-	-	-	-
Total	Male	96	01	04	68	-	-	01	-	48	-	01	40	-	-	05	-	264
	Female	73	-	-	54	-	-	-		48	-	03	43	-	-	-	-	221
G. Total		169	01	04	122	-	-	01	-	96	-	04	83	-	-	05	-	485

standard to eighth standard has been only 314 and out of which the percentage of boys was 64.17 per cent and remaining 35.03 per cent was of girls. We observe a common tendency of dropouts among the Buxa children. If we calculate it sex-wise, there we observe that the tendency of dropping out is comparatively more among girls than among boys. Besides this, we also observe the tendency of increasing cases of droppers in higher classes. It is so because at early age the children have no economic potential, rather they are treated as burden on the family. The parents, therefore enroll them in the school and become carefree from the side of the children while they are on jobs. As soon as the children grow and begin to lend their hands in economic pursuits they leave the schooling. In the case of girls this assumption is more applicable. Even some girls are married during their teenage, i.e., the schooling period which ultimately increases the percentage of drop-outs. It is only the reason that the literacy as well as the standard of education among the female is not high.

The village is well-connected by the metalled road. Telephone facility is available at the residence of the Gram Sabhapati. There is a sub-post office in the nearby market centre. But for the Buxas the telephone and post office have no meaning. They prefer to visit their acquaintances or relations personally. In the village, the villagers have installed their own hand-pumps on their own cost for getting drinking water. The government have also installed two public handpumps but the problem of maintenance is always there. The surroundings of the handpumps remains unhygienic which causes mosquito and other insect like flies carrier of different diseases. Bannakhera village is electrified but electric connections are very few. The street pole-light or the anchor the people install clandestinely at night-time to serve their needs of electricity.

Health and medicare is the prime concern of human life. This sphere has been taken up in priority basis by the government and different health policies and programmes have been framed and launched for the people in general and for the rural and tribal people in particular. In this context the Buxas of the study area have been interviewed and their responses have been sought about different health and medicare programmes. It is observed that most of the respondents have shown their awareness and acquaintance about national family welfare programme, universal immunization programme, national leprosy control programme, school health programme and control of communicable diseases programme etc. The tribal people also willing to avail the benefits of those programmes provided the programmes are made available at their door-steps. There is a sub-primary health centre in the village which is running with short staff and handicapped medical facilities. It is the reason that even the needy tribal people prefer to consult the private medical practitioners rather than go to the Govt. sub-primary health centre. The major and chronic cases are generally referred to primary health centres located at Bajpur about 12 km. far from the village as well as to Haldwani Govt. Hospital. Generally the poverty of the Buxa people is the main hindrance on the way to approach and avail of even the free medical aid. It is the reason that some chronic T.B. patients in the village could not avail even the free medical treatment provided at Soban Singh Jina Base Hospital, Haldwani- about 60 km. far from the Buxa village. Thus in spite of awareness about different national health-related programmes, the majority of the Buxa population in the village is not satisfied with these programmes. Only universal immunization programme and its implication in the village is an exception. In fact there are camps about which proper information is provided to the villagers, hence most of the immunization programmes receive positive response from the Buxas.

The other aspect of health care is related drinking water, sanitary system, dietary pattern, mother's care and infant rearing practices. In the Buxa village there is a provision for installation of 'India Marka' hand pump in the village, which is in progress. But the surrounding of the drinking water source can not be termed as hygienic. The people take their bath, wash their dirty clothes and used kitchen ware, wash their hands and feet after evacuation, make purification of the children after evacuation, and also wash their buffaloes at the source of drinking water. This process makes the surrounding of the drinking water source very unhygienic, therefore, unhealthy conditions are more prone to communicable diseases. There is a provision of installation of sanitary latrines under Indira Avas Yojana in the village. There are some latrines but not in use, because people are not used to use latrines. It is so because they have no hygienic sense of latrine use. The latrine sheet is not kept properly clean. It remains full of excreta due to lack of scavenging services. In fact the people are neither properly learned so as to know how to use latrines nor do they render their services voluntarily for this cause. It is the reason that some of the Buxas have received the latrine sheets from the department concerned but are kept unused lying in house premises. The room meant for latrine without latrine sheet is being used for keeping dry fodder for tamed animals.

The people have no knowledge of proper dietary pattern. They are very much simple and believe in satiation whatever is available and cooked in the hearth. They impose some dietary restriction on the pregnant and lactating mothers and also impose some social taboos. But the restrictions and taboos without medical sense often generate ill-effects on mother's health. The same is the case of infant-rearing practices. The people have their own beliefs, notions and practices about infant

Table 5.5. Position of the Buxa Tribal Students in Different Classes in the Last Five Years

Academic Session	Position Students	Class/Standard																														
		I		II		III		IV		V		VI		VII		VIII		IX		X		XI		XII		B.A./B.Sc.		MA/M.Sc.		Total		
		B	G	B	G	B	G	B	G	B	G	B	G	B	G	B	G	B	G	B	G	B	G	B	G	B	G	B	G	B	G	Total
1995-96	Enrolled	17	11	13	5	9	3	8	2	3	2																					
	Droppers	4	6	4	2	1	-	3	-	1	1																					
	Pass	13	5	9	3	8	3	5	2	4	1			3		5				4												
	Failure	-	-	-	-	-	-	-	-	1	-									1												
1996-97	Enrolled	15	9	13	5	5	3	7	2	3	2																					
	Droppers	2	3	8	2	-	1	4	2	-	-																					
	Pass	13	6	5	3	5	2	3	0	2	1				1	1	1									1						
	Failure	-	-	-	-	-	-	-	-	1	1																					
1997-98	Enrolled	15	12	13	6	5	3	7	2	3	0																					
	Droppers	-	2	1	-	-	1	2	2	-	-																					
	Pass	15	10	12	6	5	2	5	-	3	-						1	1	1					1		1		2				
	Failure	-	-	-	-	-	-	-	-	-	-																					
1998-99	Enrolled	7	3	15	10	12	6	6	2	5	-																					
	Droppers	3	-	7	3	8	3	-	1	-	-																					
	Pass	4	3	8	7	4	3	6	1	5	-						2		1		1		1									
	Failure	-	-	-	-	-	-	-	-	-	-											1										
1999-00	Enrolled	8	5	4	5	8	7	4	3	8	1																					
	Droppers	-	-	-	-	2	2	1	1	-	-																					
	Pass	8	5	4	5	6	5	3	2	7	1	2		4		4			2	1	1			1	2	1	1					
	Failure	-	-	-	-	-	-	-	-	-	-																					
Total	Enrolled	62	40	54	35	38	21	30	11	20	03																					
	Droppers	9	11	20	11	11	07	10	6	-	-																					
	Pass	53	26	34	24	27	14	20	5	17	2																					
	Failure	-	-	-	-	-	-	-	-	03	01																					

Note : B = Boys; G = Girls.

rearing and they prefer to follow the same in their private life. Hence the programmes related to this cause have no meaning for the Buxas. The data shown in the following Table 5.6 verify this fact.

Health and Medicare System Available in the Village

Within the periphery of Bannakhera village panchayat only an Additional Primary Health Centre is present. This centre consists of two medical officers—one allopathic MOIC and the other MOCH (Medical Officer Community Health). The sub-staff consists of one Pharmacist and one ward boy. In this Additional Primary Health Centre there is facility for first-aid only. It has been allotted only 'four beds' for emergency cases but so far a building is not built for this purpose. Hence all the cases are referred to the 'Primary Health Centre' located at Bajpur about 12 km. far from the village. The A.P.H.C. has issued medical cards to the students in the school where regular medical investigation of the school-going children is made periodically. Besides this, the centre also keeps an eye on the diseases of the people of the village in general and of the Buxa tribes in particular. Periodically immunization programmes are also carried out by the centre. The centre has only one oxygen cylinder for emergency cases and one emergency kit. Generally sterilized needle is used to inject the patients. The centre also lack medicines. The patients generally buy medicines from the private chemist and druggist. Thus the public-health sector, as such, is not up to the mark and according to the needs of the villagers. The private medical sector is also insufficient. There are some private medical practitioners on the outskirts of the market of the village. These medical practitioners may have good medical experience and the people may have faith on them but virtually they have no such medical degree or diploma which can prove their accountability and credibility and medically legalize their medical practices. In fact the people have no other option in their approachable surrounding hence they consult these practitioners and feel psychologically momentary relief. Except two private clinics, there is no polyclinic, nursing home, and dispensary in the village and its surroundings. The same is the case of the indigenous system of medicare. Ayurveda, Siddha, Unani, Tibbi, Homoeopathy etc. are not in practice. No voluntary health agency is in operation throughout the study area. Thus the poor people have no other option rather than to imprecate their destiny and to bear the sufferings. However, sometimes the health workers of the additional primary health centre visit the Buxa village and ask the tribal people about the proper nutrition pattern, ask them to take adequate and safe drinking-water, to follow the maternal and child health care practices. They also explain the benefits of family planning and immunization programme and motivate them to follow these practices in

Table 5.6. Percentage of Awareness and Attitude of the Respondents Towards Health and Medicare Programmes

Programme	Percentage of Attitude							
	Awareness		Full Satisfied	Satisfied	Unsatisfied	Fully satisfied	Uncertain	Total
	Yes	No						
Family Welfare Prog.	100%	-	-	40%	46%	-	14%	100
Universal Immunization Prog,	100%	-	-	82%	-	-	18%	100
Maternity Child Health Prog.	100%	-	-	30%	40%	-	30%	100
Malaria Eradication Programme	100%	-	-	25%	35%	10%	30%	100
Tuberculosis Programme	100%	-	-	-	-	65%	35%	100
Leprosy Control Prog.	40%	60%	-	-	-	-	100%	100
School Health programme	50%	50%	-	45%	5%	-	50%	100
Control of Communicable Disease Prog.	15%	85%	-	8%	-	-	92%	100
Installation of Sanitary Latrines	15%	85%	-	20%	-	-	80%	100
Mother & Infant Caring and Rearing Practices	60%	40%	-	30%	40%	-	30%	100
Drinking Water Supplies	100%	-	-	30%	30%	-	40%	100
Dietary Improvement Practices	65%	35%	-	40%	-	-	60%	100

their life. Besides this, the tribal people are also told about the remedial measures and follow-up referral services, first-aid treatment of minor ailments and also make monthly health examination of school children and school teachers. In fact the primary health care services are stereotyped. They just carry on the instructions made by their higher authorities and in spite of being known about the poor receptivity of the tribal people they propagate about the primary health care services in tribal areas.

In the village, the Buxa tribals use hand pump and tape water for drinking purpose. They use firewood, cow-dung cakes, kerosene oil and LPG according to their capacity for fuel purposes. As already mentioned that the Buxas are agriculturists. Today they use advanced seeds, chemical fertilizers, insecticides and organic manure in their agriculture system. In general, the tribal people are aware of different employment generation schemes like IRDP, JRY, REGS and REP only. These schemes have partially benefitted the tribals also. But majority of the tribal youths, i.e., 90 per cent is of the opinion that these schemes could not benefit the tribals. In fact the success of the self-employment generation schemes lies on the ability of the people and their enterprising quality. The Buxas by nature have no entrepreneurship quality. They also lack capital. They can become good agriculturists but not successful businessmen to start with a profit generating trade.

The Govt. has a provision for fair price shop as to make available food items on concessional rates to the Buxa tribals. As per records 07 kg. rice, 3 kg. wheat, 5 litres kerosene oil per family per-month is distributed on fair prices. Besides this the sugar is available 90 gram per unit in the family. Practically if we look into the necessity of the poor Buxas, the quantity of ration, i.e., rice, wheat, sugar etc. is not sufficient. Thus the public distribution system through fair price shops is not adequate. Even the poor Buxas buy the food items from open market where the prices are comparatively higher than at fair price shops.

The Buxa village under study is electrified. But the legal connections are very few in the village. The villagers just put on anchor at night and make light in their huts and disconnect it in the morning. This illegal practice continues even today.

The tribal people have no effective source of information that can make them known with the importance of education, health, hygiene and nutrition. However newspapers, magazines, radio and the television are some of the powerful sources of information but the first two are beyond the understanding of a common illiterate Buxas, while the remaining two may have viability for them but only a rich Buxa can afford these items, i.e., the radio and television. The behaviour pattern of the common Buxas, their attitude and likings do not favour the information about education, health, hygiene and nutrition telecast on the radio and television. They prefer rather music items, film features and other dramatic episodes. Besides this, some government personnel particularly of medical department visit the village and make the villagers aware of health, hygiene and nutrition related aspects and also provoke them to follow the precautions as well as instructions given by them. This process has some effect on the villagers. But the apathy and irregularity of the personnel and non-cooperation of the villagers due to their engagement in other jobs of daily routine, and the lack of time have reduced the viability of this process.

The Buxa village is linked to the metalled road from the market place, block, tehsil and district headquarters. The people can travel by their own conveyance or hire commercial conveyance for travelling to their destinations.

The post and telegraphic facilities are not available in the village. The people have to walk for about 2 kms. to find the postal facilities. In the village the local telephone system is also available at the house of the 'Gramsabhapati', but the use of these systems, i.e., the post office and telephone is negligible for the Buxas.

Basically the Buxa has been an omnivorous community. But with the course of time they have changed their food habits. Today the Buxas of Majara-Bhudi are fond of eating cooked rice (Bhat) with dal prepared by Masoor or Chana (gram) as per availability. In the absence of Dal, they prepare curry of potato or any other salty adhesive is used with Bhat. In the morning, at breakfast, they eat 'Roti' prepared with wheat, maize or millet flour either with seasonal vegetables like potato, spinach, gobhi, torai, lauki, kaddu, baigan, mooli, as per availability or merely with salt or any salty adhesive with chillies. Almost the same menu is repeated at night in dinner. In the lunch the people preferably eat Bhat with dal or curry of any seasonal vegetable. The Buxas are non-vegetarian. They take the flesh of fish, goat, chicken, boar, dear, rabbits, shahi, bater, peacock, pigeon etc. Even today they try to manage non-vegetarian items by any means. Even they buy the remains of chicken, fish, goat, sheep or boar etc. from butcher's meat shop in low price. In this way Bhat-fish or Bhat-meat curry is the best dish the Buxas relish and prefer to relish often. Other than staple food and meat they are fond of drinking any alcoholic drinks. The use of milk and milk products like curd, mattha, ghee, paneer ete. are rarely used by the people, because the Buxas in general do not keep milching cattle. Even the infants and the growing children are not provided milk or milk products regularly. However, if milk is available, all the family members do take the milk products.

The Buxas grow wheat, sugarcane, paddy, maize, gram, millet, masoor, urd, peas and mustard in their fields. The commercial crops like sugarcane and surplus quantity of wheat, paddy, mustard etc. is sold to the Banjaras or at the market. The money thus earned is used for other daily needs. They also grow some vegetables like spinach, methi, torai, lauki, kaddu, peas, potato, onion, garlic, brinjal, bhindi (ladies finger) and also grow some tuber like ginger, turmeric, ghuiya etc. for their own use. The Buxas also grow tobacco. Both the males and females are fond of smoking. They use Bidi, Tobacco, and cigarettes. Charas, ganja and other intoxicating drugs, as are available, are used by the male members. They get alcoholic drinks and narcotics either by buying them from the authorised or unauthorised sources. If they have no cash they barter by giving foodgrains for alcoholic drinks and narcotics.

Ratanpur; the Tharu Village

Ratanpur, the Tharu Village is located in Khatima Block of Udham Singh Nagar District in Uttaranchal Pradesh. It comes in the village panchayat area of Ratanpur Fullayya. The village may be termed as the Majara or Tok of the Ratanpur-Fullayya village Panchayat. It is predominantly a tribal village. The Tharus are the only residents of this village. Different clan groups of the Tharus are residing here. Out of which the Rana is the main clan group. Besides this some non-tribal population consisting of Kumauni hill people and people from plains are also residing in the peripheral outskirts of the village. These people have occupied and owned the tribal land since long time on the consent of both parties' on some mutually agreed terms and conditions. The total geographical areas of the village is 12760 sq. Bigha out of which 12206 sq. Bigha is cultivated land out of which 6123 sq. Bigha is irrigated land 6083 sq. Bigha is non-irrigated 469 is waste land 65 sq. Bigha is residential and the rest 20 sq. Bigha is used for roads and streets. The village is situated on the elevation of 1000 metre from the sea level. Basically the village is located in Tarai belt of Uttaranchal. Previously, when there was scanty population, this area was predominantly swampy with malarial climate. The life of human beings was very difficult. Only the Tharus used to live here. It is said that the Tharus were 'malaria proof'. Hence the people other than the Tharus were almost absent in this area and the area was known as Tharuwat or the abode of the Tharus.

The Ratanpur village is surrounded by Jasar gram in east, Bhada-Budiya village in west, Uldhan village in north and Sada-Sadiya village in south. It is well-linked to the single metalled road to the Tanakpur-Delhi national highway. The village is located about 85 km. far from Haldwani the and can be approached by motorable road. It is located besides the Haldwani-Tanakpur motor road. At about 80 km. from Haldwani there is a sub-bus station named 'Jhankat'. The village is situated about 5 to 6 km. in the north of the 'Jhankat-bus-station'. One can reach the village either on foot or by one's own conveyance may be that a taxi, car or scooter. The village is located at a distance of 68 km. from district headquarters, i.e., U.S. Nagar, Rudrapur, 11 km. from Khatima the Tehsil headquarters, 11 km. from Block headquarters, 03 km. from the Bus station, 03 km. from the local market, 11 km. from the Police station, 03 km. from the Post-Office, 11 km. from the Primary Health Centre, 11 km. from the Government hospital, 11 km. from the private hospital, 200 metres from the primary school, 200 metres from the Junior High School, 03 km from the High School, 03 km. from the Intermediate College, 11 km from the Degree College, 68 km. from the Post-Graduate College, i.e., P.G. College Rudrapur and 85 km from the People's College, Haldwani. The villagers have their own source of drinking water. The hand pumps are installed from place to place in the village for this purpose.

At present the total population of Ratanpur village is 1123 out of which the male population is 594 (52.90 per cent) and the rest population, i.e., 529 (47.10 per cent) is of females. The Age and Sex-wise details of the Tharu population of Ratanpur village may be shown in the Table 5.7.

Age and Sex-wise Educational Status of the Tharus of Ratanpur Village

The tabulated data presented in the Table 5.7 shows that out of total 1123 Tharu population 491 (43.72 per cent) are illiterate. This percentage also include the preschool childrens' population. Out of the illiterate and pre-school population, i.e., 491 (43.72 per cent), 280 (57.02 per cent) are females and 211 (42.98 per cent) are male. The educational status of the Tharu population also depicts that out of the total literate population, i.e., 632 (55.28 per cent) the percentage of the people educated up to primary standard is higher, i.e., 23.78 per cent. This percentage is followed respectively by the people who are educated up to junior high school, high school, intermediate and under-graduate level, i.e., 14.15 per cent, 10.60 per cent, 4.99 per cent, 2.50 per cent and 0.26 per cent. In the village none of the population is educated up to post-graduate level. If we correlate the educational standard of the Tharu population with 'Age-group', we find that with the increase of age the percentage of education decreases. In other words we can say that the percentage of education is more comparatively in the new generation than in the old generation. This tendency also proves the prevalence of education and its importance in the new generation which is an inevitable result of the planned process of development.

The climate of the village is very hot during summer and very cold during winter. The dry cold during winter season causes different type of diseases. Heavy fog generally covers the village during morning time. But

Table 5.7. Age and Sex-wise Educational Standard of the Tharus of Ratanpur Village

Age Group	Sex	Illiterate/ Pre-School	Primary & Preprimary	Junior High school	High School	Inter Mediate	Under-Graduate	Post-Graduate	Other	Total	Grand Total	%
0-5	M	83	11	-	-	-	-	-	-	94 (56.62%)	166	14.79
	F	82	10	-	-	-	-	-	-	72 (43.38%)		
5-10	M	7	64	4	-	-	-	-	-	75 (52.09%)	144	12.82
	F	8	59	2	-	-	-	-	-	69 (47.91%)		
10-15	M	1	10	25	19	3	-	-	-	58 (46.40%)	125	11.13
	F	7	15	37	8	-	-	-	-	67 (53.60%)		
15-20	M	5	4	12	32	12	10	-	1	75 (48.70%)	154	13.71
	F	23	18	12	09	13	03	-	-	79 (51.30%)		
20-25	M	5	1	15	20	15	04	-	1	61 (50.00%)	122	18.87
	F	34	13	09	-	03	02	-	-	61 (50.00)%		
25-30	M	11	5	18	17	04	03	-	1	59 (64.13%)	92	8.20
	F	17	9	4	3	-	-	-	-	33 (35.87%)		
30-35	M	10	3	6	8	4	-	-	-	31 (58.50%)	53	4.71
	F	18	4	-	-	-	-	-	-	22 (41.40%)		
35-40	M	13	6	6	3	-	4	-	-	32 (50.00%)	64	5.70
	F	25	6	1	-	-	-	-	-	32 (50.00%)		
40-45	M	18	9	3	-	2	1	-	-	33 (56.90%)	58	5.17
	F	22	3	-	-	-	-	-	-	25 (43.10%)		
45-50	M	13	6	2	-	-	-	-		21 (51.21%)	41	3.66
	F	18	2	-	-	-	-	-		20 (48.79%)		

(Contd.)

(Contd. Table 5.7)

Age Group	Sex	Illiterate/ Pre-School	Primary & Preprimary	Junior High school	High School	Inter Mediate	Under-Graduate	Post-Graduate	Other	Total	Grand Total	%
50-55	M	14	3	1	-	-	-	-	-	18 (52.94%)	34	3.02
	F	16	-	-	-	-	-	-	-	16 (47.06%)		
55-60	M	11	2	1	-	-	-	-	-	13 (50.00%)	26	2.31
	F	11	1							12 (50.00%)		
60-65	M	15	1	-	-	-	-	-	-	16 (66.67%)	24	2.13
	F	7	1	-	-	-	-	-	-	8 (33.33%)		
65-70	M	3	1	-	-	-	1	-	-	5 (71.42%)	7	0.62
	F	2	-	-	-	-	-	-	-	2 (28.58%)		
70 & Above	M	2	-	1	-	-	-	-	-	3 (23.07%)	13	1.16
	F	10	-	-	-	-	-	-	-	10 (76.93%)		
Total	M	211 (42.98%)	126 (47.20%)	93 (58.50%)	99 (83.20%)	40 (71.42%)	23 (82.14%)	-	2 (66.67%)	594 (52.90%)	1123	100.00
	F	280 (57.02%)	141 (52.80%)	66 (41.50%)	20 (16.80%)	16 (28.58%)	5 (17.86%)		1 (33.33%)	529 (47.10%)		
Grand Total		491	267	159	119	56	28	-	3			
		(43.72%)	(23.78%)	(14.15%)	(10.60%)	(4.99%)	2.50%)	-	(02.6%)			

with the rise of the sun it (the fog) begins to disappear and at about 12.00 Noon the weather/sky becomes almost clear, but with the setting of the sun the atmosphere begins to be misty with the effect of the rising fog again and the village and its surrounding disappears under the darkness of dense fog. There is medium rainfall in the rainy season.

The economy of the village is chiefly based on agriculture. But with the course of time some Tharus are pursuing some non-traditional jobs like government service, daily wage labour and some small scale business pursuits. Though the tribal people of Ratanpur village have been the traditional agriculturists but the growing population is facing the fragmentation of land. Everlasting indebtedness of some of the Tharus have caused the problem of land-alienation among them. This state of being has pushed them from agriculturists to agricultural labourers. Besides this the tribal people have inherent talent of handicraft. Making of baskets of different types, mat and rope-making, making of cord with twisted grass for cot weaving, manufacturing of agricultural equipment are some of their inherent talents. But the people do not commercialize their talent and prepare the things for their own needs. They also collect some forest wealth like fuel, fodder, timber and herbs for their own use. Fishing, the traditional occupation of the Tharus, still exists in the village. The people also raise some domestic animals like cow, ox and buffaloes. Thus the village economy is mainly agriculture-based. The education and occupational status of the villagers can be presented in the following Table 5.8.

Education and Occupational Status of the Tharus of Ratanpur Village

In order to present the occupational structure of the village, the total tribal population has been divided into different occupational groupings on the basis of their respective educational status. Since there is also dependent population within each of the occupational groupings, hence their population has been included separately in their respective occupational group. It is found that out of the total tribal population of Ratanpur village there are 567 people (i.e., 50.49 per cent) of the total population) who constitute the 'working population' while the rest 556 people (i.e., 49.57 per cent) are dependents. The dependent population generally consists of the pre-school, school going children and the population below 15 years of age plus above 60 years of age. It is observed that the major part of the working population, i.e., 66.12 per cent is of agriculturists while 5.99 per cent is of government servants, 1.77 per cent is of private servants, 7.24 per cent is of wage earners, 14.99 per cent is of wage-earners-cum-agriculturists, 0.18 per cent is of businessmen, 1.06 per cent is of agriculture cum service class persons and the remaining 2.65 per cent is of agriculture-cum-business class

Table 5.8. Education and Occupational Status of the Tharus in Ratanpur Village

Education	Sex	Agriculture	Service (Govt.)	Service (Pvt.)	Wage earning	Agri. Cum Wage-Earning	Business	Agri. Cum Service	Agri. & Busi.	Dependants: Agri.	Dependants: Govt. Service	Dependants: Pvt. Service	Dependants: Wage	Dependants: Business	Dependants: Agri.-wage earning	Dependants: Agri.-Ser.	Dependants: Agri.-Busi.	Total
Illiterate	Male	68	-	-	9	16	-	-	4	67	8	2	6	2	27	-	2	211
	Female	137	-	-	11	33	-	-	2	45	5	8	8	3	26	-	2	280
Primary	Male	34	01	01	4	8	-	-	2	46	1	4	-	-	19	3	3	126
	Female	48	-	-	8	8	-	-	2	40	12	3	4	-	12	3	1	141
Junior H.S.	Male	27	5	01	3	11	-	2	1	26	5	1	1	-	6	3	1	93
	Female	11	2	1	2	3	-	1	2	28	9	-	2	-	4	-	1	66
High School	Male	34	6	4	4	6	1	-	2	26	4	3	3	-	6	-	-	99
	Female	2	-	-	-	-	-	-	-	8	6	-	-	-	3	-	1	20
Inter-mediate	Male	9	9	3	-	-	-	3	-	8	2	-	1	-	2	-	3	40
	Female	4	-	-		-	-	-	-	8	2	-	1	-	2	-	-	16
Graduate	Male	01	11	-	-	-	-	-	-	4	4	-	-	-	2	-	1	23
	Female	-	-	-	-	-	-	-	-	-	2	-	1	1	1	-	-	05
Post-Graduate	Male	-	-	-	-	-	-	-	-	-	-	-	-	-	-	-	-	-
	Female	-	-	-	-	-	-	-	-	-	-	-	-	-	-	-	-	-
Others	Male	-	-	-	-	-	-	-	-	-	1	-	-	-	1	-	-	02
	Female	-	-	-	-	-	-	-	-	-	-	-	-	-	1	-	-	01
Total	Male	173	32	09	20	41	01	05	09	177	25	10	11	20	63	06	01	574
	Female	202	02	01	21	44	-	01	06	129	36	11	15	04	49	03	05	529
G. Total		375	34	10	41	85	01	06	15	306	01	21	26	06	112	09	15	1123
% of the Total		33.04	3.02	0.90	3.66	7.57	0.09	0.53	1.33	27.24	5.43	1.87	2.31	0.53	9.98	0.81	1.33	100 W
% of working Population		66.12	5.99	1.77	7.24	14.99	0.18	1.06	2.65	55.03	10.98	3.79	4.68	1.08	20.14	1.61	2.70	100 W

persons. Correspondingly out of the total dependent population the major percentage, i.e., 55.03 is of agriculturists' dependents, 10.98 per cent is of government servants, 3.78 per cent is of private servants, 4.68 per cent is of wage earners, 1.08 per cent is of business class, 20.14 per cent is of agriculturists-cum-wage-earners, 1.61 per cent is of agriculture-cum-service class and the rest 2.70 per cent dependents are related to agriculture-cum-business class families. The education-wise distribution of occupational groups also exhibit that the role of education in bringing about occupational transformation among the tribals cannot be termed as functional because in Ratanpur village even the major part of educated tribals subsists on agriculture. This trend appeals for some basic and fundamental changes in tribal education pattern so that it can present an alternate source of subsistence.

At present Ratanpur village is inhabited by 144 Tharu families. The first hand information depicts that 86 (59.72 per cent) Tharu families still live in Kachcha houses, 33 (22.91 per cent) live in pucca houses and the remaining 25 (17.36 per cent) have mixed type houses. This figure proves that mostly the tribal people of the village are still unable to afford the expenses to built pucca house. Any how they manage necessary materials for constructing their huts of traditional type. The wooden logs, grass, fine pond clay and the wooden sticks are used to construct the kachcha type of abode. While some affluent families have pucca houses made up of bricks, steel, cement, sand, gravel or crashed stone. Some medium-class families built-up mixed type of abodes. In such type of mixed abodes the wall remains of bricks, plastered over with the mud or fine clay of pond and the slopy roof is thatched over with wooden logs, wooden sticks and grass. Mostly all types of houses, have a common veranda and two or more rooms inside it. The oven is made in a corner of any room, or sometime within a separate hut but the people generally eat their meal in the veranda. Thus veranda is generally treated as a dining room where the people sit on their cots or mats and have their meal. The veranda is also used for sleeping purposes during summer while the inner-rooms of the house/hut is used for storing food-grains and other domestic items. But during winter these rooms are converted into bed rooms. Most of the families have separate cattle sheds. In general the houses, whatever their kind, are made in a row, or sometimes in round shape facing each other. The broad courtyard cleanly smeared with fine pond clay in front or amidst of the abodes serves their general necessity of storing the harvested crop for processing and also serves as threshing floor, singing and dancing place and feasting ground on the occasion of some festivals and other ritual ceremonies. Thus the Tharu families have built their abodes in a group which can be identified for a certain visible distance while their fields are scattered in different locations around or sometime very far from their abodes. Thus the group living also serves their needs of security from criminals and also from wild animals.

In fact, Tarai belt, the abode of the Tharus in general and the Ratanpur village in particular has been rich for natural resources. The level of the ground water remains nearer to ground surface. Hence there is abundance of drinking and irrigation water. For this purpose respectively hand-pumps and tube-wells are installed by the families themselves and also by the government. The fuel wood, fodder and building material can be obtained from the near by forests. The seasonal vegetables, fruits, herbs and tubers are also collected by the people from the jungles. In fact forest wealth fulfils most of the economic needs of the people. If we take into account the materials obtained from the forests we find that there are a number of varieties of vegetables collected by the people for their daily use. In rainy season the vegetables viz. Banmethi, Pathfura, Rampyare (a kind of mushroom), Narei, Lakura, Luchaka, Latfikari, Kewa etc. grow in abundance and the tribal people collect these vegetables for their daily use. There are herbs like Koro, roots of Bhanj, Banhardi, Bariyari, Chirchira, Harr, Behara, Peeper and Awanre etc. The Koro is used for the treatment of dysentery, roots of the Bhanj is used for the treatment of hot waves (Loo) during summer, Banhardi is used for the treatment of gouts, Bariyari-Chirchira is used for the treatment of snake bite, Anwara, Harr and Behara used for constipation while the peeper is used for cough and throat-related diseases. There are some fruits like Fursa, Anuwa, Kasam, Ber, Tensu and Khur-Hur which are collected by the tribals for their own use. The Tharus are inherently skilled in making mats, hand fans, cots and brooms. The material needed for these items are also collected by them from the nearby forests. The fibre of Bendu, Bebu and Moj is used for making ropes. The rope is used for knitting mats and cots while the Urai, Kans, Mirche, Motha, Chhamachha are used for making baskets of different types and brooms. Even agricultural equipments like plough, pata (leveller), Joo and handle of hoe, sickles, spade, axe, etc. are also made by the tribals themselves. For these purposes they collect the raw material from the forests. In the midst of the village there is a water-pond which serves their fishing needs. Thus the Ratanpur village has all the natural resources that can serve their basic needs.

Amidst the village there is a primary to junior high school level institution run by the government. It has three class-rooms, one principal's room and one staff-cum-school office room. On the outskirt of the school campus there are two toilets separately for males and females. Tape water and a hand pump serve the need of drinking water of the students and of the school staff. The total number of students in the current session is 195 out of which boys are 105 and girls are 90. If we take into consideration the classwise strength of the students we find that maximum number of students are in class one standard. As the standard of the class increases the number of the students decreases. In eighth class standard the total number of students is only 25. At present there are total 3 teachers in this school and the non-teaching staff includes only one fourth-class employee. The school has no library and reading-room facility. No doubt the teachers are qualified but the shortage of teachers causes disturbance in the study of students. However the approachable distance of the school attracts theTharu children and also presents an incentive to the parents for sending their children in the nearby school. The High-school and Intermediate college are located at Jhankat about 03 km. far from the village. This intermediate college is also run by the government of Uttaranchal. This college has its own school building with 06 class rooms, one principal room, one staff-cum-office room. There are facilities of toilets separately for male and female as well as of drinking water. This college has students from different villages as well as from different classes, communities and castes. But the representation of Tharu children is very discouraging. The college has total 5 teachers and 2 non-teaching staff. In the teaching staff there is one science teacher and the rest are arts teachers. The institution has a laboratory with inadequate equipment and other material needed for experiments. The non-teaching staff consists of a head clerk, a fee clerk and a peon but no sweeper is there. Hence the school surrounding and the toilets generally remain filthy and full of dirt. The teachers generally make the surrounding clean through school students under self help scheme. Some vocational courses are also run by the college. Students are taught on the courses prescribed by the Educational Board. The syllabus is of traditional pattern. It gives no better or multiple employment potential to students. Shortage of teaching staff, unbalanced student-teacher ratio, lack of proper infrastructural facilities and also the lack of vocational courses are some of the impediments which defeat the aim of the education. The undergraduate and post-graduate college are situated respectively at Khatima and Rudrapur about 14 km. and 68 km. far from the village. Since the Degree College is situated beside the motor road, students desirous to join the college and having their own conveyance or travelling capacity through rented vehicles can avail of this facility. The academic session-wise enrolment and the result of the Tharu children in different classes may present a picture of their response, receptivity and trend towards education:

Health and medicare system aim at providing medical and health related aid to the people and also has a target of achieving the goal of 'health for all' by 2000 A.D. Under this scheme a number of national programmes have been framed and launched by the Government of India. During field work, it is observed that the Tharus of Ratanpur village are known with some important programmes like, national family welfare programme, universal immunization programme, national malaria eradication programme, national tuberculosis programme, national leprosy control programme, school health programme and control of communicable disease programme etc. The people also express their reactions towards these programmes and about their implementation pattern and results. It is observed that mostly i.e. 65 per cent people are aware and satisfied with the national family welfare programme, 05 per cent are fully satisfied, 20 per cent are unsatisfied and the rest 10 per cent are uncertain. In this context, only the married couple were interviewed. The couples who have followed the national family welfare programme with its recognized means and methods only after having three and more children, express their satisfaction. They are of the opinion that during early years of their marital life they could not follow this family welfare programme and the means and methods of family planning, sometime in hesitation, sometime in passion and sometime due to the uncertainty of the survival of the begottens. When the size of the family enlarged with six and more members in all, i.e., the parents plus four or more children, then they plan to adopt the family planning. But it becomes too late to have the benefits of family planning programme. However, the people were happy for using the means and methods of family planning even after four children because it has helped them to stop further growth of the family size, simultaneously there was no interruption in conjugal love too. The five per cent couples, who are fully satisfied with national family welfare programme, accept that this programme has helped them to plan the family in a very proper manner. Each of those couples have only two children. They agreed that they were wedded after twenty-two years of age while their counterparts were above eighteen years of age. Besides this all of them are educated and well aware of the aims and objectives of family welfare programme and the use of various methods of family planning. Just after marriage they plan how to control the family size and how marital life can be enjoyed in a better and care-free manner. Resultantly they succeed. There are 19.5 per cent couples who are not satisfied with the family welfare programme and termed the family planning and its various methods unnatural and against the will of the almighty God. They are the traditional type of people and very conservative in their dealings. The birth and death, for them, are the portfolios controlled and operated by God. Any effort of intervening God's act is just a violation of God's will in which the guilty has to suffer. Those are the couples having largest family sizes. Besides this there are 10 per cent couple who are still uncertain about family welfare programmes, mainly about

Table 5.9. Academic Session-wise Enrolment of the Tharu Children in Different Classes in the Last Five Years

Academic Session	Position of the Students	Class/ Standard																										
		I	II	III	IV	V	VI	VII	VIII	IX	X	XI	XII	BA I	BSc I	B.Com I	BA II	BSc II	B.Com II	BA III	BSc III	B.Com III	MA I	MSc I	M Com I	MA II	MSc II	M Com II
1995-96	Enrolled	21	25	15	13	17	12	10	20	22	5	4	1															
	Droppers																											
	R 1st Div	-	1	1	-	1	-	-	1	-	-	-	-	-	-	-												
	E 2nd Div	13	16	10	11	13	9	5	9	3	3	3	1	1	-	-												
	S III rd	8	8	4	2	1	1	2	-	10	2	1	-	-	-	-												
	U Div																											
	L Fail	-	-	-	-	2	2	-	-	7	17	1	-	-	-	-												
	T																											
1996-97	Enrolled	15	13	16	12	13	14	19	17	17	20	6	4	-	-	-	1											
	Droppers							2																				
	R 1st Div							1																				
	E 2nd Div	15	13	16	12	13	13	14	17	13	3	2	2				1											
	S III rd	-	-	-	-	-	-	14	-	2	1	3	-															
	U Div																											
	L Fail	-	-	-	-	-	1	2	-	2	15	1	2															
	T																											
1997-98	Enrolled	13	11	14	13	15	11	16	11	25	23	6	5	3														
	Droppers	-	-	-	-	-	-	-	-	-	-	-	-	-	-													
	R 1st Div	-	-	-	-	-	-	-	-	-	-	-	-	-	-													
	E 2nd Div	12	11	14	10	10	9	10	5	13	5	2	2	2														
	S III rd	1	-	-	3	2	-	3	5	2	3	2	1	1														
	U Div																											
	L Fail	-		-	-	3	2	3	1	10	15	1	2	-	-	-	1											
	T																											

(Contd.)

(Contd. Table 5.9)

Academic Session	Position of the Students	Class/ Standard																										
		I	II	III	IV	V	VI	VII	VIII	IX	X	XI	XII	BA I	BSc I	B.Com I	BA II	BSc II	B.Com II	BA III	BSc III	B.Com III	MA I	MSc I	M Com I	MA II	MSc II	M Com II
1998-99	Enrolled	10	13	11	11	11	11	14	13	20	25	6	3	2	1			3										
	Droppers	-	-	-	-	-	-	-	-	-	-	-	-	-	-	-	-	-										
	R 1st Div	-	-	-	-	-	-	-	-	1	1	-	-															
	E 2nd Div	10	13	11	11	11	10	13	10	4	3	2	1					2										
	S III rd U Div	-	-	-	-	-	-	1	2	2	4	1	-	1				1										
	L Fail T	-	-	-	-	-	1	-	1	13	17	3	2	1	1													
1999-2000	Enrolled	11	11	12	13	13	12	12	12	19	20	6	5	3				1		3								
	Droppers	-	-	-	-	-	-	-	-	-	-	-	-	-	-													
	R 1st Div	-	-	-	-	-	-	-	-	-	-	-	-	-														
	E 2nd Div	11	11	11	10	10	10	10	10	10	5	5	2	1	11			1		2								
	S III rd U Div	-	-	-	2	3	2	1	-	-	2	-	-	2														
	L Fail T	-	-	-	1	-	-	1	2	9	13	1	3	-	-	-	-	-	-	-								

the use of various methods of family planning. They are basically silent, rather quite introvert type of people who just observe and enjoy in listening the things pertaining to the means and methods of family planning. They appear to be interested in knowing about the pros and cons, more accurately the negative aspects of family planning and are uncertain about it. However, if we calculate and analyse the things objectively, we come to the conclusion that most of the tribal people are aware of the family welfare programme and they are also aware about its benefits.

In case of universal immunization programme, most of the tribal people, i.e., 85 per cent express their full satisfaction while 5 per cent are satisfied and the rest 10 per cent are not in a position to react properly and show their uncertainly about this programme. In fact the medical department has made strict instructions to the primary health centres or sub-centres for the implementation of the vaccination programme against six vital diseases in their respective areas. The personnel of the primary health centres visit regularly in tribal villages and perform their duties. Sometimes special medical camps are also held there. The frequent visits of the concerned medical staff and the special medical camps have made the tribal people aware of the universal immunization programme against six vital diseases. Most of the tribal people of the village are also benefitted under this programme. However there are some cases of polio, about which, the case studies have been prepared and presented in the forthcoming chapters. It is observed that the carelessness of the people, their tendency of avoiding or concealing the things and their traditional pattern of treatment have been the main causes of polio and similar other vital diseases occurring in the village. In fact the tribal people in spite of being acquainted with these programmes just ignore the things and do not follow the medical practices in time, which sometimes results in polio and similar other vital diseases. Maternity and child health programme has no use in the tribal area. The health workers, mainly an 'ANM' visits the village whenever there is an emergency call from the villagers. On such occasions the ANM just asks the patients or the sufferers about the medical precautions and dietary system which a mother and the infant should take care of in their life. But the general awareness programme which is of prime concern has not been launched in the village. There is 'Malaria Control Centre' in Fulayya (a Majara of Ratanpur Fulayya village panchayat). This centre is mainly concerned with malaria eradication programme. In fact, the Tarai belt of Uttaranchal, which is regarded the most malaria prone belt is now almost free from malaria. There are hardly some exceptional cases of malaria positive. In such cases the malaria control centre plays a very functional role, with the result the Ratanpur village is almost free from malaria. It is the reason that 85 per cent villagers are fully satisfied with this programme and 5 per cent are satisfied while 10 per cent are uncertain and not in a position of responding the things. The people who are uncertain about malaria eradication programme have no experience of malaria fever hence they are not able to react about the programme meant for malaria eradication. At Primary Health Centre, Khatima (about 11 km. from Ratanpur village) has tuberculosis and leprosy control cell. The tribal people along with the general population have been benefitted from these programmes. Hence most of the tribal people, i.e., 85 per cent have expressed their full satisfaction with these programmes, while 5 per cent are satisfied and only 10 per cent are uncertain. Besides this the tribal people are also aware of school health programme as well as of the control of communicable disease programme. But they are of the opinion that both the programme are not in function these days. So far as the supply of safe drinking water, installation of sanitary latrines, improvement of dietary patterns and infant rearing practices are concerned mostly the Tharus of the Ratanpur village are not satisfied. The government has installed only two general community taps and Janta hand-pumps in the village which are insufficient to fulfil the needs of the people. The people of the village have therefore installed their own hand-pumps beside the courtyard. Mostly each family has its own handpump. But the people have no concern with sanitary latrines. Particularly the houses which are made under 'Indira Avas Yojana' have the provision of sanitary latrines but the people do not use these latrines. They prefer open grounds for evacuation purposes. Mostly agricultural fields, beside the roads and the barren land adjoining the pond are used for evacuation purposes. The people are very much traditional and follow their customary dietary pattern which can be termed as unsuitable from nutritional point of view. The people are used to rear and care for their infants in their own way. The instructions and suggestions made by the health workers during child-birth, have virtually no use for the mother and other family members. The traditional pattern of rearing and caring for the infants is effective till date. But the people have become very particular about the triple antigerms and the polio drops prescribed medically for the new-born children. The case study prepared about the polio patients also exhibits that these cases have been one to two or more decades old. In recent years mainly in the last decade no case of polio or polio-death was found in the village. In fact the old polio-cases which are still alive in the village have been functional for motivating the people to follow the medical practices for protecting their children from polio and other vital diseases.

The health and medicare system in the village is almost absent. The public health sector which chiefly consists of primary health care centres, hospitals, health insurance schemes etc. are not available in the village. The villagers approach the primary health centre located at Khatima, the block and Tehsil headquarters and find medical aid for their ailments. The primary health centre has full-fledged medical staff where the patients can have free medical investigations as well as treatment. But the medicines are not distributed free of cost. The private sector, which includes private hospitals, polyclinics, nursing homes, dispensaries, clinics and general medical practitioners etc. is also available only at Khatima. The rich Tharu tribals can avail this facility of private medicare system. The indigenous system of medicare which subsumes Ayurveda and Siddha, Unani, Tibbi, Homeopathy etc., partially exists at Khatima. But this system of medicare is not so popular among the tribals. In the village there are three unregistered medical practitioners with no degree or diploma in medical field. The patients preferably consult them in their ailments. These medical practitioners give treatment which has sometimes ill-effects on the patients. To get rid of this ill-treatment they follow exorcism-related practices. These practices go on and on with no positive results and the patients and their family members ultimately blame their own fate for the sufferings and leave the things on the almighty supernatural power. The case study of Mr. Vikki is a living example of this sort. In fact the distance of PHC, overcrowded patients, limited doctors, their treatment pattern, unavailability of medicine etc. are some of the factors which restrain the mind of the people from PHC. Rather, they prefer to consult the nearby medical practitioners who are always within their approach, who are known to them for a long time, give friendly treatment, enquire about one's welfare and thus give psychological treatment more than the desired medical treatment. This tactful handling always attracts the patients and instil confidence in them.

There is no voluntary health agency in Tharuwat area. Occasionally some Christian missionaries visit the tribal villages and give the medical treatment free-of-cost and sometime give economic aid to the needy people. But this sort of welfare services of the missionaries lead the process of religious conversion. Resultantly the people have become cautious about it and have now begun to avoid the welfare services of the missionaries. No NGO is in operation throughout the Tharuwat tribal area which is of urgent need provided it serves the people honestly.

The primary health care services which include health education, the promotion of proper nutrition, adequate and safe drinking water, proper sanitation, school health services, health appraisal of school children and school teachers with monthly checkup, remedial measures and follow up referral services, first-aid treatment of minor ailments by teachers etc. do not exist in the village only. Some health workers work for maternal and child health care, family planning and immunization programme through 'Angan Badi' institutions. But their services are felt insufficient by the villagers. The domestic and traditional exorcism practices are the first-aid treatment for all sorts of minor and major ailments. The practice of exorcism sometimes has adverse effects on the patients. For instance, whenever there is any cut wound in any organ of the body the people apply soil and try to check the bleeding. This sort of first-aid practice is more prone to tetanus. In snake bite cases the people follow exorcism and believe in sorcery rather than consulting the medical doctor. The act of sorcery sometime leads to death of the victim.

In fact health education, proper nutrition, use of adequate and safe drinking water, the sense of health, hygiene and sanitation, regular medical checkup are some of the prerequisites of a healthy life. But the Tharus have no sense of all these prerequisites. Health for them is 'fatness' or fleshly body which is possible only through stomach-full diet and frequent meal. There is no concept of safe drinking water and its use. They have locally installed hand-pumps as the source of drinking water. They use hand-pump water for all purposes and drink the water only to quench their thirst. Virtually they have no sense of pure or safe drinking water. The Tharus have no sense of proper sanitation. No awareness programme of this kind has been held so far in the village. People generally use their fields for discharging their excreta and make sit their children in front of their huts or houses for evacuation. Though the courtyard remains always clean washed with viscous soil, but during night the back portion of the hut gives the people a shelter and a safe place for urinal purposes. Virtually the urine is run over by the people while passing through there and reach their kitchens and bedrooms. Even the excreta discharged by children besides the nearby kitchen garden is also run over directly or indirectly by the people so reaches upto their kitchen and bedrooms. In this way the excreta and the disease germs are circulated between human body and the nature and become the cause of permanent diseases. This happens due to lack of sanitary and hygienic sense of the tribals. Maternal and child health care services are also not provided to the tribals. They lack proper understanding of maternal and child health care. In the absence of which the health condition of the mother and baby remain unhealthy. Even the school going children are not given proper health-related directions, practices and precautions during school time by health workers. No doubt the teachers do give some hygiene related instruction to students after morning prayer. And practically the students also follow the instructions and cut their nails, paste brush their teeth, wash their hands before and after meal. But these hygiene related instructions do never transform into habit and end with the end of schooling. During early nineties there was a provision of health appraisal of school children and of school teachers. For this purpose health workers of the nearest PHC were assigned the duties. Separate health cards were prepared of each child. They were provided necessary medical aid if needed so, and also provided nutritious food. Today in Ratanpur village school, these provisions are not in practice. Hence neither the minor nor major ailments are traced out timely nor any remedial measures and follow up referral services are carried out. In view of the present state of being the need of the hour is to implement the primary health services in tribal areas on priority basis. It will be functional for the whole of the mankind in general and for the tribals in particular to render the primary health care information through awareness programme and also through health workers to the people.

Hand-pumps are the main source of drinking water in Ratanpur village. Every family has its own hand pump at their own cost. There is no scarcity of drinking water in the village. There is also tap water facility in the village which serves the people as a subsidiary source of drinking water. A public stand post of tap water has also been put on beside the primary school, Ratanpur.

The tribal people of Ratanpur village generally use fire wood as fuel. Besides this cow-dung cakes, kerosene, LPG are also used by them. But there are only a few families who can afford kerosene and LPG but use it on some special and emergency occasions. In general days only fire-wood and cow-dung cakes are used for cooking and other purposes. The kerosene stove and LPG is treated as status symbol in the village. At present there are only 15 families who have LPG connections and 20 families have kerosene stoves. However, the families having LPC connection and kerosene stoves prefer the use of fire wood or cow-dung-cakes for cooking purposes because the taste of the items cooked in fire wood and cow-dung cakes is regarded comparatively more tasty as well as digestible. In fact it is merely an illusion and misunderstanding of the people. The same is the feeling in regard to the utilization pattern of advanced seeds, chemical fertilizers and insecticides. Today the Tharus of Ratanpur village use preferably these items in their agricultural operations. However, the organic manure and the traditional seeds prepared by the people themselves are also used. The tribal people are of the opinion that the organic manure and traditional seeds are better qualitatively as well as from the nutritional point of view. No doubt, there is scientific truth in their understanding but the cherished desire for better yield has motivated them to use advanced seeds, chemical fertilizers and insecticides. Some big tribal farmer have good yield and sell the surplus food-grains mainly wheat and paddy either to the Banjaras or in nearby Mandis and earn good benefit of it. This new agricultural system has made some tribal people better off in economic sector. Their housing condition, ownership of advanced agricultural equipment, other domestic goods and clothings etc. show their comparative prosperity in the village. This is of course the outcome of the pursuance of new agricultural pattern.

Since the emergence of community development scheme in India and particularly after 1967 when the Tharus were enlisted in the category of Scheduled Tribe, a number of rural/tribal development schemes have been formulated and launched in respective areas. As a link in the chain of various development schemes, there have been a number of employment generation schemes, viz. IRDP, JRY, REGS, REP, NREP, SFDA, MFALDA etc. for implementing in rural and tribal areas. In this regard the Tharus of the Ratanpur village responded that only some affluent people of the village have been benefitted with these schemes while the majority of the youths have been deprived so far. In fact the employment generation schemes have also some norms and conditions for the selection of the able candidate to train in some trade. But most of the illiterate tribal youths do not fulfil these norms and conditions and only for this very reason they have been unable in getting the benefits of these schemes.

In the village there is a fair price shop where only food-grains like wheat, rice and sugar and kerosene oil is distributed on concessional rates. The price of these items remains comparatively cheaper than in the open market. But there is no measurement of quality control. Even the available items are distributed according to units of the family, not according to the need of the people. Hence this fair price shop has no meaning even for the poor tribals. Generally the people are seen having kerosene and sugar of their share.

Ratanpur village is electrified. But the legal electric connections are very few throughout the village. The people still use kerosene oil lamps during night. The black smoke arising out of these lamps generally creates nosal and throat problems. In fact most of the problems related to education, health, hygiene and nutrition are due to lack of proper knowledge. The tribal people have neither any proper source of information nor they do feel its need. The newspapers, magazines and other written literature have no meaning for the illiterate and ignorant tribals. Today they have radio sets and television but they do not prefer to listen/view the education, health and hygiene related information and news. Most of their time is spent either in listening musical songs, seeing dramas or viewing pictures etc. The NGOs, media persons and health workers can have functional roles in imparting proper knowledge and information about education, health, hygiene and nutrition but these units are almost non-existent in tribal area. Hence awareness and awakening campaigns are a must for achieving the desired goal of literacy and health.

The village is well established in a plain Tarai area and linked to motorable roads to the nearest market place Jhankat about 3 km.

distance, block and tehsil headquarters, Khatima is about 11 kms. distance and district headquarter, Rudrapur about 68 kms distance. The post and telegraph facilities are available only at Jhankat and Khatima respectively. Thus the Ratanpur Tharu village having all the basic amenities in progress and within reach can be termed as a developing village inhabited by backward and ignorant people.

The villagers grow wheat, maize, barley, gram, lentil (Masoor), 'Bakula', millet, paddy, mustard and *linseed.* Correspondingly cooked rice, chapati (wheat) and bread (millet, maize, barley) are the main food items of the Tharus. Lentil, gram and Bakula are the pulses they grow and eat. Mustard and linseed oil is used by them. The people are habitual of having tea at morning time. Even they welcome visitors with tumblerful of tea. The families having milching cattle like cow, goat and buffalo also take milk and milk products like buttermilk, curd, ghee etc. Otherwise there is no compulsion and no regular use of milk and milk products. Even the infants and children are deprived of milk in early days of their life due to the non- availability of the milk and milk products in the family. There is hardly a tradition of buying and selling milk and milk products by the villagers. May be there a plenty of milk, they prefer and like to give it to their neighbourers or the needy akins free of cost but do not charge any price. There is only a 'beverage', i.e., wine/ liquor (Daru) which is compulsorily bought by the people. Because the Tharus (male) are habitual of taking liquor regularly even if they had to sell their land or any domestic utensils or agricultural equipments. In general they spend a good amount of their income in liquor and other intoxicated drugs like charas, hemp and 'Bhang'. They also have bidi, cigarettes and tobacco. The Rai-Sikhs, living amidst the adjoining Tarai forests or on the outskirts of the Tharuwat area (towards forests) are the brewers and suppliers of liquor and the Tharus are the main consumers of it. Charas, hemp and Bhang is grown, consumed and sold by the Tharus themselves.

Basaya—The Khasa Village

Jaunsar-Bawar is almost synonym of a peculiar polyandrous community known as the Khasas. A generic term 'Jaunsari' is also used to denote this community. At present the whole of the Khasa community with 81,900 population is scattered over 356 villages of Chaukrata and Kalsi Blocks of Dehradun District in Uttaranchal. The Khasa is the biggest tribal group of Uttaranchal. It constitutes 38.78 per cent part of the total tribal population of Uttaranchal. The peculiarity of the Khasa community lies in its socio-cultural and economic system. The ecology of Jaunsar-Bawar has its impact on the culture of the Khasa community which is visible as a testimony in the behaviour patterns of the Khasas on different occasions. To a large extent the basic amenities like education, health, hygiene and nutrition have deep concern with its ecology. In this very context an effort has been made for elaborating the study area, its geography, infrastructural conditions and also the demographic nature. So that the educational, health, hygiene and nutritional status of the population can be enumerated more accurately and scientifically.

In fact Basaya, the Khasa village as a whole, has been purposefully selected for the study. Basaya is basically a village-panchayat which is divided into four small villages called 'Tok' or Majara. In other words we can define it as the village panchayat of four villages, namely, the Masrar, the Lolo, the Basaya and the Garaita. The Chauhans, Das (Vermas) and Nais are the main inhabitant sub-caste groups of this village-panchayat.

This village has an area of 865.825 square hectare land. Masrar is geographically the largest Tok with 316.310 square hectare land which is followed respectively by Basaya with 210.323 square hectare land, Lolo with 165.895 square hectare land and Garaita with 173.297 square hectare land. Out of the total area maximum 479.943 square hectare (55.43 per cent) land is barren. The total cultivable land is only 126.673 square hectare (14.63 per cent) out of which 99.04 per cent is irrigated and 0.06 per cent is unirrigated. Out of the total area 190.375 (21.98 per cent) is a forest land and 2.492 square hectare (0.28 per cent) land is used for residential purposes. While the rest 66.342 square hectare land (7.67 per cent) is a waste land. The Basaya village is located at the elevation of 3300' from the sea level and surrounded by Bhairath Khai in east, Panwa gram in west, Sawani gram or Charani Danda in north and Gauthan and Hamaru gram in south. The Basaya village falls within Chakrata Tehsil of Dehradun district. The distance of the village from the district headquarters Dehradun is about 80 km. The Tehsil headquarters Chakrata is located at the distance of 20 km. from the village and Kalsi the block headquarters is located about 28 km. from the village. 'Sahaya' is the local market for the villagers which is located about 10 km. from the village. Though the village comes under the purview of revenue police, i.e., Patwari area, yet the nearest police station is located at 'Sahaya' about 10 km. from the village. The Post Office is located at a distance of 3 km. from the village at Datanu, Public health sub-centre is located at the distance of 1 km. at Sahaya while a Government Ayurvedic Hospital is located at Datanu about 3 km. from the village while a private hospital is located in Sahaya about 10 km. from the village. The primary level education is imparted at village level through primary schools located at Basaya and Masrar. There is only a Junior High School in 'Basaya' while the high school and Intermediate college is located at 'Sahaya' about 10 km. from the village. There is a Govt. Degree College with single faculty of Commerce at Dak Patthar about 35 km. from the village. Postgraduate colleges are located in the

District headquarters Dehradun now the capital of newly formed Uttaranchal state. Other facilities of technical education are available only at Dehradun. The persons desirous of having education of high school level and above are required to have a rented room nearby the educational institutions because the daily 'up and down' and travel such a long distance is not possible for them.

According to primary census survey made by the investigator, the total population of the Basaya village is 924 out of which 487 are male and 437 are female. Out of the total male population 214 (41.40 per cent) are illiterate while the rest 48.60 per cent male population is literate. Among the females 303 (58.60 per cent) are illiterate and the rest 41.40 per cent are literate. The age and sex wise educational standard of the Khasas of the Basaya village is displayed in the following Table 5.10.

It is obvious that the overall literacy among the Khasas, i.e., 55.96 per cent of the study area is still far away from the national goal of literacy. Among the literates the maximum percentage is of those people who are educated upto primary standard. Nevertheless the literacy percentage among the Khasa females is very poor. Because 69.33 per cent Khasa females are still illiterate. The ecological background and undeveloped infrastructural facilities and the prevailing poverty among the people are responsible for this poor standard of literacy. The economy of the people is more or less primitive type. So far, only 3.47 per cent persons of the Basaya village are employed in different Govt. Services, while 0.88 per cent are engaged in private sectors. The rest of the population is following wage-earning, agriculture, small scale business or animal husbandry. Generally, it is observed that the people of Basaya are performing crude type of terrace farming and its supplementary occupations like animal husbandry and agricultural labour etc. The poor agricultural yield, pressure of dependent population and the lesser percentage of unskilled working population are the main reasons of poverty in the area. The age distribution of the total Khasa population of the study area also exhibits that only 47.61 per cent population is in working position while the rest 52.39 per cent is dependent population. The following Table 5.11 shows the education and occupational status of the Khasas of Basaya village.

Basaya, the Khasa village of Jaunsar Bawar, is located in the cis-Himalayan system. The land is rugged and hilly with small patches of plain land. It is surrounded by forests. Hence the climatic conditions cannot be termed favourable for human beings. However the Khasas living for a long time in this region experience and face the adverse impacts of the climate drastically uneven throughout the year. As there is bitter cold during winter due to snowfall, but the summers are hotter. During rainy season, there are heavy rains which resulted in heavy

Table 5.10. Age and Sex-Wise Educational Standard of the Khasas of Basaya

Age Group	Sex	Illiterate/ Pre-School	Primary & Preprimary	Junior High School	High School	Inter - mediate	Under-Graduate	Post-Graduate	Others	Total	Grand Total %
0-5	M	66	16	-	-	-	-	-	-	82	167 (18.08)
	F	71	14	-	-	-	-	-	-	85	
5-10	M	12	51	-	-	-	-	-	-	63	133 (14.40)
	F	26	44	-	-	-	-	-	-	70	
10-15	M	07	20	20	08	-	-	-	-	55	94 (10.18)
	F	12	06	17	04	-	-	-	-	39	
15-20	M	05	02	07	21	08	01	-	-	44	84 (9.09)
	F	17	06	07	05	04	01	-	-	40	
20-25	M	08	11	04	04	04	02	02	01	36	80 (8.65)
	F	33	07	-	-	01	-	03	-	44	
25-30	M	14	04	07	03	09	02	02	-	41	75 (8.11)
	F	26	04	02	-	01	-	01	-	34	
30-35	M	17	05	04	-	08	01	-	-	35	59 (6.35)
	F	23	-	-	01	-	-	-	-	24	
35-40	M	16	07	03	01	02	01	01	-	31	54 (5.84)
	F	19	02	01	-	-	-	01	-	23	
40-45	M	09	03	01	-	-	01	-	-	14	21 (2.28)
	F	07	-	-	-	-	-	-	-	07	

(Contd.)

(Contd. Table 5.10)

Age Group	Sex	Illiterate/ Pre-School	Primary & Preprimary	Junior High School	High School	Inter- mediate	Under- Graduate	Post- Graduate	Other	Total	Grand Total %
45-50	M	09	04	02	02	02	-	-	01	20	43 (4.65)
	F	22	01	-	-	-	-	-	-	23	
50-55	M	08	04	-	-	-	-	-	-	12	20 (2.17)
	F	07	01	-	-	-	-	-	-	08	
55-60	M	08	03	-	-	-	-	-	-	11	25 (2.07)
	F	14	-	-	-	-	-	-	-	14	
60-65	M	35	05	-	02	01	-	-	-	43	69 (7.46)
	F	26	-	-	-	-	-	-	-	26	
Total	M	214 (41.04%)	135 (61.36%)	48 (64%)	41 (80.40%)	34 (85%)	08 (98.89%)	05 (50%)	02 (100%)	487 (52.70%)	927 (100.0)
	F	303 (58.60%)	85 (38.64)	27 (36%)	10 (19.60%)	06 (15%)	01 (1.11%)	05 (50%)	00	437 (47.30%)	
Grand Total %		517 (100.00) 55.96	220 (100.00) 23.81	75 8.11	51 (100.00) 5.52	40 (100.00) 4.32	09 (100.00) 0.98	10 (100.00) 1.09	02 (100.00) 0.21	924 (100.00) 100.00	

Table 5.11. Education and Occupation Status of the Khasas of Basaya Village

Education	Sex	Agriculture	Service (Govt.)	Service (Pvt.)	Wage earning	Agri. Cum Wage-Earning	Business	Agri. Cum Service	Agri. cum Business	Dependants								Total
										Agri.	Govt. Service	Pvt. Service	Wage earning	Agri. cum Wage earner	Agri. Ser.	Business	Agri cum Busi.	
Illiterate	Male	38	-	01	06	72	-	01	-	36	04	04	02	46	02	02	-	214
	Female	83	-	-	01	85	02	-	-	34	18	03	04	67	02	04	-	303
Primary	Male	24	-	-	04	23	02	-	01	32	09	03	02	32	02	01	-	135
	Female	07	-	-	-	07	-	-	01	22	13	01	-	27	04	03	-	85
Junior H.S.	Male	10	-	-	02	11	-	01	01	10	05	-	-	07	-	-	01	48
	Female	01	-	-	-	02	-	-	-	04	07	-	02	01	01	-	-	27
High School	Male	04	04	02	02	-	-	01	-	10	02	-	01	14	01	-	-	41
	Female	-	-	-	-	02	-	-	-	04	02	-	-	02	-	-	-	10
Inter-mediate	Male	-	18	04	01	03	-	01	-	04	-	01	-	02	-	-	-	34
	Female	-	-	-	-	-	-	-	-	02	03	-	-	-	01	-	-	06
Graduate	Male	-	06	-	-	-	-	-	-	-	-	-	-	02	-	-	-	08
	Female	-	-	-	-	-	-	-	-	-	-	-	-	01	-	-	-	01

(Contd.)

(Contd. Table 5.11)

Education	Sex	Agriculture	Service (Govt.)	Service (Pvt.)	Wage earning	Agri. Cum Wage-Earning	Business	Agri. Cum Service	Agri. & Busi.	Dependants								
										Agri.	Govt. Service	Pvt. Service	Wage earning	Agri. cum Wage earner	Agri. Ser.	Business	Agri cum Busi.	Total
Post-Graduate	Male	-	01	01	-	-	-	01	-	-	-	01	-	01	-	-	-	05
	Female	-	01	-	-	-	-	-	-	01	03	-	-	-	-	-	-	05
Others	Male	-	02	-	-	-	-	-	-	-	-	-	-	-	-	-	-	02
	Female	-	-	-	-	-	-	-	-	-	-	-	-	-	-	-	-	00
Totai	Male	76	31	08	15	109	02	05	02	92	20	09	05	105	05	03	01	487 (52.70%)
	Female	91	01	00	01	96	02	00	01	67	46	04	06	107	08	07	00	437 (47.30%)
Grand Total		167	32	08	16	205	04	05	05	159	66	13	11	211	13	10	01	924 (100%)
% of the Total		18.08	3.47	0.88	1.73	22.19	0.43	0.54	0.32	17.20	7.14	1.40	1.20	22.83	1.40	1.09	0.10	100.00
% of working Population		440 (47.61%)								484 (52.39%)								

landslides and land erosions. During May and June there is sometime heavy fall of hailstones too. In all, the climatic conditions of this area cannot be considered as favourable for agriculture. It is the reason that the economy of the people is almost of primitive type. They perform crude type of terrace farming, supplemented by animal husbandry and wage earning. Most of the economic needs are fulfilled by the people themselves. The Khasas have an inherent talent of making some handicrafts pertaining to their daily needs. They collect raw wool from sheep and weave and knit woollen yarn for making woollen stuffs for their own use. The people manufacture agricultural implements for their own use. They can make different type of baskets for daily use. They also gather some seasonal fruits and vegetables from the nearby jungles. Kafal, Kasamai, Kirmoda, Aachhu, Fedu etc. are some of the seasonal fruits gathered by the people.

The Khasas of the Basaya village live mostly in pucca and mixed type of houses. The pucca houses are built of stone bricks, pasted with mud. The roof is made up of wooden logs thatched over by black-stone slates. The pucca houses are generally two-storied. The mixed type of houses are almost identical to that of pucca houses but the only difference is of the roof. The roof of the mixed houses are generally thatched over by grass. The ground floor is used to keep tamed animals like goat, sheep, buffalos, cows and oxen while the first floor of the house is used by the family. It is the first floor that has kitchen, bed rooms and sitting-rooms. In other words we can say all the familial activities are performed in the first floor of the house.

The village surrounding is endowed with natural resources. For instance the villagers can have fuel-wood, fodder, building material etc. from the nearby forests. Besides this they can also have herbs and tubers from the forests. A peculiar tuber called 'Hatnoi' is collected by the villagers for making liquor for their daily use. They collect 'Ningal' for making baskets, 'Bhemal sticks' for lighting during night, Devdar for making wooden staff of the house. Thus we see all the natural resources needed by the villagers for their daily needs are available in the surrounding and nearby forests of the village.

The village is still deprived of various infrastructural facilities. There are two primary schools and a junior high school in the village. The schools have their own pucca buildings but the number of class-rooms is inadequate in comparison to the classes run in the schools. Resultantly there are some classes which are run in the open ground of the school. The schools lack chairs and tables for the students. Hardly a pair of chair and table is available for the principal or headmaster and other teachers. Even the mats are not available for all the students. The students just bring gunny bags or their pieces with them for their own sitting purposes. Both the primary schools have no complete teaching staff. Each school has only one teacher for teaching five classes. Whenever the teacher goes on leave or remains absent from his duty the school is closed till the teacher comes back. At the junior high school there were 'Shikshya Mitra' appointed by the BJP government which are now terminated by the new Congress government. Resultantly the only junior high school of the village is run by a single teacher. The school has no provision of a library or reading room, play ground, toilets etc. A water tap has been installed for drinking water purposes. But the upkeeping pattern of drinking water 'stand post' is quite unhygienic. There is filth and rubbish all around the stand-post. There is no incentive for the school going children. No awareness programme is launched for motivating parents for sending their children to schools. A state of general vacuum, despair and apathy is observed among the people towards education. It is the reason of poor enrolment of students in different classes. During our field work, we tried to enumerate the strength of the students in different classes in the last five years. We observed that the number of students in different classes in different years are chronologically increase the year-wise enrolment of students in comparison to the village population is comparatively lesser.

The Khasa village has no facility of health and medicare services. There is only a sub-primary health centre where an ANM is posted for providing primary medical aid and also to run the government schemes particularly family planning. There are some programmes viz. the national family welfare programme, universal immunization programme, maternity and child health care programme, malaria eradication programme, tuberculosis programme, national leprosy control programme, school health programme, control of communicable diseases programme etc., which were put before the village head and other villagers just to know about their awareness and reactions. It is observed that the common villagers are still ignorant of most of the programmes except family planning and some vaccination programme. The receptivity of the villagers towards family planning was almost nil. It is so because the Khasas of the study area are very conservative and traditional. They are God-fearing and not in a position of violating the natural processes. For them the conceptions, births and deaths are the natural processes and governed by the supernatural being. Any action against God's will may harm them. This sort of notion has always put a constraint on the way of receiving the family planning programme. Hence almost all the people are uncertain to express their views about the programmes as mentioned above. The people responded that the 'Swajal' Yojana do have positive role in running awareness programme for the last three years. With the result there is improvement in drinking water supplies. Besides this the people were also asked about the installation of sanitary latrines but they were not in favour of such system. Because they are used to follow their age old pattern of evacuation process on the one hand, and, on the other hand the problem of cleaning the latrine-pot and its surrounding is the main constraint that prevents the installation of sanitary latrines in or outside the house. Similarly, the improvement of dietary pattern and infant-rearing practices have no meaning for the Khasas. They have their own dietary pattern as well as the infant-rearing practices. The lactating mother follows the pattern of rearing and caring of the infant as experienced by her since birth. The ANM who casually visits the village and gives some precautionary suggestions to the mothers as per medical point of view are not followed, rather neglected with this notion that their age-old ways observed in the community are tested, accepted, followed and have always good results. The new ways suggested by the ANM are new and no one dare to take risk of following them.

The health and medicare system exist in the village and its approachable distance is not adequate and up to the mark. There is only an ANM centre in Basaya village with no first-aid medical facility. Casually a homoeopathic physician visits the village. The villagers stated that the doctor provides them some type of sweet pills which the children and the people suffering from different diseases take as sweets. Thus the Khasa village is deprived even of the primary health care services and necessary medical facilities. Unregistered medical practitioners are available at a distance of about 10 km. at Datanu and also in 'Sahiya' - the nearest market place of the village. The needy people visit those doctors on foot. The primary health care services which include health education, promotion of proper nutrition, adequate and safe drinking water, proper sanitation, maternal and child health care, family planning, immunizatiom programme, prevention and control of endemic diseases, school health services, health appraisal of school children etc. are absolutely absent in the village and do not have any meaning for them. It is the reason that the Khasa people of the study area still cling to their age-old traditional moorings and are very much orthodox in their thinking, dealings and behaviour.

Drinking water is another basic amenity for mankind. The Basaya village has a tap water facility for drinking water. From a distance of about 1 km., a pipeline supplies the drinking water from its natural source. There is a water tank built up amidst the village. It works as water reservoir. The villagers use it for drinking, bathing and even for cattle drinking purposes. None of the viilagers has his own water connection in his house. Fire wood, cow-dung-cakes, kerosene are used as fuel for cooking and other purposes. The people don't know about LPG and other recent sources of energy. There is no electricity in the village.

Electric poles are installed throughout the village but without electric wire. The villagers told that the work of electrification is approved by the government and is in process. The people are not prone to advanced pattern of agriculture. There is a government provision of subsidised advanced seeds, chemical fertilizers, insecticides etc. for the farmers, but the people do not dare to take risk of sowing advanced seeds and using chemical fertilizers in their fields. Even today they grow their own traditional crops and prepare seeds which have quality but not better yield. They use organic manure. No doubt some villagers have started to use fertilizers like Urea, DAP and insecticides in the cultivation of some tubers like ginger and turmeric. It was observed that they were satisfied with the yield produced after the use of the fertilizers. Some other villagers were then interviewed and asked that the people who used fertilizers and insecticides got better yield so why they do not use the same. In response to this question they replied that they can not afford the buying of the things because they are poor. In fact the people on the one hand, are ignorant and on the other hand, they are poor. This state of being has made the people lethargic towards advanced pattern of agriculture.

Since Independence the Govt. of India has an objective of rural development with the execution of different development planning with some incentives. For the tribals some more provisions are made so that the tribals can be benefitted and brought in the mainstream of the society. In this very context information were collected from the study group about the impact of various rural development schemes and also of the employment generation schemes. It was found that the villagers in general have been over burdened with debt taken from government against different schemes. They are at the verge of attachment of their property for repaying the government loan. Even the employment generation scheme could not bring relief to the unemployed youths of the village. Yet, there is certainly infrastructural development of the village. For instance, some footpaths have been constructed, a water supply pipeline has been spread out, primary school building has been renewed and electric poles have been erected to and fro. The rural development schemes like IRDP, JRY, REGS, REP, NREP, and self-help group schemes could not produce desired results.

The public distribution scheme through fair price shop is available in the village. The villagers can have foodgrains like wheat, rice as per Govt. norms directly from the Government ration shop. They can also have sugar and kerosene from the same shop on concessional rate. But the quantity of the foodgrains as well as of kerosene and sugar is limited and provided on the basis of the units of the family. Thus the villagers cannot have the food items and other goods as per their requirements from the fair price shops.

The villagers have no effective source of education, health, hygiene and nutrition related information. The newspapers, magazines have no meaning for the illiterate people living in a remote area. Even the Khasa village is far from the range of Television. The Radio is the only means of information but the illiterate people prefer to listen music programmes through radio. In the village there are hardly ten families having radio sets. Some personnel related to 'Swajal Yojana' have tried to launch an awareness programme but the adverse living conditions of the village do not sustain this endeavour of public interest. In fact the village is linked to 10 km. long bridle path from *Saiya.* A person willing to approach the village has to walk on foot for about 10 km. distance. When he reaches the village, he can not get even water, tea, breakfast, meal and shelter that can make possible his stay in the village. For all these purposes he will have to live on the mercy of the villagers. The villagers are no doubt very kind and helpful but they have their own limitations. How long can they afford the hospitality of the uninvited guests in hardship? On the contrary the person visiting purposefully the village has also his limitations of managing the things of daily needs in some unknown place. This deed, actually, need devotion, endurance and forbearance which the personnel of Govt. or non-Govt. agencies lack completely in the present day times. It is the reason that any awareness programme that can make the villagers acquainted with the basic amenities of human life has been a failure. In fact the village is aloof and cut off from road communication. The villagers can have bus services only after travelling 10 kms. on foot to approach block, tehsil and district headquarters. Even the postal service is available at a distance of 5 km. in Datanu. Thus we observe that the Khasa village under study is lacking every infrastructural facility of human life.

The Khasas are used to lead their life with the consumption of their age-old staple food-grains, pulses, oil seeds even beverages both alcoholic and narcotic produced by themselves. The coarse staple food like maze, barley, Maduwa, Jhingur, Kabari, Chuwa, are the main agricultural products of the villagers. Wheat and paddy are also cultivated but the yield remains very poor. The people make 'Roti' (Chapati) of the coarse grain— maduwa (Kodo), barley, maize at morning and evening (in Kalewa and dinner). The midday meal (lunch) consists mainly of a special cooked item called Kabari and Jhinjur Bhat, and a kind of adhesive prepared of the maduwa floor or maize floor cooked in buttermilk. Rajma, Masoor, Gahat (Kulthi), Urd, Bhat 'Frasbean' are the major pulses grown by the villagers. These pulses are cooked in different ways by the people during breakfast, lunch and dinner. The Khasa is basically a pastoral community. They rear tamed animals as to produce milk and milk products mainly 'Ghee'. The milk, curd, buttermilk are the main beverages they consume in their daily life. While the liquor made up of Maduwa and barley is brewed by themselves for their own use. The people also produce Tobacco, Bhang and Ganja for their own use. Thus, whatever they produce and whatever the quantity remains, they try to manage the things as to keep their body and soul together. In this way we observe a kind of self-sufficiency among the Khasas of the study area, even today they fulfil their needs sometimes through barter system and sometimes through local loaning of goods may be that a foodgrain, Ghee, milk, salt or pulses. In other words we can say that there is a sort of cooperative pattern observed by the people for the satiation of their basic needs.

Sample Profile

The heads of the families of the tribals under study have been sampled purposefully for study. An interview schedule as a tool for collecting first-hand information directly from the interviewees was prepared and administered on them. Our main objective was to gather general information about education, health, hygiene and nutrition of the tribal communities in general and that of the family and its members in particular. For this purpose a variety of questions regarding different aspects of the interviewee, his family and the community as a whole were structured and included in the schedule. The schedule mainly consists of the questions regarding to the introduction of the respondent, its family profile, health profile of the family members, socio-religious and environmental dimensions of health, toilet pattern, environmental and domestic hygiene, sanitary system, disposal of human excreta and other solid and liquid wastes and lastly the food habits etc. In this chapter only the sample structure which chiefly consists of the introductory information, i.e., the age and sex distribution of the interviewee and his marital, educational and occupational status and also his family profile is being presented. It is assumed that the age and sex dichotomy, marital status, education standard, occupational status and the family profile (i.e., the type of the family, size of the family, environment of the family, its economy etc.) have deep concern and positive correlation with health, hygiene and nutrition. With this hypothetical proposition in mind the tribe-wise analysis of the sample profile will be helpful in understanding the real and authentic picture of the samples. Besides this the persons suffering from any kind of morbidity particularly at the time of the field work have also been taken purposefully for study. For the study of such persons a 'Nutrition assessment interview schedule' was framed and administered on the study units. Among the Buxas we traced out eighteen persons who were ill for a long time. The description of such units has been presented separately in the forthcoming chapters.

Sample Profile : the Buxa Tribe

The total population of the Buxas of Bannakhera-Majara-Bhudi is 485 which is distributed in 96 families. Since the head of the family has been the unit of the study. Hence the total number of the respondents in the case of the Buxa tribe is only 96. The Buxa tribe is a patriarchal, patrilineal and patrilocal community. The eldest male member of the family is therefore regarded as the head (Mukhiya) of the family. Only in the case of sudden death of the eldest male member or in the absence of the male head, the eldest female, provided the rest male members are minor or very junior in age and relation to the eldest female, performs the duties of the head of the family in practical. Theoretically the next male member is regarded as the head of the family. As soon as he becomes senior and liable to perform the liability of the family he then holds practically the status of the head of the family. During our field work we found that there are 94 families with male heads while only two families had female heads. The female heads are widows and respectively 27 and 39 years of age. They have their small family of minor children. Both the females are illiterate and earn their livelihood through agricultural pursuits. Out of the total 96 Buxa respondents 59.38 per cent are illiterate, 29.27 per cent are educated upto primary standard, 7.29 per cent are upto junior high school, 3.12 per cent are up to high school and only one (i.e., 1.04 per cent) Buxa youth is educated upto post-graduate level. It is surprising the post-graduate youth is also unemployed and earning his livelihood as a daily wage labourer. In the village, most of the heads of the family, i.e., 54.16 per cent are agriculturists, 4.16 per cent have private service, only one (i.e., 1.05 per cent) is a government servant, 39.58 per cent are daily wage labourers and one (i.e., 1.05 per cent) is a businessman of small scale. If we calculate age-wise education standard of the people, we come to the conclusion that with the increasing of the age limit the educational standard correspondingly decreases. In the new generations the prevalence of education is comparatively more. However the education related facts prove that the National Policy of Complete Literacy by 2000 A.D. is far from its goal. The majority of the Buxas are still illiterate. It is evident from the Table 5.13.

The facts shown in Table 5.13 exhibit age and sex-wise marital, educational and occupational status of the family heads of the Buxas of Majara Bhudi Bannakhera village. An effort has also been made to correlate education with occupational status of the Buxas of the study area. The data pertaining to this cause are shown in the Table 5.14.

The data do not reflect any particular trend in regard to the correlation between educational and occupational status. It can be viewed as an exceptional case because the illiterate as well as the post-graduate youth earn their living either by agricultural pursuits or by daily wage earning.

Table 5.13. Sample Profile of the Buxa Respondents

Age Group	Sex	Marital Status			Educational Status								Occupational Status			
		Married	Widow	Widower	Illiterate	Primary	J. High School	High School	Inter-mediate	Under-Graduate	Post-Graduate	Agricul-ture	Service Private	Service Govt.	Labour	Business
<25	M	02	-	-	01	-	-	-	-	-	01	-	-	-	-	-
	F	-	-	-	-	-	-	-	-	-	-	-	-	-	-	-
25-30	M	15	-	-	05	06	02	02	-	-	-	03	02	-	10	-
	F	-	01	-	01	-	-	-	-	-	-	01	-	-	-	-
30-35	M	16	-	-	09	06	-	01	-	-	-	06	-	01	08	01
	F	-	-	-	-	-	-	-	-	-	-	-	-	-	-	-
35-40	M	16	-	-	04	07	05	-	-	-	-	05	02	-	09	-
	F	-	01	-	01	-	-	-	-	-	-	01	-	-	-	-
40-45	M	16	-	-	11	05	-	-	-	-	-	11	-	-	05	-
	F	-	-	-	-	-	-	-	-	-	-	-	-	-	-	-
45-50	M	06	-	01	05	02	-	-	-	-	-	05	-	-	02	-
	F	-	-	-	-	-	-	-	-	-	-	-	-	-	-	-
50-55	M	03	-	-	03	-	-	-	-	-	-	02	-	-	01	-
	F	-	-	-	-	-	-	-	-	-	-	-	-	-	-	-
55-60	M	04	-	-	-	03	01	-	-	-	-	03	-	-	-	-
	F	-	-	-	-	-	-	-	-	-	-	-	-	-	-	-
60-65	M	05	-	-	04	04	-	-	-	-	-	05	-	-	-	-
	F	-	-	-	-	-	-	-	-	-	-	-	-	-	-	-
65-70	M	03	-	01	04	-	-	-	-	-	-	04	-	-	-	-
	F	-	-	-	-	-	-	-	-	-	-	-	-	-	-	-
70 & above	M	06	-	-	06	-	-	-	-	-	-	06	-	-	-	
	F	-	-	-	-	-	-	-	-	-	-	-	-	-	-	-
Total		92	02	02	57	28	07	03	-	-	01	52	04	01	38	01
	%	95.84	2.08	2.08	59.38	29.17	7.29	3.12	-	-	1.04	54.16	4.16	1.05	39.58	1.05

Table 5.14. Education and Occupational Status of the Buxa Respondents

Education	Sex	Agriculture	Service		Business	Wage earning	Total		Grand Total	Per cent
			Govt.	Pvt.			Male	Female		
Illiterate	M	34	-	-	-	21	55	-	57	(59.37)
	%	59.65	-	-	-	36.85	96.50	-	100.00	
	F	02	-	-	-	-	-	02	-	-
	%	3.50	-	-	-	-	-	3.50	100.00	
Primary	M	13	-	-	01	14	28	-	28	(29.16)
	%	46.42	-	-	3.58	50.00	100.00	-		
	F	-	-	-	-	-	-	-	-	-
	%	-	-	-	-	-	-	-	-	-
Junior H. School	M	03	02	-	-	02	07	-	07	(7.30)
	%	42.84	28.58	-	-	28.58	100.00	-	-	-
	F	-	-	-	-	-	-	-	-	-
	%	-	-	-	-	-	-	-	-	-
High School	M	-	02	01	-	-	03	-	03	(3.12)
	%	-	66.67	33.33	-	-	100.00	-	-	-
	F	-	-	-	-	-	-	-	-	-
	%	-	-	-	-	-	-	-	-	-

(Contd.)

(Contd. Table 5.14)

Education	Sex	Agriculture	Service		Business	Wage earning	Total		Grand Total	Per cent
			Govt.	Pvt.			M	F		
Intermediate	M	-	-	-	-	-	-	-	-	-
	%	-	-	-	-	-	-	-	-	-
	F	-	-	-	-	-	-	-	-	-
	%	-	-	-	-	-	-	-	-	-
Graduate	M	-	-	-	-	-	-	-	-	-
	%	-	-	-	-	-	-	-	-	-
	F	-	-	-	-	-	-	-	-	-
	%	-	-	-	-	-	-	-	-	-
Post-Graduate	M	-	-	-	-	01	01	-	01	(1.05)
	%	-	-	-	-	100.00	100.00			
	F	-	-	-	-	-	-	-	-	-
	%	-	-	-	-	-	-	-	-	-
Total		52	04	01	01	38	95	01	-	-
		54.16	4.16	1.05	1.05	39.58	98.95	1.05	-	100.00

Mostly (59.37 per cent) the heads of the family are illiterate, out of which 35 (61.40 per cent) are agriculturists, 21 (36.84 per cent) are daily wage earners and the rest 02 women (i.e., 3.50 per cent) heads, who are widows and the guardian of minor children also subsist on agriculture. There are 28 (29.16 per cent) male heads who are educated up to primary standard only. Out of these, 14 (50.00 per cent) are daily wage labourers, 13 (35.00 per cent) are agriculturists and the remaining one is a businessman. There are only seven male heads who are junior high school pass and out of which three (42.84 per cent) are agriculturists, two (28.58 per cent) are in private service, and the remaining two (28.58 per cent) are labourers. Only three male heads are high school pass out of which two (66.67 per cent) are in private service and the remaining one (33.33 per cent) is in government service. There is only one male member in the village who has master's degree but no permanent salaried job of earning. He also subsists on daily wages. Thus it may be concluded that the level of education among the Buxas is not as much as to provide them any concrete source of livelihood. Even the literacy is below average of national literacy percentage. The people whether they are educated or uneducated are traditional in their thinking and dealings. They have general apathy and less exposure to outside world. They seem to be effortless for any kind of mobility. The people in spite of being educated are less aware about outside world. The introvert nature as well as less exposure to outside world has compelled an educated post-graduate Buxa youth to profess daily wage earning for his livelihood. The data also reflect the changing economy system of the Buxas. The percentage of agriculturists is decreasing day by day while the percentage of the daily wage labourers is correspondingly increasing. The other jobs, may be that a self employment or business and government or private services, are exceptionally having by the people in the study area. It is the reason that the family structure of the Buxas is also transforming from joint system to nuclear one. It can be proved from the data as shown in the Table 5.15.

Table 5.15
Types of Families Among the Buxas of the Village Bannakhera-Magra-Bhudi

Types of Family	*No. of Families*	%
Joint	27	28.12%
Nuclear	69	71.88%
Total	96	100.00%

Among the Buxas almost all the families are monogamous in nature. May be that a joint family or a nuclear family. In fact the Buxa tribe is known for its large vertically and horizontally extended joint family system. But today we observe that numerically the joint families are in descending order. Even the size of the joint family has been limited only upto two or three vertical nuclear families of two and more generations. In the study area only 28.12 per cent families are of joint nature while 81.88 per cent are nuclear. The size of the joint families is comparatively small. The data presented in the Table 5.16 prove this fact.

Table No. 5.16
Family Size Among the Buxas

Member	*(C.I)*	*0-2*	*2-4*	*4-6*	*6-8*	*8-10*	*10-*	*12-14*	*Total*
No. of Families	(F)	12	26	37	19	01	-	01	96
	X	1	3	5	7	9	11	13	
	FX	12	78	185	133	9	-	13	430

Mean = $\sum \frac{Fx}{N} = \frac{430}{96}$ i.e. = approximately 5 members

The family size among the Buxas has squeezed to two to twelve members only. An average Buxa family is approximately of 5 members. The parents and their children live in one abode. In fact, most of the nuclear families among the Buxas are the outcome of the familial disputes. Today most of the peace-loving Buxas separate their sons as soon as they are married so that the possibilities of familial disputes may be stopped and the cordiality among the separating nuclear families can be maintained (Bisht: 1994:125-126). It is observed that the familial disputes caused due to estrangement among brothers over property and the strained relations among the wives on the division of labour and sharing the responsibilities of the family have disorganized the joint family system among the Buxas. The education, occupational mobility and modernization process have no role in the emergence of the nuclear families among Buxas. But it can be asserted that poverty and ignorance which lead to familial disputes, are the responsible factors for transforming the joint families into nuclear families.

We have reflections about the poor economic conditions of the Buxas while we go through their occupational structure and educational level. However, we can prove it with the family-wise property ownership and income per annum. The table showing the family-wise property ownership and income per annum can be presented as follows:

Table 5.17. Family-wise Property ownership and Income Per-Annum of the Buxas of Bannakhera Village

Property	*Types*	*Nos. of Families*	*(%)*
Agricultural land-holding in Acre	Land less	38	39.59
	0-1	14	14.59
	1-3	16	16.66
	3-6	13	13.54
	6-9	8	8.33
	9-12	3	3.12
	12-15	2	2.08
	15-18	2	2.08
Tamed Animals	Cow	09	9.37
	Ox	41	42.70
	Buffalo	39	40.62
	Goat	01	1.08
	Poultry	-	-
Agricultural Equipment	Tractor	03	3.12
	Trolly	03	2.12
	Thresher	03	3.12
	Pumpset	18	18.75
	Tubewell	-	-
	Dunlop Cart	24	25.00
Other Property	Cycle	29	30.20
	Scooter/Motor Cycle	03	3.12
	T.V.	10	10.41
	Radio	15	15.62
	Tape	7	7.30
	Gun	02	2.08
House	Kachcha	40	41.67
	Pucca	30	31.25
	Mix	26	27.08
Facilities Available in the House	Electricity	15	15.62
	Hand Pump	56	58.33
	Bathroom	-	-
	Lavatory	-	-

The data shows that out of the total 96 Buxa families, 38(39.59 per cent) are landless, 14 (14.59 per cent) have less than one acre of land, 16(16.66 per cent) have one to three acres of land, 13 (13.549 per cent) have three to six acres of land, 08(8.33 per cent) have six to nine acres of land, 03(3.12 per cent) have nine to twelve acres of land, 02(2.08 per cent) have twelve to fifteen acres of land and the rest 02(2.08 per cent) have fifteen to eighteen acres of land holdings. In fact the families who are landless subsist on daily wage earnings as labourers. Whenever and wherever they find the opportunity of physical labour they perform it. We can observe them as agricultural labourers in the agricultural farms of neighbouring non-tribals, sometime in road construction under road contractors and sometimes in sugar factories. The landless Buxas hardly manage food and clothings for their family. The education, health, hygiene and nutritional aspects of life which are basically of prime importance for human beings have no meaning for them. Their only motto of life is to keep their body and soul together by any means. The Buxas also rear some tamed animals. Mostly (42.70 per cent) the families have oxen which help them in agricultural operations. The minimum percentage, i.e., 9.37 out of the total 96 families have cows not for milk but for getting bull/ox. The oxen are used for ploughing fields, carrying riped crops from fields to threshing floor and again for carrying foodgrains to market centres. 41 (42.70 per cent) families have buffalos. People get milk as well as male calves of the buffalo used for pulling cart and also for ploughing agricultural fields. Many a time a pair of a bull/oxen and a male buffalo can be seen ploughing the field and pulling the loaded cart.

There are only three families who have tractor trolleys and thrashers. These families plough their fields with the help of tractors and also plough the fields of others on contract basis and thus earn some extra income from the use of tractors. They also let out tractor with trolley and sometime thrasher on hire. Eighteen families have their own pumpsets to lift the groundwater for irrigation. Other properties which some families have are in the form of bullock-cart (25 per cent), cycle (30.30 per cent), motor-scooter (3.12 per cent), Television (10.41 per cent), the radio (15.62 per cent), Tape (7.30 per cent) and gun (2.08 per cent). The type of abodes and their condition are also not proper for healthy life. Even today 40(41.47 per cent) Buxa families have kachcha houses for living. 30 (31.25 per cent) families have pucca houses and the rest 26 (27.08 per cent) have mixed type of houses. The kachcha house are made of viscous soil, grass, wooden logs and sticks. The pucca houses are built with bricks, cement, sand, concrete and steel while there are some abodes with brick-walls and thatched roofs. Such type of houses have been termed as mixed type of houses in the present text. Almost all the houses, may be that a pucca, kachcha, or mixed, have no sufficient accommodation as is required for healthy living. There is no separate room for drawing, dining and sleeping purposes. All the activities are performed in the same room as and when it is required. In one corner of the room a oven or hearth is placed for cooking the meal. There are no proper windows and ventilations in the house. Not even a single family has its own toilet room. They are used to go in the nearby agricultural fields for evacuation purposes and wash their hands and feet with the water of the hand-pumps. Every family has its own handpump which is used as a source of drinking water and also for washing hands and feet and purification after evacuation, bathing and cleaning the used kitchen wares. No house has the provision of bathroom, lavatory and kitchen-room. There are only 15(15.62 per cent) families who have taken electric connections for their own use. Two families have bio-gas plants. But none of the families have LPG connections. The firewood and the cow-dung cakes are used for cooking meal. In brief the economic condition of the majority of the Buxas is very miserable. As 37 (38.54 per cent) families have less than ten thousand rupees income per annum. Sixteen (16.67 per cent) families have ten to twenty thousand rupees income per year, 28(29.17 per cent) families have ten to twenty thousand rupees income per year. 28(29.17 per cent) families have twenty to thirty thousand rupees income per annum. 07(7.30 per cent) families have thirty to forty thousand rupees income per annum while the remaining 08 (8.33 per cent) families have forty to fifty thousand rupees income per annum. In this way the mean average of an average Buxa family is 18020 rupees per annum, that proves that most of the Buxas are leading their lives below poverty line. The Table 5.18 presents the mean average of the income of the Buxas of Bannakheda-Bhudi.

Table 5.18. Mean Average of the Income of the Buxas of the Study Area

Income group (In thousand Rs.)	*Nos. of families*	*Mid value*	
C-I	*F*	*X*	*Fx*
0-10	37	5	185
10-20	16	15	240
20-30	28	25	700
30-40	07	35	245
40-50	08	45	360
	N = 96	$\sum Fx$ = 1730	

$$\text{Mean} = \frac{\sum Fx}{N}$$

$$M = \frac{1730}{96} = \text{Rs. } 18.02$$

Per Year Mean of the Income is Rs. 18020 only

Since an average family has an average income of Rs. 18020 per annum.

Hence the per month per family average income is Rs. 1501.67.

Since an average family has average 4.47 say 5 members.

Hence an average family per unit monthly income is Rs. 300.

Thus in view of the statistical calculation of the Buxa families, it may be concluded that they are leading their life below poverty line.

Sample Profile : the Tharu Tribe

Ratanpur, the sampled Tharu village is inhabited by 144 Tharu families with 1123 population. All the family-heads jointly constitute the study group of the present study. Out of the total 144 family-heads 137 are males and the rest 07 are females. All the female heads are widows. Since, the Tharu tribe is a patriarchal, partrilineal and patrilocal community hence the eldest male member of the family is considered as the head of the family. But in exceptional cases, particularly when the family head is dead, and the children and other male members of the family are not capable to handle the liabilities of the family, the eldest woman becomes the head of the family until the male member of the family do becomes mature enough to shoulder the liabilities of the family and hold the status of the family-head. In some other cases, particularly when the male head is absent for a long time, the eldest female holds the status of the family head till his return. In the present study all the seven female heads are windows. The age and sex-wise marital status, educational status and occupational status of the Tharu respondents is being presented in the Table 5.19.

The tabulated field data depicts that there are only two respondents below 25 years of age and 22 are more than 65 years of age. Most of the female heads are more than 60 years of age. Only one female head, who is 38 years old, is the respondent of the present study. Out of the total 137 male heads 16 (11.11 per cent) are widowers. Thus the purposefully selected respondents belong to different age groups and different marital statuses. Among the respondents, 83 (57.63 per cent) including all the seven women heads are illiterate. Only 29 (20.13 per cent) are educated upto Primary standard, 21(14.59 per cent) are Junior

Table 5.19. Sample Structure of the Tharu Respondents : Age, Sex, Marital, Education and Occupational Status

Age Group	Sex		Marital Status			Educational Status							Occupational Status			
			Widower	Widow	Married	Illiterate	Primary	J. High School	High School	Inter-Mediate	Under-Graduate	Post-Graduate	Agriculture	Service Govt.	Service Private	Labour
<25	M	2	-	-	2	-	-	02	-	-	-	-	01	-	01	-
	F	-	-	-	-	-	-	-	-	-	-	-	-	-	-	-
25-30	M	15	-	-	15	04	04	05	-	-	01	01	11	01	-	08
	F	-	-	-	-	-	-	-	-	-	-	-	-	-	-	-
30-35	M	13	-	-	13	01	01	04	-	02	-	-	11	01	-	01
	F	-	-	-	-	-	-	-	-	-	-	-	-	-	-	-
35-40	M	21	-	01	20	09	04	03	02	-	03	-	14	04	-	03
	F	01	01	-	0	01	-	-	-	-	-	-	01	-	-	-
40-45	M	24	-	02	22	15	07	01	-	-	01	-	22	01	-	01
	F	-	-	-	-	-	-	-	-	-	-	-	-	-	-	-
45-50	M	17	-	04	13	10	04	03	-	-	-	-	15	-	-	02
	F	-	-	-	-	-	-	-	-	-	-	-	-	-	-	-

(Contd.)

(Contd. Table 5.19)

Age Group	Sex		Marital Status			Educational Status							Occupational Status			
			Widower	Widow	Married	Illiterate	Primary	J. High School	High School	Inter-Mediate	Under-Graduate	Post-Graduate	Agriculture	Service Govt.	Service Private	Labour
50-55	M	16	-	02	14	12	03	01	-	-	-	-	14	-	-	02
	F	02	-	-	02	02	-	-	-	-	-	-	02	-	-	-
55-60	M	10	-	01	09	07	03	-	-	-	-	-	09	-	01	-
	F	01	01	-	00	01	-	-	-	-	-	-	01	-	-	-
60-65	M	12	-	05	07	10	01	01	-	-	-	-	12	-	-	-
	F	01	01	-	00	01	-	-	-	-	-	-	01	-	-	-
65-70	M	04	-	01	03	01	2	-	-	-	01	-	04	-	-	-
	F	01	01	-	00	01	-	-	-	-	-	-	01	-	-	-
70 & above	M	3	-	-	03	-	01	-	-	-	-	-	03	-	-	-
	F	01	01	-	00	01	-	-	-	-	-	-	01	-	-	-
Total		**144**	**05**	**16**	**123**	**83**	**29**	**21**	**02**	**02**	**06**	**01**	**123**	**07**	**02**	**12**
%		**4.87**	**11.11**	**84.03**	**57.63**	**20.13**	**14.59**	**1.39**	**1.39**	**4.17**	**0.70**	**85.41**	**4.87**	**1.39**	**8.23**	

High School pass, 02(1.39 per cent) are High School pass, 2 (1.39 per cent) are Intermediate, six (4.17 per cent) are undergraduate and the remaining one (0.70 per cent) is educated upto Post-graduate standard. Among the Tharus trend of age-wise distribution of education is viewed. As the junior or the new generation is comparatively more educated than the seniors or the old generation. This trend reflects the inclination of the new generation towards education. This trend can be verified by the educational standard of over all the population of the Ratanpur Tharu village (see Table 5.7). However the data prove that the goal of complete literacy is far beyond the reach because most of the uneducated respondents as well as the general mass of the study area do not have reading and writing capacity. Even they can not make their own signatures. The occupational distribution of the respondents show that maximum 122(85.41 per cent) are agriculturists, 07(4.87 per cent) are government servants, 02(1.39 per cent) are in private services, while the rest 12(8.33 per cent) are daily wage labourers. We have also tried to correlate education with the occupational status of the Tharus of the Ratanpur village (see Table 5.7) and found that the educated persons are inclined towards government or private salaried jobs but have not succeeded. Finally some of the educated Tharus have preferred for daily wage earning. Traditionally the Tharu is a known agriculturist tribal community of Tarai. They have been rice cultivators since time immemorial. Even today, except some educated persons, they prefer their age old agricultural occupation. Even the educated salaried job-holders have their constant linkage with their families. Most of the government personnel have left their family in the village, who perform agriculture and help in agricultural operations. It is the reason that, in spite of the impacts of modernization there is a very slow transformation on the type and size of the Tharu families. It is evident by the data presented in the Table 5.20.

Table 5.20. Types of the Tharu Families in Ratanpur Village

Types of Family	*No. of Families*	%
Joint	69	47.92
Nuclear	75	52.08
Total	144	100.00%

The data prove that even today 47.92 per cent families are of joint type and 52.08 per cent are nuclear. If we throw light on the size of the family, we come to the conclusion that most of the Tharu families are of large size comprising average 10 members in all. The Table 5.21 presents the size of the Tharu families and also the average mean of the per family number of the members.

Table. 5.21. Family Size Among the Tharus of Ratanpur Village

Memeber	*Nos. of families*	*Mid value*	
C-I	*F*	*X*	*Fx*
0-2	08	1	08
2-4	16	3	48
4-6	48	5	240
6-8	24	7	168
8-10	17	9	153
10-12	11	11	121
12-14	8	13	104
14-16	03	15	42
16-18	03	17	51
18-20	0	19	0
20-22	02	21	42
22-24	01	23	23
24-26	01	25	25
26-28	01	27	27
28 & above	01	29	29
	N = 144	$\sum Fx = 1284$	

$$\text{Mean} = \frac{\sum Fx}{N} = \frac{1284}{144} = 9 \text{ member}$$

Average members per family are approximately

Though the average mean of per family members is approximately nine persons but it is noticed that the biggest Tharu family in Ratanpur village consists of 52 members. In this family the people of more than five generations live under a common roof and eat food cooked in a common hearth. In fact the agricultural economy needs more hands for more earning and also for performing agricultural activities provided there is large agricultural land holding. The comparatively large family size among the Tharus is the outcome of their comparatively large agricultural land holdings and also a large block of tamed animals. Thus it is observed that where there is a larger land holding there is larger size of the family. The family-wise property ownership and income per annum, as shown in the Table, 5.22 and 5.23 reflects the economic status of the Tharus.

Table 5.22. Family-wise Property Ownership and Income Per-Annum of the Tharus of Ratanpur Village

Property	*Types*	*Nos. of Families*	*(%) Out of the Total 144 Total Families*
Agricultural land holding in Acre	Land less	1	7.63
	0-1	27	59
	1-3	59	4
	3-6	24	16.67
	6-9	7	4.88
	9-12	9	6.25
	12-14	2	1.39
	14-16	0	1.39
	16-18	-	-
	18-20	-	-
	20 & above	03	2.08
Tamed Animals	Cow	50	34.12
	Ox	83	57.75
	Buffalo	63	43.75
	Goat	17	11.80
	Poultry	1	7.63
Agricultural Equipment	Tractor	23	15.97
	Dunlop	63	43.75
	Pumpset	57	39.58
Other Property	Cycle	33	22.91
	Scooter/Motor Cycle	20	13.89
	T.V.	87	60.41
	VCP	-	-
	Disc	-	-
	Cooler	-	-
	Fan	68	47.22
	Radio	63	43.75
	Tape Recorder	40	27.77
	Sewing Machine	25	17.36
	Kutti Machine	15	10.41
	Generator	02	1.39
House	Kachcha	86	59.72
	Puccka	33	22.91
	Mix	25	17.36
Facilities	Electricity	98	68.05

(Contd.)

(Contd. Table 5.22)

Property	*Types*	*Nos. of Families*	*(%)*
Income per annum in thousand	0-10	37	25.70
	10-20	34	23.61
	20-30	23	15.98
	30-40	13	9.02
	40-50	7	4.86
	50-60	4	2.78
	60-70	4	2.78
	70-80	2	1.39
	80-90	3	1.09
	90-1000	6	4.16
	More than 1000	11	763

The field information collected directly from the field sources depicts that in Ratanpur village 11 (7.63 per cent) families have no land holdings. They are landless. However the government records do not confirm their landlessness. It is so because these families have sold their lands to some outsiders but due to some legal complications the land could not be transferred in favour of the purchasers. But practically they are landless and earning their livelihood as daily-wage labourers. 27 (18.75) families have less than one acre of land, 59 (41.00 per cent) have 1 to 3 acres of land, 24 (16.67 per cent) have 3 to 6 acres of land, 9 (6.25 per cent) have 9 to 12 acres of land, 2 (1.39 per cent) have 12 to 14 acres of land, another 02 (1.39 per cent) families have 14 to 16 acres of land and there are 3 (2.08 per cent) families who hold more than 20 acres of land. Thus if we categorise them according to their land holdings, we come to the conclusion that there are four categories of the Tharu families in Ratanpur village. First those who are landless, second, the marginal farmers who have less than three acres of land, third, the small farmers who hold 3 to 6 acres of land, and, fourth the big farmers who have more than 6 acres of land. Correspondingly by all the families of the four categories have also some other property which is in the form of their abodes, tamed animals, agricultural equipments, facilities available in the house and other domestic items. Table 5.22 depicts the family wise property ownership of the Tharus. The family-wise income per annum also exhibits that most of the families are below poverty line. The following table 5.23 shows the income of the Tharu families of Ratanpur village.

Table 5.23. Family-wise Income Per Annum of the Tharus of Ratanpur Village

Income group (in thousand Rs.)	*Nos. of families*				
C-I	*f*	*x*	*d*	*fd*	
0-10	37	5	-20	-1480	
10-20	34	15	-30	-1020	
20-30	23	25	-20	-460	=-3090
30-40	13	35	-10	-130	
40-50	07	45	0	00	
50-60	04	55	+10	+40	
60-70	04	65	+20	+80	
70-80	02	75	+30	+60	
80-90	03	85	+40	+120	=+1150
90-100	06	95	+50	+300	
More than 100	11	105	+60	+660	
	N=140			$\sum$fd = −1940	

$$\text{Mean} = Am + \sum \frac{fd}{N}$$

$$= 45 + \frac{-1940}{140} = 45 - 13.48 = 31.52$$

Say Rs. 31520 per annum

Since an average family has an average income of Rs. 31520 per annum

Hence the per month per-family average income will be Rs. 31520/12 = Rs. 2626.67 Say Rs. 2627

Since the average family has average 10 members

Hence the average of per family per unit monthly income comes Rs. 2627/10 = Rs. 262.70

The statistical calculation of the income of the Tharu families concludes that an average family has an income of two thousand six hundred twenty seven rupees per year. Again if the average per month income of an average family is divided by the average number of an average family members, i.e., 10, we find that an average member of an average family has only Rs. 262.70 for livelihood. If we correlate per unit per month income of the Tharus, we find that an average family is leading its life below poverty line.

Sample Profile : the Khasa Tribe

Basaya, the sampled Jaunsari village is inhabited by 924 Jaunsaris who are divided into 82 families. All the families of the sampled village are the units of the present research project and the heads of the families have further been chosen purposefully as the units for focussed interview. It is a known fact that the Jaunsari is traditionally a polyandrous community where two or more brothers used to marry a common wife. But today with the impact of modernization as well as due to the culture-contact the Khasas of Jaunsari Bawar are turning gradually towards monogamy. However the cases of polyandry, polygyny are often seen in Jaunsar area. Even in Basaya village there exists only 18 (21.96 per cent) monogamous nuclear families while the percentage of joint fraternal polyandrous families, i.e., 41.47 (34 families) is still greater than other types. 21 (25.60 per cent) families are vertically joint in nature, 05 (6.09 per cent) are polygynous and the rest 04 (4.88 per cent) families are nuclear mixed. The nuclear type of families consist of a husband, wife and their unmarried children. In such type of families both the husband and wife are literate. The joint fraternal polyandrous family comprises two or more brothers and their common one or more wives with their children (married and unmarried both). The joint-polygynous family consists of a husband and his two or more wives with children, (both married and unmarried) and also the parents of the husband. In vertically extended joint families, the people of two or more generations live together. These families are of mixed nature. Often the two or more brothers and their joint wife or wives, their married children with or without children live together. In this way, in such type of families the people more than two generations live together, share common hearth, common roof, common property and also common liabilities of any kind. Apart from these types, there is one more type in which husband, wife, their unmarried children, widow mother or widower father and father's widow sister or brother live together. In such type of families the liabilities of the family lie on the husband only. This type of family has been termed as mixed nuclear family in this text. The Table 5.24 presents the types of families among the Jaunsaris of Basaya village.

Table 5.24. Types of Families Among Khasas of Basaya Village

Types	*No. of Families*	*%*
Nuclear	18	21.96
Joint Fraternal Polyandrous	34	41.47
Joint Polygynous	05	6.09
Joint Vertical	21	25.60
Nuclear Mixed	04	4.88
Total	82	100.00

The size of the Jaunsari (Khasa) families is comparatively larger. The data presented in the following Table 5.25 proves this fact.

Table 5.25. Size of Family Among the Khasas of Basaya Village

No. of family Member	*No. of family*				
(C.I,)	*(f)*	*x*	*d*	*fd*	
0-2	01	01	-10	-10	
2-4	05	03	-8	-40	
4-6	10	05	-6	60	
6-8	08	07	-4	-32	=-178
8-10	18	09	-2	-36	
10-12	08	Am 11	0	00	
12-14	06	13	+2	+12	
14-16	07	15	+4	+28	
16-18	05	17	+6	+30	=+250
18-20	03	19	+8	+24	
20-22	01	21	+10	+10	
22-24	03	23	+12	+36	
24-26	03	25	+14	+42	
26-28	02	27	+16	+32	
28-30	01	29	+18	+18	
30-32	01	31	+20	+20	
	82		fd = 72		

$$\text{Mean} = \text{Am} + \sum \frac{fd}{N} = 11 + \frac{72}{82} + 11.87$$

Say 12 Members. Mean average of the size of an average Khasa family = 12 members.

It is evident that an average Khasa family has 12 members which is of course larger size of the family than that of the Tharus and Buxas of Udham Singh Nagar Distt. Among Khasas the economic factor has ever been determinant for deciding the type of the family. It is observed that comparatively the families who subsist on some traditional occupations and none of the members of the family is employed in any permanent Govt. or private jobs prefer to live together jointly. Even the fraternal joint family is the outcome of the backward and under-developed economy that does not allow the brothers for having separate wives to establish a nuclear family and also for further segmentation of land and property. On the contrary, the families, whose economic condition is better and some of their members are employed in some government and private jobs, allow the employed persons to establish their own nuclear families.

The sample profile of the respondents (the heads of the families) exhibit that out of total 82 household heads 81 are male and only one is female. Their marital status shows that out of 81 male heads 74 are married and 07 are widowers. The female head is a widow. Out of total 82 respondents 55 (67.09 per cent) are illiterate, 21(25.60 per cent) are educated upto primary standard, 01(1.21 per cent) is junior high school pass, 04(4.89 per cent) are high school, 01(1.21 per cent) is educated upto Intermediate standard. The majority of the respondents, i.e., 63.4 per cent are agriculturists, only 04(4.88 per cent) are employed in Govt. and private services while the remaining 26(31.71 per cent) are daily-wage labourers. The Table 5.26 presents the data pertaining to age and sex-wise marital status, educational standard and the occupational status of the Khasas of Basaya village.

Economically the Khasas are leading comparatively a miserable life. They are known as agriculturists-cum-pastoral people. Even today almost all the families subsist on agricultural economy. No doubt there are some landless people but they earn their livelihood mainly through agricultural labour. Family-wise property ownership and the income per annum of the Khasas of Basaya village reflect their economic condition. The Table 5.27 presents the family-wise property ownership and income per annum of the Khasas.

The field information tabulated as above depicts that out of the total 82 families 04(4.88 per cent) are landless, 39 (47.56 per cent) families have less than one acre of land, 32 (39.02 per cent) have one to three acres of land, 05 (6.09 per cent) have three to six acres of land and the remaining 02(2.43 per cent) have six to nine acres of land. Thus in view of the land-holdings the Khasas of Basaya village are of three types. First there are 4 landless families, second, 71 families are marginal farmers, and, 7 are small farmers. None of the families can be categorized

Table 5.26. Demographic Profile of the Khasa Respondents

Age Group	Sex	Marital Status			Educational Status							Occupational Status			
		Married	Widow	Widower	Illiterate	Primary	J. High School	High School	Inter-mediate	Under-Graduate	Post-Graduate	Agriculture	Service Govt.	Service Private	Wage Earning
<25	M	04	-	-	-	02	-	02	-	-	-	02	-	-	02
	F	-	-	-	-	-	-	-	-	-	-	-	-	-	-
25-30	M	05	-	-	03	01	01	-	-	-	-	02	-	-	03
	F	-	-	-	-	-	-	-	-	-	-	-	-	-	-
30-35	M	11	-	01	10	01	-	-	01	-	-	09	-	-	03
	F	-	-	-	-	-	-	-	-	-	-	-	-	-	-
35-40	M	12	-	-	09	02	-	01	-	-	-	05	01	01	05
	F	-	-	-	-	-	-	-	-	-	-	-	-	-	-
40-45	M	03	-	-	02	01	-	-	-	-	-	02	-	01	-
	F	-	-	-	-	-	-	-	-	-	-	-	-	-	-
45-50	M	08	-	-	04	04	-	-	-	-	-	06	-	-	02
	F	-	01	-	01	-	-	-	-	-	-	01	-	-	-
50-55	M	08	-	-	05	03	-	-	-	-	-	06	-	-	01
	F	-	-	-	-	-	-	-	-	-	-	-	-	-	-
55-60	M	05	-	-	05	-	-	-	-	-	-	04	-	-	01
	F	-	-	-	-	-	-	-	-	-	-	-	-	-	-
60-65	M	08	-	02	06	03	-	01	-	-	-	07	01	-	02
	F	-	-	-	-	-	-	-	-	-	-	-	-	-	-
65-70	M	07	-	01	05	03	-	-	-	-	-	03	-	-	05
	F	-	-	-	-	-	-	-	-	-	-	-	-	-	-
70 & above	M	03	-	03	05	01	-	-	-	-	-	05	-	-	01
	F	-	-	-	-	-	-	-	-	-	-	-	-	-	-
Total		**74**	**01**	**07**	**55**	**21**	**01**	**04**	**01**	**-**	**-**	**52**	**02**	**02**	**26**
%		**90.25**	**1.21**	**8.54**	**67.09**	**25.60**	**1.21**	**4.89**	**1.21**	**-**	**-**	**63.41**	**2.44**	**2.44**	**31.71**

as big farmer. The Khasas also raise tamed animals like cow, ox, buffalo, goat, sheep, mule, horse etc. They earn their livelihood through milk and milk products. They get wool from the sheep and prepare some woollen stuffs for their own use. Goats serve their flesh needs. Horses and mules are the main transport animals in the village. Any how the people try to fulfil their daily needs through their own efforts without going outside of the village periphery. The agricultural equipments, which are in the form of plough, comb, hoe and spade, are also prepared by the villagers themselves. In fact, the Khasas are good carpenters and craftsmen. They have sufficient skill of preparing the items of daily needs for their own use. They are good masons too. They build their house by themselves.

Table 5.27. Family-wise Property Ownership and Income Per-Annum of the Khasas of Basaya Village

Property	*Types*	*Nos. of Families*	*(%)*
Land holdings in Acre	Land less	04	4.88
	0-1	39	47.56
	1-3	32	39.02
	3-6	05	6.09
	6-9	02	2.43
Tamed Animals	Cow	61	74.39
	Ox	67	81.70
	Buffalo	57	69.51
	Goat	57	69.51
	Sheep	09	10.97
	Mule	11	13.41
	Horse	09	7.31
Agricultural Equipment	Plough	70	85.36
	Curb	70	85.39
	Hoe	75	91.46
	Speda	75	91.46
House	Pakka	65	78.04
	Kachha	04	4.88
	Mixed	14	17.08
Other Facilities	Electricity	Nil	00
	Solar Light system	13	15.85
	Own Drinking Water	17	20.73
	Public water tap	65	79.26
	Lavatory	11	13.41
	Others	-	-
Other Property	TV	03	3.65
	Radio	09	0.97
	Tape	05	6.09
	Others	-	-

(Contd.)

Property	*Types*	*Nos. of Families*	*(%)*
Income per annum in thousand	0-10	58	70.73
	10-20	21	25.60
	20-30	03	3.65
Govt. Schemes from which the families have been benefited	IRDP for Mule/horse Purchasing	0.3	3.65
	IRDP for Buffalo Pur.	11	13.41
	IRDP for Sheep/Goat purchasing	05	6.09
	IRDP for Rabbit	0.2	2.43
	Weaker Section Seheme	11	13.41
	Indira Avas Yojana	03	3.65
	Land development	03	3.65
	Old age Pension	12	14.63
	Crippled Pension	01	1.21

At present 64 (78.04 per cent) families have pucca houses, o4(4.88 per cent) have kachcha houses and 14 (17.08 per cent) have mixed type of houses. Generally in Jaunsar area the pucca houses are made up of hard stone, timber and roofed over by black stone slates. The walls are plastered over by clay and husk mixture. While the Kachcha houses are made up of straight wooden logs thatched over by grass and the mixed houses are built with the stone-walls and the roof is thatched over with grass. Since the village is not electrified so far the people are not aware of electricity. However 13(15.85 per cent) families have solar light system, 17(20.73 per cent) families have their own drinking water connections, 65 (79.26 per cent) families fetch drinking water from public water tape. Mostly, the people use open ground for evacuation purposes while there are 11 (13.41 per cent) families who have their own lavatory or toilet room meant particularly for latrine and urinal purposes. In the houses there is no provision for separate dining or drawing rooms, bed-rooms and kitchen. In double-storied houses, the ground floor is used for keeping tamed animals while the first floor is used for all familial purposes. Some people have some other property too which is in the form of television set, radio set and tape recorders etc. but the number of such families is very nominal. As only 03 families have television sets, 09 have radios and 05 have tapes only. The Khasa families belong to different income groups. Maximum 58 (70.73 per cent) families have less than 10 thousand rupees income per annum, 21 (25.60 per cent) have 10 to 20 thousand rupees per annum and 03 (3.65) families have more than 20 thousand rupees income per annum. Thus an average Khasa family has an average Rs. 57.50 per month income which denotes their poor economic condition. The Table 5.28 shows an average mean of the income of Khasa families.

Table 5.28. Per Annum Income of the Khasa Families

Per annum Income (In thousand Rs.)	No. of families		
(C.I.)	(F)	x	fx
0-10	58	5	290
10-20	21	15	315
20-30	03	25	75
	N = 82	$\sum$ fx = 680	

$$\text{Mean} = \frac{\sum fx}{N} = \frac{680}{82} = \text{Rs. } 8.29$$

M = 8.29 Say 8.29 × 1000= Rs. 8290/-

Average Mean of per annum income is Rs. 8290 only.

An average family has an average income of Rs. 8290

Hence the per month per family average income comes Rs. 690 only.

Since an average family has average 12 members

Hence an average family per unit monthly income comes to Rs. 57.50.

Thus, it may be concluded that an average Khasa family is leading its life below poverty line.

Resume

The sample structure of the present study is constituted by 347 respondents out of which 144 (41.50 per cent) respondents are from the Tharu tribe, 96 (27.67 per cent) are the Buxas, 82 (23.63 per cent) are the Khasas and remaining 25 (7.20 per cent) are the Rajis. Out of the total 347 respondents, 332 (95.69 per cent) are male and 15 (4.31 per cent) are female. All the females are widows and out of the total male respondents 305 (91.87 per cent) are married and 27 (8.13 per cent) are widowers. None of the respondents is unmarried. The age and sex wise marital status of the tribe-wise respondents is given in the Table 5.30.

The respondents are of different occupational statuses. The maximum percentage i.e. 66.00 is of the agriculturists which is followed by the daily-wage labourers whose percentage is 27.95. The percentage of government and private service personnel is comparatively lower, i.e., 3.46 and 2.31 per cent respectively. While the businessmen are only 0.28 per cent. Besides this, the daily wage labourer constitute 27.95 per cent of the total respondents. The Table 5.30 presents the occupational status of the tribe-wise respondents of the study.

Table 5.29. Age and Sex-wise Marital Status of the Tribe-wise Respondents.

Age Group	Sex	Marital Status of the respondents														
		Tharus			Buxas			Khasas			Rajis			Total		
		Mr.	Wd.	Wr.	Mr.	Wd.	Wr.	Mr.	Wd.	Wr.	Mr.	Wd.	Wr.	Mr.	Wd.	Wr.
<25	M	2	-	-	4	-	-	04	-	-	01	-	-	09	-	-
	F	-	-	-	-	-	-	-	-	-	-	-	-	-	-	-
25-30	M	15	-	-	15	-	-	05	-	-	02	-	01	37	-	01
	F	-	-	-	-	01	-	-	-	-	-	01	-	-	-	-
30-35	M	13	-	-	16	-	-	11	-	01	01	-	-	41	-	01
	F	-	-	-	-	-	-	-	-	-	-	-	-	-	-	-
35-40	M	20	-	01	16	-	-	12	-	-	02	-	01	50	-	02
	F	-	01	-	-	01	-	-	-	-	-	02	-	-	04	-
40-45	M	22	-	02	16	-	-	03	-	-	-	-	-	41	-	02
	F	-	-	-	-	-	-	--	-	-	-	-	-	-	-	-
45-50	M	13	-	04	06	-	01	08	-	-	05	-	-	32	-	05
	F	-	-	-	-	-	-	-	01	-	-	-	-	0	01	-
50-55	M	14	-	02	-	-	-	08	-	-	01	-	-	26	-	02
	F	-	01	-	-	-	-	-	-	-	-	-	-	-	02	-
55-60	M	09	-	01	04	-	-	05	-	-	04	-	-	22	-	01
	F	-	02	-	-	-	-	-	-	-	-	-	-	-	02	-
60-65	M	07	-	05	5	-	-	08	-	02	02	-	-	22	-	07
	F	-	01	-	-	-	-	-	-	-	-	-	-	-	01	-
65-70	M	03	-	01	03	-	01	07	-	01	-	-	-	13	-	03
	F	-	01	-	-	-	-	0	-	-	-	-	-	-	01	-
>70	M	03	-	-	06	-	-	03	-	03	-	01	-	12	-	03
	F	-	01	-	-	-	-	-	-	-	-	-	-	-	02	-
Total	M	121	-	16	92	-	02	74	-	07	18	-	02	305	-	27
	%	-	-	-	-	-	-	-	-	-	-	-	-	91.87	-	8.13
	F	-	07	-	-	02	-	-	01	-	-	05	-	-	15	-
	%	-	-	-	-	-	-	-	-	-	-	-	-	-	100	-

Abbreviation : Mr = Married, Wd = Widow, Wr =Widower

Table 5.30. Occupational status of the Tribe-wise Respondents

Occupation	*Tribes*				
	Tharu	*Buxas*	*Khasas*	*Rajis*	*Total %*
Agriculture	123	52	52	02	229 (66.00)
Service Pvt.	02	04	02	00	08(2.31)
Service Govt.	07	01	02	02	12(3.46)
Business	00	01	00	00	01 (0.28)
Daily Wage Labourer	12	38	26	21	97 (27.95)
Total	144	96	82	25 .	347 (100.00)

The respondents are of different educational statuses. The tebulated data show that out of the total respondents 197(59.34 per cent) male and all the 15 female respondents are illiterate, 83 (25.00 per cent) are educated up to primary standard, 32 (9.64 per cent) are of junior high school level, 09 (2.71 per cent) are high school pass, 03(0.90 per cent) are intermediate, 06 (1.81 per cent) are graduates and 02 (0.60 per cent) are post-graduates. Tribe-wise calculation of the educational status of the respondents is given in the following Table 5.31.

Table 5.31. Educational Status of the 'Tribe-wise Respondents'

Education	*Sex*	*Tribes*					*Grand Total %*
		Tharus	*Buxas*	*Khasas*	*Rajis*	*Total %*	
Illiterate	M	76 (55.48)	55 (58.51)	54 (66.67)	12 (60.00)	197 (59.34)	212
	F	07 (100.00)	02 (100.00)	01 (100.00)	05 (100.00)	15 (100.00)	61.10
Primary	M	29 (21.16)	28 (29.79)	21 (25.92)	05 (25.00)	83 (25.00)	83
	F	-	-	-	-	-	23.92
J. H. School	M	21 (15.33)	07 (7.44)	01 (1.24)	03 (15.00)	32 (9.64)	32
	F	-	-		-	-	9.22
High School	M	02 (1.46)	03 (3.20)	04 (4.93)	-	09 (2.71)	09
	F	-	-	-	-	-	2.59
Intermediate	M	02 (1.46)	-	01 (1.24)	-	03 (0.90)	03
	F	-	-	-	-	-	0.86
Graduate	M	06 (14.38)	-	-	-	06 (1.81)	06
	F	-	-	-	-	-	1.73
Post-Graduate	M	01(0.73)	01(1.06)	-	-	02(0.60)	02
	F	-	-	-	-	-	0.58
Others	M	-	-	-	-	-	-
	F	-	-	-	-	-	-
Total	M	137 (100)	94 (100)	81 (100)	20 (100.00)	332 (100.00)	347
	F	07 (100)	02 (100)	01 (100)	05 (100.00)	15 (100.00)	100.00

Besides this, the types of family and also the size of families of the tribe-wise respondents have also been presented quantitatively. It is observed that 156 (44.96 per cent) respondents still live in joint families, 187 (53.89 per cent) live in nuclear families and 04 (1.15 per cent) live in mixed nuclear families. There is tribe-wise variation in the type and size of the families, which is evident from the following Table 5.32 and 5.33, and this variation is mainly due to variation of the economic, educational and traditional background of the tribals concerned.

In fact it is assumed while planning for this research project that the age, sex, marital status, occupational status, educational status, family profile, socio-religious tenets as well as the ecological background have deep concern with health, hygiene and nutritional pattern of the community concerned. Hence all these variables have been taken into consideration and are also being analysed through this chapter. Besides this some case studies are also prepared for presenting the nutritional assessment of the respondents of different tribal groups. The forthcoming chapters will present the over all factual and objective scenario of the education, health, hygiene and nutritional status of the tribals under study.

Table 5.32. Size of the Family of the Tribe-wise Respondents

No. of Members	*No. of Families*				
	Tharus	*Buxas*	*Khasas*	*Rajis*	*Total*
0-2	08	12	01	01	22 (6.35)
2-4	16	26	05	04	51 (14.70)
4-6	48	37	10	17	112 (32.28)
6-8	24	19	08	3	54 (15.57)
8-10	17	01	18	-	36 (10.38)
10-12	11	-	08	-	19 (5.48)
12-14	08	01	06	-	15 (4.32)
14-16	03	-	07	-	10 (2.89)
16-18	03	-	05	-	08 (2.30)
18-20	-	-	03	-	03 (0.87)
20-22	02	-	01	-	03 (0.87)
22-24	01	-	03	-	04 (1.16)
24-26	01	-	03	-	04 (1.16)
26-28	01	-	02	-	03 (0.87)
28-30	01	-	01	-	02 (0.58)
30-32	-	-	01	-	01 (0.29)
Total	144	96	82	25	347 (100.00)

Table 5.33. Types of Families of the 'Trible-wise Respondents'

Types of Family	*No. of Respondents*				
	Tharus	*Buxas*	*Khasas*	*Rajis*	*Total%*
Nuclear	75	69	18	25	187 (53.89)
Joint	69	27	60	00	156 (44.96)
Mixed Nuclear	-	-	04	00	04 (1.15)
Total	144	96	82	25	347 (100.00)

6
Education, Health, Hygiene and Nutritional Status of Tribals

Educational Status

For an objective evaluation of the educational status of the tribals, their perception towards education; what they really think of education and its significance; what is their opinion about the existing educational facilities and what sort of educational facilities they need in their area; for them, which are the implications of education in priority basis and what are the multiple functions of education for them etc. are some of the research questions which were discussed and shared with the respondents during field work for this very purpose, first of all the literacy percentage and the educational standard of the tribal population of the study area were studied. The data pertaining to their education are being presented in the Table 6.1.

The tabulated data depict that the literacy percentage among the tribals is 41.11 per cent which is comparatively less than the general literacy of the newly-formed Uttaranchal, i.e., 72.28 per cent. The male tribal literacy is 58.53 per cent while the general male literacy in the state is 84.01 per cent and the female tribal literary is 34.23 per cent while the general female literacy in the state is 60.26 per cent. If we correlate the tribals literacy of the study area with the national tribal literacy, we observe that the tribal literacy in Uttaranchal is comparatively more than the national tribal literacy; that is, only 29.60 per cent only. Among the tribals under study we observe that the literacy among the Buxas, i.e.,31.94 per cent is lower than other tribals of Uttaranchal. The Khasas have 44.04 per cent literacy while Tharus have maximum 56.28 per cent and the Rajis have only 52.33 per cent literacy. Thus the literacy percentage among the Tharus is comparatively more than among other tribals viz. the Rajis, the Buxas and the Khasas. In view of the national literacy policy which aims at providing education for all by 2000 A.D. is far beyond its goal particularly in regard to the tribal literacy of the study area of the present research project. More so if we take into account the family head-wise literacy of the tribals of the study area we observe that most of the family heads 59.34 per cent are illiterate. The illiteracy among the Rajis is maximum 68.00 per cent which descends among the Khasas 67.07 per cent, the Buxas 59.38 per cent and the Tharus 57.63 per cent respectively. Almost the same situation is with other family members of the tribals (see Table 5.31). But if we take into account the overall literacy in different age-groups we come to the conclusion that the literacy graph climbs up comparatively in lower age-group. And it is maximum in between 10 to 20 years of age. The following Table 6.2 exhibits that in higher age-groups the literacy percentage and the standard of education among the respondents is in descending order. Viewing the accuracy of the information pertaining to education the total universe has been divided tribe-wise in different age-groups—the preschool children, i.e., below 05 years of age have been separated into, i.e., preschool category. After the deduction of the preschool children the tribal literacy scenario becomes somewhat different as is shown in Table 6.1. In this context we observe that among the Tharus there are 166(14.79 per cent) preschool children and the percentage of illiteracy is 30.81 while 54.40 per cent population is literate. In the case of the Buxas, 59(12.17 per cent) are preschool children, 271 (55.88 per cent) are illiterate and 155(31.95 per cent) are literate. Among the Khasas there are 167(18.07 per cent) preschool children, 380(41.13 per cent) are illiterate and the rest 379(40.40 per cent) are literate. Among the Rajis 08(7.48 per cent) are preschool children, 48 (44.85 per cent) are illiterate and the remaining 51 (47.67) are literate. If we make a comparative evaluation of the literacy of the tribals under study we come to the conclusion that among the Tharus the literacy percentage is comparatively more than the Buxas the Khasas and the Rajis. This literacy percentage of the Tharus is followed respectively by the Rajis with 47.67 per cent literacy, the Khasas with 40.40 per cent and the Buxas with 31.95 per cent only.

It is evident that there is a variation in the educational status among the tribals of Uttaranchal. The facts show that this variation is due to the difference of ecological background of the tribals, their economy, their intensity towards economic need, infrastructural variation, outlook and psychology of the tribals towards education. The Rajis, who are still in semi-nomadic stage, spend most of their time in the arrangement of food for daily need. The education, which is a long term process and needs investment, devotion and toil, cannot give them instant relief, hence they prefer and expect for some economic pursuits even from the children above six years of age. The infrastructural facilities related to schools absolutely absent in the village and its approachable surrounding. At a time there was a 'Agan-Badi' school run by Harijan and Social

Table 6.1. Educational Status of the Tribals Under Study

Name of the Tribe		Illiterate	Education							
			Primary	Jr. High School	High School	Intermediate	Graduate	Post-Graduate	Others	Total
Raji	M	21 (37.50)	38 (84.44)	05 (100.00)		-	01 (100.00)	-		65 (60.74)
	F	35 (62.50)	07 (15.56)	-	-	-	-	-	-	42 (39.26)
Total		56 (52.33)	45 (42.06)	05 (4.68)	-	-	01 (0.93)	-	-	107 (100.00)
G.Total	M	583 (41.82)	374 (59.18)	180 (64.29)	153 (83.60)	74 (77.09)	32 (84.21)	06 (54.54)	04 (80.00)	1406 (53.28)
	%	41.47	26.60	12.80	10.88	5.26	2.28	0.43	0.28	100.00
	F	811 (58.18)	258 (40.82)	100 (35.71)	30 (16.40)	22 (22.91)	06 (15.79)	05 (45.46)	01 (20.00)	1233 (46.72)
	%	65.77	20.92	08.11	02.43	01.79	00.49	00.41	0.08	100.00
Over-all		1394 (100)	632 (100)	280 (100)	183 (100)	96 (100)	38 (100)	11 (100)	05 (100)	2639 (100)
Total	%	52.83	23.95	10.62	6.93	3.63	1.43	0.42	0.19	100.00

(Contd.)

(Contd. Table 6.1)

Name of the Tribe		Illiterate	Education							
			Primary	Jr. High School	High School	Intermediate	Graduate	Post-Graduate	Others	Total
Buxa	M	137 (41.51)	75 (75.00)	34 (82.92)	13 (100.00)	-	-	01 (100.00)		260 (53.60)
	F	193 (58.49)	25 (25.00)	07 (17.08)	-	-	-	-	-	225 (46.40)
Total		330 (68.04)	100 (20.62)	41 (8.45)	13 (2.69)	-		1 (0.20)	-	485 (100.00)
Tharu	M	211 (42.98)	126 (47.20)	93 (58.50)	19 (83.20)	40 (71.42)	23 (82.14)	-	2 (6.67)	594 (5290)
	F	280 (57.02)	141 (52.80)	66 (41.50)	20 (16.80)	16 (28.58)	05 (17.86)	-	1 (3.33)	529 (47.10)
Total		491 (43.72)	267 (23.78)	159 (23.78)	119 (10.60)	56 (4.99)	28 (2.50)	-	3 (2.6)	1123 (100.00)
Khasa	M	214 (41.40)	135 (61.36)	48 (64)	41 (80.40)	34 (85.00)	08 (8.89)	05 (50.00)	02 (100)	487 (52.70)
	F	303 (58.60)	85 (38.64)	27 (36)	10 (19.60)	06 (15.00)	01 (1.11)	05 (50.00)	-	437 (47.30)
Total		517 (55.96)	220 (23.81)	75 (8.11)	51 (5.52)	40 (4.32)	09 (0.98)	10 (1.09)	02 (0.21)	924 (100.00)

Table 6.2. Literacy Percentage in Different Age-groups of the Tribal Population

Name of the Tribe	Age Group														
	0-5	5-10	10-15	15-20	20-25	25-30	30-35	35-40	40-45	45-50	50-55	55-60	60-65	65-70	70-	Total
Tharus																
Pre School	166	-	-	-	-	-	-	-	-	-	-	-	-	-	-	166
%	100	-	-	-	-	-	-	-	-	-	-	-	-	-	-	14.79
Illiterate	-	15	8	28	39	28	28	38	. 40	31	30	22	22	5	12	346
%		10.41	6.40	18.19	31.97	30.43	52.83	59.38	68.97	75.60	88.23	84.61	91.67	71.42	92.30	30.81
Literate		129	117	126	83	64	25	26	18	10	04	04	02	02	01	611
%	-	89.59	93.60	81.81	68.03	69.57	47.17	40.62	31.03	24.40	11.77	15.39	08.33	28.58	7.70	54.40
Buxa																
Pre-school	59			-	-	-	-	-	-	-					-	59
%	100.00															12.17
Illiterate		46	19	20	21	29	26	25	19	13	11	09	06	08	19	271
%	-	69.70	34.54	40.60	55.27	63.04	65.00	71.42	82.60	72.22	100.00	90.00	85.71	100.00	10.00	55.88
Literate	-	20	36	30	17	17	14	10	04	05	00	01	01	00	00	155
%		30.30	65.46	60.00	44.73	36.96	35.00	28.58	.17.40	27.78		10.00	14.29			31.95

(Contd.)

(Contd. Table 6.2)

Name of the Tribe	Age Group														
	0-5	5-10	10-15	15-20	20-25	25-30	30-35	35-40	40-45	45-50	50-55	55-60	60-65	65-70	70-	Total
Khasas																
Preschool	167	-	-	-			-	-	-	-	.	-		-	-	167
%	100.00															18.07
Illiterate	-	38	19	22	41	40	40	35	16	31	15	22	61			380
%	-	28.58	20.21	26.19	51.25	53.33	67.80	64.81	76.20	72.09	75.00	88.00	88.40		-	41.13
Literate	-	95	75	62	39	35	19	19	05	12	05	03	08	-	-	377
		71.42	79.79	73.81	48.75	46.67	32.20	35.19	23.80	27.91	25.00	12.00	11.60	-	-	40.80
Rajis																
Pre-school	08	-	-	-	-	-		-	-	-	-		-	-	-	0.8
%	100.00	-	-	-	-	-	-	-	-	-	-	-	-	-	-	7.48
Illiterate		03	05	02	04	02	02	05	05	07	01	07	02	-	03	48
%	-	13.63	26.31	22.22	57.14	33.33	100	162.50	100	87.50	100	100	100	-	100	44.85
Literate	-	19	14	7	3	4	-	3	-	1	-	-	-	-		51
	-	86.37	73.69	77.78	42.86	66.67	-	37.50	-	12.50	-	-	-			47.67

Welfare Department of U.P., which is not functioning for the last five years. The 'Ashram Type School' is located at Baluwakat (Dharchula) has no doubt functional utility even for the Rajis. But the percentage of their enrolment in ATS (particularly of the Rajis of Kimkhola village) is very nominal. The Buxas have only 31.95 per cent literacy. Maximum Buxa population is still illiterate. Even the educational standard among the literate Buxas is also very low. It is observed that in the Bannakhera Buxa village, the main stress of the tribals remain on economic activities. No motivational factor effectively provokes the tribals and their children towards education. The mid-day meal consists of biscuits and porridge etc. do not have much attracting effect on the children. However some parents prefer to send their minor children to the school while they are at work in agricultural fields. Sometimes it appears that the village primary school also works as creche. But when the children grow up and become capable for performing some familial task, they just drop from the schooling. The age-wise descending percentage of the literacy among higher age-groups is the result of their reluctance towards education. Even today the Buxas could not assess the importance of the education and its multiple functions in personality development. But among the Tharus and the Khasas, the situation is somewhat different. The people have begun to know the importance of education. They are now aware and provoke their children for education. Comparatively the higher literacy percentage among the Tharus and the Khasas is the result of their awareness of education.

But if we take into account the overall scenario of the tribal education, we come to the conclusion that most of the grand-parents and parents of the respondents were illiterate. Even most of the respondents (61.10 per cent) are still illiterate. But they are inclined to send their children for schooling. The literacy percentage as well as the educational standard in new generation is comparatively higher than in the old generation. It is the result of inclination of their parents. The trend does reflect the positive outlook of the tribals towards education. But there still appears rigidity, conservativeness and ignorance in their perceptions about education and its implications. The gender biases are there. The people preferably want to educate their male children and also to give them higher education so that they can be able to seek government salaried jobs. But they have almost contrary opinions about female education. The low percentage of female literacy is the result of their conservative outlook and gender prejudices. For them, the male child, when grown up, is liable to shoulder the responsibility of the family. Education helps him in performing his duties particularly towards family and its members. The respondents were asked about their aspirations for the education of their children (son and daughter), it is found that maximum 31.1 per cent respondents were desirous to educate their male children at least up to high-school standard, 30 per cent wish upto intermediate standard, 9 per cent for graduation, 06 per cent for post-graduation and 24 per cent respondents were in the state of uncertainty, even they were of the opinion that male children should be educated. In regard to the female education, most of the respondents, i.e., 25.94 per cent were desirous to educate their daughters or any female child of the family at least up to primary standard so that they can read and understand the things written and also can make their signatures whenever needed. So 14 per cent want to educate the female up to junior high school level, 16 per cent up to high school, 5 per cent upto graduation and 2 per cent up to post-graduate level. There are 29 per cent respondents who kept mum in regard to the female education. They are the people who think that the school-going girls get into bad habits, hence they are not in favour of women's education. Thus we obviously observe gender prejudices in the reactions of the respondents. The data presented in the following Table 6.3 show tribe-wise educational aspirations of the respondents towards their children.

The tribe-wise analysis of the data pertaining to the educational aspirations of the respondents show that among the Tharus maximum 24.30 per cent respondents are not in a position of making any reaction about the education standard of the male child. However there are 31.25 per cent Tharus who expect at least high school level education for their male children, 29.87 per cent expect for intermediate level education, 9.02 per cent for graduation and 5.56 per cent for postgraduate level education. In the case of female child, 29.16 per cent Tharu respondents are not certain about their education, 9.72 per cent are not in favour of educating the female children while 25.00 per cent expect for at least primary level education for females, 13.89 per cent want to give junior high-school level education to girls, 15.98 per cent wish for high school level education to daughters, 4.17 per cent are in favour of intermediate level education and 2.08 per cent respondents are desirous for post-graduate level education for their daughters. In the case of the Buxa respondents, 16.67 per cent are not in favour of women's education and state that no education should be provided to them, 23.95 per cent Buxas are in favour of giving at least primary level education to the female child, 16.67 per cent expect for junior high school level education, 6.25 per cent want to educate their female child up to Junior-high school level and the remaining 36.46 per cent respondents are in a state of uncertainty. Contrary to this the Buxa respondents have different opinions about men's education. Almost all the respondents are desirous to educate their sons (male child), however 32.30 per cent cannot express to what level they wish to educate their male children, 15.62 per cent respondents want to educate their son(s) up to primary level, 14.59 per cent expect

Table 6.3. Aspiration of the Respondents Towards Their Chilren's Education

Respondent	*Children/ Gender*	*Educational Aspiration*								
		No Education	*Primary Only*	*Upto Jr.High School*	*Upto High School*	*Upto Intermediate*	*Upto Graduation*	*Upto Post-Graduation*	*Not certain*	*Total*
Tharu	Son (M)	-	-	-	45	43	13	8	35	144
	%	-	-	-	31.25	29.87	9.02	5.56	24.30	100.00
	Daughter(F)	14	36	20	23	6	3	-	42	144
	%	9.72	25.00	13.89	15.98	4.17	2.08	-	29.16	100.00
Buxa	Son (M)	-	15	14	24	6	4	2	31	96
	%	-	15.62	14.59	25.00	6.25	4.16	2.08	32.30	100.00
	Daughter (F)	16	23	16	06	-	-	-	35	96
	%	16.67	23.95	16.67	6.25	-	-	-	36.46	100.00
Khasa	Son (M)	-	6	7	24	20	7	1	17	82
	%	-	7.30	8.54	29.27	24.40	8.54	1.22	20.73	100.00
	Daughter (F)	11	24	14	19	-	-	-	14	82
	%	13.41	29.27	17.08	23.17	-	-	-	17.07	100.00
Raji	Son (M)	-	6	4	3	2	2	2	6	25
	%	-	24.00	16.00	12.00	8.00	8.00	8.00	24.00	100.00
	Daughter (F)	2	7	4	4	3	-	-	5	25
	%	8.00	28.00	16.00	16.00	12.00	-	-	20.00	100.00
Total	Son (M)	-	27	25	96	71	26	13	89	347
	%	-	7.78	7.20	27.67	20.46	7.49	3.75	25.65	100.00
	Daughter (F)	43	90	54	52	09	03	-	96	347
	%	12.39	25.94	15.56	14.99	2.59	0.86	-	27.67	100.00

for junior high-school level education, 25.00 per cent make advocacy for high school level education, 6.25 per cent make for intermediate level education, 4.16 per cent for graduation and the remaining 2.08 per cent want to educate their son(s) upto post-graduate level. Among the Khasas 20.73 per cent respondents are not certain about the educational standard of the male child but all of them want to educate their male child. Besides this there are maximum 24.40 per cent respondent who want to provide at least intermediate level education, 29.27 per cent make plea for high school level education for the male children, 8.54 per cent make for junior high school level education, 7.30 per cent for primary level only. 8.54 per cent want to provide upto graduation level education to their male children while the rest 2.08 per cent wish for post-graduation. Almost the same reactions we received from the Raji respondents. Thus we can conclude that the respondents have different outlook about male and female education. As all the respondents are willing to educate their male children while there are 12.39 per cent respondents who are not in favour of women's education. Even in the case of educational standard their opinion is different for male and female. Most of the respondents want to provide higher education to the boys in comparison to girls. This sort of gender bias is the outcome of traditional rigidity and conservative outlook of the respondents.

In order to make an intensive and objective analysis of the opinion of respondents towards education and its implications, some functional options of the education were presented before them. The respondents were then asked to give their answers in preferential order. Their reactions in quantitative form are presented in the Table 6.4.

It is observed that there are tribe-wise variations about the expected functions of education but maximum average percentage of respondents, i.e., 70.97 per cent give first preference to education as a source of employment. Now the tribal people are fully aware of education and its importance and confident that no employment can be achieved without proper education. 29.27 per cent respondents give first preference to education as a means of achieving high social status, 25-60 per cent consider education as a means of welfare of the family, 14.63 per cent are of the opinion that education is helpful in establishing good relations with higher out-groups. Second preference is given by the maximum 27.96 per cent respondents to the welfare of the family. Almost the same percentage, i.e., 27.45 give third preference to the welfare of the family. Every function of education has been considered by the respondents in one way or the other. It appears that the tribal people are now conscious about the significance of education and its functions for human society. There are average 4.59 per cent respondents who are of the opinion that education is helpful in personality development which ultimately paves way for better living. There are some respondents who

Table 6.4. Reaction of the Tribe-wise Respondents Towards Some Expected Functions of Education.

Tribe-wise reaction in prefe-rential order	*Expected Function of Education*												
	Source of Emplo-yment	*Enligh-tenment*	*Helpful in removing Ignor-ance*	*Achieving high social status*	*Helpful in Creating confi-dence*	*Helpful in welfare of the family*	*Removes super-sition*	*Means of perso-nality devel-opment*	*Source of high prestige*	*To have good relation with higher in-group*	*To have good relation with out-group*	*Not certain*	*Total*
Buxa	1	2	3	4	5	6	7	8	9	10	11	12	13
1st preference	69 (71.88)	-	05 (5.20)	-	-	11 (11.45)	-	3 (3.123)	4 (4.17)	2 (2.09)	2 (2.09)		96 (100.00)
2nd preference	-	-	-	23 (33.95)	-	49 (51.05)	4 (4.17)	5 (5.20)	3 (3.12)	-	-	12 (12.50)	96 (100.00)
3rd preference		-	18 (18.76)	15 (15.62)	-	34 (35.41)	5 (5.20)	6 (6.26)	3 (3.12)	4 (4.17)		11 (11.46)	96 (100.00)
Tharu	1	2	3	4	5	6	7	8	9	10	11	12	13
1st preference	108 (75.00)	-	9 (6.25)	7 (4.86)	-	16 (11.11)	-	-	-	4 (2.78)	-	-	-
2nd preference	22 (15.28)	-	28 (19.44)	30 (20.83)	-	38 (20.39)	10 (6.94)	-	6 (4.17)	4 (2.78)	-	6 (4.17)	144 (100.00)
3rd preference	-	-	9 (6.25)	14 (9.72)	4 (2.78)	53 (36.80)	13 (9.03)	19 (13.20)	9 (6.25)	7 (4.87)	4 (2.78)	12 (8.33)	144 (100.00)
Raji	1	2	3	4	5	6	7	8	9	10	11	12	13
1st preference	19 (76.00)	-	-	01 (4.00)	-	03 (12.00)	-	-	-	-	-	03 (8.00)	25 (100.00)
2nd preference	08	-	-	6	-	06 (24.00)	-	01 (4.00)	-	01 (4.00)	-	14 (56.00)	25 (100.00)
3rd preference	-	-	-	-	-	03 (12.00)	-	01 (4.00)	-	-	-	21 (84.00)	25 (100.00)

(Contd.)

(Contd. Table 6.4)

Tribe- wise reaction in prefe-rential order	Expected Function of Education												
	Source of Emplo-yment	Enligh-tenment	Helpful in removing Ignor-ance	Achieving high social status	Helpful in Creating confi-dence	Helpful in welfare of the family	Removes super-sition	Means of perso-nality devel-opment	Source of high prestige	To have good relation with higher in-group	To have good relation with out-group	Not certain	Total
Khasa	1	2	3	4	5	6	7	8	9	10	11	12	13
1st preference	59 (71.95)	-	-	-	-	-	-	13 (15.86)	-	6 (7.31)	3 (3.66)	1 (1.21)	82 (100.00)
2nd preference	26 (31.71)	-	5 (6.10)	-	-	11 (13.41)	-	8 (9.77)	-	6 (7.31)	2 (2.43)	24 (29.24)	82 (100.00)
3rd preference	-	-	4 (4.88)	24 (29.27)	-	21 (25.60)	-	7 (8.53)	-	10 (12.21)	12 (14.63)	4 (4.88)	82 (100.00)
Total I	255 (83.60)	-	14 (17.95)	08 (6.96)	-	30 (12.25)	-	16 (25.40)	04 (16.00)	12 (27.28)	05 (21.73)	03 (2.80)	347 (33.33)
II	50 (16.40)	- -	33 (42.30)	54 (46.95)	- -	104 (42.45)	14 (43.75)	14 (22.22)	09 (35.00)	11 (25.00)	02 (8.70)	56 (52.34)	347 (33.33)
III	- -	- -	31 (39.75	53 (46.09)	04 (100)	111 (45.30)	18 (56.25)	33 (52.38)	12 (48.00)	21 (47.72)	16 (69.57)	48 (44.86)	347 (33.33)
Grand Total	305 (100.00)	-	78 (100.00)	115 (100.00)	04 (100.00)	245 (100.00)	32 (100.00)	63 (100.00)	25 (100.00)	44 (100.00)	23 (100.00)	107 (100.00)	1041 (99.99)
%	(29.30	-	(7.50)	(11.04)	(0.39)	(25.53)	(3.08)	(6.06)	(2.40)	(4.22)	(2.20)	(10.28)	(100.00)

stated that education has different functions viz. it removes ignorance and superstitions, it is helpful in achieving high social status and high prestige in the society. It provides a high social status to the people in the 'in group' as well as in 'out group' social spectrum. In brief, it may be concluded that the tribals do realize the importance of education but their deep-rooted poverty, conservative pattern of living, traditional outlook, motivational vacuum and finally the intensity of economic needs etc. have obstructed their way to education. In this very context we have made thorough and intensive observation about the available educational facilities in the study area and also tried to know the opinion of respondents towards the existing educational facilities they preferably desire. In this regard we came to know that educational facilities existing at present in the study area are not upto the mark. In the Raji village the school is not in functioning order for the last five years as there is no teaching staff at present. In order to know the real and objective information the teachers posted for teaching were consulted and interviewed thoroughly. It was informed that the Raji children were not regular in the classes, the staff was not paid salary even for months together, no infrastructural facilities were there and ultimately the school was closed. Even in the Tharu, Buxa and Khasa study areas the schools are running with insufficient teaching staff, classrooms, seating facilities, toilets and other basic infrastructural facilities. At this, when the tribal people were asked what sort of facilities they wish for the better schooling of tribal children. The tribal people unanimously responded for scholarship and stipend for school-going children as an incentive, so that the parents can have an alternative source of earning and also compensate the loss of their children's contribution in economic pursuits. When the respondents were asked about the existing incentives provided to the school-going children in the form of midday meal, stationery and school uniform etc., they react that the incentives being provided are in the name only and quite insufficient to attract the children for schooling. For example, the Buxas are basically agriculturists. They manage food-grains for their own need but for the fulfilment of other needs like clothings, shelter, medical treatment, schooling, the children and performing the rituals and other festivities they need money. The agricultural yield does not provide them surplus value as to meet out their necessities. Even the employment-generation schemes could not provide them instant economic relief which they desire. Hence they demand assistance only in the form of cash. The same is the notion with 'scholarship' in education. The Buxa people have no patience, no endurance and no stability in nature. These are the personality characteristics of the Buxas which detain them from any sort of long-term enterprises. Though they are aware of the importance of education and also understand that education can provide them a permanent source of livelihood, enlightenment, high social status, better living, high prestige and also an opportunity to have good relations with higher 'in group' and 'out group' members but they feel that education is a long-term process having no instant output for the person concerned and also for the family as a whole. Hence in spite of being aware about the importance and multiple functions of education they do not send their children for schooling. The poverty, in real sense, does not allow them for schooling.

The respondents were also asked to express their reactions about a statement, i.e., "Education is helpful in alround development of mankind". In response to this question there were maximum 51 (53.13 per cent) respondents who agreed, 10 (10.42 per cent) were fully agreed, 15 (15.62 per cent) do not agree and remaining 20 (20.83 per cent) were uncertain. It is observed that literate parents express their consent towards the statement presented before them and the illiterate and less educated parents were uncertain while the respondents who were illiterate and comparatively poorer do not agree with this statement. They are of the opinion that it is money that all alone can make alround development of mankind. It is money that makes a man educated, brings happiness in man's life and also makes him able to do everything for one's well-being. The data pertaining to the reactions of the respondents of different tribals under study can be presented in the following Table 6.5.

Table 6.5. Reactions of the Respondents Towards the Statement, "Education is Helpful in Alround Development of Mankind"

Tribe-wise Respondents	*Reactions*					*Total*
	Fully agree	*Agree*	*Do not agree*	*Fully do not agree*	*Uncertain*	
Buxa %	10 (10.42)	51 (53.13)	15 (15.62)	-	20 (20.83)	96 (100.00)
Tharu %	32 (22.22)	85 (59.02)	13 (9.03)	-	14 (9.73)	144 (100.00)
Raji %	02 (8.00)	03 (12.00)	05 (20.00)	-	15 (60.00)	25 (100.00)
Khasa %	24 (29.27)	52 (63.41)	-	-	6 (7.32)	82 (100.00)
Total	68 (19.60)	191 (55.04)	33 (9.51)	-	55 (15.85)	347 (100.00)

Among the Tharus, maximum 85 (59.02 per cent) respondents express their consent towards the statement, i.e., 'Education is helpful in alround development of mankind'. There are 32 (22.22 per cent) respondents who fully agree with this implication of education, 13 (9.03 per cent) do not agree while 14 (9.73 per cent) are uncertain and not in a position of reacting accurately. In fact those are the people who do not have any sort of expectations from education. Education for them is the thing of some affluent people. Among the Khasas 24 (29.27 per cent) respondents fully agree, 52 (63.41 per cent) agree and only 6 (7.32 per cent) are uncertain about the statement. In regard to the Rajis, most of the respondents, i.e., 15 (60.00 per cent) were uncertain, 05 (20.00 per cent) did not agree while 03 (12.00 per cent) and 02 (8.00 per cent) respectively agree and fully agree with this statement. When the same statement, 'Education is helpful in alround development of mankind' was presented before the Khasas, it is observed that most of the respondents, who were literate, aware and known with different provisions made for the welfare of the Scheduled-Tribe people, react that education is a must for achieving benefits meant for the STs. Without education no one can achieve the best of one's life may be that Scheduled Tribe. The person who has at least minimum qualification can avail the facilities under the constitutional provisions. Only the illiterate and very poor people were in a state of dilemma while they were asked for their reactions about the 'statement'. In fact it is the economic and educational status of the people which determines their outlook, attitudes, aspirations and expectations. The same thing was noticed while the respondents of different economic and educational categories were interviewed and asked to express their reactions towards education and its role in personality development. The educated and comparatively well-off respondents expressed their positive reactions of the functions of education in personality development.

The respondents were also asked a question, i.e., "Having achieved high and prestigious post due to higher education, whether any of the tribal members became capable to have ones relation with higher non-tribal caste group?" In response to this question the respondents were of the opinion that the educated persons of their community have good acquaintance with out-group members whether they are in service or not. Only due to education they (the educated persons) have been able to have interactions with out-group members may be they are officials or non-officials. But at the same time the respondents also reacted that none of their educated community members has any socially recognized commensal and connubial relations with non-tribal caste groups. In this matter they appealed to be traditionally rigid and committed for maintaining their socio-cultural and ethnic identity. Thus in view of the objectives of the study we can conclude that the 'National goal of literacy for all by 2000 A.D., has not been achieved so far particularly in the tribal areas under study. Even the perception of the tribals towards education is also exhibited that most of the tribal people are not aware of the implications of education and its function in human life. Hence a general awareness programme as well as a policy oriented scheme is needed for the dissemination and propagation of education in tribal areas. These efforts can be fruitful in attracting the tribals towards education.

Health Status

Health status of the people, in general determines the average expectation of life, number of persons in the productive age bracket, production, productivity, earning capacity, employment and family welfare. On the other hand, several economic variables like income, employment, purchasing power and poverty determine the health status of the people (Gopal : 1961:1-2). It is the health status that determines the nature and state of human resource development and finally ascertains the form of a society. There are some determinant factors as to ascertain the heath status of the people. These factors include food, nutrition, hygiene, medical facilities, socio-cultural implications of health, environmental aspects, education, psychology and the world view of the people etc. The health status of any society is manifested in the form of prevalent infant mortality rate, life expectancy, morbidity of the people, maternal mortality, level of fertility and mortality etc. In other words we can term those factors as the indicators of health. By and large the health status of a community determines the nature of human resource development and finally ascertains the wellbeing of the people and a community as a whole. In true sense 'Health is wealth' is an appropriate saying.

In the present research work the health status of the tribals has been studied in terms of the various indicators of health. In this context first of all the infant mortality rate prevalent among the tribals at its pre-natal, post-natal and pre-school stage is enumerated. The crude deaths occurred in the study area has also been studied. The reasons of different deaths have also traced out with thorough investigations and enquiry. The life expectancy of the tribals has also been enumerated through the average age of the people living in the family. For this purpose necessary information of the last five years related to infant mortality, life expectancy, incidence of sickness in the family have been collected through intensive interview conducted with the respondents and other family members.

In the case of the Raji Tribe, we observed that in last five years, i.e., from 1996 to 2000 A.D. there were total 19 deaths in Kimkhola Raji village. The date presented in the Table 6.6 depict that out of the total deaths maximum 42.11 per cent were post-natal deaths, 31.58 per cent were pre-school deaths (i.e., between 1 to 3 years of age), 15.79 per cent were crude deaths and the rest 10.52 per cent were pre-natal deaths.

In view of the different deaths it can be asserted that most of the deaths among the Rajis took place at post-natal and pre-school level. It means the newborn children particularly below three years of age are more prone to mortality. In this matter the Raji people were thoroughly interviewed. We made deep observations of the community and tried to understand the reasons of deaths. It is observed that the respondents were not consensus about the causes of deaths. In the case of the prenatal mortality, though there were only two deaths in the last five years, the parents who experienced the agony of the pre-natal deaths as well as other family members and neighbours were asked about the probable causes of the prenatal deaths. We observed that the parents who experienced this anguish are of the opinion that they were married at a very early stage and the pregnancy was held at the age of 14 years of the wife. Virtually both the wife and husband were not aware of the pregnancy, hence all the routine sexual activities and the familial jobs were usually performed by them, which resulted in abortion at a very early stage. While the other respondents have different opinions. For

Table 6.6. Infant Mortality Among the Tribals in the Last Five Years

Tribes	Years	Yearwise Infant Mortality				
		Pre-natal	*Post-natal*	*Pre-school*	*Crude deaths*	*Total*
Rajis	1996	-	-	01	-	01
	1997	01	01	01	01	04
	1998	01	03	02	01	07
	1999	-	02	02	01	05
	2000	-	02	-	-	02
	Total	02 (10.52)	08 (42.11)	06 (31.58)	03 (15.79)	19 (100.00)
Buxas	1996	-	-		-	-
	1997	01	01		-	02
	1998	02	01	-	-	03
	1999	02	-	-	-	02
	2000	02	-	01	-	03
	Total	07	02	01	-	10
Tharus	1996	02	04	01		07
	1997	01	04	-	-	05
	1998	04	02	02	-	08
	1999	05	05	01		11
	2000	-	-	-	-	-
	Total	12	15	04	-	31
Khasas	1996	01	03	-	-	04
	1997	01	-	-	01	02
	1998	02	04	01	01	08
	1999	03	.	01	01	05
	2000	03	01	-	01	05
	Total	10	08	02	04	24
	G. Total	31	33	13	07	84

instance, as the data presented in Table 6.7, shows, 48.00 per cent Raji respondents were of the opinion that overburden of work and heavy physical labour during pregnancy period is the cause of prenatal mortality, 20.00 per cent respondents talk about morbidity as the cause of prenatal mortality, 16.00 per cent stated the lack of primary health care services during pregnancy period as the cause of pre-natal mortality while 4.00 per cent were not certain about the causes of prenatal mortality. Besides these causes, a general notion of the respondents was that it is the will of God. (*Upper wale ki ichchha*) that determines the births and deaths of any creature may be that a human being on the earth. Hence, the people do express their worries whenever there is any death of any kind but pacify themselves too because the things are beyond their will and capacity.

Among the Rajis during the last five years the total cases of conception were 28. Out of the total cases of conceptions only 26 cases were mature because there were 2(7.14 per cent) pre-natal deaths. Thus out of the total conception cases only 9 (32.15 per cent) were turned into living cases while the rest 19 (67.85 per cent) were deaths in different stages. As the data show that there were 08 (28.58 per cent) post-natal deaths in the last five years. In this matter, concerning parents and the family members were interviewed first. Consequently, all of them stated that the lack of maternity services and post-natal treatment caused the post-natal deaths. Besides this, maximum 28.00 per cent Raji respondents told that the Home-delivery as well as the traditional delivery practices are the causes of post-natal deaths, 12.00 per cent respondents were of the opinion that the lack of maternal and child heath services in tribal areas are the cause of post natal deaths while the remaining 16 per cent were uncertain and not in the position of any reaction about it. (See Table 6.8). There were 6(31.58 per cent) preschool deaths (i.e., the deaths below 03 years of age). Mostly the informants are of the opinion that malnutrition is the cause of preschool deaths. In their own words, how they utter '*Khano-pino Bhau nya, Khurak Bhai nya Dawai bhai nya, Aaphi marya*', means there is no proper diet, no energetic balanced diet, no medicine, no medical aid, hence death is inevitable'. The people alive are due to their own destiny. The people are very uncertain about the causes of deaths. Now their age-old traditional pattern of treatment has no utility. It is no longer effective. Hence some respondents blame the almighty for such immature deaths. The people having such feelings, are traditionally very sensitive and left even their place of residence whenever there is such immature death of children. This is one of the various causes that has perpetuated their nomadic nature. In the case of the crude deaths which are 3(15.79 per cent) in numbers during last five years almost all the respondents consensually replied that due to the wrath of the supernatural power such deaths are occurred. The people believe that there are some invisible spirits throughout the high Himalayan peaks. Some evil spirits, goblins and demons do exist in their adjoining forest and hill areas too who become active whenever they view any one or two persons aloof and at a lonely place. Such incidents occur mainly early in mornings, at summer-noon, at evening time or at about midnight. The people have their notion that these are the timings when the free souls, evil spirits, goblins and demons ramble about in their respective areas. At the lime whenever any person with weak will-power comes in their purview, he falls a prey to the evil spirits and becomes the victim of their wrath. The victim sets free from the prey only when the systematic offerings is made to the evil spirit. Sometimes the victim die by the wrath of evil spirits. Mostly the Raji people do not think about the medical treatment of the illness of any patient. Preferably they perform the exorcism practices first, then they consult the traditional medicine man, and finally to the medical doctors for the treatment of the patients. Till then the disease comes to its chronic stage and is declared irremediable by the doctors. In fact when we interviewed the family members as well as the doctors about the symptoms of the deceased man's illness and also about the cause of deaths, we came to the conclusion that the crude deaths occurred due to tuberculosis that has become chronic due to the carelessness of the patients. Among the Rajis the Tuberculosis is still very common. Because of the infectious nature, the disease transfers from one person to the other. And due to conservative nature the people sometimes are heard saying that the evil spirit has an overall effect on the village and its people. While in reality the people are affected more or less by tuberculosis, asthma and other respiratory diseases.

We have also tried to understand the year-wise type of pre-natal and post-natal mortality in the family. We came to know that among the Rajis during the last five years, i.e., from 1996 to 2000, total cases of conceptions were 28 out of which there were 02(7.14 per cent) pre-natal deaths, 8 (28.50 per cent) post-natal deaths, 6 (21.42 per cent) were pre-school deaths, 3 (10.27 per cent) were crude deaths and thus the total deaths were 19 (67.86 per cent) while the rest 09 (32.14 per cent) remained alive. Thus as the data presented in the following Table 6.9 depicts the mortality rate among the Rajis is comparatively more than any other tribal groups under study. Even the total mortality rate among Rajis which is 64.28 per cent per thousand per year is more than the general mortality of the state. On the contrary out of the total 28 conceptions in five years duration the living cases are 09 (31.14 per cent) persons which stand about 6.42 per cent of total conceptions. This percentage is really alarming. Thus, literally we can enumerate the population growth among the Rajis of the study area like this: Since the total existing

Table 6.7. Reactions about the Causes of Pre-natal Mortality

Tribes	*Respondent*	*Causes*					
		Conception in early age	*Lack of PHC services*	*Over-burden of Physical Labour*	*Morbidity*	*Not certain*	*Total*
Rajis	M	02	04	10	03	01	20 (75%)
	%	10.00	20.00	50.00	15.00	5.00	100.00
	F	01	-	02	02	-	05 (25%)
	%	20.00	-	40.00	40.00	-	100.00
	Total	03	04	12	05	01	25 (100%)
	%	12.00	16.00	48.00	20.00	4.00	100.00
Buxas	M	24	35	20	11	04	94 (97.92)
	%	25.53	37.23	21.28	11.70	14.26	100.00
	F	-	-	02	-	-	02 (02.08)
	%	-	-	100.00	-	-	100.00
	Total	24	35	22	11	04	96 (100.00)
	%	25.00	36.46	22.92	11.46	4.16	100.00
Tharus	M	36	52	37	06	06	137 (95.14)
	%	26.27	37.96	27.01	4.38	4.38	100.00
	F	-	02	03	-	02	07 (4.86)
	%	-	28.57	42.46	-	28.57	100.00
	Total	36	54	40	06	08	144 (100.00)
	%	25.00	37.50	27.78	4.16	5.56	100.00
Khasas	M	08	-	66	07	-	81 (98.78)
	%	9.88	-	81.48	8.64	-	100.00
	F	-	01	-	-	-	01 (01.22)
	%	-	100.00	-	-	-	100.00
	Total	08	01	66	07	-	82 (100.00)
	%	9.76	01.22	80.48	8.54	-	100.00
Grand Total	M	70	91	133	27	11	332 (95.68)
	%	21.08	27.41	40.06	8.13	3.32	100.00
	F	01	03	07	02	02	15 (4.32)
	%	6.67	20.00	46.67	13.33	13.33	100.00

population of the study area is 107. The population which added in last five years is 09 only. It means before five years, i.e., in 1996 the population of the study area would have been 98 only. During the last 05 years span only 09 persons were added to the population. In other words we can say that the population grows at the rate of 1.83 per cent per year which is less than any community or the tribe in the state. On the contrary, out of the total 29 conceptions, 19 were mortal cases. It means 67.86 per cent cases demised in five years which stands about 13.57 per cent per year. If we enumerate the death rate at the post-natal stage and above we come to the conclusion that the people die at the rate of 3.59 per cent per year. Thus the death rate is comparatively more than the birth rate. The variation in birth and death rate is 3.57 -1.83, i.e., 1.74 persons per year.

Table 6.8. Reactions about the Causes of Post-natal Mortality

Tribes	*Respondent*	*Causes*					
		Home delivery	*Traditional way of delivery Practices*	*Lack of maternity and post-natal treatment*	*Lack of maternity and child health care services*	*Not certain*	*Total*
Rajis	M	05	05	06	03	01	20
	%	25.00	25.00	30.00	15.00	5.00	100.00
	F	02	-	-	-	03	05
	%	40.00				60.00	100.00
	Total	07	05	06	03	04	25
	%	28.00	20.00	24.00	12.00	16.00	100.00
Buxas	M	15	26	22	15	16	94
	%	15.96	27.66	23.40	15.96	17.02	100.00
	F	-	-	-	-	02	02
	%	-	-	-	-	100.00	100.00
	Total	15	26	22	15	18	96
	%	15.63	27.08	22.92	15.63	18.74	100.00
Tharus	M	23	14	74	10	16	137
	%	16.79	10.22	54.01	7.30	11.68	100.00
	F	02	-	02	02	01	07
	%	28.57	-	28.54	28.57	14.29	100.00
	Total	25	14	76	12	17	144
	%	17.36	9.72	52.78	8.33	11.81	100.00
Khasas	M	16	03	61	-	01	81
	%	19.75	3.70	75.31	-	1.23	100.00
	F	01	-	-	-	-	01
	%	100.00	-	-	-	-	100.00
	Total	17	03	61	-	01	82
	%	20.73	3.66	74.39	-	1.22	100.00
G. Total	M	59	48	163	28	34	332
	%	17.77	14.46	49.10	8.43	10.24	100.00
	F	05	-	02	02	06	15
	%	33.34	-	13.33	13.33	40.00	100.00

Rate of Fertility and Mortality Among the Tribes

The rate of fertility and mortality is positively correlated with the health status of a given community. In conservative societies, where the level of education and literacy percentage among the people remains comparatively low and the people are governed by traditions, control over fertility is regarded as violation of nature and natural laws. In such types of conservative societies the people observe strictly the institutional norms, social taboos and all the restrictions laid down by the society and do not care about institutional goals. This state of being generates a variety of anomalies even in man's life. Frequent conceptions, more

Table 6.9. Year-wise Cases of Conception and Infant Mortality Among the Tribe

Tribes	Years	Causes						
		Conception	Pre-natal	Post-natal	Pre-school	Crude deaths	Total deaths	Total alive
Rajis	1996	03	-	-	01	-	01	02
	1997	07	01	01	01	01	04	03
	1998	08	01	03	02	01	07	01
	1999	06	-	02	02	01	05	01
	2000	04	-	02	-	-	02	02
	Total	28	02	08	06	03	19	09
	%	100.00	7.14	28.58	21.42	10.71	67.85	32.15
Buxas	1996	08	-	-	-	-	-	08
	1997	15	01	01	-	-	02	13
	1998	11	02	01	-	-	03	08
	1999	21	02	-	-	-	02	19
	2000	05	02	-	01	-	03	02
	Total	60	07	02	01	-	10	50
	%	100.00	11.67	3.33	1.67	-	16.67	83.33
Tharus	1996	14	02	04	01	-	07	07
	1997	26	04	01	-	-	05	21
	1998	26	04	02	02	-	08	18
	1999	15	05	05	01	-	11	04
	2000	16	-	-	-	-	-	16
	Total	97	12	15	04	-	31	66
	%	100.00	12.37	15.46	4.12	-	31.96	68.04
Khasas	1996	26	01	03	-	-	04	22
	1997	28	01	-	-	01	02	26
	1998	35	02	04	01	01	08	27
	1999	49	03	-	01	01	05	44
	2000	13	03	01	-	01	05	08
	Total	151	10	08	02	04	24	127
	%	100.00	6.62	5.30	1.32	2.65	15.89	84.11
Grand		336	31	33	13	07	84	252
Total	%	100.00	9.23	9.82	3.87	2.08	25.00	75.00

births without restrictions, observance of various traditional taboos and superstitions (which by definition are irrational and unscientific) during menstruation, pregnancy at neo-natal stage, during lactation and the taboos related to dietary intake during gestation period and even after pregnancy have generally ill-effects on the health of the person concerned. On the contrary, in progressive and advanced societies the people are more rational and have scientific approach and world view. They are very particular and prompt in every walk of life. In such societies the rate of fertility and mortality remains normal and restricted. In the context of the aforesaid hypothetical propositions, we have tried to understand the level of fertility and mortality among the Tribes of Uttarakhand. The information collected through interview schedule method are presented in the Table 6.10 and 6.10 (b).

Table 6.10. Tribe-wise Rate of Fertility and Mortality in the Last Five Years

Tribes	*Fertility/ Mortality*	*Years*					*Total*
		1996	*1997*	*1998*	*1999*	*2000*	
Raji	Births	03	07	08	06	04	28 (100.00)
	Deaths	01	04	07	05	02	19 (67.86)
	Alive	02	03	01	01	02	09 (32.14)
Buxa	Births	08	15	11	21	05	60 (100.00)
	Deaths	-	02	03	02	03	10 (16.67)
	Alive	08	13	08	19	02	50 (83.33)
Tharu	Births	14	26	26	15	16	97 (100.00)
	Deaths	07	05	08	11	0	31 (31.96)
	Alive	07	21	18	04	16	66 (68.04)
Khasa	Births	26	28	35	49	13	151 (100.00)
	Deaths	04	02	08	05	05	24 (15.89)
	Alive	22	26	27	44	08	127 (84.11)
Grand Total	Births	51	76	80	91	38	336 (100.00)
	Deaths	12	13	26	23	10	84 (25.00)
	Alive	39	63	54	68	28	252 (75.00)

The data depict that among the Rajis, out of the total 26 births during last five years, only 9 (34.61 per cent) are alive and the rest 17(65.39) demised after birth. In other words we can say that the fertility rate among the Rajis is comparatively more but the percentage of the survivals is only 34.61 in five years. If we enumerate it annually we come to the conclusion that average 1.8, say two persons, are added to the population every year. Out of the total births 65.39 per cent died. It means the mortality rate among the Rajis is comparatively more than in other tribes. It is so because the Rajis are very conservative, traditional and introverted by nature. They are still very nearer to nature and dominated by natural laws. For them the births and deaths are not under the control of human beings. If the persons use any contraceptive they virtually dishonour the supernatural power and thus become the receptacle of divine vengeance. This notion provokes them to keep on their natural course which results in frequent conceptions. Furthermore, the traditional

Table 6.10 (b) Year-wise Cases of Prenatal and Post-natal Mortality Among the Tribes

Tribes	Year	Conception and type of death occurred									
		Live Birth	Abortion	Still Birth	Total	Neo-natal	Infant	Pre School	School age	Total	Grand Total
Rajis	1996	-	-	-	-	-	-	01	-	01	01 (5.26)
	1997	-	01	-	01	01	-	01	01	03	04 (21.05)
	1998	01	-	-	01	01	02	02	01	06	07 (36.85)
	1999	-	-	-	-	01	02	02	-	05	05 (26.32)
	2000	-	-	-	-	-	01	-	01	02	02 (10.52)
	Total	01	01	-	02	03	05	06	03	17	19 (100.00)
	%	5.26	5.26	-	10.52	15.79	26.32	31.58	15.79	89.48	100.00
Buxa	1996	-	-	-	-	-	-	-	-	-	-
	1997	01	-	-	01	01	-	-	-	01	02 (20.00)
	1998	01	01	-	02	01	-	-	-	01	03 (30.00)
	1999	02	-	-	02	-	-	-	-	-	02 (20.00)
	2000	02	-	-	02	-	-	01	-	01	03 (30.00)
	Total	06	01	-	07	02	-	01	-	03	10 (100.00)
	%	60.00	10.00	-	70.00	20.00	-	10.00	-	30.00	100.00

(Contd.)

(Contd. Table 6.10(b))

Tribes	Year	Conception and type of death occurred									
		Live Birth	Abortion	Still Birth	Total	Neo-natal	Infant	Pre School	School age	Total	Grand Total
Tharus	1996	01	-	01	02	03	01	01	-	05	07 (22.58)
	1997	01	-	-	01	03	01	-	-	04	05 (16.13)
	1998	03	-	01	04	02	-	02	-	04	08 (25.81)
	1999	05	-	-	05	04	01	01	-	06	11 (35.48)
	2000	-	-	-	-	-	-	-	-	-	-
	Total	10	-	02	12	12	03	04	-	19	31 (100.00)
	%	31.26	-	6.45	38.71	38.71	9.68	12.90	-	61.29	100.00
Khasas	1996	01	-	-	01	02	01	-	-	03	04 (16.67)
	1997	01	-	-	01	-	-	-	01	01	02 (8.33)
	1998	02	-	-	02	02	02	01	01	06	08 (33.33)
	1999	02	01	-	03	-	-	01	01	02	05 (20.83)
	2000	03	-	-	03	01	-	-	01	02	05 (20.83)
	Total	10	01	-	10	05	03	02	04	14	24 (100.00)
	%	41.67	4.17	-	41.67	20.83	12.50	8.33	16.67	58.33	100.00
Grand		27	03	02	31	22	11	13	07	53	84 (100.00)
Total	%	32.14	3.57	2.38	36.90	26.19	13.10	15.48	8.33	63.10	100.00

beliefs and customs detain them from following the health and medicare services meant for them. In fact there was a casualty of a pregnant Raji woman in labour room at the 'Baluwakot Sub-primary Health Centre'. The case was being handled by A.N.M. It was first ever case consulted by the Rajis to A.N.M. for delivery. But the casualty of the pregnant woman during delivery has created a sort of fear and distrust among the Rajis towards A.N.M. and modern medical practices. Since then the whole of the Raji community did not consult the A.N.M. and other medical practitioners particularly in the case of maternity matters. They have firm belief on their traditions and natural way of life. Hence every thing among the Rajis goes in natural course which ultimately results in prenatal and post-natal deaths. These deaths are viewed by the Rajis as the wrath of the supernatural power and also an ultimatum for them to escape from further mishappening. With this view in mind the Rajis generally left their places of residence when there is any immature death and fled to some unknown place in search of a proper settlement. Even today the semi-nomadic nature of the Rajis is the result of their superstitions related to births and deaths.

Among the Buxas, there have been only 60 births in the last five years. Out of which only 02(3.33 per cent) died and the remaining 58(96.67 per cent) are alive. It shows that the mortality rate among the Buxas is comparatively lower than in other tribes mainly the Rajis. The annual enumeration of the birth-rate shows that the Buxas of the Bannakhera village do add 2.83 per cent persons in their population every year but out of which 0.67 per cent persons die due to different reasons. In this way approximately 2.16 per cent persons are added every year in the population of the Buxas. In fact the agriculturist Buxas have sufficient staple food for their daily consumption, they are better aware of maternity and child health-care services. They are more prone to modern medical practices. Hence the mortality rate among the Buxas is lesser than among the Rajis. Contrary to this, there are the Tharus who added 94 persons in their population during the last five years. Out of which 31(31.96 per cent) persons demised and the rest 66 (68.04 per cent) were alive. In other words, we can say that mortality rate among the Tharus is 6.39 per cent per year and the population growth rate is 13.61 per cent per year.

Among the Khasas, there were total 151 births in the village during the last five years. Out of which 34(22.52 per cent) demised and the rest 177(77.48 per cent) are alive. Thus the mortality rate among the Khasas is only 4.50 per cent while the growth rate of the population is 15.50 per cent persons per year. Thus it may be concluded that the mortality rate among the Rajis is maximum in comparison to other tribal communities of Uttaranchal. The overall scenario of the tribals of Uttarakhand shows that there were total 334 births among the tribals in the last five years out of which only 74 (22.16 per cent) demised while 177 (77.48 per cent) were alive. Thus the mortality rate among the tribes is 4.43 per cent per year while the rate of population growth is 15.57 per cent persons per year, which is more than the growth rate of the general population. An outstanding trend of demographic nature of the tribal population also came into notice during the field work. We observed that there is variation in the survival percentage of the children of different tribal groups. For example, among the Rajis out of the total conceptions only 32.15 per cent could survive but this percentage goes up to 68.84 per cent, 83.33 per cent and 84.11 per cent among the Tharus, Buxas and the Khasas respectively. But in all matters there was a similarity in conception trend which is almost unrestricted rather very natural in all the tribal communities. The respondents were, then, asked about the causes of more conceptions. It was found that maximum 44.09 per cent conceptions took place as a result of desire for sons 27.09 per cent respondents were of the opinion that the conception cases mature in a natural course because the husband and wife when conjugate they hardly think of the result, i.e., conception. It is nature that makes concception, birth and the death possible. There are 26.23 per cent respondents who are of the opinion that more hands lead to more earnings and it is possible only through frequent conceptions. Particularly among the Rajis there is a notion, '*Kya Khanan Koon Hyo jo Ko Khanan Koon Jan Ho*' means, 'better to say what to eat', rather than who to eat', similarly -'*Kan Ranan Koon Hyojo, Ko Ranan Koon Jan Ho*' means 'better to say where to live rather than who to live'. These are the notions that always provoke and pacify mentally the Raji couple for having more conceptions, more births and more survials. But its destiny that causes more deaths which result in slow rate of population growth among the Rajis. The Table 6.10 (b) illustrates the facts pertaining to notions about more conceptions.

We have also tried to understand about the trend of mother or maternity mortality among the tribes. Surprisingly it is noticed that except two exceptional cases of maternal mortality found in the Raji community, none maternal mortality case was traced out in any tribal community of Uttaranchal during the last five years. So far as the two cases of maternal mortality are concerned, the Raji respondents stated that in both the cases, the deliveries were made by untrained and inexperienced persons. One of the cases was taken by a newly-appointed and less experienced ANM posted at Baluwakot Sub-primary Health Centre, while the other one was the home delivery. In both the cases after giving birth, the bleeding of the mother did not stop and finally it became fatal. During our field work we observed that deliveries among the tribal communities take place often very normal. We tried to understand the reason of these normal and natural deliveries and found that the women are very much

Table 6.10 (c) Notions About More Conceptions

Tribes	Sex	Notions						
		Desire for son	*More hands More earning*	*By nature*	*High infant Mortality*	*High Child Mortality*	*Uncertain*	*Total*
Raji	M	07	05	01	07	-	-	20
	%	35.00	25.00	5.00	35.00	-	-	100.00
	F	01	01	01	02	-	-	05
	%	20.00	20.00	20.00	40.00	-	-	100.00
Tharu	M	81	15	41	-	-	-	137
	%	59.12	10.95	21.93	-	-	-	100.00
	F	07	-	-	-	-	-	07
	%	100.00		-	-	-	-	100.00
Buxa	M	40	25	29	-	-		94
	%	42.55	26.60	30.85	-	-	-	100.00
	F	02	-	-	-	-	-	02
	%	100.00	-	-	-	-	-	100.00
Khasa	M	15	45	21	-	-	-	81
	%	18.52	55.56	25.92	-	-	-	100.00
	F	-	-	01	-	-	-	01
	%	-	-	100.00	-	-	-	100.00
Total	M	145	90	92	07	-	-	334
	%	43.41	26.95	27.54	2.10	-	-	100.00
	F	08	01	02	02	-	-	13
	%	61.55	7.69	15.38	15.38	-	-	100.00
Grand		153	91	94	09	-	-	347
Total	%	44.09	26.23	27.09	2.59		-	100.00

active and punctual in their physical working. They remain throughout mobile during their gestation period and their physical movements help in normal deliveries. There are cases when a pregnant woman gives birth to a baby on way to forest for collecting fodder or working in an agricultural field. They were asked why the people take such a risk of not going to maternity homes for deliveries. They flatly refuse saying that there is no risk felt by the people. They are used and accustomed of having deliveries at home. In most of the cases, both the mother and new-born baby remain healthy. No maternal casualty during the last five years particularly among the Tharus, the Buxas and the Khasas is itself an evidence of this fact.

Life Expectancy

For the enumeration of the life expectancy among the tribes we have taken information related to the date of births and deaths in the family. Since there was no birth and death register maintained in the village so we asked the respondents one by one the date of birth of his/ her family members who died, for example, an approximate date of birth and death of the grandfather, grandmother, father, mother, husband/ wife, son(s), daughter(s), brother(s), sister(s) and others. Most of the respondents were unable to tell exactly the date of birth and death of the family members, however, they were confident that the different deaths in the family occurred at what age. As per their information based on memories, the life expectancy is enumerated. The concerning data have been presented in the Table 6.11 to 6.15.

Table 6.11 depicts that among the Rajis there were 123 deaths occurring in the village as per family-wise information gathered through the family heads. It is observed that out of the total 123 deaths, maximum 30.09 per cent occurred at the age group of 60-70 years which preceded respectively by 18.70 per cent at the age-group of 70 years and above, 17.89 per cent at the age-group of 50-60 years, 15.44 per cent at the age-group of 0-10 years of age, 10.57 per cent at the age-group of 40-50 years, 3.26 per cent at the age-group of 30-40 years, 2.43 per cent at the age-group of 20-30 years and the rest 1.62 per cent at the age group of 10-20 years. We have also calculated an average mean of the age lived by the deceased people and we come to the conclusion (which is shown in Table 6.12), that among the Rajis the average life expectancy is 50.93 years, say 51 years only. In other words we can say that the average age of a Raji person is only 51 years while the latest data pertaining to general life expectancy show that it is 58 years. Thus the life expectancy among the Rajis is comparatively lower than general life expectancy.

In the same way we have also enumerated the life expectancy prevalent among the Buxas, the Tharus, and the Khasas. In the case of all the tribes, we could not get the written records about births and deaths of the people. Because any such record is not maintained at village level by any agency. However the tribe-wise purposefully selected respondents gave the information more confidently as is preserved in their memory. The data presented respectively in the Table 6.11 to 6.15 exhibit that among the Buxas out of the total 75 deaths 4.64 per cent occurred at the age-group of 0 to 10 years, 3.02 per cent at the age-group of 10 to 20 years, 1.16 per cent at the age-group of 20 to 30 years, 2.78 per cent at the age-group of 30 to 40 years, 16.47 per cent at the age-group of 40 to 50 years, 30.16 per cent at the age-group of 50 to 60 years, 23.21 per cent at the age-group of 60 to 70 and the remaining 18.56 per cent deaths occurred at the age-group of 70 years and above. The mean average of life expectancy, as calculated in Table 6.13, among the Buxas is 54.95, say 55 years. It means an average Buxa person lives approximately 55 years of age.

Among the Rajis there are total 123 deaths in the village. Out of the total deaths, 19(15.44 per cent) occurred at the age-group of 0-10 years, 02(1.62 per cent) in the age-group of 10-20 years, 03 (2.43 per cent) in the age-group of 20-30 years, 04(3.26 per cent) in 30-40 years of age, 13 (10.57 per cent) in the age-group of 40-50 years, 22 (17.89 per cent) in the age-group of 50-60 years, 37(30.09 per cent) at the age-group of 60-70 years and the rest 23 (18.70 per cent) deaths occurred at the age of 70 years and above. The mean average of life expectancy as calculated in Table 6.12 depicts that an average Raji lived an average 51 years of age which is less than that of the Buxas, the Tharus and the Khasas. Among the Tharus only 697 persons died, out of which 90 (12.91 per cent) died in the age-group of 0-10 years, 14 (2.01 per cent) in the age-group of 10-20 years, 16 (2.31 per cent) were in the age-group of 20-30 years, 17 (2.44 per cent) in the age-group of 30-40 years, 53 (7.60 per cent) died in the age-group of 40-50 years of age, 102 (14.63 per cent) in the age-group of 50-60 years, 200 (28.69 per cent) in the age-group of 60-70 years of age and the rest 205 (29.41 per cent) at the age of 70 years and above. Thus the average mean of an average Tharu person as shown in Table 6.14, is 54 years. Among the Khasas only 364 persons were recorded as dead. Out of the total deaths 41(11.26 per cent) occurred at the age-group of 0-10 years, 05 (1.37 per cent) at the age-group of 10-20 years, 04 (1.10 per cent) at the age-group of 20-30 years, 29(7.97 per cent) in 40-50 years of age, 46(12.64 per cent) in the age-group of 50-60 years, 114 (31.32 per cent) at the age-group of 60-70 years, while the rest 125 (34.34 per cent) deaths occurred at the age of 70 years and above. Thus the life expectancy among the Khasas is 57 years. Finally we come to the conclusion that life expectancy among the Khasas is maximum which is preceded respectively by the Buxas with 55 years, the Tharus with 54 years and the Rajis with 51 years respectively.

Table 6.11. Life Expectancy Among the Tribes

Total Age Lived (Age-Group)	*Tribes*			
	Rajis	*Buxas*	*Tharus*	*Khasas*
0-10	19 (15.44)	20 (4.64)	90 (12.91)	41 (11.26)
10-20	02 (1.62)	13 (3.02)	14 (2.01)	05 (1.37)
20-30	03 (2.43)	05 (1.16)	16 (2.31)	04 (1.10)
30-40	04 (3.26)	12 (2.78)	17 (2.44)	00 (00.00)
40-50	13 (10.57)	71 (16.47)	53 (7.60)	29 (7.97)
50-60	22 (17.89)	130 (30.16)	102 (14.63)	46 (12.64)
60-70	37 (30.09)	100 (23.21)	200 (28.69)	114 (31.32)
70 & above	23 (18.70)	80 (18.56)	205 (29.41)	125 (34.34)
Total	123 (100.00)	431 (100.00)	697 (100.00)	164 (100.00)

For the calculation of the tribe-wise life expectancy, it is necessary to enumerate the tribe-wise mean average of the people, who died in different age-groups. The life expectancy thus can be enumerated as follows:

Table 6.12. Life Expectancy Among the Rajis

Age Group CI	*Frequency f*	*x*	*fx*
0-10	19	5	95
10-20	02	15	30
20-30	03	25	75
30-40	04	35	140
40-50	13	45	585
50-60	22	55	1210
60-70	37	65	2405
70 & above	23	75	1725
Total	N=123		$\sum$fx = 6265

$$\text{Mean} = \frac{\sum fx}{N} = \frac{6265}{123} = 50.93 \text{ Years}$$

thus the life expectancy among the Rajis is 50.93 say 51 years

Table 6.13 Life Expectancy Among the Buxas

Age Group CI	*Frequency x*	*f*	*fx*
0-10	5	20	100
10-20	15	13	195
20-30	25	05	125
30-40	35	12	420
40-50	45	71	3195
50-60	55	130	7150
60-70	65	100	6500
70 & above	75	80	6000
Total		N=431	$\sum$fx = 23685

$$\text{Mean} = \frac{\sum fx}{N} = \frac{23685}{431} = 54.95 \text{ Years.}$$

Thus the life expectancy among the Buxas is 54.95 say 55 years.

Table 6.14. Life Expectancy Among the Tharus

Age Group CI	*Frequency x*	*f*	*fx*
0-10	5	90	450
10-20	15	14	210
20-30	25	16	400
30-40	35	17	595
40-50	45	53	2385
50-60	55	102	5610
60-70	65	200	13000
70 & above	75	205	15375
Total		N=697	$\sum$fx = 38025

$$\text{Mean} = \frac{\sum fx}{N} = \frac{38025}{697} = 54.56 \text{ Years.}$$

Thus the life expectancy among the Tharus is approximately 54 years.

Table 6.15. Life Expectancy Among the Khasas

Age Group CI	Frequency x	f	fx
0-10	5	41	205
10-20	15	05	75
20-30	25	04	100
30-40	35	00	0
40-50	45	29	1305
50-60	55	46	2530
60-70	65	114	7410
70 & above	75	125	9375
Total		N=364	$\sum$fx = 21000

$$\text{Mean} = \frac{\sum fx}{N} = \frac{21000}{364} = 57.69 \text{ years.}$$

Thus the life expectancy among the Khasa is approximately 57 years.

So far as the cause of death is concerned different tribes have their different opinions. Among the Rajis the deaths in adult and old age were caused mostly by respiratory diseases like Asthma and lung-related diseases like tuberculosis. In old age, as the Raji people told, the persons generally become the victims of lung-disease. Due to Asthma, they become out of breath. Sometimes they become the victim of severe cough and cold. While some deaths are caused by snake bites. Lung diseases like tuberculosis used to be the most prevalent disease in the Raji area. In old age, swelling in the body, chest pain, severe cough with bleeding, to be out of breath, dyspepsia, loss of hunger, joint pains, hydroceles, rheumatism, gout, general fatigue, etc. are some of the general bodily ailments. These symptoms indicate towards tuberculosis and other chest and liver related diseases, which ultimately cost the lives of the people. Moreover there are some deaths due to falling down from rocks and from trees while at work. In fact the Rajis are the poorest among the poor people. They are the victims of malnutrition from womb to tomb. The longing of stomach-full diet is a dream for them. Scarcity of food stuffs, milk and milk products, vegetables etc. causes a number of deficiencies in their body which results in loss of resistance power that ultimately invite the diseases of various kinds. The deaths in early age are caused by pneumonia, typhoid, whooping cough, tansilitis, measles, diptherea, mums, dysentry and diarrhoea. There are some respondents who do not agree with the causes of death as are being narrated by most of the respondents. They are of the opinion that births are inevitable. The causes, as narrated, are simply a pretence. However the diseases mentioned here, have ever been a life killing impact on the Rajis. The other aspect of their life-style is concerned with their day-to-day routine work in a harsh and unfavourable ecological conditions which sometimes takes the human life. The dense forests and rocks generally prove to be a lurking danger for them. It is the reason that the population growth and the health status of the Raji people is below normal till the date.

The Rajis who still subsist on jungle products just go for collecting food from the forests. Their frequent visit to jungle sometimes for vegetable, fruits, tubers, sometimes for fuel and fodder, and, sometimes for trapping small games and collecting the eggs of some birds like red-legged partridge and so. During this period, sometimes the people have to become the victim of some lurking dangers, for instance, there are some birds who web their nest amidst of the rocks' cavity and lay their eggs. The people looking for the eggs just put their hands in the cavity of the rocks to search out the nest and the eggs there in. But there are cases, while the snake sitting on a coil within the cavity of rocks, just pricks with a stings to the person, who ultimately dies for having no medical aid. There are also some cases of snake-biting while sleeping within the hut. It is known fact that the Raji people build their abodes by themselves. Even today most of them live in mixed type of houses. There are incidences when snake enters into the abodes and bite the person at sleep. The non-availability of medical first-aid causes the death of the victim. Even in other cases when any person suffering from measles, typhoid, diarrhoea, cowpox, mums and other life-killing diseases, which needs instant medical treatment, cannot have medical aid. Because the Raji area lacks absolutely medical facility on the one hand, and on the other hand, they prefer to apply the traditional method first for the treatment of the ailment. This process delays the proper medical diagnosis and treatment and ultimately proves to be fatal.

Besides this, the consumption of some poisonous jungle products becomes the cause of deaths because the people remain ignorant of the poisonous nature of these products. The unknowingly use of these items generates some bodily abnormalities and ultimately takes the toll of persons. There are some casualties occurring due to chronic jaundice (locally known as 'Kamalbye fever'), respiratory problems and gout. Some have no answer to the causes of deaths occurring in their families. But they were confident that death is inevitable, it may come at any age and at any time and place. It depends on the will of God. In brief it can be concluded that the Rajis have no scientific approach towards births and deaths of persons. They treat it as a natural process and therefore appear to be careless about their health and health-related aspects. They have their notions and assumptions about births and also a traditional pattern of treatment to the ailments. They exceptionally visit the primary health centres for consulting the medical practitioners for their illness and other health problems. Hence, the most of the cases of sickness have proved to be fatal in the last five years.

Even some of the causes of illness they mentioned during our discussions were fictitious. As a matter of fact except some accidental cases like deaths due to falling from the rocks and trees, and snakebite etc. all the diseases have not been properly diagnosed by the authorised medical practitioners and no permanent treatment was provided to the patients. Almost all the sickness cases, therefore, resulted into deaths.

Among the Buxas most of the cases of sickness are running under treatment. The people are suffering from respiratory diseases, cough, tuberculosis, hypertension, asthma, heart related problems, fits due to sudden attack of fever, polio, paralysis, leprosy, psychiatric problems, hydrocele, sexually transmitted diseases or venereal diseases among women, cancer, jaundice, colic pain, dyspepsia, gastric problems, malaria, urinary disease etc. In most of the cases the sick person is observed under treatment. Mostly the tuberculosis cases are result in deaths. The general disease, particularly among the women, has always proved to be fatal. It is so because the women do not disclose the general ailments even to the family members due to hesitation which ultimately become the cause of various other serious diseases like cancer. In the village there are women who are suffering from breast cancer. In the family most of the old-age deaths are caused due to respiratory, lung and liver-related diseases. Some of the deaths were occurred due to smallpox, measles and typhoid. General weakness, anaemia, constant fever, cough, swelling in the body, gastric problems, loss of appetite are some of the general problems of the Buxas. These problems gradually develop to chronic stage only then the people consult the doctor. But till then it was too late to cure the disease. In fact the Buxas are superstitious people. They firmly believe in sorcery and magical practices. Some traditional sorcerer and sorceress are known for their exorcism practices and occult arts. In other sense they can be termed as the traditional medicine persons who are consulted first by the patient. Naturally it is difficult to get rid of the grip of these traditional medicine men. But when the diseases becomes incurable and fatal then the traditional medicine men blames the patient for not having precautions suggested by them and for bidding for any further treatment. Then the patient, flabbergasted, approaches and consults the medical practitioners available in the village who remain untrained. For sometime they also give their treatment and lastly refer them to other hospitals for treatment. This long process starting from patients' own forbearance and own treatment, then consultation of traditional medicine men, then untrained medical practitioners and lastly trained and authorised medical doctors virtually exhaust the patient physically, mentally as well as economically and proves fatal in most of the cases. While in some cases the patients do have positive results of the treatment but with some perpetual handicaps. In fact the Buxas are the conservative people, they even today believe in sorcery, occult practices, traditional practices of treatment and prefer to follow them first. It is so because of their illiteracy, lack of awareness, pervading ignorance and overall firm believe in divine power that is supposed to be the only cause of all happiness and worries. This is the notion that leads to a number of sufferings and foster them generation to generation.

The Tharus, who have comparatively more literacy and more education in comparison to the Rajis and the Buxas, have somewhat different notion about bodily ailments, other physical morbidities and deaths of the people. Though there are not written records and visible proofs of the causes of diseases and deaths but what the family members, particularly the respondents told according to the best of their recollections prove that deaths in their families were caused by their ignorance, non-availability of proper medical aid and ill-treatment given by the untrained medical practitioners. The case studies of some polio affected persons in Ratanpur village can be treated as a scientific proof of this kind, (see case study No. 1, 2, 3 and 4).

The polyandrous Khasas have some additional problems in relation to former three tribal communities. It is so because of the types of the marriages they practise in their social life. There are people who observe polyandry on the one hand, and polygyny and monogamy, on the other hand. The polyandry and polygyny are the manifestation of traditionality and economic backwardness while the observance of monogamy indicates modernity and affluence. Besides this the double standard of measurement for the married and unmarried females as well as for the female as a daughter and daughter-in-law. In fact in Basaya village, the female is known as 'Dhyan' while she is at her parents' place and the same female is known as Rain at in-laws place. According to the social postulations of the Khasas the women as 'Dhyan' are free from all sorts of normative conditions while at in-laws' place they are supposed to follow different ethical values and certain standard of morality, modesty and chastity. The observance of double standard of morality, one for wife and another for daughter, leads to a number of health-related anomalies in females' health which has far reaching impacts even on the men-folk. In fact the laxity in sexual behaviour, the polyandrous and polygynous form of marriage and conservatism, shyness, hesitation and the tendency of hiding the facts altogether generate, preserve and transmit various sexually transmitted diseases among the people. This is a known fact that an ailment in the body and its prolonged stay causes several other ailments and anomalies in human body. Most of the deaths in the Khasa families, as the respondents uttered, are caused by some unknown force. However the symptoms, what the respondents told about, indicate about the ailments which proved to be fatal for the patients.

The nature of work which the people perform and also the working conditions at work's place have also positive correlation with health status of the people concerned. In Tribal area we observe three main seasons in a year; these are : the summer season which starts from March and ends in June, the rainy season that starts from July and ends in October, and, the winter season that starts from November and ends in February every year. All the three seasons are of different nature according to which the tribal people change their routine of work, fooding, clothing and even the working hours. In other words, we can say that the 'time factor' has an effective role in the determination of the nature of work and the routine of day-to-day activities. Among the Rajis, as already mentioned, most of the population subsist on the traditional type of crude cultivation, daily labour work, food gathering from jungles etc. In a year the Raji people harvest only two crops, namely, Rabi and Kharif. The agricultural fields where they work is hilly, rugged and slopy land. The soil is dry, sandy and barren. The agricultural yield completely depends on rainy water because there is no facility of irrigation. The insufficient agricultural yield leads to a number of supplementary jobs like gathering jungle products, earning daily wages as labour, trapping small games and fishing etc. The Rajis go for collecting fuel wood and fodder from the jungle all the year round. Only a small part of fuel and fodder is kept for their own use while the major part of the collection is sold by them in the nearby market place at Jaulajibee. The money thus earned is spent on meeting out their daily needs of fooding, clothing and others. But hardly a nominal part of their income is spent on treatment of health related ailments. Besides this, they also collect some tubers like 'Bhekuna, Gethi, Tarud and also some fruits like Hisalu, Kirmoda, Bamuri, Kafal and the vegetables like Luna, Sinna and Mushroom etc. The jungle products consisting of tubers, fruits and vegetables are consumed by them according to availability as well as of the intensity of hunger. The intensity of hunger makes them eat the jungle products without assessing their side effects on body. Sometimes the consumption of some poisonous jungle products ends the life of the people. There were several cases of this type in past. Thus we can conclude that the nature of work and the working conditions where the Raji people work as such are not unhygienic and unhealthy but their health-related repercussions are not always positive and functional.

The occupational structure among the Buxas and the Tharus show that the tribal people have to work as landless labourers, as agriculturists they also have to work in the forests for collecting jungle products. There are some tribal people who work in the adjoining industrial areas. In all the places the nature of work, the working conditions and the environmental conditions of the region remain almost different from each other. As we observe three seasons in the hilly area of Uttaranchal so is the case of the Uttaranchal Tarai—the dwelling place of the Tharus and the Buxas. It is a known fact that the Uttaranchal Tarai is known as a bowl of rice. It was basically a swamp region with contrast climatic conditions. In summer the mercury rises to its extreme and adversely falls down to its bottom in winter. In rainy season the climate becomes malaria prone. Having comparatively shallow level of ground water the people just install their own tubewells for irrigation purposes. In some areas the ground water comes up to its surface and makes the land swampy and sometimes ponds crop up. In the Ratanpur village, there is self-made pond amidst the village which is permanently a breeding ground of mosquitoes. In agricultural fields where the landless agricultural labourers as well as the agriculturists have to work throughout the year the working condition of the working place remain unsuitable for health particularly during rainy season when muddy grounds are prepared for transplanting paddy seedlings and the people have to work continuously in the muddy grounds with long stay. In peak season sometimes the people enter the muddy ground for transplanting paddy seedlings at about 8.00 a.m. and come out by 4.00 p.m. This long stay in muddy ground for transplanting paddy seedlings plants some serious ailments in human body also which gradually transforms into serious disease.

The tribal people also go for collecting fuel wood, fodder, timber seasonal vegetables, fruits and tubers from the nearby forests. In Tarai area the forests are mostly dense with humid climate. No doubt the forests have functional importance to the tribal people in general but the attack of some poisonous insects, as well as the consumption of some poisonous vegetables, fruits and a type of mushroom become fatal to them. The Buxas are the main labour force in sugar factories established in Bajpur area. The industrial refuse, smoke and stinking garbage have always ill-effects on their health. Lung diseases, respiratory problems and various other bodily ailments are caused by polluted environment of the factory area.

Basaya is a hilly Khasa village. Most of the people subsist on their age-old traditional occupation of agriculture and its supplementary jobs like animal husbandry, rearing sheep and goats, collection of jungle products and brewing etc. Mostly, the land is unirrigated and sandy. The hilly and rugged land need rainy water as to make it cultivable. The people have to work in agricultural fields and also in jungles for earning their livelihood. Because of the clear-cut division of labour, the family members start their routine work with the break of the day. At night, generally when dinner is over, the family members sit together and the head of the family assigns them duties for the following day. According to the instructions of the family head some people go for performing agricultural tasks, some for collecting jungle products, while some of the family members go for daily wage earning as labourers, some for opening shops and some remain at home for performing the familial jobs like cooking meal, feeding children, sweeping and washing the house-courtyards, rooms and also for cleaning cattle-sheds. The persons at home are liable for doing all the familial tasks.

Thus, some of the Khasa people work at home, some in agricultural fields, some in jungles, some in pastures while some in the nearby market place at Sahaya. The nature of work and the working conditions remain almost different of members of the family. Due to backward agricultural economy, pervading illiteracy, poverty, unawareness of various essential aspects of health and hygiene the traditional Khasas just carry out the instructions, liabilities and duties assigned to them by the heads of families even in adverse situations. Geting up early in the morning, fetching water from the water source, milking the cattle (buffalos and cows), cleansing the cattle sheds, then cleaning the rooms, kitchen, and preparing breakfast, feeding the children are some of the jobs performed by the women who are supposed to work at home. In fact she has no time for herself. Only after performing her jobs, she takes her meal. Working in cattle shed, cleansing cow-dung and other rubbish from cattleshed, storing the dung and other rubbish are some of the unhygienic tasks which has always ill-effects on human body. The pastoral Khasas have to pass their maximum time with their tamed animals and related jobs which are unhygienic such tasks have far reaching ill-effects on them. Going to agricultural fields for performing agricultural tasks and forests for collecting fuel-wood and fodder are very tedious jobs which require balanced food conducive to good health, but it is quite impossible in most of the Khasa families. The working conditions are very hard and the working places are not favourable for good health. Even in winter mornings, the people go in their duties as usual and even in summer noons they can be seen working in fields and pastures. Such adverse climatic conditions have always ill-effects on human body. Just to pull on the life, people have acclimatized themselves with the physiology of the region but the ill-effects of it can in no way be ignored. It is the reason that a person at the age group of 25 to 35 begins to look like of sixties. Their thin built, untimely wrinkled face, emaciation of cheeks etc. are some of the manifestations of their ill-health and also the repercussions of their hard life.

Socio-Religious and Environmental Aspects of Health

Health has some socio-religious and environmental aspects which have crucial role in determining the health status of a community as a whole. Keeping to this assumption in mind we have tried to understand the notion prevalent among the tribals about morbidity and sickness of persons of different categories viz. aged, adult, young, children and infants. In this very context the respondents were also asked about the causes of illness they assumed and also their notions about disease. We have different opinions of different tribal people. Even in the same tribal community the respondents were of different opinions about the causes of morbidity and sickness. They have different notions as well as different concepts of diseases. The reactions we had from the respondents were thoroughly generalized and then classified in the groups according to similarities. There are people who consider divine power and its displeasure as a cause of morbidity and sickness of the people. While some other consider the effect of evil eye and evil spirit as the cause of morbidity and sickness. Besides this, the effect of 'hot or cold', 'excess or shortage' of food and drinks, excess physical work and shortage of food items, excess work and use of intoxicant but not sufficient diet, fate, sorcery, wrath of deities, violation of socio-religious taboos, result of one's deeds, intemperance and lack of medical facilities are some of the factors the tribal people consider as the cause of morbidity and sickness of the people. But there is a variation of opinion percentage in regard to different factors. As in the case of the aged persons the people are of the opinion that morbidity and all sorts of suffering are nothing but the result of one's deeds. While there are people who stated that they (the aged persons) can neither adjust with, seasonal variations due to bodily weakness nor do they have receptivity in digesting the food items available and provided to them for eating. Some are of the opinion that shortage of food items and excess of work load causes different types of morbidity among the aged persons. In the case of the adult and the youth, the tribal people have different opinions. They state that the adult and the youth have maximum work load in the family but not sufficient balanced diet they can have due to poverty. Besides this, they (the adult and the youth) have a sort of intoxication of youth which provokes them to work hard as well as leads to intemperance and also for using intoxicants and ultimately resulting in a sort of weakness that paves the way for morbidity and sickness. There are number of cases of tuberculosis which started with weakness, then loss of appetite, then loss of weight and everlasting physical fatigue of physical work and lastly, bleeding in cough. Such cases, when contacting to medical practitioners, were declared tuberculosis positive at a very advanced stage. It is the real position of morbidity and its causes. But the members of the family interpret it in some other way. They are confident that it was the ill-practice of the sorcerer who made them eat some magical things with sweet which caused incurable illness.

The data presented in Table 6.16 show the tribe-wise reactions about the cause of morbidity and sickness of persons of different categories. Almost all the respondents belonging to different tribal communities have approximately similar views and notions about the causes of morbidity. As most of the respondents have stated that it is fate as well as one's deeds which altogether lead to morbidity and sickness in old age, while the children and infants fall sick or suffer from morbidity only due to ill-effects of evil spirits, evil eyes, wrath of deities, sorcery and bad luck of the parents. There is exceptionally a nominal percentage of the respondents who asserted that the inadequate medical facilities and health services as the cause of morbidity and sickness. In the case of youths and adult persons, the respondents have different opinions. In this regard, they stated that excess physical work, inadequate and unbalanced diet, intemperance and use of intoxicants are some of the causes of morbidity and sickness, have morbidity and sickness of the youth and the adult, while pregnant women have morbidity due to violation of socio-religious taboos, intemperance, excess physical labour, sorcery, her own fate and deeds. In fact, there is a general notion about the aged sick person that he/she had misdeeds in his/her youth or in young age which have resulted in morbidity and sickness in old age. In other words, we can say that morbidity and sickness, particularly in old age, is the result of one's deeds and fate. The respondents have different opinions about morbidity and sickness of the youth and the adult. They stated that in youth and in adult age the persons have energy of work. In real sense they are the working people of any community naturally they have more liabilities. They are supposed to fulfill the expectations of the family members. This situation provokes them to work hard. But the poor economy does not provide them sufficient and proper diet which results in weakness. Sometime the young and adult persons are addicted to intoxication and do not care for their health. This state of being results in morbidity and sickness. Children and infants are more prone to the effect of evil eye, evil spirits, wrath of deities and sorcery. To verify the notion prevalent about morbidity and sickness of persons of different categories a counter multiple choice question was put to the respondents. The responses as presented in the following Table 6.17, make it proves that their notion about morbidity and sickness of persons is almost the same. See Table 6.16 and 6.17.

There are respondents who held that lack of medical facilities in their area is also a cause of all sorts of illness but the percentage of such respondents is very nominal. Thus the results show that the health has some socio-religious concerns which determine the health status of the people in the community.

The tribal people have a notion of 'hot and cold'. They are of the view that certain things are of 'hot' nature while some are of 'cold' nature.

Correspondingly there are people who have receptivity towards things of 'hot' nature. By the way if those persons eat some thing of 'cold' nature they fall ill vis-a-vis the persons who have more receptivity to cold items, just fall ill with the consumption of hot items. For example, among the Rajis, Tadud, Gethi, Bhaikuna, (edible roots) are of cold natured edible roots but they form an important part of their food habits. Since they have no other option, the consumption of these items is therefore inevitable which ultimately causes digestive problems among the people. Among the Tharus and the Buxas the cooked rice is treated as of 'cold nature' food item, in spite of that they are used to take cooked rice twice a day, i.e., in lunch and in dinner. This tendency ultimately causes some bodily ailments. Among the Khasas the 'Ghuyan' an edible root and 'urd' (a pulse) are of cold nature. The use of those items causes some bodily ailments. Needless to say the notion of 'hot and cold' is based on the experience of the tribal people. But there is no scientific base of such notions. It is merely their own interpretation which can more accurately be termed as superstitious. The observance of such superstitions has always ill bodily effects. Besides this the tribal people have their own interpretation of 'abstinence' and 'intemperance'. As for instance, among the Raji and the Khasa community the use of the things with 'heat engymes' is treated always harmful to pregnant women. Hence they are provided very simple unfried food free from all sorts of spices and fat. Even the lactating mothers are denied to have cold water may be she is thirsty because it can cause cold to the sucking baby. Even the newly born baby is not provided water until the performance of 'Anna-prashan' ceremony. Birth to Anna-prashan ceremony has at least six months interval. The observance of such unscientific notions leads to a number of ailments in human body. If any person does not follow these notions, it is treated as intemperance for which the person concerned is treated as responsible and therefore neglected by the family members. No treatment is provided to those persons whose sufferings result from intemperance. They are, virtually, left to their own destiny. There is an example that in tribal areas every new-born baby is not attired with new costumes. It is a prevalent notion that wearing new clothes by the new born-baby is always harmful to him/her. It has always ill-effects. Hence, there is a tradition to attire the baby with worn-out clothes or the new-born is put on rags or wrapped in tatters. Since the tribals have no sense of hygiene, the use of dirty, filthy, stinking tatters always have unhealthy effects on the new-born child. In fact those notions have no scientific basis, however, they are observed by the people, and non-observance of such notions is treated as 'intemperance' for which the person concerned is held at fault and is not given any proper care. Such a practice invites and correspondingly multiplies the morbidity and sickness

Table 6.16. Tribe-wise Notion Prevalent about Morbidity and Sickness

Tribe	Category of Persons	NOTIONS											
		Displeasure of Divine Power	Evil Eye and Evil Spirit	Concept of Hot and Cold	Excess Physical Work, no proper diet and use of intoxicants	Fate	Sorcery	Wrath of deities	Violation of socio-religious taboos	Lack of medical facilities	Intemper-ance	Result of one's deed	Total
Raji	Aged	01 (4.00)	03 (12.00)	05 (20.00)	— —	04 (16.00)	— —	— —	— —	— —	— —	12 (48.00)	12 (100.00)
	Adult	02 (8.00)	06 (24.00)	01 (4.00)	11 (44.00)	3 (12.00)	— —	— —	— —	— —	— —	02 (8.00)	25 (100.00)
	Young	02 (8.00)	03 (12.00)	— —	11 (44.00)	— —	02 (8.00)	— —	04 (16.00)	— —	03 (12.00)	— —	25 (100.00)
	Child	04 (16.00)	10 (40.00)	01 (4.00)	— —	03 (12.00)	02 (8.00)	04 (16.00)	— —	01 (4.00)	— —	— —	25 (100.00)
	Infant	01 (4.00)	08 (32.00)	07 (28.00)	— —	02 (8.00)	03 (12.00)	01 (4.00)	— —	03 (12.00)	— —	— —	25 (100.00)
	Pregnant Mother	— —	— —	— —	— —	03 (12. 00)	02 (8.00)	05 (20.00)	06 (24.00)	03 (12.00)	06 (24.00)	— —	25 (100.00)
Tharu	Aged	— —	— —	17 (11.80)	— —	35 (24.31)	— —	— —	13 (9.03)	— —	32 (22.22)	47 (32.64)	144 (100.00)
	Adult	11 (7.64)	— —	— —	63 (43.75)	24 (16.67)	— —	18 (12.50)	— —	16 (11.11)	12 (8.33)	I	144 (100.00)
	Young	26 (18.06)	28 (19.44)	— —	53 (36.81)	18 (12.50)	08 (5.56)	—	05 (3.47)	—	06 (4.17)		144 (100.00)

(Contd.)

(Contd. Table 6.16)

Tribe	Category of Persons	NOTIONS											
		Displeasure of Divine Power	Evil Eye and Evil Spirit	Concept of Hot and Cold	Excess Physical Work, no proper diet and use of intoxicants	Fate	Sorcery	Wrath of deities	Violation of socio-religious taboos	Lack of medical facilities	Intemperance	Result of one's deed	Total
	Child	27 (18.75)	51 (35.42)	29 (20.14)		16 (11.11)	02 (1.39)	10 (6.94)		5 (3.47)	4 (2.78)	I	144 (100.00)
	Infant	28 (19.44)	53 (36.81)	12 (8.33)	—	10 (6.94)	03 (2.08)	20 (13.89)	—	13 (9.03)	05 (3.48)	I	144 (100.00)
	Pregnant Mother	—	—	—	72 (50.00)	15 (10.42)	—	—	36 (25.00)	09 (6.25)	10 (6.94)	02 (1.39)	144 (100.00)
Buxa	Aged	—	—	18 (18.75)	—	28 (29.17)	—	—	14 (14.58)	04 (4.17)	07 (7.29)	25 (26.04)	96 (100.00)
	Adult	4 (4.1 7)	—	—	44 (45.83)	14 (14.58)	10 (10.42)	12 (12.50)	—	02 (4.17)	08 (8.33)	—	96 (100.00)
	Young	6 (6.25)	22 (22.92)	—	35 (36.46)	24 (25.00)	04 (4.17)	—	—	—	05 (5.20)	—	96 (100.00)
	Child	—	32 (33.33)	18 (18.75)	—	07 (7.29)	10 (10.42)	21 (21.88)	—	—	8 (8.33)	—	96 (100.00)
	Infant	06 (6.25)	38 (39.58)	—	—	12 (12.50)	11 (11.46)	12 (12.50)	—	—	17 (17.71)	—	96 (100.00)
	Pregnant Mother	—	—	—	21 (21.88)	23 (23.96)	—	—	28 (19.27)	11 (11.46)	13 (13 53)	—	96 (100.00)

(Contd.)

(Contd. Table 6.16)

Tribe	Category of Persons	NOTIONS											
		Displeasure of Divine Power	Evil Eye and Evil Spirit	Concept of Hot and Cold	Excess Physical Work, no proper diet and use of intoxicants	Fate	Sorcery	Wrath of deities	Violation of socio-religious taboos	Lack of medical facilities	Intemperance	Result of one's deed	Total
Khasa	Aged	—	—	23 (28.05)	22 (26.83)	12 (14.63)	—	—	—	—	04 (4.88)	21 (25.61)	82 (100.00)
	Adult	—	—	16 (19.51)	36 (43.90)	16 (19.51)	—	—	—	—	10 (12.20)	04 (4.88)	82 (100.00)
	Young	—	05 (6.10)	03 (3.66)	40 (48.78)	14 (17.07)	05 (6.10)	11 (13.41)	4 (4.88)	—	—	—	82 (100.00)
	Child	08 (9.76)	25 (39.49)	12 (14.63)	—	06 (7.32)	20 (24.39)	—	—	11 (13.41)	—	—	82 (100.00)
	Infant	06 (7.32)	26 (31.70)	13 (15.85)	—	07 (8.54)	13 (15.85)	—	—	07 (8.54)	10 (12.20)	—	82 (100.00)
	Pregnant Mother	05 (6.10)	—	—	18 (21.95)	07 (8.54)	15 (18.29)	04 (4.88)	11 (13.41)	02 (2.44)	20 (24.39)	—	82 (100.00)

Table 6.17 Notion About what Leads a Person to Illness

Tribe	*Reactions*							
	Super Natural force	*Sorcery*	*Mystical Power*	*Wrath of deities*	*Evil & Evil Eye Spirit*	*Violation of Socio-religious taboos*	*Unavailability of Medical facilities*	*Mal-Nutrition*
Rajis	10	09	10	10	25	10	07	09 3
%	40.00	36.00	40.00	40.00	100.00	40.00	28.00	6.00
Tharus	91	13	92	48	132	54	43	69
%	63.89	9.03	63.89	33.33	91.67	37.50	29.86	47.92
Buxas	16	35	16	45	82	42	19	58
%	16.67	36.46	16.67	46.88	85.42	43.75	19.79	60.42
Khasas	19	53	19	15	56	15	20	30
%	37.17	64.63	23.17	18.29	68.29	18.29	24.39	36.39

among the people. Among the Tharus a woman, when undergoes mensturation or when gives birth to a baby, is kept in a room dark and aloof. She is provided dry-cut-stalks of paddy with a quilt made up of worn-out tatters for bedding. She is treated untouchable for five and nine days respectively. She is not permitted to have a bath daily. She is given a very simple unfried food with plain salt or sometime unfried 'dal' or vegetables. Such a notion leads to morbidity and other ailments in human body. Among the Buxas, a woman when gives birth to a baby, is made confined to a room and is not allowed to come out even for evacuation and other natural discharges. She makes evacuation and urinary discharge in the corner of that very room, and its a duty of the husband or any other family member to throw it out. She comes out only after the period of nine days are over for a sacred bath. Till then, both, the mother and the infant, are not allowed for taking bath. Such type of notions and practices generate a number of morbidities.

The health care system available in the village or elsewhere and the utilization pattern of these health services have been discussed village-wise in chapter-4. However in brief we can state that the Khasas and the Buxas have the facility of primary health care services in their own villages while the Rajis and the Tharus have to travel 04 to 11 km. respectively for availing of the services of primary health centres because the government health centres are located at Balwakot (Dharchula) for the Rajis and Khatima for the Tharus. Almost all the health centres have shortage of medical officers and other subordinate staff as well as machines and medicines. Hence they are hardly capable of providing even the first-aid services to the patients. It is the reason that the tribal people mainly the Tharus and the Buxas consult preferably their traditional medicine-men first and then the private medical practitioners available in the approachable distance nearby to their villages but do not want to consult the Govt. Health Centres. While the Rajis and the Khasas are used to tolerate their ailments or they prefer to make their treatment by themselves through traditional practices rather than approaching the primary health centres. Because the people know it better that when they approach the primary health centres, the medical officer(s) or the subordinate staff do investigate the patient but do not give any medicine. During investigation their behaviour and treatment with the patients remains sympathetic and cooperative but due to nonavailability of medicines in the centre they just write the prescription and ask the patient for buying the medicine from the market dispensary. Hence they prefer to visit private medical practitioners who not only investigate the patients but also provide them medicine at the clinic and charge nominal fees for it. It is the reason that the tribal people do not prefer to consult the government doctors and health centres even for delivery cases.

The respondents were asked, where the deliveries of different women in the family take place. For example, we asked the respondent to tell about the places where the deliveries of their wives took place. They were given five options for the places of deliveries, these were Home, PHC, Sub-PHC, Govt. Hospital and Private Maternity Home. They were further asked to tell about the places where the deliveries of their brother's wife and their daughter-in-law's took place. Our main aim was to observe the change in attitudinal trend in different generations. In this context, the respondent's wife was treated as the old generation in comparison to brother's wife and of the daughter-in-law who were regarded the second and the third generation respectively in comparison to respondent's wife. It is observed that maximum deliveries, i.e., 1779 (99.32 per cent) out of total 1795 deliveries of the three generations took place only at home. There are exceptionally 12 (0.67 per cent) cases of deliveries out of which four among the Rajis, three among the Tharus, one among the Buxas and four among the Khasas took place at Primary Health Centres and four cases (0.23 per cent) of deliveries of the daughters-in-law of the Buxas took place in private maternity homes at Bajpur. But this percentage does not present any trend in attitudinal changes of the tribals. The deliveries having taken place out of home were really of complicated nature, as the respondents were asked and it was inevitable for them to consult the doctor (See Table 6.18)

In most of the delivery cases held at home the birth attendants were the indigenous untrained aged women who are believed to have enough experience of making the deliveries normal by their own traditional means and methods while the cases taken up by the medical practitioners at Primary Health Centres and the doctors at Private Maternity Homes were thoroughly attended by trained midwives, ANM and nurses respectively. But the tribal people particularly the Rajis reiterated that the cases taken up by the Primary Health Centres remain failure while there is hardly any maternity case held at home was a failure. Thus even today the tribals prefer to have home deliveries. After delivery they cut the umbilical cord with scissors, sickle or blade and dress up it in their own way. Among the Rajis just after the birth of a baby the umbilical cord is tightly bound with thread and then cut down with sickle or blade. Then the end of the umbilical cord is dressed up generally with ash or dry soil. Among the Tharus first of all mustard oil is applied to umbilical cord and then it is bound with thread at about its bottom and the rest part is cut with scissor or blade and the end of the remaining umbilical cord is dressed up in mustard oil again. It is believed that remaining part of the umbilical cord will dry-up within a week or so and fall off itself. The Buxas use only thread for binding tightly the umbilical cord and then cut it with a blade. In due course of time the remaining part falls off and the

Table 6.18 Tribe-wise deliveries held on

Tribe wise deliveries held on		Wifes deliveries							Daughter-in-law's deliveries					Brothers wifes deliveries					Total
		1st	IInd	IIIrd	IVth	Vth	VIth	VIIth	1st	IInd	IIIrd	IVth	Vth	1st	IInd	IIIrd	IVth	Vth	
Raji	At Home	24	20	15	04	02	01		—						—	—	—	—	66
	In PHC	01	01	—	—	—	—	—	02	—	—	—	—	—	—	—	—	—	04
	Sub PHC	—	—	—	—	—	—	—	—	—	—	—	—	—	—	—	—	—	—
	Govt. Hospital	—	—	—	—	—	—	—	—	—	—	—	—	—	—	—	—	—	—
	Pvt. Hospital	—	—	—	—	—	—	—	—	—	—	—	—	—	—	—	—	—	—
	Total	25	21	15	04	02	01	—	02	—	—	—	—	—	—	—	—	—	70
Tharu	At Home	144	136	108	63	24	09	02	96	85	62	08	—	25	18	09	05	—	794
	In PHC	—	—	—	—	—	—	—	01	01	01	—	—	—	—	—	—	—	03
	Sub PHC	—	—	—	—	—	—	—	—	—	—	—	—	—	—	—	—	—	—
	Govt. Hospital	—	—	—	—	—	—	—	—	—	—	—	—	—	—	—	—	—	—
	Pvt. Hospital	—	—	—	—	—	—	—	—	—	—	—	—	—	—	—	—	—	—
	Total	144	136	108	63	24	09	02	97	86	63	08	—	25	18	09	05	—	797
Buxa	At Home	85	72	65	50	06	04	01	32	15	15	10	02	15	09	06	04	01	392
	In PHC	01	—	—	—	—	—	—	—	—	—	—	—	—	—	—	—	—	01
	Sub PHC	—	—	—	—	—	—	—	—	—	—	—	—	—	—	—	—	—	—
	Govt. Hospital	—	—	—	—	—	—	—	—	—	—	—	—	—	—	—	—	—	—
	Pvt. Hospital	—	—	—	—	—	—	—	01	02	01	—	—	—	—	—	—	—	04
	Total	86	72	65	50	06	04	01	33	17	16	10	92	15	09	06	04	01	397

(Contd.)

(Contd. Table 6.18)

Tribe wise deliveries held on		*Wives deliveries*							*Daughter-in-law's deliveries*					*Brother's wives deliveries*					*Total*
		1st	*IInd*	*IIIrd*	*IVth*	*Vth*	*VIth*	*VIIth*	*1st*	*IInd*	*IIIrd*	*IVth*	*Vth*	*1st*	*IInd*	*IIIrd*	*IVth*	*Vth*	
Khasa	At Home	82	64	55	38	28	11	05	75	62	39	22	02	15	13	07	06	01	525
	In PHC	—	—	—	—	—	—	—	01	01	—	—	01	—	01	—	—	—	04
	Sub PHC	—	—	—	—	—	—	—	—	—	—	—	—	—	—	—	—	—	—
	Govt. Hospital	—	—	—	—	—	—	—	—	—	—	—	—	—	—	—	—	—	—
	Pvt. Hospital	—	—	—	—	—	—	—	—	—	—	—	—	—	—	—	—	—	—
	Total	82	64	55	38	28	11	05	76	63	39	22	03	15	14	07	06	01	529
G. Total		335	292	243	155	60	25	08	203	164	116	40	04	55	40	22	15	02	1779 (99.10)
Govt. Hos/PHC		02	01	—	—	—	—	—	04	02	01	—	01	—	01	—	—	—	12 (0.66)
Pvt. Hospitals		—	—	—	—	—	—	—	01	02	01	—	—	—	—	—	—	—	04 (0.22)

dries umbilical cord comes to an end. The Buxas do not use any material for dressing up the cord. While the Khasas use thread and blade for separating the umbilical cord from the navel and dress it up with mother's breast milk. The mother just puts a drop of her breast milk twice or thrice daily until it does not dry up. But in no case the medicated material is used by any tribal community to dress-up the cord.

However, certainly there is change in the attitude and awareness of the tribes towards medical practices and the medical aid needed particularly in pregnancy period. Even among the Rajis 19(76.00) respondents reacted that the pregnant mothers consult ANM visiting in their area and have tetanus injections, iron tablets and also try to follow other instructions as suggested by ANM. Only 06 (24.00) respondents expressed their ignorance of any medical aid needed during pregnancy. Among the Tharus 98 (68.06 per cent) respondents were aware and prefer to have medical aid as is required during pregnancy. Among the Buxas only 41.67 per cent respondents were aware of the medical aid needed during pregnancy while among the Khasas 52.55 per cent have acquaintance with medical aid needed during pregnancy. In fact the propagation made by the medical and health department in tribal areas have positive results. Now most of the people are aware of the medical aid needed during pregnancy and they are willing to have every medical and health care services provided to them at pre-natal as well as post-natal stage. The following Table 6.19 shows the reaction percentage of the respondents towards medical aid they are willing to have during pregnancy.

Table 6.19
Reaction About Medical Aid Needed During Pregnancy

Tribes	*Willing to have medical aid as needed during pregnancy*	*Unwilling to have medical aid as needed during pregnancy*
Rajis	19/25 (76.00)	06/25 (24.00)
Tharus	98/144 (68.06)	46/144 (31.94)
Buxas	40/96 (411.67)	56/96 (58.33)
Khasas	43/82 (52.44)	39/82 (47.56)
Total	200/347 (57.64)	147/347 (42.36)

In fact there is a great difference of being willing and practising the things or to be willing but not getting into practice. To verify this state of being, lastly the respondents were asked a counter question, i.e., 'state preferentially from where you receive health services, medical advice and medical aid or treatment in different situations like pregnancy, delivery, infant's illness, children's sickness, general sickness of the family members, epidemics and other diseases the people suffer from'. At this, the respondents have different preferential responses. It is tried to present these responses in the Table 6.20 (See Pages 247-248).

The information as denoted quantitatively in Table 6.20 shows that the tribal people of Uttaranchal even today trust on the indigenous method of treatment, traditional medicine-men, sorcery and finally they prefer to consult the trained medical practitioners for seeking medical advice, or treatment in different situations as cited in the table. Here by indigenous method we mean the self-medication, belief in supernatural being and offering of worship and sacrifice, performing other ritualistic ceremonies to local deities, goblins and ghosts and also trusting in superstitions and wrath of the deities and spirits. As the tribal people have still firm belief on supernatural powers, deities, spirits etc. and they also have the notion that the happiness and sufferings or ailments take place due to the pleasure or displeasure of these powers. Besides this, by traditional medicine men means the person of the respective community having the knowledge and experience of occult-art, herbs, medicinal plants and also an ability of diagnosing the causes of sufferings, ailments and other things related to human life. Among the tribes particulary the Khasas, the Buxas and the Tharus have firm belief on the effect of sorcery and the person having knowledge of sorcery is known in different names with different communities. For example, among the Tharus and the Buxas it is known as 'Bharare' and among the Khasas it is known as 'Dankan'. The sorcerers have still important role and effect on the tribes. For a long time they have been used to have the service of those persons and the medical science of today could not overcome these practices even now. The preferential responses we got from the study units make it prove that almost all the tribal communities have first choice for getting indigenous ways into practice in spite of their willingness to have modern medical practices in different situations. There are some more results that came out from the study. The preferential choice and its percentage varies according to variations of situations and ailments. For example, most of the respondents, irrespective of any community, have their first choice to get into practice the indigenous methods in case of pregnancy and delivery cases. Only in some complicated matters they think of consulting the trained medical practitioners. Rather they prefer to consult their traditional medicine men before approaching the trained medical practitioners. On the contrary in the case of infants and children's sickness they also consult the sorcerers rather than traditional medicine-men and lastly to trained medical practitioners. While in the case of general diseases and epidemics the percentage of choice seems increasing towards trained medical practitioners. Thus the overall scenario reflects the dominance of traditional pattern of treatment in tribal communities. In all the situations the modern medical pattern of treatment is their third and the last choice. At the same time and in the same situation their first choice is the indigenous method then traditional medicine-men, then sorcery and finally modern medical practices.

Thus in view of the 'Health Status' of the tribal people of Uttaranchal, as the aforesaid interpretation of data exhibit that the goal of 'Health for all by 2000, A.D.' is not achieved and there is still more to be done in policy planning and also in practice for reaching to this enthusiastic target. The goal of 'Health for All', can be achieved only through (i) framing the eco-based policies for health, (ii) time-bound execution of the policies, (iii) Establishing infrastructural facilities corresponding to the policies and practices, (iv) launching awareness programmes in the respective areas, (v) periodic evaluation of the task by competent and just bodies, and, finally, (vi) inculcation of humane dimensions of development in health policies, planning and practices and also the provision of incentives for better response, work and results of the concerning components of the 'health and medicare system' and also the punishment for their bad response, workings and results. For the execution of the policies and plans the target area should be divided into two clear-cut zones and should be allotted in the charge of government and non-government agencies separately. This procedure will help in the assessment of the workings and results of both the agencies simultaneously provoke them for better workings so that they can prove their competence and ability to work.

Hygienic Condition and Nutritional Status

Health status has deep concern with hygienic conditions and nutritional status of a person. Hence, in order to know the health status of the tribal people of Uttaranchal the study of the hygienic conditions and the nutritional status is just a pre-requisite for the scientific attainment of results. In this context an attempt has been made for understanding the hygienic conditions of the tribal people. Here the hygienic conditions have been referred in terms of personal hygiene, environmental hygiene, domestic hygiene and community hygiene. The personal hygiene denotes the bathing system of the person, dress pattern, their habits of cleanliness, pattern of caring feet, nails and teeth, their spitting, coughing and sneezing behaviour etc. It is evident that personal hygiene has direct relation with the health status of a person. The study of personal hygiene is therefore immensely important for understanding health status of the person or community concerned. The environmental and domestic hygiene consists of ecological background of habitations, type of houses, their upkeeping pattern, facilities available in the house, the food habits of the people,

Table 6.20. Sources of Medical Advice and Treatment sought Preferentially by the Tribal People in Different Crisis Situation

Tribe	*Situations*	*Preferential Choice for Treatment/ medical Advice*	*Source of Medical Advice and Treatment*			*Trained medical Practitioners*
			Sorcerer	*Traditional Medicinemen*	*Indigenous Method*	
Rajis	I. Pregnancy	Ist Choice	—	06/25 (24.00%)	18/25(72.00%)	01/25 (4.00%)
		IInd Choice	—	18/25(72.00%)	01/25(4.00%)	06/25(24.00%)
		IIIrd Choice	—	01/25(4.00%)	06/25(24.00%)	18/25(72.00%)
	2. Delivery	Ist Choice	—	—	22/25(88.00%)	03/25(12.00%)
		IInd Choice	—	20/25(80.00%)	03/25(12.00%)	02/25(08.00%)
		IIIrd Choice	—	03/25(12.00%)	02/25(08.00%)	20/25(80.00%)
	3. Infants' illness	1st Choice	—	06/25(24.00%)	02/25(08.00%)	17/25(68.00%)
		IInd Choice	—	17/25(68.00%)	06/25(24.00%)	02/25(08.00%)
		IIIrd Choice	—	02/25(08.00%)	17/25(68.00%)	06/25(24.00%)
	4. Childrens' illness	1st Choice	—	02/25(08.00%)	19/25(76.00%)	04/25(16.00%)
		IInd Choice	—	19/25(76.00%)	04/25(16.00%)	02/25(08.00%)
		IIIrd Choice	—	04/25(16.00%)	02/25(08.00%)	11/25(44.00%)
	5. General Disease	1st Choice	—	02/25(08.00%)	05/25(20.00%)	18/25(72.00%)
		IInd Choice	—	05/25(20.00%)	18/25(72.00%)	02/25(08.00%)
		IIIrd Choice	—	18/25(72.00%)	02/25(08.00%)	05/25(20.00%)
	6. Epidemics	1st Choice	—	15/25(60.00%)	6/25(24.00%)	04/25(16.00%)
		IInd Choice	—	04/25(16.00%)	15/25(60.00%)	6/25(24.00%)
		IIIrd Choice	—	6/25(24.00%)	04/25(16.00%)	15/25(60.00%)

(Contd.)

(Contd. Table 6.20)

Tribe	Situations	Preferential Choice for Treatment/ medical Advice	Source of Medical Advice and Treatment			Trained medical Practitioners
			Sorcerer	Traditional Medicinemen	Indigenous Method	
Tharus	1. Pregnanacy	1st Choice	—	8/144(5.56%)	113/144(92.36%)	03/144(2.08%)
		IInd Choice	—	133/144(92.36%)	03/144(2.08%)	18/144(5.56%)
		IIIrd Choice	—	03/144(2.08%)	8/144(5.56%)	33/144(92.36%)
	2. Delivery	1st Choice	—	18/144(12.50%)	93/144(64.58%)	133/144(22.92%)
		IInd Choice	—	93/144(64.58%)	33/144(22.92%)	18/144(12.50%)
		IIIrd Choice	—	33/144(22.92%)	18/144(12.50%)	193/144(64.58%)
	3. Infants illness	1st Choice	39/144(27.08%)	41/144(28.47%)	58/144(40.28%)	106/144(4.17%)
		IInd Choice	41/144(28.47%)	58/144(40.28%)	06/144(4.17%)	1139/144(27.08%)
		IIIrd Choice	—	06/144(4.17%)	39/144(27.08%)	199/144(68.75%)
	4. Childrens illness	1st Choice	54/144(37.50%)	15/144(10.42%)	71/144(49.31%).,	04/144(2.78%)
		IInd Choice	19/144(13.19%)	50/144(34.72%)	15/144(10.42%)	60/144(41.67%)
		IIIrd Choice	24/144(16.67%)	9/144(6.25%)	7/144(4.86%)	04/144(72.22%)
	5. General Disease	1st Choice	06/144(4.17%)	30/144(20.83%)	69/144(47.92%)	19/144(27.08%)
		IInd Choice	39/144(27.08%)	30/144(2083%)	14/144(9.72%)	61/144(42.36)
		IIIrd Choice	12/144(8,33%)	17/144(11.81%)	22/144(15.28)	93/144(9.03)
	6. Epidemcs	1st Choice	10/144(6.94%)	38/144(26.39%)	45/144(31.25%)	51/144(35.42%)
		IInd Choice	18/144(12.50%)	27/144(18.75%)	51/144(35.42%)	48/144(33.33%)
		IIIrd Choice	08/144(5.56%)	19/144(13.19%)	21/144(14.58%)	96/144(66.67%)

(Contd.)

(Contd. Table 6.20)

Tribe	Situations	Preferential Choice for Treatment/ medical Advice	Source of Medical Advice and Treatment			Trained medical Practitioners
			Sorcerer	Traditional Medicinemen	Indigenous Method	
Buxa	1. Pregnanacy	1st Choice	13/96(13.54%)	43/96(44.79%)	20/96(30.21%)	11/96(11.46%)
		IInd Choice	11/96(11.46%)	29/96(34.38%)	33/96(22.92%)	23/96(23.95%)
		IIIrd Choice	07/96(7.29%)	15/96(15.63%)	11/96(11.46%)	63/96(65.63%)
	2. Delivery	1st Choice	03/96(3.13%)	33/96(34.38%)	52/96(54.17%)	08/96(8.33%)
		IInd Choice	08/96(8.33%)	45/96(46.88%)	22/96(22.92%)	21/96(21.88%)
		IIIrd Choice	02/96(2.08%)	08/96(8.33%)	11/96(11.46%)	75/96(78.13%)
	3. Infant's illness	1st Choice	15/96(15.63%)	48/96(50.00%)	23/96(23.96%)	10/96(10.42%)
		IInd Choice	10/96(10.42%)	27/96(28.13%)	44/96(45.83%)	15/96(15.63%)
		IIIrd Choice	05/96(5.21%)	08/96(8.33%)	12/96(12.50%)	71/96(73.96%)
	4. Childrens illness	1st Choice	07/96(7.29%)	36/96(37.50%)	39/96(40.63%)	14/96(14.58%)
		IInd Choice	12/96(12.50%)	33/96(34.38%)	27/96(28.13%)	24/96(25.00%)
		IIIrd Choice	03/96(3.13%)	09/96(9.38%)	08/96(8.33%)	76/96(79.17%)
	5. General Disease	1st Choice	06/96(6.25%)	14/96(14.58%)	34/96(35.42%)	42/96(43.75%)
		IInd Choice	11/96(11.46%)	18/96(18.75%)	19/96(19.79%)	48/96(50.00%)
		IIIrd Choice	07/96(7.29%)	17/96(17.71%)	24/96(25.00%)	48/96(50.00%)
	6. Epidemics	1st Choice	09/96(9.38%)	24/96(25.00%)	29/96(30.21%)	34/96(35.42%)
		IInd Choice	04/96(4.17%)	16/96(16.67%)	18/96(18.75%)	58/96(60.42%)
		IIIrd Choice	02/96(2.08%)	18/96(18.75%)	12/96(12.50%)	64/96(66.67%)

(Contd.)

(Contd. Table 6.20)

Tribe	Situations	Preferential Choice for Treatment/ medical Advice	Source of Medical Advice and Treatment			Trained medical Practitioners
			Sorcerer	Traditional Medicinemen	Indigenous Method	
Khasa	1. Pregnanacy	1st Choice IInd	05/82(6.10%)	22/82(26.83%)	48/82(58.54%)	07/82(08.54%)
		Coice IIIrd	07/82(08.54%)	26/82(31.71%)	22/82(26.83%)	27/82(32.93%)
		Choice	05/82(6.10%)	12/82(14.63%)	15/82(18.29%)	48/82(58.54%)
	2. Delivery	1st Choice IInd	08/82(9.76%)	28/82(34.15%)	35/82(42.68%)	11/82(13.41%)
		choice IIIrd	11/82(13.41%)	22/82(26.83%)	21/82(25.61%)	28/82(34.15%)
		Choice	04/82(04.88%)	10/82(12.20%)	14/82(17.07%)	54/82(65.85%)
	3. Infant's illness	1st Choice IInd	16/82(19.51%)	23/82(28.05%)	31/82(37.80%)	12/82(14.63%)
		choice IIIrd	12/82(14.63%)	16/82(19.51%)	23/82(28.05%)	31/82(37.80%)
		Choice	03/82(3.66%)	11/82(13.41%)	17/82(20.73%)	51/82(62.20%)
	4. Childrens[1] illness	1st Choice IInd	12/82(14.63%)	25/82(30.49%)	30/82(36.59%)	15/82(18.29%)
		choice IIIrd	10/82(12.20%)	18/82(21.95%)	21/82(25.61%)	33/82(40.24%)
		Choice	04/82(04.88%)	08/82(9.76%)	15/82(18.29%)	55/82(67.07%)
	5. General Disease	1st Choice IInd	07/82(08.54%)	19/82(23.17%)	31.82(37.80%)	25/82(30.49%)
		choice IIIrd	06/82(07.32%)	11/82(13.41%)	25/82(30.49%)	40/82(48.78%)
		Choice	02/82(02.44%)	06/82(07.32%)	09/82(10.98%)	65/82(79.27%)
	6. Epidemics	1st Choice IInd	03/82(3.66%)	30/82(36.59%)	35/82(42.68%)	14/82(17.07%)
		choice IIIrd	05/82(6.10%)	27/82(32.93%)	14/82(17.07%)	36/82(43.90%)
		Choice	04/82(04.88%)	17/82(20.73%)	15/82(18.29%)	46/82(56.10%)

(Contd.)

their commensal system, the up-keeping pattern of tamed animals and the cattle sheds, the disposing pattern of domestic refuse and other waste materials etc. The community hygiene refers to the source of drinking water, surrounding of the drinking water-source, sanitary services available at community level, disposing pattern of human excreta and other solid and liquid wastes and lastly the dietary pattern of the community in general. In the context of the variable as cited above the hygienic conditions of the tribal people of Uttaranchal has been studied.

Hygienic Conditions; Personal Hygiene

Routine of bathing practice is an important part of personal hygiene. During our field study we have tried to understand the routine of bathing practices of the tribal people. In this regard, first of all, the respondent units were consulted and interviewed when, where, how and in which manner they take a bath. In view of their reactions, we then observed the bathing behaviour of the family members of the respondents. In this way the personal hygiene of the whole of the tribal community was studied and the responses of the respondents, as recorded, are being presented quantitatively in the Table 6.21.

Table 6.21. Bathing Pattern of the Respondents

Tribes	*Routine of Taking Bath*							
	Every day	*Every alternate day*	*Every Sunday*	*Once in a Week*	*Once in a fortnight*	*Once in a month*	*Not certain*	*Total*
Rajis	—	—	—	11 (44.00)	—	05 (20.00)	09 (36.00)	25 (100.00)
Tharus	03 (2.08)	18 (12.50)	—	06 (4.17)	—	—	117 (81.25)	144 (100.00)
Buxas	12 (12.50)	54 (56.25)	04 (4.17)	06 (6.25)	—	—	20 (20.83)	96 (100.00)
Khasas	03 (3.66)	08 (9.76)	—	49 (59.75)	—	—	22 (26.83)	82 (100.00)

It is observed that every tribal community has its own notion about routine of bathing practices. The climatic conditions, the availability of water, the motivating factors and the model group, have crucial role in determining the bathing practices. For instance, among the Rajis mostly the people do not take daily bath. Maximum 44.00 per cent Raji people prefer to take bath once a week, 20.00 per cent once in a month, 36.00 per cent people take bath whenever they feel so. There is no regular routine of bathing practices observed by the Rajis. Comparatively, the cold climate, lack of motivating factors and ineffective model group are the responsible factors of this practice. To some extent the non-availability of source of water at their door-steps is also a constraint of this practice.

For the Rajis daily bath or regular bathing has no meaning for healthy life. They are of the opinion that taking bath daily is one of the major causes of cold-related ailments like catarrh, cold-cough, pneumonia. Even the indigestion and constipation is also caused by cold. Hence the Raji people do not take bath regularly. Even they do not think it necessary to wash the face at morning. Due to cold climate the Rajis use hot or luke-warm water for bath. They fetch water from the nearby water source, make it hot on a large kettle and then prefer to take bath at noon while the sun is on the head. They bring the hot or lukewram water in the courtyard of the hut and make the children take bath first. The children are quite frightened and avoid the bath. They just run way to avoid the bath and the mother runs after them and gets hold of them any how. As soon as she put off the torn wearings of the children, they wail loudly and resist. In one way or the other she makes them take bath. After taking a bath the child shivering with cold is made to sit in the sun by covering her/his body with the towel/ bedsheet/Dhoti/Saree. The child keep on wailing until he/she is not given something to eat preferably 'Gurh', Mishree or a piece of bread. While wailing the sucking child keeps on flowing nasal discharge. After giving bath to the child/children the mother also takes a bath. One more thing we observed that among the Rajis the women generally wash their heads and hairs only comb them sitting in the sun. While combing the hair the other female member of the family or of neighbourhood helps in killing lice and lice eggs. On some other day woman wash only her body. Hence for them taking a bath means to wash the body only which excludes the washing of head and hairs. The same pattern is also followed by menfolk. For the Rajis, the head, hair and face are the visible parts of the body which are supposed to be kept clean while the hidden parts have no meaning of cleanliness. Hence they just try to keep their visible parts clean and wash them whenever they feel it necessary. At noon generally before lunch, i.e., the mid-day-meal (Chha-Kala-Ko-Khano) they perform this job.

Generally the aged, adult, small children and infants do take bath in courtyards of houses or huts while the teenagers, young man and women prefer to go at the natural spring or the water-tank for taking bath. Those who go to spring or water tank use only cold water for bath. The Raji people have no particular choice of bathing soap and its brand. Whatever the soap, may be that a detergent or any other soap available, is used by them even for taking bath. The people lacking soap use ash or bitter butter-milk or sour-curd-water for bath and particularly for washing head and hairs. It is believed that these items help in killing the lice and also in removing the dandruff. After every bath the Raji people change their under-garments provided they have it. Otherwise the Raji women having no petticoat just cover their body with a piece of sari and take bath, while men take bath wearing underwears. The wet garments used for bathing are washed after bath and dried up in sun for further use. The men having undershirts do not think necessary to change it after every bath. This habit provides a suitable situation for flourishing lice even in the inner garments of the people.

The Rajis can not afford two and more pairs of dress at a time. Most of the family members have only one pair of dress. Anyhow they manage its washing. Hence the clothes they wear are generally washed once or twice in a month. But in some particular cases while any person plans to visit one's relation or a fair and or attend a festival the clothes are compulsorily washed. The people use any detergent soap for washing clothes. The people having no washing soap just use ash or buttermilk (if available) for washing clothes.

Exceptionally if any person has two or more pairs of dresses he/ she washes the used one generally in a week or fortnight or when the clothes become filthy and begin to stink. Besides this, they change their dresses only when they prepare a new one. Among the Rajis the new clothes are bought compulsorily at least twice a year. First on the occasion of 'Anthu festival' in August or September and second in the month of February or March. Persons having purchasing capacity buy woollen garments during winter. But in general most of the Raji persons are viewed wearing two or more torn rags as to protect themselves from the winter cold. During winter the Raji people avoid bath in general. But married women take bath compulsorily when the menses period is over. Thus so far as the routine of bath and dress pattern are concerned the Rajis are not so particular about it. Rather the bathing practices for them is just a curse. They wish to have new clothes but their economic condition does not allow for it. Whatever garments they have are not properly kept neat and clean. In another sense the garments of the Rajis are just a seeding bed for insects like bed-bugs and lice. This state of being has naturally ill-effects on the Raji people and reflect their unhygienic habits. The following Table 6.22 and 6.23 present the reactions of tribe-wise respondents in regard of the bathing pattern.

Table 6.22. Type of Water used for Taking a Bath in Different Seasons

Tribes	*Summer season*				*Winter season*			
	Hot water	*Luke warm*	*Cold water*	*Total*	*Hot water*	*Luke warm*	*Cold water*	*Total*
Rajis	—	09 (36.00)	16 (64.00)	25 (100.00)	18 (72.00)	07 (28.00)	—	25 (100.00)
Tharus	—	—	144 (100.00)	144 (100.00)	—	—	144 (100.00)	144 (100.00)
Buxas	—	11 (11.46)	85 (88.54)	96 (100.00)	11 (11.46)	—	85 (88.54)	96 (100.00)
Khasas	—	56 (68.29)	26 (31.71)	82 (100.00)	13 (15.85)	45 (54.88)	24 (29.28)	82 (100.00)

Among the Tharus the people have different opinion about bath as well as different bathing behavioural patterns. The observations show that only 2.08 per cent Tharus take bath daily. 12.50 per cent take every alternate day, 4.17 per cent take bath once in a week and the rest 81.25 per cent have no particular routine. They take bath whenever they like it. Mostly cold water is used by them for bathing purposes and they prefer to take bath near the water-source, i.e., the hand-pump installed generally at the corner of the courtyard. The persons habitual to take a bath daily generally get up early in the morning and go far evacuation in the nearby fields or on the outskirt of the village. On return they just wash hands and feet in the hand pump first and then take a bath before taking even a cup of tea. Only after taking bath their daily routine begins. The people who take bath every alternate day generally prefer the noon-period for it because they prefer to perform their daily routine tasks first. They get up at morning, wash their hands, feet and face, then take tea then visit the cattle shed, then go far evacuation (if feel so), and after purification they take their breakfast and then go for the work assigned to them. At about noon they return from the work, then go for taking bath. It is the duty of the women to make bath the small children and the infants. But the majority of the population has no particular routine pattern of bath. Generally leisure time is utilized for this. There is a seasonal variation in the frequency of bathing behaviour. During summer mostly the people take bath daily or every alternate day. But the timings remain almost uncertain, on the contrary, during winter the frequency decreases and the people take bath sometime in a week or twice in a month. Among the Tharus, a woman while goes under menstruation, compulsorily takes a bath when the menses period is over. Generally the aged and the infants avoid the bath during winter. They feel that the bath may cause them cold, fever and pneumonia. In fact the summer and the rainy season in the Tarai plain, the abode of the Tharus, remains very hot and sultry, hence the people in general take bath daily so as to get relief from the heat. But there we observed a state of extremism that the youths generally have bath twice and sometime thrice a day, and the children ranging from 6 to 13 years of age are seen swimming in the village ponds which are in real sense storage of polluted water. These are the ponds where tamed animals particularly buffalos are made to drink water and also washed by their masters. The same pond and the stored water is then used by the children for taking bath. The children can be seen swimming and playing in the ponds for hours. Some time the young women also have a dip. They go in group for catching a small variety of fishes and remain within the pond's water for hours. Some flirting young boys also go for fishing and play in the pond's water for hours. But this state of

which the ignorant people remain unaware and unknown. In fact this process gives temporary relief to the people from heat and sultry weather but its latent adverse impacts generate sometime uncurable bodily ailments and infested canker. Almost the same state of extremism we also observed during winter. In fact winter in the Tarai plain remain very cold and foggy. The whole of the Tarai region remains under the hitting range of cold waves. The people therefore avoid bath throughout the winter season. This state of being generates a number of skin problems and a favourable ground for the germination of insects like bedbugs, lice, lice-eggs and fleas etc. which have always ill-effects on human body. The persons who take bath in winter generally use warm water.

The Tharus have no choice for a particular brand of bathing soap. They do not care about the soap, its type, quality and brand. They use any soap available at home for bathing. Even the detergent soap, which is meant for washing clothes, is used by them for bathing. But some rich people do take bath with bathing soap like Lux, Life-bouy etc. If the bathing soap is not available, they do not hesitate to use detergent or any other soap available in the house for bathing purposes. Today, the Tharus have a deep sense of under-garments too. They make their children wear the undergarments mainly underwear and change it after every bath. The other persons of the family do have undergarments which are changed only on bathing. While the other garments are washed on being filthy and the previously-washed clothes are worn in place of them. During field study we have also tried to investigate the bathing pattern of the family members. We found that the aged persons have least frequency of bathing. They generally take a bath once in a week during summer and hardly once in a month during winter provided it is necessary. Otherwise the whole of the winter season passes with no bath. The women have slightly different bathing behaviour. They generally wash only their head and hairs at a time and the rest body on any other day. Hardly there are some occasions when the whole of the body, including head and hairs are washed at a time by them. Asking about this pattern they simply answer that they have learnt this habit from their elders and further state that it is rather a simple and less time consuming process. Hence women follow this pattern in normal conditions. But at the occasion of fairs, festivities and ritualistic performances they take bath in full at-a-time. Besides this the women also take bath in full, when their menses period is over. Infants and children (less than six years of age) are given bath by their mother or grandmothers. During summer/ winter the mother and the grand mother take respectively cold/warm water in a bucket or in a large pan and make their infants and children bathe in the courtyard of the house. While teenagers, and the young

Table 6.23. Place where the Bath is Taken

Tribes	Place						Total
	Courtyard	In the pond	In the river	In the spring	At drinking water point	Others	
Rajis	17 (78.00)	—	—	08 (32.00)	—	—	25 (100.00)
Tharus	30 (20.83)	24 (16.67)	—	—	90 (62.50)	—	144 (100.00)
Buxas	33 (34.38)	12 (12.50)	—	—	40 (41.67)	11 (11.46)	96 (100.00)
Khasas	52 (63.41)	—	—	22 (26.83)	8 (9.76)	—	82 (100.00)

bathe in the courtyard of the house. While teenagers, and the young have bath according to their choice, sometimes in the pond, sometimes at the hand-pumps, sometimes at the tube-wells and sometime near the water-tap installed for supplying drinking water. But there is not even a single bathroom built within the house by any family. Even the women make their own arrangement for verbal bath. The rear of the house is the best. 'Purdah'/veil for women to have bath. In fact women while taking bath at any place is overseen by menfolk and this tendency makes an automatic veil to the women and also provides them an environment guarding their modesty.

The Tharus have their own distinct dress pattern. The traditional costumes have almost disappeared from the cultural system of the Tharus and the young generation particularly the womenfolk look down upon the traditional woman's attire, which chiefly consists of a 'Ghagara in lower part and a full sleeve 'Angia' with Pichhora in the upper part'. The young new generation of menfolk also have the same attitude towards their traditional dress pattern which included 'Payajama' in lower part and full sleeve Kameej in upper part and a white cap on head. Men and women like to wear modern costumes as are worn by neighbouring non-tribal Hindus. For instance the school-going children are bound to have school dresses as prescribed during school hours while in normal course boys wear 'Pant and Shirt' and the girls wear 'Salwar-Kurta', while the married women wear 'Saree and Blouse' and the men wear Pant/Payajama and shirt according to situation. The people generally wash their used clothes once in a week. Almost all the family members in the Tharu community have at least two dresses which are worn in alternate ways. Some well-off people have also a provision of a separate dress for each of the family members which is worn only on some special occasion like fairs, festivals, ritualistic ceremonies and for visiting markets and relations. In normal course the people change their used clothes only when they become filthy and wear the washed dress in place of the used

visit the market place or any relation or join any feast or festival or take part in ritual ceremonies. Thus we came to the conclusion that the Tharus have receptivity towards the material culture and a sense of cleanliness. To look attractive has developed in their habits and psyche. This is the psychology that provokes the people for keeping atleast their dresses neat and clean, even if, they do not bathe for weeks.

The Tharus do not have any particular choice for washing material. However the cheaper detergent powders and detergent cakes are used for washing clothes. Lacking the washing material they use their indigenous materials like 'ash' and sometime just dip the clothes in water, thresh them without using any washing material and lastly rinse out and dry up in the sun.

Among the Tharus there is no clear-cut difference between summer and winter dress. Only the number of clothes increases during winter. In general the cheap pullovers or jerseys is added in summer-dress during winter. It means the summer dress plus a jersey or a pullover equals to winter dress vis-a-vis the winter dress minus a jersey or a pull-over equals to summer dress. The persons who can not afford jersey or a pull-over during winter generally put on double clothes at a time and thus protect themselves from the winter cold. Today the Tharus prefer to wear cheap synthetic clothes, because the synthetic clothes have comparatively better looks, easy wash, better finishing and durability. The cheap synthetic woollen stuffs (acrylic woollen clothes) are used in winter.

Almost all the members of the family compulsorily wear undergarments. The male under garments includes undershirt and underwear while the female undergarments consist of petticot/underwear and bra. The undergarments particularly underwears are changed only on bath while undershirts/bra are changed when it becomes filthy. The persons generally have a pair of underwears while undershirts/bras etc. remain in singles. The dress pattern of the Tharus, thus, reflects their proclivity towards modern fashionon the one hand, and ignorance and unawereness of personal hygienes on the other hand. Even the bathing behaviour of the Tharus exhibits the lack of hygienic sense in their personal life.

Among the Buxas only 12.50 per cent person take daily bath, 56.25 per cent prefer to take bath every alternate day, 4.17 per cent person take bath every Sunday, 6.25 per cent take once in a week and the rest 20.83 per cent do not have any particular routine rather they have bath whenever they like. In summer 11.46 per cent people use lukewarm water for bath and 88.54 per cent use cold water. During winter 11.46 per cent use hot-water for bath and the rest majority of the people, i.e.,

cent use hot-water for bath and the rest majority of the people, i.e., 88.54 per cent use cold water for bath. The courtyard artisan tubewell and the drinking water hand-pumps are the suitable places and sources preferred by the Buxas for bathing purposes. The people generally like to take bath with some bathing soap like Lux, Hamam etc. provided it is available in the house. Otherwise whatever the soap may be that a simple detergent soap, available at home is used even for bath. The people lacking any kind of soap generally bath with water alone. The bathing behaviour of the Buxas thus does not reflect their sincerity and seriousness towards, bathing pattern. They appeared rather ignorant and very careless about the functional importance of bathing in the personal life of the people. Even children and infants do not take bath for weeks. The same is the case of the aged persons. For the Buxas, daily and frequent bath in general may cause cold and cold related-ailments in human body. The infants, children and the aged persons are more prone to cold and cold-related diseases hence they avoid bath with cold water. The infants, young children and the aged persons do not follow any particular routine for bath. While the young and adult persons take compulsorily bath atleast once in a week in general. During summer this frequency increases to twice or sometime thrice a week. Even the infants and the aged do have bath in summer but the routine remains almost uncertain and depends on the persons who make them take bath or initiate for bathing. Generally cold hand-pump water is used for bath. But the aged and infants bathe with luke-warm water. During winter the frequency of bath decreases. Even the youths and the adults do not prefer to take bath. The foggy weather causes bitter cold in the Buxars area during winter hence the tribal people anyhow try to manage to protect themselves from the impacts of cold waves. But some persons like women going under menstruation period do take bath when the period is over. But the use of hot or warm water is strictly prohibited for them while other persons who occasionally take bath can use hot water. It is believed that the use of hot water for bath after menses can extend the monthly discharge of blood and the cold water helps in stopping this discharge. This notion, which is outright unscientific, forbids the women in using hot water for bathing purposes specially for a sacred bath taken after the menses period. They just take cold water in a vessel and go out of the range of the source of drinking water, i.e., the hand-pump and house-premises, generally in their own agricultural fields or kitchen gardens, and take bath and also wash their used clothes. This process particularly during winter may cause some bodily ailments which have far reaching ill-effects on the body.

Today the Buxas also have a fashion of wearing under garments which in the case of male members include a pair of underwears and have underwear and bra. The person having a pair of undergarments, changes the used ones after every bath. The data show that 50.00 per cent of the male members change their undergarments in every bath, while the remaining 50.00 per cent male population, who have only one pair of undergarments, change whenever they feel that the undergarments have become filthy and have begun to stink. In the case of the female members we have some startling information. The female having a single pair of undergarments, i.e., petticoat/underwear and bra, just put-off them before bathing and wrap a piece of torn Dhoti or Saree around the middle-lower part of the body covering breast to knee point and thus take their bath. And after bath they again put on the already used undergarments. The undergarments are washed only when they become dirty and start giving out foul smell of sweat. Sometime when there is breeding of louse in the dirty undergarment the people then plan to wash them. On the contrary, there are exceptionally few women having two pairs of undergarments, for alternate use. Those women change their used undergarments in every bath and wear the washed ones.

The Buxas have very limited clothes to wear. Mostly the people have two pairs of dresses for wearing alternately. Generally 60 per cent persons change their dress once in a week. While the rest 40 per cent are quite uncertain about it. The clothes are washed when they become filthy and begin to stink. Sometime the people willing to visit market place or any relation or to participate in any festival, feast and religious ceremony also wash their dress and thus put on the clean and washed clothes. This trend of dress pattern eventually does show the sense of cleanliness that exists among the Buxas but more for the sake of ostentation and less for hygienic reasons. The Buxas use washing soap or detergent powder, whatever available at home for washing clothes. They have no particular choice for the washing material but it must be cheaper.

The polyandrous Khasas living in hilly region with comparatively cold and temperate climatic conditions have their own peculiar pattern of personal hygiene. The information shows that their bathing behaviour changes with the change of the season and the workload of the person concerned. In general, only 3.66 per cent Khasas have expressed their positive response towards daily bath, 9.76 per cent stated that they take a bath every alternate day, 59.75 per cent once in week while the remaining 25.33 per cent have no particular routine, rather they are uncertain about it and state that whenever they have spare time and favourable situation they take bath. The persons who are very much particular and have daily bath prefer morning time, generally before breakfast for this purpose. While majority of the persons have bath before mid-day-meal. We observed that the Khasas begin their routine work

mid-day-meal. We observed that the Khasas begin their routine work with the dawn. Every person of the family preferably performs first his duty as assigned by the head of the family. Then they have time for themselves. At morning, having breakfast, some member of the family goes for agricultural tasks, some for collecting fuel and fodder from the forests, some for grazing tamed animals while some remain at home for performing familial tasks. The person staying at home along with various jobs cook food for the family members, looks-after infants and also the milching cattle left at home. Virtually they have also no time for themselves until all the family members do have their mid-day-meal. At about noon the family members come back home. Some of them like to have bath before meal, while the rest just wash their hands, feet and face and sit for having meal. Thus it is the choice of the persons whether they take bath or not. But it is decided that the person willing to bath will take before mid-day-meal. The drinking water source, that is a water-tank amidst the village or somewhere, a water tap-stand-point, is the only place where persons go for bath. During summer the people use cold tap-water for bath and lukewarm water for infants and children who are given a bath at home by a mother or a senior woman of the family. During winter the Khasas have rare bath, because it is bitter cold in the Jaunsar Hills during winter. However, the persons who compulsorily take bath use hot water for this purpose. During winter the courtyard or the backyard of the house is the suitable place for having a bath. Mostly the aged, infants and small children do not have bath throughout the winter season because the Khasas are of the view that bath during winter can cause cold-related problems to the people. The Khasas have no choice for a particular brand of bathing soap, rather they use any soap, may be that of a cheap quality detergent soap available at home for bath. After having bath the people compulsorily wash the inner-garments and wear the washed ones. In a question, the Khasas responded that they do not compulsorily have undergarments. Only those persons have under garments who can afford them. Otherwise the persons have generally no inner wears. Even the women wear just one fold Dhoti without petticoat. The same is the case of the males who wear only trousers or pant or Dhoti without underwear. The infants, children and teenagers also do not compulsorily have the under garments. This state of being is the result of the acute poverty among the Khasas. It is the reason that the well-off Khasas do have compulsorily undergarments which include underwears, undershirts in the case of male and petticoat/underwears, bra in the case of the female. But the percentage of persons belonging to this category is exceptionally low. The dress of the Khasas also reflects their poor economic condition which has various health and hygiene-related implications. Mostly the Khasas have one to two pairs of dresses

wear are washed at least within a fortnight while during winter this duration extends to a month. The people preferably wash their garments only when they become filthy and start giving out foul smell. But on some particular occasion, like feast and festivals the used clothes are necessarily washed. For washing the garments and other-clothes the Khasa people use generally detergent cakes. Thus the bathing behaviour and the dress pattern among the Khasas reflect their ignorance and unawareness of the importance of personal hygiene in human life.

The pattern of toilet and cleansing hands and feet also have deep concern with personal hygiene. When the people go far evacuation, what is the method of purification after evacuation, availability of latrine facilities, the method of discharging excreta, the availability and quality of scavenging services, the method of cleansing hands and feet after evacuation as well as before and after meal etc. are some of the focal points which are to be observed intensively as to analyse the status of personal hygiene of a person or a community as a whole. Viewing this thirst in mind we have also tried to analyse the status of personal hygiene of the tribal communities of Uttaranchal through observation method. We have different observations about different tribal communities. For instance the Raji community do not have any regularity of evacuation. Mostly the persons of the Raji community prefer to go for evacuation in morning time provided they feel so. In the eastward of Kimkhola the Raji village there flows a small stream of water.

The tribal people get up in the morning and go for fetching water from the hilly spring and also make evacuation there. After evacuation they just wash their hands, feet and face with spring water and then fill the vessel with water and come back home. This is a normal process observed mainly by those youths or adults of the family who go for fetching water at morning. While the rest of the population, may be infants, children and elderly persons, do not have any particular routine for evacuation. They do it whenever they feel the pressure. The children and the elderly people just sit beside the footpath or nearby terraces meant for growing vegetables or crops for discharging excreta. In other words we can say that infants, children and elderly people discharge the nature's call in a very natural way. There is uncertainily in regard to evacuation. None of the family has lavatory or latrine facilities available in the house or the hut. In the open ground under cover a rock or shrubs or terrace wall or drain the people sit for egestion and discharge the nature's call may be that a major or minor. The excreta is not covered by any means. There is no scavenging services available in the village. Hence the excreta in open turns into a germinating ground for flies the permanent agents of germs carrier. In most of the cases the persons are seen using a piece of stone or vegetable leaf or grass for cleansing

are seen using a piece of stone or vegetable leaf or grass for cleansing the remains of excrete in their anus. In rare cases the people use water for purification after egestion. Most of the people even use a piece of stone or a twig of grass or a leaf for cleaning but do not use water instantly for washing hands. Only those persons using water for purification just wash their hands with water without the use of any detergent or soap. In some cases the people were seen using soil or ash for washing hands after purification. The Raji people are not in habit of washing their hands before meal but after meal they wash their hands and mouths with water. The toilet pattern and ways of cleaning hands reflect the absence of hygienic sense among the Rajis. This is the reason of various type of morbidities they are suffering from.

The scenario of the Tharus is somewhat different from the Rajis. The egestion pattern shows that 47.45 per cent Tharus prefer to go for natural ablution at morning time after having a cup of tea, 48.17 per cent do not bother about it and are of the view that whenever the body needs so we make discharge the excreta, while the rest 4.38 per cent are uncertain and responded that there is no particular time meant for it. Sometime they go at morning time and sometime at evening. About 99 per cent Tharus even today make egestion either in agricultural fields or on the bank of the village pond or beside the footpath/bridle path or in the outskirt of the village. Since there is only one family which has a facility for lavatory in the house.

But the people compulsorily take a bottle-full of water with them while going for ablution and make purification with water. While returning they also bring some soil with them for washing their hands in the hand-pump. But the people who prefer to go beside the village pond do not take water with them. Just after egestion they make evacuation with pond water and also wash their hands with clay of pond. Agricultural fields, outskirt of the village, pond site are seen with excreta because the people are not in habit of covering the excreta after discharge. The infants are made to sit in the courtyard or sometime in the backyard of the house/hut, while the small children, ranging about three to nine years old are made to sit in the nearby kitchen gardens. The excreta of infants is then thrown on the road side or besides the village pond because the tribal village absolutely lacks scavenging services. The infants are then purified with water but in the case of the children purification after ablution is not certain. It is so because the children go themselves for egestion whenever they feel so and avoid purification. The ignorant children can be seen with excreta sticking in their buttocks and sometime in their feet. The Tharus are used to wash their hands before and after meal but the children are not aware of it. They do not use any sort of material for washing hands. Thus it is evident that a sense of cleanliness is certainly

and methods of cleanliness. It is the reason that they could not cultivate the hygienic sense in their children so far.

The Buxas of the Bannakhera village are also unaware of and careless about personal hygiene. Majority of the Buxa population (57.45 per cent) does not follow any regular and particular time schedule even for natural ablution. So far only 37.23 per cent population has developed the habit of egestion at morning time before breakfast. The rest of the population has uncertain of time-schedule. This category of persons includes generally the infants, children and the aged people. The youths and the adults are used to go for evacuation at morning. The Buxas also use any open ground for natural ablution. It may be an agricultural field, outskirt of the village, surrounding of the forest land and along side of footpath or village route. It is so because there is no tradition of making lavatory and latrine within the house/hut or within the house premises. Exceptionally only two Buxa families have so far lavatories for evacuation purposes. Excreta can be seen alongside the foot path as you enter into the Buxa village because the Buxas neither cover the excreta after ablution nor any scavenging service is available in the village. The young and the adults Buxas, in general, use water for purification after evacuation while the children, infants and the elderly are viewed wiping and extricating excreta from their anus with grass or leaves. The persons of this category do not wash even their hands after ablution. The Buxas are not used to wash their hands before meal but certainly wash after meal. Generally soap of any kind is used for washing hands, otherwise they do not hesitate to use ash, soil or clay for washing their hands particularly after evacuation. Thus it is observed that the toilet pattern and cleansing activity of the Buxas do not have any concern with their hygienic sense. All the processes goes in a very natural course. Even the Buxa people do not think about the ill-effect of the unhygienic practices they often perform.

The polyandrous Khasas of the Basaya village have different opinion about the toilet pattern and cleansing practices. Though the majority of the Khasa population, i.e., 69.14 per cent prefer to go for ablution at morning after having a cup of tea. But in practice almost all the working population does not have any provision of spare time for petty jobs like egestion. They proceed to their routine jobs and make evacuation during this period whenever they feel so. For example, the persons just release the pressure on the way while going to jungle for collecting fuel and fodder, or sometime during gazing animals or working in agricultural fields. Even the children are seen discharging excreta on the way to school. In all the cases as soon as the people feel any pressure they under cover the shrub, rocks or hillock, sit alongside the foot path and release the pressure. In such cases the people just use stone piece for

release the pressure. In such cases the people just use stone piece for wiping excreta from their anus. After ablution they do not think it necessary to wash their hands. On the contrary, the Khasas who have lavatory facilities in the house, generally make ablution at morning and purify with water and wash their hands with soap. But the percentage of those families is very low. At present, there are only 14.81 per cent families having lavatory facilities available in the house. Besides this, the children and infants egest alongside the foot path. The buzzing flies on the excreta with foul smell make an easy inkling of carelessness and unhygienic sense of the tribal people. In fact neither they cover the excreta after ablution nor is there any scavenging service available in the village. This state of being causes a number of diseases about which the people remain almost unaware. Thus the over all scenario of the toilet pattern as observed by the tribals of Uttaranchal shows the lack of hygienic sense and also the ignorance of tribal people of the importance of personal hygienes for healthy life.

Care of feet, nails and teeth is also an important dimension of personal hygiene. To a large extent the pattern of caring feet, nails and teeth affect and determine the status of personal hygiene of a person or a community as a whole. It is empirically proved that the habit of caring for feet, nails and teeth has deep concern with health status of a person. The cleanliness and regular care make the organs healthy and lastly pave the ways for better health status of the persons concerned and also sets them free from various infectious diseases. While carelessness and irregularity weakens these organs which may at last causes various unseen and latent infectious diseases with far reaching fatal consequences. With this hypothetical propositions in mind the pattern, how the tribal people care for their feet, nails and teeth, has been studied during the investigation so that the role of personal hygiene in determining the health status can be understood objectively.

The field information shows a certain variation of opinion, the tribal people have towards caring pattern of the organs as well as the practices they observe for this purpose in normal course. As for instance we put a number of questions and observations directly related to the caring system of the bodily organs related to personal hygiene. At this the different tribal communities responded in different ways. We have instances of difference of opinion within the community. As some people are very particular about caring their feet, nails and teeth while others are very careless and do not give any importance to this cause. Among the Rajis we observed that the people are now in habit of wearing footwears not with the notion of protecting their feet but for the sake of fashion. Even the Raji women, who can afford it, prefer to wear sleepers but some women can be seen wearing canvas shoes while going to work as well the children are seen wandering barefooted. The poor Rajis anyhow manage two-time meal first, if they can able to save some money they buy clothes for the family members and lastly think about footwears. The Rajis do not have any particular routine of washing feet. They do not have any notion of cleansing feet while returning from routine work and long foot walking or before going to kitchen, bed or going for meal. Some adult persons are seen just pouring water on their feet before meal. Even the infants and children are not made to wash their feet. But the people certainly wash their feet while taking bath. The Rajis do not apply anything like mustard oil, vaseline and ghee etc. as to care for their feet. Cracked heel, chilblain on feet and fungal infection on fingers speak about carelessness of the Rajis and also reflects their unhygienic sense towards personal hygiene. They are not used to cut their nails of hands and feet. The blackish ends of finger nails tell the story of their ignorance. Sometimes the women, whenever relax on way to their routine job, are seen casually cutting their nails with sickle. On a question, the Rajis responded that they prefer to grow-long nails not because of the fashion and applying nail polish or mehandi as to make the nails attractive but because long nails have some functional importance in their life. To tear up the things, to kill lice and to work in the fields and forests, long finger nails help them in many ways. Even the parents and the elderly persons do not motivate the youngsters for cutting their nails and cultivating habit of washing hands and feet before and after meal. In fact the uneducated and ignorant jungle people are not aware of the clean habits and its importance for personal hygiene. How can they make their children learn about it? Besides this, the Rajis are not used to cleansing mouths through brushing teeth. Casually some Raji persons are seen cleansing their teeth with charcoal which has far reaching iil-effects on their teeth. But the Rajis are not aware of it. The untimely decay of teeth is the inevitable outcome of this ignorance.

The Tharus are comparatively more aware of the importance of cleanliness of feet, nails and teeth. Almost all the Tharu people have foot wears. They prefer to wear sandal and shoes while going for work or outside of the house. But at home only some persons are seen wearing sleepers while the majority of the persons are not used to wear any kind of footwears. Generally the people use footwears while going to work. The Tharu youths are very fond of wearing footwears of latest fashion but they lack hygienic sense as the stockings they wear give out foul smell because they are not particular about its washing. The children and the elderly people do not cut their nails regularly. The worn out nail-ends full of dirt give an impression of their ignorance of cleanliness of nails. The Tharus casually cut their nails of feet and hands. They often use blade, sickle, knife or scissors for this purpose. Chilblains, fungal

use blade, sickle, knife or scissors for this purpose. Chilblains, fungal and cracks are the general ailments found in the feet of the elderly Tharus. The constant work in agricultural fields particularly in raining season causes a type of skin problem amidst the foot fingers of the people working in fields. For the treatment of the skin problem the people preferably make some indigenous efforts. The people wash their feet while returning from work, long on foot walks and evacuation and also before going to bed and before taking the meal. There is a routine of washing feet and hands at evening time. The people generally do not use any soap for washing hands and feet. They do not apply any thing like mustard oil or vaseline in their feet. The nails of the foot-fingers are not cut regularly. No social taboos are observed for cutting nails. The young girls do not follow any technique for making their nails more beautiful. The people are not aware of the unhygienic effects of the long nails full of dirt. Even the parents and the elderly people do not have any sense of inculcating the habits of washing hands and feet before and after meal and also cutting and cleansing nails regularly. It is so because the Tharus are not fully aware of the importance of cleanliness of feet and nails. Besides this the pattern of caring for teeth is also different among the Tharus. There is different opinion and behaviour of the persons. The elderly people do not follow any practice as to keep their teeth clean and strong. While the youths prefer to use tooth powder or tooth paste for cleansing their teeth provided they can afford it. The infected teeth are cured through indigenous methods. A mixture of salt and mustard oil is rubbed around the infected tooth regularly for its treatment. Sometimes, the people also consult the traditional medicine-man or the sorcerers for the treatment of infected teeth who on the basis of occult art make the treatment. However the tribal people do not think about proper cleansing practices as to keep their teeth clean and healthy. Hence, because of the ignorance of the hygienic sense the Tharus could not cultivate practices for cleaning feet, hands, nails and teeth in their children.

Almost the same hygienic status is of the Buxa community. The poor Buxas are leading their life in ignorance. Their main concentration remains on earning their livelihood. The people even do not know the art of expending their earnings. Their priority is to manage food, clothes, shelter, medicine etc. Footwears for them is not meant for protection of feet but just an imitation by nodding acquaintance. Hence most of the Buxas do not wear any sort of footwears while at home. But they, particularly the adult and the elderly Buxas (male only), put on cheap type of canvas or plastic shoes. The females are seen wearing sleepers while going to work. The school-going children wear canvass or the plastic shoes as prescribed by the school authority. The youths preferably wish to wear sleepers while at home and the shoes at work or outside of the home, 19.79 per cent shoes, 6.25 per cent sandals and the remaining 11.46 per cent do not use footwears while at home. The last category consists of the elderly persons while the youths and adults are habitual of wearing footwears while at home. We observed that the children of the Buxas do not prefer any footwears, they feel comfort in barefooted. But the parents and the elder persons of the family make them wear the shoes, sandals or sleepers while going to school or anywhere outside the house premises. The poor Buxas, in spite of their willingness, cannot afford footwears. Chilblains and fungal infection is very common among the Buxas.

They take indigenous treatment for it. In fact the Buxas are neither aware and particular about caring their feet nor have they a sense of health hazards. All their decisions are made mainly by economic considerations. Even in buying footwears their priority is that it must be cheaper and durable. By and large we observed that only the cheaper plastic footwears fulfil their requirement as well as their considerations. But the ignorant poor Buxas are not aware of the unhygienic effects of plastic footwears. They are not particular about washing their feet. They casually wash their feet when they come back from work, fields and evacuation. They use no material for washing their feet. Exceptionally some women are seen rubbing stone or brick pieces to remove chilblains from their heels. They do not wash their feet before going to kitchen, meal and bed. No prophylactic material like crack-cream, vaseline etc. is applied as to keep their feet free from ailments. The Buxas are not regular in cutting their finger nails of feet and hands. Casually, in leisure time they are seen cutting their nails with sickle or scissors or the blades. Otherwise due to constant work their finger nails worn-out themselves. Only the blackish ends of finger nails full of dirt make it realize that they also need to be removed. The ignorant Buxas are not aware of it and its ungygienic repercussions. Thus we can conclude that the Buxas in general are not particular about cutting their nails. They neither observe any taboo for nail cutting nor follow any particular technique to remove them. The women do not follow any technique for making their nails more beautiful. They are also unaware of the ill-effects of long nails. Hence they do never even motivate their children for cutting nails and also for keeping them clean. The Buxas are not aware of keeping their teeth clean through brushing them with toothpaste or tooth powder or any indigenous material like fibrous twigs of neem etc. They just clean the mouth superficially with water while washing the face at morning and after having meal. In some cases when teeth turn to infection the people use a mixture of salt and musturd oil and rub it in and around the infected teeth. When the pain becomes intolerable they rush to the doctor and then take the treatment as prescribed by him. Exceptionally we also

then take the treatment as prescribed by him. Exceptionally we also observed the Buxa youths rubbing their teeth with charcoal. On a question they responded that the charcoal whitens the teeth and also keeps them strong. This notion ultimately paves way for various teeth-related ailments because charcoal has always ill-effects on teeth and gums.

Every community has its own pattern of caring for feet, nails and teeth. Washing with water is a general one. Besides this, different materials and things are used, as per-capacity of the person concerned and his likings. Wearing footwears, cutting nails, cleansing its ends and brushing the teeth either with tooth paste/tooth powders or with fibrous twigs of neem and other plants and trees are some other refined ways of caring for these important organs. In fact the teeth, nails and feet have hygienic importance in human life. Taking care of these organs may cause good health vis-a-vis carelessness will have adverse effects. The polyandrous Khasas have their own ways and notions about caring for feet, nails and teeth. They generally wash these organs with water as to keep them clean. But merely the water cleansing has no hygienic meaning. Besides water cleansing almost all the Khasas also wear footwears to protect their feet mainly from cold particularly during winter and thorn and other rough and pricking materials in general. For this purpose an average Khasa wishes to purchase footwears of any kind. But their ultimate consideration is the cheap cost of the footwear. Their poor economy permits them to buy only a cheaper convas or plastic footwears. The footwears of course protect the feet of the wearers but chilblains, fungal infection between the fingers and the cracks on the heels explain the story of the ailing feet which is inevitable result of the carelessness of the Khasas. In fact the people are seen to pour water on their feet in the name of washing. But they are never seen extricating the dirt by rubbing their feet with a stone-piece, detergent and other bathing soap. The gradual deposition of dirt, layer after layer, ultimately causes cracks even on the forefront of ankles. This state of being indicates the lack of hygienic sense pervading among the Khasas. The field observations show that the Khasas living in cold climatic conditions are not much particular about washing their feet very carefully. They just complete the formality of washing feet by pouring water on feet when returning from fields, forests, long walks and also before taking a meal, going to bed and kitchen. Sometime the people are seen applying fat of goat or ghee in the infected part of the feet, i.e., chilblains and cracks. The Khasa people also apply mustard oil in their feet and hands. They are not serious and habitual of cutting nails of feet and hands regularly. The school going children are asked by their teachers for cutting nails and brushing teeth but the parents and the elders of the family do not care of it and also do not motivate the cihldren. Some children are seen

But the innocent children are not aware of its ill-effects. However, the Khasas while in leisure casually cut their nails with sickle. They do not follow any socio-religious taboos for cutting nails. Even the women are not desirous of following any technique for making their nails clean and more attractive and their teeth shining. Though the tradition of hospitality prevading among the Khasas even today makes us recollect the period of the Mahabharata, when Lord Krishna washes the feet of his poor friend, Sudam at the threshold of the palace. Even today the Khasa women wash the feet and hands of the new-comers at the threshold of the house and also before and after every meal but this pattern implies more the observance of tradition of hospitality but not the sense of personal hygiene. The Khasa community passes on this tradition to their new generations but they never know the real implication, i.e., the hygienic sense of it. It is the reason that the Khasas just perform their formality by washing superficially the hands and feet and also cleansing the mouth with water only.

Spitting, coughing and sneezing behaviour is also an important dimension of personal hygiene. But it is experienced during our investigation that these habits differ man to man and do not exhibit any community-wise trend. Irrespective of any community the tribal people are not aware of decent ways of spitting, coughing and sneezing behaviour. Among the Rajis most of the people are uncertain about these habits. They spit, cough and sneeze whenever and wherever they feel so. While spitting they do not mind the place. The inner side of the wall of the huts proves this fact. The fresh and the dried cough sticking with walls shows that the Rajis, who are generally the sufferers from cold, cough, asthma, catarrh and tuberculosis, just spit sputum on the walls or beside the bed while sleeping inside the house. When they are in the corridor or courtyard of the hut they spit either side of their seating place. Almost the same pattern we observe among the Khasas and the Buxas. But the Tharus have somewhat decent ways of spitting. They always mind the place while spitting and try to avoid the places used for general activities. Most of the tribal people were in the habit of covering the cough. They do not use spittoons. They do not have any sense of covering the mouth while coughing and nose while sneezing. They discharge the nasal waste with their fingers and then wipe out the fingers with their attires. The children are seen sucking the nasal waste and sometime they wipe out their nasal waste with their sleeves of clothes. Thus we observe that the tribal people have neither any decent sense of spitting, coughing and sneezing nor are they aware of the ill-effects of it.

In view of the aforesaid observations we also have tried to understand the perceptions of the tribals towards the correlation between health and hygiene and also their views about the term hygiene. We

health and hygiene and also their views about the term hygiene. We found that the tribal people are not aware to the positive correlation of health and hygiene. In some matters they express their views that there is a negative correlation between health and hygiene. For instance, they are of the views that bathing during winter causes cold-related ailments. Besides this the 'neat and clean' appearance of a person, mainly of the children, may be a curse for them because such persons easily become the victim of evil eyes and also of evil spirits. It is the reason that the Rajis and the Khasas, in particular, do not prefer to keep their children neat and clean. In fact the tribals do not understand hygiene and its implications for a healthy life. The 'hygiene' has no meaning in their life. Keeping the children dirty, does not make them wear the new clothes at their 'Naming ceremony' merely to protect them from evil eye and also from the ill-effects of evil spirits are some of the examples which prove that they have rather misconception about hygiene. More so, following the practices of occult art for the treatment of illness of children and also the use of superstitious remedies as to set free the children from the effects of the evil-eye and evil-spirit are some other examples of their misunderstanding of the term 'hygiene'. Among the tribals, the traditional medicine-man just put five chillies along with mustard seeds in the burning coal in a vessel and make the small rising smoke to the children suspected to be under the spell of evil-eye and evil-spirit. This practice may cause some side-effects on the child and can not be termed good from hygienic points of view.

Environmental and Domestic Hygiene: The environmental and domestic hygiene is an important dimension of the 'Hygienic System'. In the present study we have used the term environmental and domestic hygiene in terms of the nature of the dwellings the tribals live in, the facilities available within the abodes, the provisions made within the house for the convenience of the family members, the surrounding of the house/hut, the provision for domestic animals, the pattern of cleaning abodes, the storage of food-grains and the method for keeping intact the stored food-grains, the notion of the people towards the stale and rancid food, the pattern of preserving the cooked food and its consumption, the pattern of disposing of the sweepings and the waste of the house etc. It is observed that the tribals have different types of abodes. Among the Rajis almost all the population live in mixed type of houses. Every family has only one abode out of which 28.00 per cent are single storeyed and the rest 72.00 per cent are double storeyed 20.00 per cent family have joint system of dwellings for human beings and of tamed animals. In 72.00 per cent houses, the ground floor is used for keeping animals and the first floor is used for human beings. Only 8.00 per cent families have separate cow sheds. In Raji abodes there is no provision for separate rooms. Generally a corner of the room is used as kitchen. There is no provision of toilet and store room in the abode. Almost all the activities of the family are performed in single room abodes. The people hardly sweep room once in a day and smear the room with the mixture of cow-dung and ruddle once in a week. No bactericide is used in the mixture made for smearing the floor. The abode does not have proper ventilations. The Rajis have hardly surplus food-grains to store. Hence they do not have any problem of storing food-grain and to make it insect free. The sweepings and the waste of the house is just pushed to courtyard of the abode through broom. The courtyard of the abode is casually swept to keep it clean. But the overall condition of the abode and its surrounding can not be regarded suitable from the hygienic point of view. The Rajis are not in practice to keep covered the cooked food. As soon as the food is cooked the members of the family take their part and devour it instantly. There is no surplus cooked food. Hence the problem of preserving the cooked food does never arise before them. However, if it happens, they do not hesitate to eat stale and rancid food, provided that it is cooked at their own kitchen. The children when return from school are often provided stale food because the timings of meal does not suit the children. Thus the Rajis do not have suitable environmental and domestic hygienic conditions. They absolutely lack hygienic sense.

The Tharus have comparatively different position of environmental and domestic hygiene. No doubt the majority of the Tharus, i.e., 59.72 per cent are living in Kachcha houses, yet there are 22.91 per cent and 17.36 per cent Tharus who dwell respectively in Pacca and mixed type of houses respectively. Mostly the Tharu abodes, whatever their type is, are single storeyed. Only the ground floor is constructed by the people. The inner rooms are used for storing food-grains and also for sleeping. While the corridor is used for seating and dining purposes. The Tharus have separate arrangement for keeping tamed animals. Almost all the families who have tamed animals construct separate cattle sheds. The abodes have no proper provision for light and ventilation facilities. But the remarkable feature of the Tharu abodes is its cleanliness. Both the inside and the outside of the dwellings is smeared every day with the mixture of cow-dung and viscous soil. They sweep the rooms, corridor and courtyard of the abode daily. They do not mix up any bactericide in the mixture used for smearing the floor. But the mixed and Kachcha type of abodes remain closed from all sides. No provision for light and air is made. However the inner side of such abodes remain comfortable in all seasons because grass roofs and mud walls protect the inner side of abodes from hot as well as from cold. The Tharus make earthen structure called 'Kutheya' for the storage of food-grains. Being an agriculturist community they need a store for storage for surplus food-

agriculturist community they need a store for storage for surplus food-grains. They use insecticide to keep food-grains insect free. The Tharus have the sense of cleanliness. They keep clean their house surroundings. The sweepings and the waste of the abode and its surroundings is thrown in the nearby agricultural fields or alongside of the road. They keep the cooked food items covered. Generally the agriculturist Tharus cook food at morning in surplus and set off to their jobs of daily routine. The children and other members of the family when return from their assignment take food items of their share. Thus they are used to take stale food. They simply preserve the remaining cooked food in any of the vessels they use for cooking and just cover it with a plate or a large brass dish in the kitchen. If the food is left uncovered they do not hesitate to consume it. The school-going children and also the persons on their routine work when return, normally eat the stale food. Generally the Tharus have comparatively better environmental and domestic hygienic conditions. It is so because the cleanliness of the house and its surroundings is their age-old habit and not because of any cause which has virtually better hygienic effects on the people.

The Buxas have somewhat different environmental and domestic hygienic conditions. Mostly 41.67 per cent Buxas live in Kachcha houses, only 31.25 per cent have pucca houses and the rest 27.08 per cent persons live in mixed type of abodes.Almost all type of the Buxa abodes are single storeyed with single fold. The front part consists of the corridor and the inner part consists of the rooms. One corner of the corridor is used for kitchen while the rest part of corridor is used for dining and sitting purposes. The rooms are used for sleeping purposes and keeping intact their movable property and also for storage of the food-grains.There is no provision for light and ventilation in 'kachcha' and 'mixed type' of abodes. The Buxas are also used to smear their rooms, corridor and courtyard with a mixture made up of cow-dung and viscous soil. They sweep the rooms and the surrounding of the abodes daily. On some occasions they also smear the walls with ruddle and carve different figures lying in their conscience. In fact, keeping clean the abode and making it attractive is the inherent tradition of the Buxas which has ultimately positive hygienic effects on the community as a whole. The people do not use any bactericide in the mixture made for smearing the abode and its surroundings. The Buxas have separate settlement for domestic animals. Normally the other end of the courtyard is used for making the cattle-shed. The dung and other organic waste of the cattle is stored along side the cattle shed and used as organic manure when decomposed. Even the sweepings and waste of the house is disposed of with the organic waste of the cattle. But the stench coming out of the putrefied waste has ill-effects on the human body about which the Buxa

constant foul smell of the waste cannot be ignored from the hygienic point of view. Today the Buxas also use different types of insecticides for keeping their stored food-grains insect-free but they are not aware of the ill-effects of the food-grains kept with poisonous insecticides. Nor the people know the techniques for making food-grains free from poisonous effects of insecticides. This process may cause silent and slow poisoning in human body and create different anomalies.

The Buxas are used to take stale and rancid food.They cook food in surplus and keep it for children and other persons of the family to eat whenever they like it. They do not use any almirah, box or refrigerator as to preserve the cooked food, they just cover it with a large dish and uncover while eating. But sometime the cooked food is left uncoverd by mistake and becomes infected due to the sitting of house-flies, nevertheless the stale food is consumed by persons as usual. It seems the Buxas are not aware of the ill-effects of the use of the stale and rancid food and also of the infected food items. The hungry children when come back home from schools and the family members from their routine jobs do not care about the quality of food, they just satiate their hunger. This state of being reflects the lack of hygienic sense among the Buxas. They are basically conventionalists and carry on the things they have acquired from their ancestors.

The Khasas have different situation of domestic and environmental hygiene. Today majority of the Khasas (78.04 per cent) live in pucca houses, 17.08 per cent live in mixed type of houses and the rest 4.88 per cent live in huts. Except the huts all the houses are two storeyed. The pucca and mixed type of houses have provision of light and ventilation. The Khasas are used to sweep their rooms once in a week. The women supposed to perform the domestic tasks usually sweep the rooms at morning time and smear with the ruddle mixed with cowdung. No bactericide is mixed with the smearing material. The houses do not have separate provision for kitchen, dining-room, sitting-room and bed rooms. The people manage anyhow their abodes for all familial tasks. Generally the ground floor of the house is used for keeping tamed animals. Along side of the courtyard they dump the cow-dung, other animal waste, sweepings and the refuse of the house. This process of dumping the dung and other wastes goes on throughout the year and during winter the decomposed dung and other waste is carried to agricultural fields and used as manure. The objective analysis of the situation exhibits that the vicinity of the tamed animals and dumping of the wastes nearby the house is not good from the hygienic point of view. But the age-old prevalence have made the people follow the pattern of keeping tamed animals in the ground floor of the house and the cow-dung near the courtyard. The foul smell coming out of the decomposed animal waste

courtyard. The foul smell coming out of the decomposed animal waste and flies, insects and other germs germinated out of the decomposed manure have ill-effects on human body. But the Khasas have no understanding about it.

The Khasas follow the indigenous methods for storing food-grains. They do not use any insecticide for keeping food-grains insect-free. The people use mouse-trap as to get-rid of the mouse. The Khasas are used to eat stale and rancid food. They preserve the surplus cooked food in any vessel or dish and eat whenever they are hungry.The Khasas have no refrigerator, almirah and box for preserving surplus cooked food. They dry up the flesh of goat for preserving it for future and hang it with a wooden-staff of the roof. The people are not in habit of keeping the food covered. The environmental and domestic hygiene have no meaning for the Khasas. They are ignorant and unaware of the functional importance of environmental and domestic hygienes in man's life.

Community Hygiene: The source of drinking water, quality of drinking water, upkeeping pattern of the surrounding of the source of water, drainage system, awareness of the people towards water borne diseases, and the measures of water purification system etc. deal partially with the community hygiene. Besides this, the sanitary services, the method of disposal of human excreta and other solid and liquid wastes also have deep concern with community hygiene. In the present project work the community hygiene of the tribals of Uttaranchal has been taken into consideration for scientific investigation. It is observed that the hill tribes namely the Khasas of Basaya village and the Rajis of the Kimkhola village use tap-water for drinking. The government has made a provision for supplying drinking water at their villages. Within the reach of every tribal family a water-tank has been constructed in the tribal village which acts as a water reservoir. On some occasions the hill tribes also use natural water source, springs and rivulets while the Tharus and the Buxas use hand-pump water for drinking and other purposes. Almost all the Tharu and the Buxa families have installed hand-pumps at their abodes. In the hilly areas, particularly in the Raji and the Khasas villages, the water-tanks are basically constructed beyond the source of contamination and comparatively in the higher elevation. A platform of cement concrete was also made around the tank so that the villagers can have bath and can also wash their clothes on the clean hard surface and the contaminated water can flow uninterruptedly. But gradually, it is observed, the surrounding of the water tank turned itself into a contaminated source because the constant discharge of human waste, such as, cough, nasal discharge, urine etc. around the water-tank has become a source of contamination, even the people coming for fetching drinking water at early morning are seen making purification with drinking water-tap after the water tank under cover of the wall of the tank and make purification after ablution while some do not hesitate using the cemented platform for this purpose. There was a provision of a pucca drain for carrying the spilled water but due to lack of proper upkeeping and constant cleansing the drains are chocked with filth and other waste materials. This state of being also causes permanent source of contamination around the water-tank. The top of the tanks is certainly covered when it was newly constructed but with due course of time the people began to remove it, sometime for cleaning the water tank, sometime to observe the water level and sometime for fetching water directly, particularly when the water-level remains below the tap of water supply. This process may be inevitable for the time being but the innocent children take it otherwise and take a bath by going inside the water-tank. At summer noon, when elders of the village are in their daily routine, the children are seen swimming and jumping within the water tank. In fact the children, particularly in summer noons just come in group, remove the top cover of the tank and enter it and then take a bath in their own way. This process makes the drinking water more contaminated. The tribal people do not take any precautionary measures for purifying drinking water. Only some people just avoid the tank-water and fetch from the natural source for drinking purposes. Among the Buxa and the Tharus the water source, i.e., the hand-pump is kept clean only by making a small cement concrete platform. There is a kachcha drainage system that carries the spilled water, but within a short distance of the hand-pump the spilled water collects and turns into a quagmire and become a permanent breeding ground of insects like mosquito and flies, and other worms. In fact the water level in the Tarai plain remains high and, the abode of the Buxas and the Tharus, remain nearer to the ground surface, hence the absorbing capacity of the earth remains very weak. Hence the used and spilled water of hand-pumps submerge the surrounding which has ultimately unhygienic effects on the people.

The tribal people are not aware of the water-borne diseases like viral hepatitis A and E, poliomyelitis, rotavirus, diarrhoea (all viral diseases), Typhoid, paratyphoid fever, bacillary dysentery, coli-diarrhoea, cholera (all bacterial diseases), amoebiasis, giardiasis (protozoal disease), weils disease (lepto-spiral disease) round worm, thread worm, hydatid disease (helmintic disease) etc. It is the reason that the tribal people do not apply any measure of water purification system. They do not know the proper storage of safe drinking water, filtration system and the method of disinfecting the drinking water. Resultantly they often use the contaminated water. It is, of course, the ignorance of the tribal people that makes them perform various activities like personal ablution, washing of clothes and tamed animals, (like buffalo) dumping of refuse and waste

of clothes and tamed animals, (like buffalo) dumping of refuse and waste and also menstrual bath in the vacinity of the source of drinking water. All the tribal villages under study lack safe and pure drinking water facilities. There is no proper drainage system. No motivating agencies exist in the area, no awareness programmes have so far been launched and no health, hygiene and nutrition related education is imparted to the tribals. The people therefore lead their life in ignorance and suffering from various kinds of diseases.

Disposal of human excreta and other solid and liquid wastes. Sanitary services, methods of disposing of human excreta and other solid and liquid waste have direct concern with human health and hygiene. The tribal areas lack the sanitary services and any other scientific method of disposing of human excreta and solid and liquid waste. Even today most of the tribal population do not have sanitary latrine system. Today only twelve families among the Khasas, one family among the Tharus and two families among the Buxas have sanitary latrines at their houses. Rest of the tribal population follow the traditional pattern of disposing of excreta and other solid and liquid waste. They use open grounds for evacuation but do not cover the excreta and other waste. In fact the soil pollution, water pollution, contamination of food and propagation of flies are some of the 'Health Hazards' caused by improper disposal of excreta and other wastes. Hence the degree of awareness of the tribal people towards health hazards caused due to improper disposal of excreta and other human waste. The following Table 6.24 exhibits the awareness of the tribal people.

It is observed that most of the Raji and Buxa respondents are unaware of the expected health hazards caused by improper pattern of disposing of human excreta and other waste. They are unaware that the excreta and other solid and liquid waste causes soil and water pollution and also contaminate the food. They do not know that the house flies are the agent of germs and may cause epidemics at community level. It is the reason that the Rajis and the Buxas, as a whole, are very careless about it. Rather they have misunderstanding that excreta and other waste are the best manure, hence they preferably dispose it of in nearby fields or kitchen gardens. On the contrary, the Tharus and the Khasas do have a little understanding about the health hazards caused by the improper disposal of the excreta and other waste. However, they do not take any precaution about it because the majority of the population of the respective communities is of the opinion that the excreta and other solid and liquid waste are the things to be disposed of and it is better to dispose it in the agricultural fields for manure. In real sense the tribal people are not ignorant of about the direct and indirect ill-effects of pollution caused by improper disposal of excreta.

Table 6.24. Awareness Towards Health Hazards Caused by Improper Excreta Disposal

Respon- dent	Health Hazards	Degree of Awareness					
		Fully aware	Aware	Un- certain	Un- aware	Fully un- aware	Total
Raji	Soil, Pollution	—	—	18	04	03	12
	%	—	—	72.00	16.00	12.00	100.00
	Water Pollution	—	—	19	04	02	25
	%	—	—	76.00	16.00	08.00	100.00
	Contamination of food	—	—	14	09	02	25
	%	—	—	56.00	36.00	8.00	100.00
	Propagation of flies	—	—	16	07	02	25
	%	—	—	64.00	28.00	08.00	100.00
Tharu	Soil, Pollution	—	—	97	46	01	144
	%	—	—	67.37	31.94	0.69	100.00
	Water Pollution	—	52	52	39	01	144
	%	—	36.11	36.11	27.09	0.69	100.00
	Contamination of food	—	04	92	47	01	144
	%	—	2.78	63.89	32.64	0.69	100
	Propagation of flies	—	21	81	42	—	144
	%	—	14.59	56.25	29.16	—	100.00
Buxa	Soil, Pollution	—	—	82	14	—	96
	%	—	—	85.41	14.59	—	100.00
	Water Pollution	—	—	82	14	—	96
	%	—	—	85.41	14.59	—	100.00
	Contamination of food	—	—	82	14	—	96
	%	—	—	85.41	14.59	—	100.00
	Propagation of flies	—	—	82	14	—	96
	%	—	—	85.41	14.59	—	100.00
Khasa	Soil, Pollution	—	01	43	38	—	82
	%	—	1.22	52.44	46.34	—	100.00
	Water Pollution	—	08	36	38	—	42
	%	—	9.76	43.90	46.34	—	100
	Contamination of food	—	05	39	38	—	82
	%	—	6.09	47.57	46.34	—	100.00
	Propagation of flies	—	13	34	35	—	82
	%	—	15.86	41.46	42.68	—	100.00

dysenteries, diarrhoeas, cholera, hookworm disease, ascariasis, viral hepatitis, intestinal infections and parasitic infections which are caused by the pollution arising out of improper disposal of the excreta and other solid and liquid wastes. But the tribals are not aware of it. Most of the respondents are not in a position to respond about the probable diseases caused by the pollution arising out of improper disposal of excreta. They are either fully unaware or partly unaware of it. There are some exceptions among the Tharus, the Khasas and the Buxas who expressed their awareness of some of the diseases like diarrhoeas, ascariasis, and hookworms which are caused by polluted soil and water, but they do not have any understanding of precautionary measures. The Table 6.25 exhibits

have any understanding of precautionary measures. The Table 6.25 exhibits the degree of awareness of the respondents pertaining to diseases caused by the pollution arising out of improper disposal of excreta. (See Table 6.25)

It is observed that most of the respondents are either uncertain or unaware or fully unaware of the health hazards and their scientific causes. Even they are unaware of the ill-effects of improper disposal of the excreta and other solid and liquid waste. We, therefore tried to understand their opinion about the causes of diseases the people are suffering in their respective communities. We found that mostly the respondents were uncertain about the causes of illness. This percentage was followed respectively by those respondents who consider the destiny, notion of hot and cold, excess work load and lack of stomach full diet as the cause of different diseases. The data pertaining to tribe-wise responses are presented in the Table 6.26.

The dress pattern, foods, beverages, vegetables and beddings have also deep concern with human beings in general and with the females under menstruation or during gestation and delivery period in particular. The health of women under pregnancy and of the lactating mothers determines the health of infants too. Hence the food, clothing, bedding she uses and also the intake of beverages and vegetables have by and large important role in determining the health status of the mother as well as the infant during gestation period and also after delivery. In view of this hypothetical proposition, we made an attempt to investigate the general pattern of dress, food, drinks, vegetables, bedding and also the routine work of the women who are under menstruation, pregnancy, and delivery period and also of the lactating mothers. It is observed that the women under menstruation period generally wear the dress as usual. There is no change observed in the dress pattern of the women during menstruation period. Even they do not make any arrangement for abstaining from the stains of the menstrual bleeding. The stains on the Dhoti and any other worn clothe in the lower portion clearly exhibits the menstrual status of the women. There is no prevalence of sanitary napkins as used by the women during menstruation period. They are given the food items and vegetables as usual but the milk and milk products are strictly prohibited these days because the use of milk and milk products may cause harm to the milching cattle. It is merely a derivation but almost all the tribal people under study in general profess this notion. The pregnant mother has certainly a different situation. The well off or comparatively economically sound tribal families provide nutritious food which consists of milk and milk products but not ghee or any food item with hot effects and properties. The spices are strictly prohibited during pregnancy. The poor tribal families provide food as usual to the pregnant

Table 6.25. Degree of Awareness Towards the Disease Resulted Out of the Improper Excreta Disposal

Respondent	*Disease*	*Degree of Awareness*					
		Fully aware	*Aware*	*Uncertain*	*Unaware*	*Fully unaware*	*Total*
Ranji	Typhoid, Paratyphoid fever	-	-	19	-	06	25.00
	%	-	-	76.00	-	24.00	100.00
	Dysenteries	-	-	14	08	03	
	%	-	-	56.00	32.00	12.00	
	Diarrhoeas	-	-	12	09	04	
	%	-	-	48.00	36.00	16.00	
	Cholera	-	-	11	12	02	
	%	-	-	44.00	48.00	08.00	
	Hookworm disease	-	-	11	09	05	
	%	-	-	44.00	36.00	20.00	
	Ascariaisis	-	-	09	12	04	
	%	-	-	36.00	48.00	16.00	
	Viral hepatitis	-	-	11	10	.4	
	%	-	-	44.00	40.00	16.00	
	Intestinal infections	-	-	14	05	06	
	%	-	-	56.00	20.00	24.00	
	Parasitic infection	-	-	14	05	06	25
	%	-	-	56.00	20.00	25.00	100.00
Tharu	Typhoid, Paratyphoid fever	-	08	40	35	61	144
	%	-	05.00	27.77	24.30	42.38	100.00
	Dysenteries	-	-	103	41	-	
	%	-	-	71.52	28.48	-	
	Diarrhoeas	-	04	95	41	04	
	%	-	2.78	65.97	28.47	2.78	
	Cholera	-	-	93	41	10	
	%	-	-	64.58	28.78	6.94	

(Contd.)

(Contd. Table 6.25)

Respondent	Disease	Degree of Awareness					
		Fully aware	Aware	Uncertain	Unaware	Fully unaware	Total
	Hookworm disease	-	02	62	40	20	
	%	-	1.38	58.94	27.77	13.89	
	Ascariaisis	-	12	86	41	05	
	%	-	8.33	59.72	28.47	3.48	
	Viral hepatitis	-	-	106	29	09	
	%	-	-	73.61	20.13	6.26	
	Intestinal infections	-	-	101	43	-	
	%	-	-	70.13	29.87	-	
	Parasitic infection	-	-	90	38	16	144
	%	-	-	62.50	26.39	11.11	100.00
Buxa	Typhoid, Paratyphoid fever	-	-	35	46	15	96
	%	-	-	36.45	47.92	15.63	100.00
	Dysenteries	-	-	36	42	18	96
	%	-	-	37.50	43.75	18.75	100.00
	Diarrhoeas	-	02	27	57	20	
	%	-	2.08	28.12	59.37	20.83	
	Cholera	-	03	29	35	29	
	%	-	3.12	30.21	36.46	30.21	
	Hookworm disease	-	02	34	33	27	
	%	-	2.08	35.42	34.38	28.12	
	Ascariaisis	-	07	32	36	21	
	%	-	7.30	33.33	37.50	21.87	
	Viral hepatitis	-	-	28	43	25	
	%	-	-	29.16	44.80	26.04	
	Intestinal infections	-	-	29	42	25	
	%	-	-	30.21	43.75	26.04	

(Contd.)

(Contd. Table 6.25)

Respondent	*Disease*	*Degree of Awareness*					
		Fully aware	*Aware*	*Uncertain*	*Unaware*	*Fully unaware*	*Total*
	Parasitic infection	-	-	32	29	35	96
	%	-	-	33.33	30.21	36.46	100.00
Buxa	Typhoid, Paratyphoid fever	-	-	28	32	22	
	%	-	-	34.15	39.02	26.83	
	Dysenteries	-	08	32	32	10	
	%	-	9.76	39.02	39.02	12.20	
	Diarrhoeas	-	08	17	15	42	
	%	-	9.76	20.73	18.30	51.21	
	Cholera	-	04	44	20	14	
	%	-	4.88	53.65	24.40	17.70	
	Hookworm disease	-	08	40	22	12	
	%	-	9.76	47.79	26.82	14.63	
	Ascariaisis	-	06	55	21	-	
	%	-	7.31	67.08	25.61	-	
	Viral hepatitis	-	-	43	18	21	
	%	-	-	52.43	21.96	25.61	
	Intestinal infections	-	-	50	21	11	
	%	-	-	60.68	25.61	13.41	
	Parasitic infection	-	-	48	22	12	
	%	-	-	58.53	26.83	14.64	

Table 6.26. Causes of Disease for the Tribals

Respondent		Reaction-about the cause of disease						
		Destiny	*Lack of Stomach full diet*	*Notion hot and cold*	*Excess work load*	*Pollution*	*Lack of medical facility*	*Uncertain*
Rajis	M	05	10	-	-	-	-	10
	%	20.00	40.00	-	-	-	-	40.00
Tharus	M	30	-	31	27	-	29	27
	%	20.83	-	21.52	18.76	-	20.13	18.76
Buxas	M	-	16	-	-	-	-	80
	%	-	16.67	-	-	-	-	83.33
Khasas	M	36	06	18	08	05	-	09
	%	43.90	7.31	21.96	9.76	6.10	-	10.97
Total	M	71	32	49	35	05	29	126
	%	20.47	9.22	14.12	10.09	1.44	8.35	36.31

dainty Indian dish prepared with ghee, wheat floor, sugar and water. Besides this, ghee, gaggery, chapati and Dal is provided. The milk and milk products, other than 'ghee', is not provided to the woman until she takes a sacred bath after ten or twelve days of the delivery. The lactating mothers have to follow some taboos related to food and drinks. Generally the food items and the drinks which are supposed to cause some ailments in infants, as per their prevalent notions, are strictly prohibited. For example, the lactating mother is not allowed to take cold water, she is not given spiced as well as fried food because these items may cause cold and cough to the infant. The routine work of the tribal women during menstruation and pregnancy period go on as usual, but certainly there is curtailment in their diet as well in other spheres too. In those days they are supposed to follow different taboos related to food, clothes and beddings. For instance, the tribal women among the Buxas and the Tharus under menstruation and delivery period are given light beddings consisting of a carpet/Dari, bed-sheet and blanket. A woman is not permitted to change the dress before a sacred bath.

The Khasas permit the women under delivery after sixth day for washing their clothes. Only then they can change their dresses. The overall situation exhibits that tribals have no hygienic sense. They share their age-old assumptions, notions and benavior patterns which have no concern with health and hygiene. However, the people follow them without caring for their repercussions.

Conclusion

In view of the objective of the present project work it can be asserted that the target, "Health for all by 2000 A.D." is still beyond reach particularly with reference to the tribal communities of Uttaranchal. The health status of the tribal people cannot be said well. The majority of the population is suffering from different kinds of ailments. They do not have proper facilities of medicare system. To a large extent the traditional attitude of the tribal people is responsible for their ill-health. Even today the majority of the tribal people have deep faith in their age-old health care practices. The unhygienic conditions and the lack of hygienic sense among the tribals is also a cause of their ill-health. Besides this the motivational vacuum, ignorance pervading among the tribals, unawareness, illiteracy and also the predominance of traditional ethos are some of the responsible factors of their ill-health, on the one hand, and also of the ineffectiveness of government machinary on the other hand. Only the motivational efforts, awareness programme along with relevant incentives, medical facilities within the easy approach of the tribals can produce positive results and help in achieving the national goal of 'Health for All'.

Nutritional Status

There are various methods for assessing objectively the nutritional status of any individual or a community as a whole. But there are some technical constraints in observing these methods in field studies. For instance there are some clinical examinations which take into consideration the assessment of the general appearance of the person concerned, condition of his/her hair, face, eyes, lips, tongue, teeth, gums, glands, skin, nails, oedema, rachitic changes and internal system. But, in field studies like ours, it is equally impossible to make clinical examinations of the study units because establishing a laboratory in the study field, taking samples, preservation of the samples in conditioned situations and to have technical know-how as to make clinical examination possible are really impossible. However, the nutritional assessment through anthropometric measurements, dietary pattern of the study units, quality and quantity of food items consumed by them in general, is possbile. These techniques can present a general assessment of the nutritional status of the study units. The ethnic food, its nutritional value, food preferences and food avoidance, food types and food status are valuable and determining criteria for assessing nutritional status of a given society. With this assumption in mind the nutritional status of the tribals under study has been enumerated in terms of the dietary intake and the food habits of the tribal people of the sampled villages.

The quality and quantity of the staple food, pulses, oil seeds, milk products, vegetables, flesh food, drinks and narcotics consumed by the people have deep and direct concern with their nutritional status. The nutritional status, by and large, determines the health status of a person or a community as a whole and also determines the caste and class status in social and economic ranking.There are historical evidences of varient tribal food patterns rather than the rest of the non-tribals. During the medieval period the Rajputs and the Brahmins had about thirty-six varieties of sweets and as many as sixteen vegetables including edible nuts and seeds. While there was much difference in the number of food consumed by the tribals in comparison to the non-tribal higher groups. This variation is also conditioned by ecological factor. The people living in rural areas have certainly different food ideology different from the people living in urban areas.

The tribals under study have different food ideology that reflects their nutritional status and also their health status. The general dietary intake and the season-wise preparation of food has not much difference among the tribals. Among the Tharus and the Buxas the cereals that consist of wheat, rice and maize constitute their present diet. The pulses like gram, urad, peas, beans, masur which are consumed along with cereals altogether constitute the source of protein, carbohydrate, vitamin B and other minerals. Throughout the Tharuwat and Buxar areas the cereal crops and pulses have great adaptability to climatic conditions and yields is more per acre. Of all the cereals wheat and paddy are popularly associated with the Tharu and the Buxa regions. The swampy land had ever the adaptability to the rice cultivation which has made the tribals habitual of taking rice and its preparations. In this way it was time when the rice used to be the primordial diet of the Tharus and the Buxas. In other words we can say that the food ideology of the Tharus and the Buxas was conditional with the climatic conditions of the region. This ideology, with the passage of time, transformed into different food habits and then food pattern. Even today the tribal people living in Tarai plain, undoubtedly, cultivate various cereal crops and pulses other than paddy but only for commercial purposes because even today the consumption of rice is comparatively more than of other cereals. There are tribal people who prefer to have rice preparation twice daily rather than bread made up of wheat or maize and other preparations. This food pattern does not provide balanced nutrients intake.

The Tharus and the Buxas have almost similar ecological conditions. Hence the food pattern and the cropping of cereals are approximately the same. Other than the cereals and pulses they also cultivate mustard and use mustard oil with their diet. But consumption of milk and milk products is the least and irregular among them. They do not use milk and milk products. Even the infants and the children are not compulsorily and regularly given milk. They are undoubtedly agriculturists and raise cows and buffalos but mainly for the purpose of dung and male calves. The male-calves help them in pulling the cart and ploughing the fields. There was a time when squeezing out milk from the milching cattle was a social taboo for the Tharus and the Buxas. It was the notion prevalent throughout the tribal region that to milk the milching cattle is a sin against the calf. The people violating this taboo are supposed to suffer its consequences. Hence the tribals used to set free the calf for sucking its mother's milk uninterruptedly. A nodding aquaintance with their neighbouring non-tribals some of the Tharus and the Buxas have started to milk the milching cattle but the regular consumption of milk and milk products has not penetrated into their food ideology. Hence the consumption of cereals, pulses and oil seeds compensate the nutrients supposed to be supplied by the consumption of milk and the milk products.

The Tharus and the Buxas, the known omnivorous tribal communities of the time are still used to have flesh food. They are fond of flesh food may be a mutton, chicken, fish and the flesh of a bore, deer, partridge, hare or porcupine and relish it with great ardour. Fishing and trapping of small game from the nearby jungles is the age-old habit of the Tharus and the Buxas. Even today they try to manage the flesh food any how. Some of the Buxas just buy parts of head, beak, paw of the chicken and also intestine of the slaughtered goat from the butcher's shop and thus fulfil their desire of relishing flesh.

The Rajis and the Khasas (the Hill tribes) have some limited cereals like maize, barley, maduwa (kodo), Jhingur (all coarse grains) as to fulfil their food needs. They consume rice and its preparations in a very scanty manner and on some particular occasions because the cultivation of paddy is less as its yield in the hilly region is very poor. The low purchasing capacity of the tribal people does not allow them to buy rice according to their demands and needs. Hence the tribal people make their indigenous preparations as to keep their body and soul together. They cultivate urad, beans, masur, soya (Bhat) but in a very scarce quantity. The poor yield of pulses does not fulfil their demands and needs. The hilly region has no favourable agro-climatic conditions for the cultivation of oil seeds. The tribal people, generally buy mustard oil, rapeseed oil, vegetable ghee from the market for their own consumption. But some of the poor tribal families cannot afford the consumption of these edible oils in their dietary intake. The Rajis, in particular, are used to have their meals without the use of oil and oil preparations but the Khasas compensate it with ghee and fat of goat they prepare and preserve in their own indigenous ways. There is a limited, rather nil consumption of milk and milk products among the Rajis. The Rajis, who are still very backward and very nearer to the primitive stage do not know the art of raising tamed and milching cattle. Today they do raise cows, oxen, goats and buffalos in a very limited number but for selling purpose. They are not aware of the nutritional value of the milk and milk products. Hence the consumption of milk and milk products is absent from their food ideology. On the contrary Khasas, the pastoral community, has sufficient milk and milk products like curd, butter milk, butter and ghee. The milk and milk products are the main items in their dietary intake. Even milk products mainly ghee and butter milk compensate respectively the scarcity of oilseeds, its product and pulses and their preparation. The Khasas use 'ghee' in place of edible oil in their food system. Buttermilk with salt is used in place of 'dal' and cooked vegetables. The pastoral Khasas are very fond of flesh food may be that mutton, chicken or the flesh of the deer, partridge, porcupine etc. Besides this, they also collect fat from slaughtered animals and use it in the preparation of dal and other vegetables. They dry up the flesh of goat and preserve it for further use.

The Rajis are also fond of flesh food. They manage it by trapping small games from the jungle or by fishing from the nearby rivers and rivulets. The goats they raise sometime also fulfil their need of flesh food. The consumption of flesh food depends on its availability. Thus we come to the conclusion that coarse grain is the main source of dietary intake of the Rajis. There is rare consumption of pulses, oil, fat and the flesh food which are the rich source of protein, carbohydrate, vitamins and various minerals. The nutritional dominance of cereals consist of coarse grains only which does not provide balanced diet. An average Raji, therefore, appeals to be a case of under-nutrition. Their thin built, easily pluckable hair, diffused depigmented face, eyes with bitot's spots, angular stomatitis lips, pale and flabby tongue, teeth with mottled enamel, spongy gums with bleeding, dry and scaly skin, bow legs, light weight and short stature in comparison of age are some of the physical characteristics which show their malnutritional status.

But the nutritional status of the Khasas is comparatively better than the Rajis. The general assessment of dietary intake among the Khasas exhibits that there is of course nutritional dominance of cereals like maize, kodo, Jhingur, paddy, wheat etc. in their food system, yet they have a consumption of milk and milk products and also of flesh food. Such a dietary intake has more or less good nutritional value to the people.

The agriculturists Tharus and the Buxas have cereals, pulses and oil seeds for consumption. They are fond of flesh food but the milk and milk products are absent from their food habits. The people, may be that an infant, a child, youth, adult or aged, just prefer to take stomach full staple food but do not care for its nutrient value. Their basic need is to satiate hunger by any means mindless the food is nutrient or not. They do not care about the nutritious value of the food they take. Even small children are given same staple food which is consumed by other members of the family. As soon as the child leaves breast milk, he/she is fed with the staple food as is cooked in the family for its members. This food pattern causes malnutrition among the children because the consumption of limited variety of staple food does not have balanced quantity of nutrients as is required for the proper development of the physique of a child. It is the reason that children among the Tharus and the Buxas appear physically to be victims of malnutrition.

The tribals have not much difference between food habits and food pattern they follow in winter season and summer season. The routine of the dining time certainly changes but it has no nutritional concern. During winter season mostly the hill tribes (the Khasas and the Rajis) have cooked rice, dal or the like at morning time at about 10 a.m. and maize or kodo bread or the like in the evening. Only two-time meal is taken during winter while in summer they take breakfast at morning, lunch in the noon and dinner at evening. Generally maize or kodo or the kodo-wheat mix bread is taken with salt powder and salty butter milk (if available) in breakfast. The cooked rice with dal or Chudakani or Palau and Bhatiya or Phano (all local preparations) are taken in lunch and again bread with vegetable is taken at night in dinner. Thus we observe that lunch time shifts about 2 to 3 hours earlier and simultaneously the breakfast is dropped in winter season.

The Tharus and the Buxas also change slightly the routine of their dietary pattern with the change of seasons. In summer they take breakfast at morning, lunch at noon and dinner at night. But in winter they take only lunch at about 9 to 10 a.m. and evening meal at about 6 p.m. or before sunset. Thus they suspend one time meal, i.e., breakfast during winter. So far as food preparation is concerned they irrespective of any season, prefer to have rice preparation twice a day, i.e., in lunch and dinner together with wheat or maize bread. They generally prepare 'Dal of Masoor' and also prepare seasonal vegetables like potato, brinjal, spinach, radish, tomato and the vegetables collected from nearby jungles. Besides this the flesh food is also prepared casually or whenever it is available.

So far as the quantity and quality of food is concerned almost all the tribals under study have the same attitude and behaviour. Irrespective of age and sex difference all the family members are dish up the same food items as is cooked in the common hearth. The quantity intake varies according to the capacity of diet of the persons concerned, yet the people take as much as is provided to them by the cook (i.e., the female head of the family in general) who dish up the food. While serving the meal it hardly matters that who is the eater because it is presamed that the person whether he performs sedentary work or moderate work or heavy work consumes as per one's diet capacity hence dished up as much as is required by the person. Even the children of different age-groups are dished up according to their choice. There is no special provision for hard workers, males, females, boys and girls separately. The quantity of food items is determined as per its availability particularly among the people some take their food only once in a day and sometime they tolerate hunger patiently because their uncertain earnings and poor agricultural yields do not provide them two times meal. On the contrary sometime they take meal twice or thrice in a day. It totally depends on the availability and quantity of food items at home. The poor Khasas also manage anyhow two-time meal for the family. While the Tharus and the Buxas depend on the cereal crops they cultivate in their fields and the earning they earn as daily wage labourers. By and large, the staple food which consists of wheat, maize, barley, paddy or rice is the first priority of the food ideology of the tribals. The consumption of pulses, milk, milk products, flesh food is their second choice.Their main concentration remain on the stomach full diet whatever be its quality.

Even the pregnant and lactating mothers are not provided any additional allowance. But they are supposed to observe some dietary restrictions and taboos during pregnancy and lactation period. The pregnant mother is not allowed to take any food item which has hot properties. Flesh food, spiced food fried in ghee and jaggery is strictly prohibited during pregnancy. On the contrary, drinking cold water and consumption of fried food is restricted during lactation period. The infants have only one source of food and that is breast feeding. The weaning food has no meaning for the tribal infants. For about two to two and a half years of age they take breast feeding along with staple food the family members take in general. In fact the tribal infants after six months of their birth are fed in a little way the staple food cooked in the family hearth. Gradually this quantity increases with the increase of their age. Except the breast-feeding and staple food no extra allowance is provided to the infants. Bottle-feeding and other ready made nutritious food as is available in the market are not in prevalence throughout the tribal areas under reference. The school-going children are also provided the same food as is available at home. No special provision for extra nutritious food is made for the school going children. The thin built, moon face, pale conjunctiva eyes, angular stomatitis lips, dry and scaly skin, pigeon chest etc. are the general physical traits of the tribal-school-going children which proves their malnutritional status.

The tribals are very fond of taking alcoholic drinks and narcotics. The Khasas brew ale in their own way for their own consumption. The coarse foodgrain jaggery and a certain kind of vegetable roots called 'Hatnoi' are used for preparing alcoholic drinks. The surplus ale is sold out to the needy drunkards. Thus they satiate their drinking needs, on the one hand, and also earn some extra income through brewing on the other. The Rajis, the Buxas and the Tharus are also fond of taking alcoholic drinks but they do not brew it by themselves. They manage it anyhow from the local illegal breweries. In Tarai plains, the role of 'Rai-Sikhs' who live in the adjacent areas of Buxar and Tharuwat, has been crucial. Initially they were the motivators, who made the Tharus and the Buxas addicted to alcoholic drinks. With the passage of time, the alcoholic drinks have become the part of their drinking habit. Even the poor Rajis, who can hardly manage their two-time meals are addicted to alcoholic drinks which they manage anyhow from the local brewers. The maximum part of their earnings is spent in alcoholic drinks. Almost all the tribal male and female except young children take alcoholic drinks. The same is the case of narcotics. Almost all the adult male and female take Bidi and Tobacco while the youths take it sometime covertly and sometime overtly. But the school-going children certainly do not take any kind of narcotics. Besides this the tribal people are used to take some intoxicated drugs like 'Charas' and 'Bhang'. The addicted persons buy these intoxicated drugs anyhow even if they are reduced to penury. We have sufficient evidences of adverse effects of alcoholic drinks and narcotics on the health of the tribals as well as on their economy. The respiratory diseases, asthma, tuberculosis and other lung diseases are the repercussions of drinking and smoking habits of the tribals.

Lastly, the respondents were asked about nutritious food items they think necessary for the persons of different age-groups and also of different categories. At this, most of the respondents responded that first of all stomach full diet of whatever quality, is a must for persons of every age group and category. After that, they stated, infants should be given some nutritious weaning food as is available in the market. Since the tribal people cannot afford it, hence prefer to give only staple food cooked at home as a weaning food. For school-going children some additional food in the form of boiled eggs, milk and milk products like ghee, etc. are felt essential but the poor tribal people can not afford it. But for other members of the family irrespective of their age, nature of work they perform and the status they wield they expect atleast stomach full diet twice a day. They do not have any aspiration for extra nutritious food for the youths, adults and aged persons in general. Certainly they expect some extra allowance for the pregnant and also for the lactating mothers. They prefer to provide milk and milk products to the pregnant mothers. In addition to that they wish for stomach-full diet consists of bread, rice, dal and vegetables etc. for the lactating mothers. Overtly the tribals under study do not observe any sort of discrepancy in dietary pattern for male and female. They make every possible effort for providing food to every member of the family as much as is required by them. The consumption of fruits, vegetables and any other nutritious food have no meaning for them. Thus the food pattern, food habits, food ideology and overall the dietary intake of the tribals of Uttaranchal reflect their nutritional status. And the objective analysis shows that an average person of the tribal community is suffering from malnutrition.

7
The Conclusion

Education, health, hygiene and nutrition are the prime concerns of human life and of human existence. These are the attributes that make difference between human beings and animals. Education is conducive to the creation of equality in general. And for the down-trodden section of the society it has become immensely important as to bring about development and transformation towards the well versed civilized and cultured social system. Even the proper sense of health and healthy life, hygiene and hygienic conditions, nutrition and nutrients is cultivated only through education. It is the education that permits development of a scientific and objective outlook. It is the reason that the role of the State in providing education to the people in general and to weaker sections of society in particular is acknowledged all over the world. The campaign for the 'education for all' at international level defines well the functional importance of education for human beings irrespective of the difference of caste, class, race, region, language, religion, and sex. On the other hand 'Health' is also equally important factor for a healthy life. 'Health is wealth' is the old saying that makes us realise the importance of health for a healthy life. It creats an ability to work and also generates positive thinking and broader world view. 'Sound body sound mind' is an another saying that indicates about the essence of good health. The world community therefore had made a campaign for 'Health for All' and constantly making all possible efforts in this direction.

In this very context an assessment of the real situation of 'education and health' among the tribes of India with special reference to the tribal community of Uttaranchal has been presented.

The main thirst of this writing is:

1. To study the existing education health and nutritional status of the tribal areas with a view to finding out the impediments amenable for the problem related to education, health and nutrition,
2. Role and perception of the tribals towards the education, health and nutritional pattern,

3. to study the role of the state government and non-government organizations in the field of health and nutrition of the tribals particularly in normal and critical situations,
4. to study the newly-emerged class (tribal elite class) from among the tribals particularly in the context of its role and perception towards the health and nutrition and also to study the patterns of social mobility and
5. to provide viable policy-oriented solution to eradicate the causes responsible for the problem related to education, health and nutrition and also for their betterment.

The primary data shows that most of the tribal population, i.e., 52.83 per cent is illiterate, 23.95 per cent tribal pupulation is educated upto primary standard only, 10.62 per cent up to junior high school level, 6.93 per cent up to high school level, 3.93 per cent up to Intermediate level, 1.43 per cent up to graduate level, 0.42 per cent is up to post-graduate level and the rest 0.19 per cent population has some technical education.

Besides this, the sex-wise literacy shows that among females, maximum 58.18 per cent population is illiterate while among the male population 41.82 per cent are illeitrate. The literacy percentage thus proves that the target of literacy mission i.e. 'education for all by 2000 A.D.' is still beyond its reach. The poverty pervading among the tribals, lack of education facilities in tribal areas, unawareness and ignorance of the tribal people, motivational vacuum, traditional outlook of the tribal people are some of the responsible factors which have obstructed their way to education. It is the reason that a major part of the tribal population is still illiterate.

The health status of the tribals under study has been studied in terms of various indicators of health. For example, the fertility and mortality rates, life expectancy, incidence of sickness etc. Even the role of the government agencies meant for providing primary health services is also evaluated. The study comes to the conclusion that the goal of health for all by 2000 A.D. is not achieved so far. Both the policies and their execution pattern are responsible for it.

The hygienic condition existing throughout the tribal area is beyond expectation. They lack the hygienic sense may be that personal hygiene, environmental hygiene, domestic hygiene or community hygiene. The ignorance, unawareness and motivational vacuum towards hygienes have been amenable for a number of morbidities prevalent among the tribes. The tribal people do not know nutritious food and the uses of various nutrients for making good health. The food pattern, food ideology and drinking habits do not have any positive concern with their nutritional status. The only motto of an average tribal family is to achieve stomach-full diet of any nature and quality. The unscientific conception about food, the consumption pattern of food stuffs, nonavailability of balanced diet, over and above, the drinking habit of the tribal people have caused malnutrition among them. Thus, the inhygienic conditions of the tribal areas and pervading malnutrition among the people have defeated the goal 'Health for all by 2000 A.D.' of the government. It is, therefore, inevitable to take the hygienic conditions and the nutritional aspects into account in addition to the health services while making health policies for the people in general and the tribal communities in particular.

Generally there are two situations viz. the normal situation and crisis situation of health and nutrition. In both the situations, the role structure and role intensity differ corresponding to the situation. We have made an attempt to evaluate the role of the government agencies and also of non-government organizations in normal and crisis situations of the tribal communities. It is well understood that a number of national programmes related to health and nutrition are being carried out in tribal areas. The tribals are aware of the programmes like national family welfare programme, maternity and child health care programme, malaria eradication programme, national leprosy control programme, etc. They are willing too to avail the facilities being provided under these schemes with certain conditions. But the overall handicap of infrastructure system' deprive them of their rightful privileges of having government-sponsored health services. It is observed that the government agencies, supposed to make available health services to the tribals, are not in a position to provide them the facilities under different health and nutritional schemes. The lack of medicines, tools, equipment and the shortage of working staff have ever been the main hindrance on the way of the implementation of programmes. Generally in normal situation, an ANM used to visit the tribal areas and provide them necessary information about the programmes related to health and medicare system. She also renders her services to those people in need. Even in the crisis situations the ANM is supposed to visit the tribal areas because most of the primary health centres are running with short staff. Only in some exceptional cases, the district medical staff is instructed by the district authority to take care of the crisis situation. For instance, in the first week of January 2000 there was a casualty of a Raji woman due to some unknown disease, as is propagated in local daily newspapers. At this, the district authority of Pithoragarh ordered the medical department to look into the matter. Only then a team of doctors made a trip to the Raji tribal area and looked into the matter. The author also visited that tribal area with a research team and a medical officer. It is found that the paper news has no weight. In fact the 'Raji woman' was under treatment for about two years. She was suffering from tuberculosis that was in a chronic stage and therefore could not be cured. The research team made its case history and found that the woman was ill and used to have constant fever with cold. Sometime there was shivering in her body. The husband of the deceased woman told that they were of the opinion that she was under the effect of some evil spirit and correspondingly given traditional treatment by traditional medicineman for about one year. But she could not get well. Then they made worship of the deities and offered sacrifice of a cock and a goat but all in vain. Lastly, when the woman had her body swelling, the pepole consulted the medical officer of the adjoining health clinic who made investigations and referred her to district hospital Pithoragarh. After medical examination and tests she was declared tuberculosis positive at its last stage by the doctors. And lastly she died. Thus case history makes it prove that the health-related programmes do not have much impact on tribal areas. The medical staff just performs its formal duties in normal situations and appears to be active in crises situation only. On the contrary, the tribals in spite of their willingness of having medical aid, prefer first to have the traditional practices. Lastly when they do not get any relief from traditional practices they follow the modern medical practices. Thus it may be concluded that the government agencies have not much functional role in normal as well as in crisis situations among the tribals. So far as the role of non-government organizations is concerned the tribal areas till the date are untouched and beyond the clutches of the NGOs. Exceptionally a Christian missionary used to be active in Tharuwat area but it did more for conversion of the Tharus to Christianity. Hence the Christian missionary was outright rejected by the Tharuwat. Nevertheless, it succeeded in consolidating its position in Tharuwat by establishing a church in the area. But with the interference of the people the activities of the missionary are absolutely stopped and overtly it is in the state of non-function at present. Thus the NGO's have no role in providing any sort of services related to education, health, hygiene and nutrition to the tribals of Uttaranchal so far.

An attempt was also made to study the newly emerged class i.e. the tribal elite class from among the tribals particularly in the context of its role and perception towards health and nutrition. In this context it was tried to understand the pattern of social mobility in the newly emerged tribal elite class. It is observed that among the tribes under reference there is no existence of any such elite class emerging out of the tribals so far. It is proved by the statistics we gathered in regard to the educational standard of the tribes, their occupational groupings, property ownership and the general way of life. As for instance the data exhibit that among the Khasas of the Basaya village only 0.98 per cent and 1.09 per cent population is educated upto graduate and Post-graduate level respectively. Besides this, 4.32 per cent are educated upto intermediate and 5.52 per cent are only high school pass. Even the occupational status of the Khasa village exhibits that most of the population is engaged in agricultural and its subsidiary jobs like pastoral work or wage-earning etc. There is only 3.47 per cent and 0.88 per cent population which is engaged respectively on government and private salaried jobs. The property ownership and income perannum of the Khasas also exhibit that an average Khasa family leading its life in scarcity. No trend of emerging an elite class is viewed in the village. Almost all the villagers educated or uneducated have more or less the same perception towards health and nutrition because they are governed equally by the traditional norms and values. It is the reason that the pace of social mobility is viewed in the state of stagnation so far. Besides this, the Khasas appear to be committed to keep their social identity intact. This notion has also interrupted the pace of social mobility. No doubt, we certainly observed the reflections of the political scenario of Indian democracy. Today the tribal people have their political voice. They know their political importance. They are aware of their rights and privileges. This awareness has certainly produced a new political class which has its political aspirations but no perception of health and nutrition apart from the villagers. Almost the same situation is viewed among the Rajis, the Buxas and the Tharus. At least, the tribal villages under study do not have any such elite class emerging out of the respective tribal communities which has its own perception about health and nutrition. No remarkable social mobility is observed, rather the contemporary political trend, reservation policy and the feeling of existentialism have motivated them for maintainng their status quo and social identity intact. The emergence of regional tribal organizations like Tharu-Rana-Parishad, Ran-Kalyan Parishad etc, and their objectives are the living examples of this kind.

8

Constraints of Education, Health, Hygiene and Nutrition in Tribal Areas and Expected Suggestions, Solutions and Remedial Measures

It is evident from the aforesaid interpretation that the status of educaton, health, hygiene and nutrition of the tribal communities under reference is below normal and far beyond the national goal. The constraints traced out are numerous but these can be categorised into the following six major categories:

First: The constraints pertaining to government policies.

Second : The constraints related to execution system of the policies, plan and programmes meant for the tribals.

Third : The constraints pertaining to the psychology of the tribals.

Fourth: Ecological constraints.

Fifty: Socio-economic constraints, and, lastly.

Sixth: Lack of objective assessment of the work done by the agencies and lack of incentives for better work.

In fact the uniform policies meant for the tribals living in backward hilly areas with their age-old pattern of living and also for the tribals living in Tarai plain area with comparatively more advanced technology have no viable relevance because the general trend reflects that the degree of receptivity and resistance in both the cases can never produce approximately the same results. It is the reason that the government policies could not yield positive results as to meet their targets in the tribal areas of Uttaranchal.

The government have proposed enthusiastic schemes and programmes pertaining to education and health but could not correspondingly raise the infrastructure as to achieve the targets. The shortage of teaching and medical staff in schools, colleges and health centres, lack of teaching materials in educational institution and medicines, medical equipments etc. in health centres have defeated the objectives as targeted by the government. The lack of infrastructural facilities has been a gigantic problem on the way to reach the target of 'education and health for all.'The lethargic, apathetic and conventional attitude of the personnel/officers shouldering the responsibility of executing the government policies, programmes and schemes is the other aspect of the problem. The bureaucratic network, more indulgence in paper work and importance of documentary proofs rather than grass-root level facts are the invisible but more damaging constraints on the way to the targets.

The psychology of the tribals that is predominantly conservative, traditional and superstitious is also responsible for their illiteracy, low standard of education, ill-health and malnutrition. The aspirations, attitudes, short-sighted worldview, limited ambitions and comparatively more faith on the traditional way of the life vis-a-vis lesser receptivity towards modernity are some of the psychic attributes of the tribal personality which have posed impediments in achieving the national goal of education and health.

The ecological background of the tribals in general and mainly of the hill tribes (the Khasas and the Rajis) is not only a major factor that has interrupted as well as defeated the national policy of education and health but it has also provided a suitable situation to the shirker and maligner personnels shouldering the liabilities of executing the concerned policies, plans and programmes in remote tribal areas. Besides this, there are policies, plans and programmes unsuitable to the ecology of the tribals and therefore do not produce desired results.

The socio-cultural ethos have ever been a deciding role in tribal social system. The deeply rooted ethos still has a functional role for the tribals but has no relevance to the corresponding contemporary education and health related policies. The tribals, predominantly governed with this ethos, have lesser receptivity towards the policies and therefore could not receive the desired benefits. Besides this the pervading poverty has made constant indulgence of the tribals in economic pursuits for earning their livelihood and pushed back education and health related priorities to secondary preference. The dire need of the tribals is to satiate hunger first. The nonavailability of the stomach-full diet, lack of nutritious food items and balanced diet, ignorance of health, hygiene and nutrition related pre-requisites, have made the tribals apathetic towards the immensely important policies of education and health which are inevitable for the overall development of mankind. More so, the food and drinking habits of the tribals is another factor responsible for malnutrition and ill-health.

Lastly, the working of the agencies shouldering the responsibilities of implementing the government policies are needed for objective periodical assessment with ground realities, facts and figures. But the pattern of assessment does not appear scientific because it is based merely on paper-work done by the concerning department and the agencies. Besides this, there is no provision of incentives meant for the units who have better quality of work and who have been capable to achieve the targets or are nearer to targets. This sort of dealing has ever been an impediment on the way of achieving the targets in real sense.

Suggestions, Solutions and Remedial Measures

In view of the aforesaid constraints and pondering over the ground realities we have some suggestions, solutions and remedial measures for viable policy framing and also for the eradication of the causes responsible for the problems related to education, health, hygiene and nutrition of the tribals of Uttaranchal. These are as follows:

1. Framing Eco-based Zone-wise Policies, Plans and Programmes

It is a ground-reality and empirically tested fact that the uniform policies, plans and programmes are not viable universally. The zonal ecological variations have their own conditions and demands which should be taken into consideration while framing the policies. It seems, most of the government policies are the outcome of the mental exercise of the bureaucrats nescient and unacquainted with the ground realities and ecological condition of the region for which the policies, plans and programmes are being framed. The zone-wise policies should be framed. The services of the academicians having scientific understanding of the region concerned, their suggestions and expert opinion must be taken into consideration, and incorporated while the policies are made. The uniform policies have no viable relevance universally. The zone-specific policies are needed. The goal and targets are conditional with the means, methods and infrastructural network. Hence the goal and targets must be ascertained as according to means, methods and infrastructural network. Nevertheless the priority must be in establishing the eco-based infrastructure first and correspondingly to the goal and targets be ascertained. Merely the slogan and declaration of the goals and targets without factual assessment of means, methods and infrastructural network do not yield positive results. The resultant effect of the national policy, "Health and education for all by 2000 A.D." particularly in regard to the tribal communities under study is a striking example of it.

2. Periodic Contract Basis Execution of the Policies, Plans and Programmes with Personal Accountability of the Unit/Person Concerned and Objective Assessment of the Work Done

The execution of the government policies, plans and programmes should be carried out by the concerning department but on contract basis. For this purpose the non-government organization with certain government norms as decided by the govt. itself, should equally be treated eligible and given on merit basis the liability of implementing the programmes with their personal accountability on contract basis. The periodic targets should be fixed and further assignment should be granted only on the successful completion based on objective assessment of the previous assignment.

3. To Ensure an Objective, Unbiased, Impartial Assessment of the Work done and the Provision of Awards, Incentives as Well as Punishment Respectively For Target-oriented Work and Inferior and Incomplete Work Would be Helpful in Achieving the Targets

4. Launching Effectively the Awareness Programme as to Change the Psyche of the Tribals

The tribals are still conservative, traditional and superstitious in their dealings in different walks of life. As long as their psyche is not changed the implementation of government policies, plans and programmes in tribal areas is not more than an apparition and indirect nourishment of the corrupt personnel and the mediators. Target oriented awareness programmes by some selected and devoted organizations, known activists, social workers and social scientists can produce positive results. We will have to make the tribals mentally aware of the welfare policies meant for them. We will have to educate them, train them and finally build them. Only then the policies like education and health can be meaningful for them.

5. Inclusion of Socio-Cultural Dimensions in Education and Health Policies Meant for the Tribals, and Launching of Time and Space-Specific Anti-Poverty Programmes Preferably on the Line of the Inherent Talents of the Tribals with Their Full Participation

It is ever known fact that the tribals have their own specific and peculiar socio-cultural ethos and they are not in a position of ignoring them at any cost in their socio-cultural milieu. Particularly the tribals are not much influenced by modernity. They have, firm faith and infatuation with their age-old traditions, even if they are irrelevant and have proved unsuitable in the present day context. The same is the case of the tribals under study. Hence any policy hurting the spirit of the tribal ways of life has minimum possibility of being success. It is, therefore, inevitable to incorporate the corresponding socio-cultural ethos, tenets and postulations of the tribals while framing policies for their wellbeing and development. If we are really serious for the education and health of the tribals, we will have to give first priority to the formation and implementation of 'Time and Space-Specific Anti-Poverty Programmes' for the tribals. Atleast the satiation of minimum basic economic needs, i.e., the stomachfull food of whatever kind, clothes of whatever quality and the shelter of whatever type, make the tribals think for further issues like education and health. Imparting education in their own milieu should be the second priority of the policies. It is merely the education that can make the tribals aware of the importance of health, hygiene and nutrition. Only an educated person can understand the essence of the policies pertaining to health, hygiene and nutrition and also gain some benefits out of them. The health and nutrition related policies have no meaning for the penniless and starving illiterates. It is the reason that the National Goal, "Health And Education For All by 2000 A.D." in spite of massive outlay could not be achieved as per its target particularly in the tribal areas of Uttaranchal under study.

Annexure- I

Case Studies of the Polio Affected Cases Traced out in Ratanpur Village

At present only four major cases of Polio victims have been traced out in the Ratanpur village. The facts have been collected intensively and extensively through case study method. The patients' parents and grant parents who were alive, other members of the family and the maid servant or 'Dai' who made delivery of these cases, the medical practitioners who gave treatment and the traditional exorcism practitioner consulted for treatment and other concerning persons were the main informants. Through intensive and focussed interview method, the information were collected. The case-wise description of the cases is being presented as follows:

Case Study No. 1

Name of the Polio-affected person is 'Vikki' who is about eighteen year old. He is the eldest son of Mr. Kashmir Singh who is forty-two year old. His mother Mrs. Sakuntala is thirty eight year old. Both the husband and wife are illiterate and were married at the age of 14 year and 12 year respectively. According to age, both were minor and immature physically and mentally at the time of marriage. But due to prevalent tradition of child marriage, the guardians of both the parties had wedded their minors. Soon after marriage the 'Gauna' rite was performed and the bride, i.e., Mrs. Sakuntala Devi departed to her in laws in Ratanpur village. The minor Sakuntala was now being treated as a responsible female member at the groom's place. Her first priority was to fulfil the expectations of the in-laws as well as of the husband. It was basically an agriculturist family. Mr. Kashmir Singh was the eldest son of his parents. Hence his liabilities along with his wife were comparatively more than that of other members of the family. It was a time when the family of Mr. Kashmir Singh was large in size. The persons of more than three generations used to live together. In such a type of large joint family the work pattern and the work load remains comparatively more on the shoulders of married women of the family than on the others. Mrs. Shakuntala had to play the role of different nature. She was now a wife, a daughter-in-law, a grand-daughter in-law, and also a sister-in-law. Correspondingly there were expectations of the people. With the break of the day her hands used to start working and stopping with the sleeping of the family members. But her one task was more to perform, i.e., the duty of a wife to her husband. In this way the early days of her marital life was very complicated. She had no time for herself. Her sufferings and minor ailments were always secondary. She remembers the days and says bashfully that she was virtually unknown when she became pregnant. It was a new experience for her. For about two or three months she concealed this fact. But the symptoms, her bodily structure, the way of eating, drinking and living, even her likings soon reflected her state of being pregnant. She further says hesitatingly that in early two or three months her routine work went on as usual. Even the process of cohabitation with husband went on as usual. But as soon as the family members came to know about her pregnancy a number of taboos, restrictions and precautions were imposed on her. She again remembers that she was free to perform her duties but the eating and drinking related restrictions were followed strictly. The mother-in-law, grandmother-in-law (who was alive that time) and the so-called experienced old women of the community used to give her different cautions sometimes overtly and sometimes covertly. Some time their cautions and suggestions used to be contradictory. It was really a situation of dilemma for her, what to follow and what not to was really critical to her. Due to hesitation she had concealed many health-related problems to her in-laws. Once she did ask her husband about her bodily discomfort and the pain in her lower part of the body-abdomen, but he told for tolerating the pain and argued that it happens when a woman goes under pregnancy for the first time. Then, covertly she told her mother-in-law, who made some local and traditional treatment she also made her consult to the experienced old women of the community but they simply pacified her with some suggestions and consolations. While the father-in-law of Mrs. Shakuntala kept mum because he was ignorant on this matter nor he enquired by anybody. Anyhow, ten months of pregnancy lasted and a baby was born to Mrs. Shakuntala. It was really a joyous moment in the family. Mr. Kashmir Singh is now a father. His parents and grandparents have the honour of becoming grand and great grand parents respectively.

The baby was born after six years of their marriage. Naturally the age of Mrs. Shakuntala was about seventeen to eighteen years while her husband's age was about nineteen to twenty years. The baby was, underweight, as Mr. and Mrs. Kashmir Singh describe, but it was quite healthy and active. The delivery was made at home by a so-called trained old woman of the same community. The *navel* string was cut with scissors. The parents told that the scissor were brought by that woman and was not boiled before use. The mother began to feed her milk to baby. During child birth the precautions, whatever suggested by parents-in-law, grand-parents-in-laws as well as the so-called experienced women of the village, were followed by the mother. Under the instructions the mother and the child spent about one year of age of the child. But one day child caught the cold and suffered from high fever. It was for the first time when it did not suck mother's nipple and did not make any physical motion. The baby was almost unconscious throughout a day and a night. He was devoid of mobility and become like a wett cotton cloth. All the local efforts, made by the so-called experienced aged persons of the village were in vain. Lastly a medical practitioner, who had virtually no degree or diploma of medical practice but used to be in the village as a medical doctor for a long time, was consulted at about evening time. He gave some treatment and also injected the baby. Then the baby was brought home. About an hour after this treatment the baby opened his eyes and began to suck mother's nipple. The mother felt relieved as her begotten was alive and the tension caused by baby's illness as well as the discomfort due to not-feeding the breast milk was released. But after sometime the mother found that her baby returned to consciousness but his physical motions were almost nil. He had become motionless. Next morning the parents again approached the same doctor (untrained medical practitioner) who gave him a treatment and also suggested the parents for consulting exorcism practitioner. Then the 'Bharare' (a traditionally well-informed person of occult arts) was consulted. The Bharare regularly made practices of occult arts for the treatment of the baby, simultaneously the medical treatment of the local medical practitioner went on. Both the practices of treatment went on for about two years. With this treatment the baby began to sit for itself, and also began to move its hands. But the lower part of his body, i.e., lower than his waist remained motionless. Then the parents put a stop to the treatment and consulted the physician nearby PHCs located at Khatima, Rudrapur and then in Bareilly. The physicians declared that it was basically a 'polio attack' and due to not having proper precautions and timely treatment the disease had become chronic so incurable. It was for the first time when the parents and the guardians of the baby came to know about polio and its causes.

In response to a question, the mother told that she was not given any medical aid while she was under pregnancy. Even the tetanus injection was not received by her. After birth the infant was not provided polio-drops nor other necessary medical aid. The mother had to take a number of precautions before and after birth of the child. Today this child has become

18 year old. The mother herself feeds him food, and drink. She also makes him evacuate whenever he feels so and also change his clothes. Mother also makes a complaint that every night her eighteen year old son discharges urine in the bed and it is the mother who washes and cleans the bedding every day. Viewing her perplexities and the helplessness of the patient, the 'Bharare' one who made practices of occult art for his treatment, asserts that it would have been better for the child to die rather than to lead such a hellish life. However the mother is happy and utters, "I am happy at least my first issue is alive and remains before my eyes. He is the eldest son of ours and in one sense he is the Mukhiya of the family after his father". She proudly adds, that her son is grown up now, even if he can not walk freely but his senses are alive. He can drink wine (she smiles), and also run in the tricycle. But ultimately she blames her destiny and console herself. In response to a question, we came to know that it was the first polio case in the family of Mr. Kashmir Singh and his wife's parents' place. After this issue, Mr. Kashmir Singh and Mrs. Shakuntala have three more children out of which a daughter died at the age of one and a half year. But she took every possible medical aid and precautions during next pregnancies and the children were born normal.

The case history of Mr. Vikki concludes that (i) the ignorance prevalent among the Tharus and lack of proper knowledge of maternal and child health care (ii) lack of maternal and child health care services (iii) predominance of traditional way of doing the things, non-availability of proper medical aid in time and lack of health, hygiene and nutritional sense among the tribals have been the major causes of polio.

Case Study No. 2

Mr. Rohit, son of Sri Parushram and Smt. Muskamini is eight year old polio patient of Ratanpur village. He is the second issue of the parents. At present Mr. Rohit is studying in second standard in the nearby Junior High School, Ratanpur. His father, thirty years old, and mother twenty eight year old, are agriculturists by occupation. They were married respectively at the age of 10 and 8 years. In fact, as both the spouses told, earlier they were unknown with the concept of marriage. Wedding ceremony for them was just a trifling matter or a childrens' affair. Both were illiterate. Soon after marriage, that is to say atter four months of marriage, the Gauna rite was performed and Mrs. Muskamini departed to her in-laws for living there permanently. She says, it was of course a good rather exciting experience that her brother accompanied her to see her off to in-laws house. My husband (Mero Adami) was also with us. He actually came to our place for calling her back to his house. But when her brother come back and left her there to live with her in-laws I felt really very sad. Every one was unknown to her there. Only her husband, who used to avoid meeting her before other family members, was her companion. Gradually her parents like in-laws, other family members accommodate her with the new family surrounding. Soon she got adapted herself with her husband's family. And a new chapter of life began with new experiences of life. She bashfully reply that in earlier days of her marital life she was ignorant of conjugal love. But gradually with the passage of time, the nature itself made her learn the truth of marital life. About six years after her marriage she became pregnant for the first time and gave birth to a girl child. To a question she answers that she was given tetanus injection while she was under pregnancy. The polio drops were also given after birth to the girl child. The medical aid as needed was received and the girl child remained healthy. When the child was only two year old the next issue (a male child) was born. Mrs. Muskamini was the mother of two children.

The mother had taken all the precautions as advised by health worker (ANM). She had tetanus injection in time and the child was also provided polio drops and other vaccine of DPT. Both the deliveries were made at home with the help of the ANM and experienced women of the village. In fact a trained maid-servant in 'Agan Badi' school, used to visit her twice in a week. The male child was quite healthy and active. He depended on mother's milk only. One day when he was about one year old, he caught fever and a gland cropped up at his thigh joint. There was severe pain in the gland. To get rid of this pain all the indigenous prescriptions were made. Some magical practices were also performed. Under this process the traditional medicine-man uproots particular vegetable plant with some magical spell. It is believed that with this process the gland also uproots and disappears from the affected part. As soon as the uprooted plant gets dried the gland also dries up. But this magical treatment was not a success. After some days the gland disappeared from the thigh joint and come out at right outer corner of his right eye and soon the gland was converted into an abscess. There was pus formation in a boil and the affected part was painful. The child used to moan in pain. When indigenous treatment proved unable to cure the abscess, the physicians were consulted. During this period a medical doctor was consulted first, for fifteen days at Nanakmatta (a small town). The doctor gave some medicines and also injected the affected part but the treatment was not a success. Then a physician at PHC Khatima was consulted. He also gave necessary treatment with some medicines and injections. There was even a minor operation on the abscess but in vain. No doubt with the effect of the medicine the abscess disappeared for sometime but again cropped up with pus formation. The pus used to come out continuously. The treatment was given for about two and a half year. Ultimately the parents stopped the treatment. They used to make some indigenous efforts and also dressed-up the wound by themselves. As the mother says, one day when she was dressing up the abscess a hard bone type part come out from the abscess. She just pulled that part and threw it out. With this part some pus mixed with blood began to ooze. After a few minutes the oozing of pus stopped. She further stated, 'Since then the abscess began to dry up. Gradually the abscess disappeared and the pus formation process also stopped itself.' This whole process took about two years and half of their child and snatched the happiness of the family.

The mother stated that for sometime the family as a whole heaved a sigh of relief. But soon their momentary relief was converted into an ever lasting agony. In fact the chest as well as the upper back portion of the child began to come out. His normal growth stopped. At present there is no correlation between its height, width and weight. Now the child is eight year old. He goes to school. He can walk and run himself. But his length is below normal. The anthropometric measurement and the nutritional assessment report exhibit that it was basically a case of malnutrition since birth. The mother also tells us that the child was very underweight and very weak when born. In fact the second issue (this child) was born just before two years of the first delivery. Since, it was a male child, hence the mother had to follow a number of food-related taboos and restrictions. Even she was not permitted to drink cold water during early days of this delivery. Because drinking of cold water may cause cold to the new-born child as he sucks the breast of mother. She was provided only some luke warm water to drink, unfried cooked rice and dal in lunch as well as in dinner. Both the child and the mother used to have a bath once in a fortnight. The people are of the belief that daily bathing may cause cold related ailments which is not good in the interest of the health of lactating mother and the infant. Hence they, the mother and the new born baby, were advised to avoid daily bathing. The mother tells that she has no sufficient milk to feed the child. Sometimes the elder daughter who was only two years old, used to suck the breast and the new born baby had to suffer from hunger. These days the outer feeding of new born child was neither permitted nor the milk was available in the family. Because that time, no milching cattle was tamed by them. Whenever the baby used to cry in hunger, "I just put the nipple to his mouth but there was no secretion of milk from my breast". But when the baby grew up to six months of age the 'Annaprasan rite' was performed and he (the baby) was permitted to have a cooked food for eating. Since then whatever the mother took in lunch, dinner or other times was, provided to the child also. But in spite of following a number of precautions and taboos the baby fell ill. Sometime fever, sometime vomitting, sometime loose motions and lastly there was a severe attack of fever which ultimately deformed the child. But today the parents, grand parents (who are still alive) and the family members are happy that the child is alive and present before their eyes. In fact it was the case of malnutrition. The mother who had already a girl baby of about one year old when she conceived second time. She had to feed two lives at a time, one in the womb and the second, by breast feeding. Naturally, due to insufficient nutrition the baby in the womb, was born weak. This undernutrition transformed into malnutrition and the new-born child had to pay its cost. In fact the doctor who made its treatment told that it was basically a case of malnutrition. The case study comes to the conclusion that (i) socio-religious notions implied with food and nutrition, the taboos, precautions and restrictions socially imposed on mother and child, (ii) lack of proper knowledge of mother and child health-care system, (iii) preference of traditional way of treatment pattern, (iv) conception, resultantly the ill-health of the mother, (v) nutrition-related complication etc. have been the causes of malnutrition and related ailments.

Case Study No. 3

This case study deals with a polio patient. His name is Mr. Atul Singh, age twelve years. His father's name is Mr. Mahesh Singh Rana who is thirty seven years of age and his mother Mrs. Jagjeewan Devi is thirty five years old. The grandparents and great-grand mother of Mr. Atul Singh are still alive. The grandmother is sixty year old and grandfather is sixty-five. His great-grandmother is more than hundred years old and it is said that today she is the eldest living person in the village.

Mr. Mahesh Singh Rana has four sons and a daughter. The polio patient is the second issue of Mr. Mahesh Rana. The mother of Mr. Rana tells that he was married at the age of 14 years while his wife was only 12 years at the time of marriage. After five years of marriage the first delivery of Mrs.Rana matured. It was a male child. He was quite healthy. Just after two years of the first delivery the second child was born. It was also a male child. This delivery was held at home. The experienced old women of the community and a so-called trained maidservant of the same community who was working in the Agan Badi school of the 'Ratanpur village', helped in delivery. The *navel* string was cut with scissors by the trained maidservant. Everything was normal for about one and a half year of the child birth. The grand-mother states that one night the child suddenly fell ill and became almost unconscious due to severe attack of fever. Throughout the night they made every possible indigenous efforts for the treatment of the child. But there was no positive sign of effect on the patient. It was a sleepless night passed by the parents and the grand parents of the child. The child look like an inanimate squeezed item. He was badly exhausted. Next morning, Mr. and Mrs. Mahesh Singh Rana took the child to a private medical practitioner. The known villagers told that this medical practitioner had no degree or diploma of medical practice but the tribal people have deep faith on him. Since he was doing this job for a long time there. His private clinic was in the same village. Mr. Rana says while they reached the doctor, he was busy in his consulting the patients. But due to the seriousness of the case, he called Mr. Mahesh and made necessary investigation of the child and gave five injections to the child with an interval of a few minutes. The same treatment was given regularly for twenty days. In this way the child received hundred injections and some oral suspension. His fever abated but the body of the child was almost motionless. Then the doctor, who was giving treatment to the patient suggested to Mr. Mahesh Rana to consult the 'Bharare', i.e., the traditional practitioner of exorcism practices. The 'Bharare' was called upon for the treatment of the patient. This indigenous treatment also went on for a month but in vain. Then the 'Bharare' himself suggested the parents for consulting any expert physician. On this the patient was taken to 'Bareilly' Mission Hospital. Again the treatment went on for about one month. The treatment given by the doctors at Mission Hospital has made the patient worth to move about but his left leg was paralysed, told the parents. But the parent's grand-parents, the great-grand-mother and other family members were happy to find Atul Singh alive. Today he is studying in sixth standard and limps with the help of the paralysed leg.

On a question, the grand-mother, i.e., the mother-in-law of Mrs. Jagjeewan Devi said that during pregnancy her daughter-in-law was not given any medical aid. Even the tetanus injection was not in prevalence that time in their area. Even after delivery no medical aid was given. The child was not given polio drops. The grandparents told that they had no experience of this kind. There was no such type of possibility because the first delivery of Mrs. Jagjeewan Devi was normal and the child was healthy and did not fall ill. We were thinking that the second child would also be normal. The same was the opinion of child's mother and father. However, they have little repentance of having very little interval between the deliveries. Today they have five children within nine and a half years duration. Thus there is approximately one and a half years to two years interval between the two deliveries. However they blame more to nature or supernatural power for the births and a little to themselves for not timely adopting any means of family planning. Today Mrs. Jagjiwan Devi has sterilized herself with an operation under family planning scheme. There are a number of such cases in Tharuwat area when the women have got themselves sterilized after having four or more children alive. But such type of family planning has no meaning virtually as it does not fulfil the objectives of the family planning programme.

The 'Bharare' said that he had cured a number of polio patients in past only through his exorcism practices. But Master Atul's case was altogether different and complicated. His practices had no effect on him. As he used all the tricks and also made some magical spells but all that went in vain. Lastly, he suggested the parents to consult the medical doctor.

In the context of the facts gathered through case study method and the practices followed in priority for the treatment of the polio-patient, it can be said that general ignorance of the tribal people, unawareness of medical care and maternity and child-health care services, apathy of the health workers, blind faith on supernatural power and traditional medicine men and also in exorcism practices, the indigenous pattern of food and nutrition, have been the responsible factors of any kind of ailments in tribal area in general and the polio- related ailments in particular. As the tribal people say that it was a time when there had been no tradition to consult specialist doctors even at nearby hospital or PHCs. Ailments of different kinds were there. The people themselves had their own treatment pattern sometimes by themselves and sometime, particularly in some complicated cases, through the traditional medicine-man, i.e., the 'Bharare'. But in due course of time the incurable diseases entered the tribal area with the entrance of the outside intruders as well as of the so-called development schemes and the related machinery. In fact the tribal people have never been serious about the vital diseases like polio. They had never been conscious and particular about health, hygiene and nutrition. For them the stomach full intake of diet of whatever kind is a good nutrition and a fleshy body is a good health. They are not aware about the positive correlation of health and hygiene. The hygienes of whatsoever kind have no meaning for them. The medical care, is of prime importance in the present day context when there is adulteration everywhere and in every food item and beverage. This particular case was the result of that very socio-psychological situation of the Tharus.

Case Study No. 4

This is a case study of an unmarried twenty one year old girl. She is a daughter of Mr. Virodh Singh Rana who is forty five year old. Her mother Mrs. Mankali Devi is forty two year old. Both the parents are illiterate. Mr. Virodh Singh and Mrs. Mankali were married at the age of eleven and eight years respectively. Their first delivery took place after seven years of marriage. At that time Mrs. Mankali was fifteen and Mr. Virodh Singh was eighteen year old. The first baby child was female and healthy. The growth of the first baby was very normal. Just after two years of the first delivery, the second one matured and again a girl child was born to Mrs. Mankali. She was already perplexed for having a girl child. The delivery of the second girl child added some more socio-psychological worries of the family in general and the parents in particular.

At the time of the birth the child was weaker than the previous one. But she was quite active. Mother used to feed her milk to the child. Mrs. Mankali tells that the breast-feeding was not sufficient to the child because the lactation of milk was comparatively lesser this time. Hence at the age of the six months the child was given outside food. The mother used to feed her the food items whatever she took in lunch and dinner. Sometimes the baby was given stale food. However the baby was normal and active. Once the baby had a severe attack of dysentery. Instantly the indigenous treatment was given. It relieved her but since then the baby began to lose her health and become weaker. After a few months of this happening she had to face another sever attack of fever. The fever made her unconscious and afflicted. 'She was virtually motionless', said the mother. Throughout the day and night she was sitting beside her. The mother made all the possible efforts to bring back the baby into consciousness. The baby did not suck even mother's milk. The aged and experienced persons of the village also made efforts for the wellbeing of the child. Even the indigenous treatment pattern did not respond positively. The parents then took the child to the private doctor who had a small clinic in the outskirt of the village. As already mentioned the doctor had no degree or diploma as to prove his legal medical practice. But he had a good hold on the villagers. He had won the trust of the villagers.

The untrained medical practitioner has made medical investigations and gave some prescription. He injected the baby for the subsidence of high bodily temperature. The prescription of the doctor that consists of a number of doses of medicine and injections continued throughout the month but the condition of the baby did not improve. No doubt, the father says, there was no high temperature, no fever but the weakness of the baby remained as usual. Almost all the organs of the baby turned motionless. She used to discharge even her excreta remaining in a prostrate position on the bed. At last the medical practitioner advised the parents for consulting the 'Bharare', i.e., the indigenous practitioner of occult art. The grandfather of the baby called on the 'Bharare' from the nearby village. He was non-tribal. For about a month treatment of the 'Bharare' went on. But there was no improvement in the condition of the child. Lastly, the 'Bharare' suggested the grandfather for consulting the medical doctor. Then they took the baby to the primary health centre, Khatima, then Nanakmatta and then Rudrapur. With the medical treatment of the doctors in primary health centres, the baby began to walk here and there limpingly. The doctors gave their opinion that it was basically a polio case. Since the patient was already given a mistreatment and the case was referred at a very late stage of the disease, hence it could not be cured successfully. However the life of the baby is safe. Today she walks limping as her right leg had polio effect.

The polio affected baby, who later on named as Ku. Reena Rana when grown up to six years age, was enrolled at the village primary school. Since then she is continuously studying and at present she is twenty-one year old and studying Hindi, Sociology and Economics in undergraduate level in the nearby Government Degree College, Khatima about eleven kms. far from the village. She is not disheartened. She wants to have higher education and also wants to do any government job preferably a teaching job for self-reliance. She further utters that it was illiteracy of her parents, their ignorance and the lack of health, hygiene and nutrition-related understanding, which made me lame. Hence, her priority is to educate the people first. For this very purpose she wants to become a teacher in future.

Thus the case study shows that general ignorance, absence of maternity and child health care system in the village, blind faith on indigenous pattern of treatment as well as the presence of the untrained so-called medical practitioner in the tribal area, lack of awareness of some vital diseases and the related precautions and not having the medical aid by the pregnant mothers, and the babies, are some of the responsible factors of general ailments and also of the polio.

Besides this the case study of Mr. Dhurb Singh Rana who is twenty two year old and a polio victim case, also tells almost the same story as is narrated in aforesaid cases. Mr. Dhurb Singh Rana is educated up to Intermediate and limps as his right leg is polio affected so very weak to walk properly. He wants to have a government job. For his state of being, he blames his fate first and also blames the social setup of that time when he fell ill and also blames insufficient medical facilities. Thus it may be concluded that whatsoever been the cases but the causes are almost the same.

Bibliography

Ahmed, P.I. and Coelho, G.V., 1979 : *Towards a New Definition of 'Health'*, Pleum, New York.

Aykroyd, W.R., 1970: *Conquest of Deficiency Diseases, FFHC Basic Study*, No. 24, Geneva, WHO.

Aykroyd, W.R., 1966 : *The Nutritive value of Indian Foods and the Planning of Satisfactory Diet*, Sixth revised edition by C. Gopalan and S.C. Balasubramaniam, ICMR, New Delhi.

Akhtar, Rais and Yola Verhasselt, 1990 : *Disease, Ecology and Health*, Rawat Publications, Jaipur (Rajasthan).

Ackrknecht, E.H., 1995. *A Short History of Medicine*, Ronald Press, New York.

Atkinson, E.T., 1996 : *The Himalayan Gazetteer* Vol. III (Reprint), Natraj Publishers, Dehradun.

Burman, B.K. Roy, 1972 : "Tribal Demography" in, *Tribal Situation in India*, ed. by K.S. Singh, Indian Institute of Advanced Study, Simla.

Bisht, B.S. 1993 ; *Raji: A Tribe of Indo-Nepal Border of Uttarakhand*, Vivek Prakashan, Delhi-7.

Bisth, B.S., 1997 : *Uttaranchal - Gramin Samuday, Pichhadi Jati Avam Janjatiya Paridrasya*. Almora Book Depot. Mal Road, Almora.

Bisht, Sarojani, 1999 : "The Buxas of Uttarakhand"- Habitat, Society, Economy and Transformation, in *Backward Communities in India*, ed. by. B.S. Bisht, Gyan Publishing House, New Delhi.

Bisht, B.S., 1994 : *Tribes of India, Nepal, Tibet Border Land*, Gyan Publishing House, New Delhi.

______1996 : "Uttarakhand Ki Janjatiyan Avam Janjatiya Samikaran", in, *Uttarakhand Today* (ed.) by K. S. Valdiya, Shree Almora Book Depot, Almora.

Behura, N.K. 1992 : "Constraints in Tribal Culture for Formal Education", in *Tribal Transformation in India* ed. by B.D. Chaudhuri, Inter-India Publications, Delhi-15.

Basu, Salil, 1995 : "Health Status of Tribal Women in India"; in, *Tribal Women in India*, (ed.) by Bhupender Singh and N. Mahanti, Inter-India Publications, New Delhi-15.

Bairathi, S., 1991 : *Tribal Culture, Economy and Health*, Rawat Publications, Jaipur.

Basu, S.K., 1989 : "Factors Affecting Fertility and Mortality Behaviour Among Tribal Population Groups of Bastar District (M.P.)", in, *Health and Family Welfare Services in India* (ed.) by B. Jena and R.W.Pati, Ashish Publishing House, New Delhi.

Basu, S. K., Jindal, A., Kshatriya, G., Chetlapalli, S.K., and Khan, A.S. 1990: *Genetic and Socio-Cultural Determinants of Tribal Health : Kutia Konds of Phulbani District*, Orissa, Annual Report, NIHFW, New Delhi.

Bhowmick, P.K., 1994 : *Primitive Tribal Groups in Eastern India*, Gyan Publishing House, New Delhi-2.

Barua, I., Phukan, R., 1998 : Socio-Religious Aspects of Health Among Sonowal Kachari, in, *The Eastern Anthropologists*, ed. by J.S. Bhandari et al, Ethnographic and Folk Culture Society, Lucknow-24.

Barman, P.B., 1992 : Education Among the Lepchas of Darjeeling : A Sociological Study, in, *Tribal Transformation in India*, Vol. IV, ed. by B.D. Chaudhuri, Inter-India Publications, Delhi-15.

Berman, B.K. Roy, 1992 : Pattern of Tribal Education, Status of Research and Sociological Dimensions for Projecting the Future, in, *Tribal Transformation in India* Vol. IV, ed by B.D. Chaudhuri, Inter-India Publications, Delhi-15.

Chandra, R., 1992 : Education in Nilgiris Tribes - An Appraisal, in, *Tribal Transformation in India*, Vol. IV. ed. by B.D. Chaudhuri, Inter-India Publications, Delhi-15.

Chakrabarti, P., 1998 : Health Management and Care for the Elderly, in, *The Eastern Anthropologists*, Vol. 51, No. 3, ed by J.S. Bhandari et. al., Ethnographic and Folk Culture Society, Lucknow.

Clements, F.E., 1932. *Primitive Concept of Disease*, University of California Publications in American Archaeology and Ethnology, pp. 185-252.

Chaudhuri, B.D., 1994 : Tribal Health and Medicine : Socio-Cultural and Environmental Dimensions, in, *Tribal Economy, Health and Waste Land Development*, ed. by Neeti Mahanti, Inter-India Publications, New Delhi-15.

Chaudhuri, Buddhadev, 1992: *Tribal Transformation in India*, (ed), Inter-India Publications, New Delhi.

Crooke, W., 1973 : *Races of Northern India*, Cosmo Publications, New Delhi.

Chatterjee, B.B., 1975 : *Bhotiyas of Indo-Tibetan Border of Uttarakhand*, RP, ICSSR, Documentation Centre, New Delhi.

Crooke, W., 1846 : *Tribes and Castes of North-West Provinces and Oudh Region,* Vol. II, Calcutta.

Chaudhuri, Buddhadeb, 1990 : *Tribal Development in India-Problems and Prospects* (ed.) Inter-India Publications, New Delhi-15.

Dhebar, U.N., 1961 : *Report of the Scheduled Areas and Scheduled Tribe Commission.*

Danda, A.K., 1992: Response of Scheduled Tribes Students to Special Provisions; in, *Tribal Transformation in India*, ed. by B.D. Chaudhari, Inter-India Publications, Delhi-15.

Dave, P., Divakaran, M., and Majhithir, V., 1983 : *Nutritional Status of Under Fives in Limkhada, Panchmahals, Gujarat.* Report from the Department of Child Development, M.S. University, Baroda.

Das, A.K., 1992 : Education and Economic Achievements and Trend thereof among the Scheduled Tribes of West Bengal, in, *Tribal Transformation in India*, Vol. IV, ed. by B.D. Chaudhuri, Inter-India Publications, Delhi-15.

Devadas, R.P., Chandrasekhar, V. and Bhooma, N., 1984: Nutritional Outcomes of a Rural Diet Supplemented with Low Cost Locally Available Foods. Impact on Preschool Children from a Tribal Community, *Indian Journal of Nutrition Dietetics.*

Das, N.P. and Shel, U., 1991: Contraceptive Prevalence and Maternal and Child Health Care Status among Tribals, in, *Tribal Demography in India*, ed. by R.N. Pali and Lalitendu Jagatdeb, Ashish Publishing House, New Delhi-26.

Dubos, R.C., 1965 : *Man Adapting,*New Haven, Yale University Press.

Dissanayake, C. B., 1990 : Human Health Problems in Sri-Lanka, in, Disease, *Ecology and Health* (ed.) by Akhtar and Verhasselt, Rawat Publications, Jaipur, Rajasthan.

Doshi, S.L., 1995 : *Anthropology of Food and Nutrition*, Rawat Publications, Jaipur. Dube, S.C., 1965 : Manav orSanskriti, Raj Kamal prakashan, Delhi.

Dube, S.C., 1998 : *Antiquity to Modernity in Tribal India-Continuity and Change Among Indian Tribes*, Vol. I, Inter-India Publications (ed.) New Delhi-15.

Eckstein, Eleanor F., 1980 : *Food, People and Nutrition,* AV Publishing Company, Inc. West Port, Connecticut.

Eberst, R.M. 1984 : *Jr. School Health*, 54 (3).

Elvin, Varrier, 1960 : *Report of the Committee on the Special Multi purpose Tribal Blocks*, Calcutta.

Fillenbaum, G.G. 1984 : *The Well-being of the Elderly*, WHO Offset Publ. No. 84.

Freund, Paul J., 1990 : Child Health and Nutrition in Zambia in, *Disease Ecology and Health* (ed.) by Akhtar and Verhasselt, Rawat Publications, Jaipur, Rajasthan.

Furer-Haimendorf, Vonc. 1975 : Himalayan Traders, Murray : London.

____1981: *Asian Highland Societies*, Sterling Publishers, New Delhi.

Galtung, J., 1967: *Theory and Methods of Social Research*, London.

Goode, WJ. and Halt, P.K., 1952 : *Methods in Social Research*, Mc-Graw Hill Book Co, New York.

Gopal, K. Rani, 1996 : *Health Status of Tribals*, A.P.H. Publishing Corporation, New Delhi-2.

Gopal, K. Rani; 1996 : *Tribals and Their Health Status*; A.P.H. Publishing Corporation, New Delhi - 2.

Goyal, S. and Goyal, N., 1997 : Health and Disease of the Tribal Elderly, in *Bulletin, Tribal Research Institute*, Bhopal, ed. K. V. Singh, Director Tribal Research Institute, Bhopal, M.P.

Guha, B.S., 1944: *Racial Elements in Indian Population*, Oxford Pamphlet on Indian Affairs, Oxford University Press, Bombay.

Goyal, S., Goyal, S. and Goyal, N., 1998 : "Health and Social Aspects of Tribal Adolescent Girls in Betul District of Madhya Pradesh", in *Bulletin of the Tribal Research Institute*, Bhopal, ed. by T.R. Sahani, Vol. XXVI, No. 1.

Garg, S.K., R.S. Negi and A.R. Sankhyan, 1981: *A Serological Analysis of the Bhoksa: A Scheduled Tribe of Uttar Pradesh*, Acta Anthropo Genetica, 5 (3).

Guha, B.S., 1944: *Racial Elements in Indian Population, Oxford Pamphlet on Indian Affairs*, Oxford University Press, Bombay.

Hanumantha Rao, D., Brahman, G.N.V., and Prahlad Rao, N., 1989 : Diet and Nutrition Survey Among the Onges. *Nutrition News* 1988.

Harper, Laura Jane and Maryellen Spencer; 1987 : "Food for Thought: An Approach to the Study of Food in Culture", in, *Food and Nutrition*, Vol. 13, No 1, FAO, UN.

Hankel, Reinhard; 1990: Health Care Services in Zambia, in *Disease Ecology and Health*, ed. by Akhtar and Verhasselt, Rawat Publications, Jaipur, Rajasthan.

Hasan, Amir, 1979 : *The Buxas of the Tarai*; B.R. Publishing Corporation, Delhi.

Haddon, A.C., 1919: "The Wondering People, in, *Social Anthropology* ed. by D.N. Majumdar and T.N. Madan, Asia Publishing House, Bombay.

Iyun, F., 1990 : Health Care Planning and Distribution of Health Services in Oyo State, Nigeria, in, *Disease, Ecology and Health* ed. by Akhtar and Verhasselt, Rawat Publications, Jaipur-Rajasthan.

Jahoda, M., and Cook, S.W., 1969 : *Research Methods in Social Relations*, Mathew and Co. Ltd. 11 New Fitter Lane, E.C.4., U.S.A.

Joshi, N.D., 1982: *Tribal Education in Kerala—Adult Education and Development*, Kerala.

Jelliffe, D.B., 1966 : The Assesssment of the Nutritional Status of the Community, *World Health Organization*, Monograph, Series, 53, Geneva; WHO.

Karkal, Malini, 1995 : "Women and Health in India", in, *Health Hazards, Gender and Society* (ed.) by Indu Mather and Sanjay Sharma, Rawat Publications, Jaipur.

Kohli, Y. P., 1995 : Moral Values through Informal Education, in, *Tribal Education in India*, (ed.) by, Bhupendra Singh and N. Mohanti, Inter-India Publications, Delhi-15.

Kurup, A. M., 1992: Extent and Problems of Tribal Education, in, *Tribal Transformation in India*, ed. by B.D. Chaudhuri, Inter-India Publications, Delhi-15.

Kharkwal, S.C., 1971 : "The Uttar Pradesh Himalaya", in-R.L. Singh ed. *India: A Regional Geography, National Geographical society of India*, Varanasi.

Lakshmaiah, T, 1995 : "Educational Facilities, Problems and Impact- A Comparative Study of Two Blocks in Ranchi District in Bihar State", in, *Tribal Education in India* (ed) by B. Singh and N. Mohanti, Inter-India Publications, Delhi-15.

Lakshmaiah, T., 1992: "Problems of Education in Tribal Areas," in, *Tribal Transformation in India*, ed. by B.D. Chaudhuri, Inter-India Publications, Delhi-15.

Lakshmaiah, T., 1987 : *Educational Facilities, Problems and Impacts; A Comparative Study of Two Blocks in Ranchi District of Bihar state*, NIRD, Hyderabad.

Lakshmaiah, T, and Aravind Yadappanavar, 1986 : *A Study of Educational Facilities for Tribal Students- Problems and Impact in Paderu Samithi, Visakha Patanam Distt.* A.P., NIRD, Hyderabad.

Lakara, I., 1997 : "Health Status of Women of Khairwar Tribes of Surguja District", in, *Bulletin of the Tribal Research Institute, Bhopal*, M.P., ed. by S.K. Sood, Director Tribal Research Institute, Bhopal, M.P.

Luzzi, G. Eichinger Ferro, 1980 : "Food avoidances at Puberty and Menstruation in Tamilnadu", in, *Food Ecology and Culture* (ed.) by, J.R.K. Robson, Gordon and Breach Science Publishers, New York.

Maro, P.S., 1990 : "Population Distribution and Health Facilities", in, *Disease Ecology and Health* ed. by Akhtar and Verhasselt, Rawat Publications, Jaipur, Rajasthan.

Mathur, P.R.G., 1992 : "Tribal Education in Kerala", in, *Tribal Transformation in India*, Vol. IV., ed. By B.D. Chaudhuri, Inter-India Publications, Delhi-15.

Mishra, D.K., Pandey, G.D., and Sinha, P.K., 1991: "Some Aspects of Curative Health Care Among the Aged; A Study in a Tribal Block of Madhya Pradesh," in, *Tribal Demography in India*, ed. by R.N. Pati and Lalitendu Jagatdeb, Ashish Publishing House, New Delhi-26.

Mahanti, N., 1995 : "Tribal Health in India: Retrospect and Prospect", in, *Tribal Health in India* (ed.) by, Bhupender Singh and Neeti Mahanti, Inter-India Publications, New Delhi-15.

Mishra, C.P., Reddy, D.C.S., and Tiwari, I.C., 1986 : "Some Epidemiological Determinants of Anthropometrically Determined Grades of Malnutrition Among Harijan and Tribal Pre-school Children", in, *Indian Journal of Nutrition and Dietetics*.

Majumdar, D.N., 1963 : *An Introduction to Social Anthropology*, Asia Publishing House, Bombay.

____1955 : *Races and Cultures of India*, Asia Publishing House, Bombay.

Malzke, Gordon; 1990 : "Health Consequences of Tsetse Zone Expansion in Zambia", in, *Disease Ecology and Health* (ed) by, Akhtar and Verhasselt, Rawat Publications, Jaipur, Rajasthan.

Maulik, S. K., Ghosh and Anita Ghosh Maulik, 1992 : "Mode of Subsistence and Response to Elementary Education in Some Tribes of Orissa", in, *Tribal Transformation in India.*, ed. by B.D. Chaudhuri, Inter-India Publications, New Delhi-15.

Morris, R.T., 1960 : *The Tow-Way Mirror, Cultural Status in Foreign Student Adjustment*, University of Minnesota, Press.

Mahalanobis, P.C., et. al, 1949: *Anthropometric Survey of the United Provinces—A Statistical Study*, Sankhya IX.

Mishra, S.N., 1998 : *Antiquity to Modernity in Tribal India—Ownership and Control of Resources Among Indian Tribes*, Inter-India Publications, New Delhi-15.

Majumdar, D.N., 1963 : *Himalayan Polyandry*, Asia Publishing House, Bombay.

Majumdar, D.N., 1994 : *Races and Cultures of India*, Asia Publishing House, Bombay.

Majumdar, D.N., 1942: "The Tharus and Their Blood Group", in, *Journal of Royal Asiatic Society of Bengal*, Vol. III, part I.

Narayan, S., 1992 : "Education; Then and Now Among Oraon Children", in, *Tribal Transformation in India*, ed. by B.D. Chaudhuri, Inter-India Publications, New Delhi-15.

Nagla, B.K., 1992 : "The Problem of Tribal Education in Southern Rajasthan", in, *Tribal Transformation in India*, ed. by B.D. Chaudhuri, Inter-India Publications, New Delhi-15.

Naidu, V.N. and Gurumurthy, G., 1991 : "Determinants of Infant Mortality in Relation to Health Practices Among Sugali Tribals in Andhara Pradesh", in, *Tribal Demography in India*, ed. by R.N. Pati and L. Jagatdeb, Ashish Publishing House, New Delhi-26.

Naryana, K.V.; 1997 : *Health and Development*, Rawat Publications-Jaipur, Rajasthan.

NCERT, Delhi 1986: *Report of the Empirical Evaluation of Academic Aspects of Non-Formal Education Programme in Bihar*, Delhi.

Nesfield, J.C., 1885 : *Description of Manners, Industries and Religion of the Tharu and Buxa Tribes of Upper India*, Calcutta.

Patel, M. L., 1995 : "Awareness of Tribal Health and Medical Care in Madhya Pradesh", in, *Tribal Health in India* ed. by Bhupender Singh and N. Mahanti; Inter-India Publications, New Delhi 15.

Patnakar, M., 1994: "Diet and Nutritional Status of Tribals in India with Special Reference to Children", in, *Tribal Economy, Health and Wasteland Development*, ed. by Neeti Mahanti, Inter-India Publications, New Delhi-15.

Palta, Arun, Vishwakarma, M., Sharma, N., 1998: "Impact of Nutrition and Health Education on the Kamars", in, *Bulletin of the Tribal Research Institute*, Bhopal., ed. by T.R. Sahni (IAS), Vol. XXVI, No. 1.

Palla, A., 1988 : "A Study of the Food Consumption Pattern of the Baigas in Baigachak Region of M.P.", in, '*Bulletin of the Tribal Research and Development Institute*, Bhopal, ed. by V.K. Jajoria, Govt. of M.P., Bhopal.

_____1993 : "A Study on the Food Consumption Pattern and Nutrient Intake of the Oraons of Jaspur Nagar State,in, *Bulletin of the Tribal Research and Development Institute,* Bhopal, Vanya Prakashan Bhopal, M.P., ed. by K. Devgan, Director, Tribal Research Institute, Bhopal.

Patil, A.D., 1993 : *Koraku Janjati*, Vishwabharati Prakashan, Nagpur.

Palta, A. and Aghaniwansi, M., 1999: "Anthropometric Profile of the Hill-Korwas of Surguja District", in, *Bulletin of the Tribal Research Institute*, Bhopal, M.P., ed. by T.R. Sahani, Director, Tribal Research Institute, Bhopal.

Park,K., 1997 : *Preventive and Social Medicine*, Banarasidas Bhanot, Jabalpur, 001.

Phillips, David R.; 1990 : "Health Care Planning in Hong Kong", in, *Disease Ecology and Health*, ed. by Akhtar and Verhasselt, Rawat Publications, Jaipur, Rajasthan.

Pant, B.R., 1996: "Physical Geography and Demographic Characteristics of Uttarakhand", in, *Uttarakhand Today*, by. K.S. Valdiya, Shree Almora Book Depot, Almora.

Pant. S.D., 1935 : *The Social Economy of the Himalayas*, London, George Allen and Unwin.

Ratha, S.N., 1992: "Literacy in Tribal India: An Evaluation", in, T*ribal Transformation in India*, Vol. IV, (ed) by Buddhadeb Chaudhuri, Inter-India Publications, Delhi-15.

Risley, H.H.; 1969 : *The People of India*, Delhi.

Rahul, R., 1970 : *The Himalayan Border Land*, Vikas Publications, New Delhi.

Risely, H.H., 1915 : *People of India*, Delhi.

____1997 : *The Scheduled Tribes*, Oxford University Press, Delhi.

Raha, M.K., 1989 : *Tribal India-Problem, Development, Prospect*, in two Vols. (ed.), Gian Publishing House, New Delhi.

Singh, Bhupender, 1995 : "An Overview of Tribal Health", in, *Tribal Health in India*, ed. by Bhupender Singh and N. Mahanti, Inter-India Publications, New Delhi-15.

Srivastava, A.L. and A. North, 1995 : "Galaxy of health Hazards in Various Socio-cultural Scenario", in, *Health Hazards, Gender and society*, ed. by Indu Mathur and Sanjay Sharma, Rawat Publications, Jaipur.

Sarvpriya, S., and Mathew, S., 1988 : Nutritional Status of Tribal Adolescents of Village Gogunda, Rajasthan, *Indian Journal of Nutrition and Dietetics*.

Sharma, K.K.N., 1997 : "Prevalence of Protein Calorie Malnutrition Among the Tribal School Children of Shankerpur and Churcha Villages of Baikunthpur Tehsil of Surguja District, Madhya Pradesh", in, *Bulletin of the Tribal Research Institute*, Bhopal, Vanya Prakashan, Bhopal, M.P., ed. by K.V. Singh, Director, Tribal Research Institute, Bhopal.

Sharma, K.L., 2001 : *Reconceptualizing Caste, Class and Tribe*; Rawat Publications, Jaipur.

Sonwat, R., and Singh, V., 1997 : "Nutritional Status of Rag Pickers and Agarbatti Makers in Indore City", in, *Bulletin of the Tribal Research Institute, Bhopal*, ed. by K. V. Singh, Director, Tribal Research Institute, Bhopal.

Sartorius, N., 1983 : *Bulletin.* WHO, 61(1)5.

Sheehan, G. and Hopkins, M., 1979 : *Basic Needs Performance*, ILO, Geneva.

Simoons, Frederick J., 1991; *Food in China :A Cultural and Historical Inquiry*, CRC Press, Boston.

Swain, S., 1998 : Health and Nutrition in Tribal Areas", in, *Antiquity to Modernity in Tribal India*; by S.C. Dube, Inter-India Publications, New Delhi.

Singh, B., 1995 : Tribal Education in India; Inter-India Publications, New Delhi-15.

Singh, B.S., 1995: *Tribal Education in India*, Inter-India Publications, New Delhi-15.

Sachchidanand, 1995 : "Non-Formal Education in Tribal Areas", in, *Tribal Education in India* (ed) B. Singh and N. Mohanti, Inter- India Publications, New Delhi-15.

Steward, George, H.; 1954 : *Sex and Social Order*, Penguin Books.

Sachchidanand; 1954: "The Morung and Dhumkuria : A Study in Contrast", *Journal of Bihar Research Society*, Vol. XL, Part-4.

Sinha, A.K., 1992 : "University-Education Among the Tribals of Chotanagpur- A Case Study", in, *Tribal Transformation in India*, Vol. IV, ed by B.D. Chaudhari, Inter-India Publications, Delhi-15.

Sachhidanand, 1992 : "Structural Constraints in the Education of Scheduled Tribes and Scheduled Castes", in *Tribal Transformation in India*, ed. by B.D. Chaudhuri, Inter-India Publications, Delhi-15.

Signerist, H.E., 1951. *A History of Medicine*, Vol. I, Oxford University Press, Fair Lawn. N.J.

Singh, S.N., 1996 : Reservation Policy for Backward Classes, Rawat Publications, Jaipur.

Singh, K.S., 1994 : *The Scheduled Tribes*, Oxford University Press, Walton Street, Oxford, New York.

Singh, V.P. and Shukla, B.K., 1990 : "Buxa Janjati Me Jeevan Sathi Ka Chayan", in *Manav*; Year -18, Vol. 3,1990, Ethnographic and Folk-culture Society, Lucknow.

Smith, W. Robertson, 1903 : *Kinship and Marriage in Early Arabia*, London.

Sherring, C.A., 1906: *Notes on the Bhotiyas, Almora and British Garwal*, Calcutta, Asiatic Society, Bengal.

Sashi, S.S. 1979 : *The Nomads of the Himalayas*, Sundeep Prakashan, New Delhi.

Singh, Bhupender, 1998 : "Antiquity to Modernity" in *Tribal India— Tribal Self-Management in North-East India* (ed.), Inter-India Publications, New Delhi-15.

Singh, K.S., 1998 : "Antiquity to Modernity in *Tribal India—Tribal Movements in India* (ed), Inter-India Publication, New Delhi.

Thompson, Della, 1995 : *The Concise Oxford Dictionary*, Oxford University Press, Delhi.

Thurnwald R., 1933 : "Nomads", *Encyclopedia of Social Sciences*, Delhi.

Verma, R.C., Das, G.P. and Kaur, M., 1995 : "Genetic and other Health Problems of Tribal Communities", in, *Tribal Health in India*, ed. by B. Singh and N. Mahati, Inter-India Publications, New Delhi-15.

Vaishnav, T.K., 1995: "Bio-cultural Study of Diet and Nutrition on Gamit Tribe of Gujrat", in, *Bulletin of the Tribal Research Institute, Bhopal*, M.P., ed. by K. Devagan, Director Tribal Research Institute, Bhopal, M.P.

Verma, R.C,, 1995 : *Indian Tribes through the Ages*, Publication Division, Ministry of Information and Broadcasting, Govt. of India, New Delhi.

Vaishnava, Y.D., 1983: *Land and People; Himalayan Districts of Uttara Pradesh*, Sri Almora Book Depot, Almora.

WHO, 1986 : Concepts of health behaviour research, Reg. Health paper No. 13, SEARO, New Delhi.

WHO; 1978: *Bulletin*. WHO 56(4)519.

WHO, 1981 : *Health for all,* Sr. No. 6.

Wilson, R.W. and T.F. Drury, 1984 : Ann Rev. Pub. Health. Quoted from K. Park, *Preventive and Social Medicine*, Banarasi Das Bhanot, Jabalpur, 01.

WHO, 1989, *Global Nutritional Status: Anthropometric Duplicators* Update.

Index

E

F

G

H

N

Q

R

S